COMMUNISM
AND DEVELOPMENT

COMMUNISM
AND DEVELOPMENT

Robert Bideleux

Methuen
London and New York

First published in 1985 by
Methuen & Co. Ltd
11 New Fetter Lane, London EC4P 4EE

Published in the USA by
Methuen & Co.
in association with Methuen Inc.
733 Third Avenue, New York, NY 10017

Typeset by Scarborough Typesetting Services
and printed in Great Britain at the
University Press, Cambridge

British Library Cataloguing in Publication Data

Bideleux, Robert.
Communism and development.
1. Communism – 1945–
I. Title.
335.43   HX73

ISBN 0–416–73410–3

Library of Congress Cataloging in Publication Data

Bideleux, Robert.
Communism and development.
Bibliography: p.
Includes index.
1. Communism – developing countries.
2. Developing countries – economic policy.
3. Communism.   4. Economic development.
I. Title.
HX517.8.B54   1985
335.43' 091724   85–4819

ISBN 0–416–73410–3

For Alison

Contents

Preface

This book offers a wide-ranging and radical reappraisal of the remarkably diverse communist development strategies which have helped to shape the destinies of a third of mankind. It highlights the fallacious presuppositions and the often appalling human and economic costs of the most widely adopted Stalinist and neo-Stalinist strategies of forced industrialization and collectivization; and it radically reconsiders the powerful economic and non-economic arguments in favour of the most cost-effective socialist alternatives to Stalinism: the varieties of village communism advocated by Herzen, Kropotkin, Chayanov, Gandhi and Marx; and the forms of market socialism advocated by Bukharin, Bazarov, Kondratiev and Trotsky. Several chapters show how forced industrialization has further entrenched hierarchy, inequality, corruption and the abuse of monopolistic power under avowedly communist regimes; how centrally planned economies have been comparatively wasteful in their use of resources; how this has been exacerbated by a lopsided emphasis on producer goods industries whose products are mainly consumed by other producer goods industries, against the interests of agriculture and ordinary consumers; and how the problems of centralized economic planning have become more rather than less intractable as industrialization proceeds. The book also yields unconventional and sometimes controversial perspectives on Marx, Engels, the Russian Revolution, Mao's China, Castro's Cuba, Tito's Yugoslavia, Nyerere's Tanzania, Soviet Central Asia, international and intertemporal variations in peasant poverty and mortality, the very diverse forms and functions of rural collectivization, theories of unbalanced growth, economic nationalism and the state as an obstacle to socialism. The book's main theses also draw upon Polish, North Vietnamese, North and South Korean, Taiwanese, Japanese, Irish, Danish, Hungarian, Indian and Mongolian experiences. My approach is comparative, interdisciplinary, empirical and thematic, and I try to avoid esoteric theoretical abstraction and the kinds of biographical and historical narrative which already abound in the literature on communism. I offer no narrow, sectarian definition of communism. It is more fruitful to recognize the *diversity* of avowedly communist aspirations. Although I have been greatly influenced by some of the ideologists considered in this book, I find only Herzen wholly sympathetic. Herzen's sympathies were always with the underdogs and victims of society, irrespective of the regime. He clearly believed that people matter much more than abstract principles; that revolutions step on a very slippery slope when they sacrifice people on the altar of principle; and that communism is *only worth having* if it can be attained through overwhelming, non-violent popular support, gradually building on existing auspicious institutions 'from the bottom upwards', rather than by imposition.

The book's structure is very simple: Chapters 1 and 2, which reappraise the main arguments in favour of village communism as a communist alternative to large-scale industrialization, establish the standpoint from which I assess Lenin's basic economic tenets (Chapter 3), and the wide range of development strategies which have shaped the destinies of the existing communist states (Chapters 4–11). Finally, in Chapter 12, I assess the diverse results of rural collectivization and show how Soviet Central Asia, in particular, seems to vindicate my initial arguments in favour of village-based development.

When dealing with major socialist thinkers, I have tried as far as possible to let them speak for themselves, through extensive quotations from their writings. However, limitations of space often obliged me to eliminate much of the repetitiveness and verbosity of the original, especially when making my own translations into English, but I do not think this has resulted in any substantive misrepresentation.

Finally, I welcome this opportunity to thank the people who have helped to make this book possible: my parents, Maude Mayne, Joyce Bideleux, Beryl Williams, Professor Geoffrey Best, John Gooding, Dr Ian Blanchard, Professor Tibor Barna, Gavin Kitching, Derek Heater, Hector Blair, Dr Richard Newman, Professor Max Cole, Ben Bradnack, David Howie, Professor François Duchêne, Dr Edward Szczepanik and Professor S. B. Saul. Swansea's Centre for Russian and East European Studies financed the necessary travel. Gavin Kitching, Dr Eleanor Breuning, Professor Alec Nove, Professor Roger Pethybridge, Dr Ian Jeffries and Nancy Marten offered many helpful comments on and corrections to my typescript. My interaction with Gavin Kitching was made the more fruitful by the fact that we have approached similar subjects from different standpoints, with very different expectations and preconceptions. Above all, I am grateful to my wife Alison for her forbearance, support, humour and sense of proportion during the stresses and strains of the past few years.

Swansea, March 1984

1 The fate of peasant societies: Marx versus Engels

Avowedly Marxist movements have won power and influence mainly in peasant societies whose industrialization has barely begun and where peasant needs and aspirations should be prime considerations. Yet Marx and Engels were not renowned for respectful solicitude towards peasantries. Their *Communist Manifesto* (1848) envisaged an ineluctable progression through capitalist industrialization towards a proletarianized society in which 'a considerable part of the population' would be 'rescued' from 'the idiocy of rural life'. Thus the proletariat could 'win the battle of democracy' and 'wrest, by degrees, all capital from the bourgeoisie' and 'centralize all means of production in the hands of the State, i.e. the proletariat organized as the ruling class'. It fiercely criticized 'petit bourgeois socialism', which feared 'the inevitable ruin of the petit bourgeois and the peasant' and aspired 'either to restore the old means of production and exchange, and hence the old property relations and the old society, or to cramp modern means of production within the framework of the old property relations, which have been inevitably exploded by those means'.

Marx on peasant societies: France, India and Russia

Marx's most damning characterization of peasants as a social class occurs in his conclusion to *The Eighteenth Brumaire of Louis Bonaparte* (1852):

> Peasant smallholders form a vast mass, whose constituents live in almost identical conditions, yet scarcely enter into mutual relations. Their mode of production isolates them from one another. . . . Their smallholdings practically preclude division of labour, application of science . . . diversification. . . . Thus the great mass of the French nation is made up of homologous entities, much as potatoes in a sack make up

a sack of potatoes. Inasmuch as millions of families live in economic conditions which distinguish their way of life, interests and culture from those of other classes, rendering them antagonistic to the latter, they constitute a class. But inasmuch as their connections are merely local and their identity of interests hasn't found expression in a community, a national association or a political organization, they don't constitute a class. So they are unable to assert their class interests in their own name. . . . They cannot represent themselves; they must be represented. Their representative must appear as their master, lording it over them, wielding unlimited governmental power, protecting them against other classes. . . . So the political influence of smallholders ultimately finds expression in the executive subordinating society. . . . By its very nature, smallholder property forms a suitable basis for an omnipotent, innumerable bureaucracy. It fosters uniformity, facilitating uniform action from the centre upon every part of this homogeneous mass. . . . But in the nineteenth century feudal extortion has been replaced by urban usury, feudal obligations by mortgages, and aristocratic landlordism by bourgeois capital. The peasant's smallholding is now only the pretext enabling capitalists to draw profits, interest and rent from the land. . . . Hence the peasants find their natural ally and leader in the urban proletariat, whose mission it is to overthrow the bourgeois order. . . . With the progressive undermining of smallholder property, the State structure erected thereon collapses.

However, it can be argued that France's Third Republic (1870–1940) *defended* peasant interests by promoting a remarkably durable and peasant-oriented parliamentary democracy, universal education, cheap transport and agricultural protectionism. Perversely, it has often received a bad press precisely because it *did* protect peasant and petit-bourgeois interests – those of the majority. In 1852 Marx evidently underestimated how far industrialization was already expanding opportunities for intensive, small-scale livestock-rearing, dairying, horticulture, viticulture, etc., granting a new lease of life to independent smallholder agriculture; and how far mortgage debt is an index of credit rating rather than impoverishment. Generally big mortgages are obtained by successful farmers, whereas the poor have little to mortgage.

Nevertheless, with substantial assistance from Engels, Marx advanced a similarly dismal caricature of 'Oriental' peasant societies in his major prospectus for India (1853):

There have been in Asia, generally, from immemorial times, but three departments of government: that of Finance, or plunder of the interior; that of War, or plunder of the exterior; and . . . the department of Public Works. Climate and territorial conditions . . . constituted artificial irrigation . . . the basis of Oriental agriculture. . . . This prime necessity of an economical and common use of water . . . necessitated, in the Orient where civilization was too low and territorial extent too vast to call into life voluntary association, the interference of the centralizing power of Government. . . . These two circumstances . . . brought about . . . the so-called village system. . . . These small stereotype forms of social organism are disappearing, not so much through the brutal interference of the British tax-gatherer and the British soldier, as to the working of English steam and English free trade. Those family-communities were based on . . . that peculiar combination of hand-weaving, hand-spinning and hand-tilling agriculture, which gave them self-supporting power. English interference . . . dissolved these . . . communities by blowing up their economical basis. . . . Now, sickening as it must be . . . to witness those myriads of industrious, patriarchal and inoffensive social organizations disorganized and dis-solved . . . we must not forget that . . . these idyllic village communities . . . had always been the solid foundation of Oriental despotism, that they restrained the human mind within the smallest possible compass, making it the unresisting tool of superstition, enslaving it beneath traditional rules, depriving it of all grandeur and historical energies. . . . We must not forget that this undignified, stagnatory and vegetative life . . . evoked . . . aimless, unbounded forces of destruction . . . that these little communities were contaminated by distinctions of caste and by slavery, that they subjugated man to external circumstances instead of elevating man. . . .

England has to fulfil a double mission in India: one destructive, the other regenerating – the annihilation of old Asiatic society, and the laying of the foundations of Western society in Asia. . . . The political unity of India . . . imposed by the British sword, will now be strengthened and perpetuated by the electric telegraph. The native army, organized and trained by the British drill-sergeant, was the *sine qua non* of Indian self-emancipation. . . . The free press, introduced for the first time into Asiatic society . . . is a new and powerful agent of reconstruction. The zemindari [intermediaries transformed into landlords by the British in Bengal] and ryotwari [peasants estab-lished on heritable smallholdings by the British in southern India], abominable as they are, involve two distinct forms of private property in land – the great desideratum of Asiatic society. From the natives, reluctantly and sparingly educated at Calcutta under English superintendence, a fresh class is springing up, endowed with the requirements for government. . . . Steam has brought India into regular and rapid communication with Europe . . . and has revindicated it from the isolated position which was the prime law of its stagnation. . . . The millocracy [British industrialists] have dis-covered that the transformation of India into a reproductive country has become of vital importance to them and, to that end, it is necessary above all to endow her with means of irrigation and internal communication. . . . You cannot maintain a net of railways over an immense country without introducing all those industrial processes necessary to meet the immediate and current wants of railway locomotion, out of which there must grow the application of machinery to branches of industry not immediately connected with railways. . . . All that the English bourgeoisie may be forced to do will neither emancipate nor materially mend the social condition of the mass of the people, depending not only on the development of productive powers, but on their appropriation by the people. But what they will not fail to do is to lay down the material premises for both. (*New York Daily Tribune*, 25 June and 8 August 1853)

Note that Marx obviously took great pains over this incisive prospectus and that, unlike more simplistic and/or xenophobic writings on 'imperialism' and 'dependency', it rightly emphasized that the *overall* results of British rule and economic penetration were bound to be *positive* (cf. the provocative theses advanced

4   Communism and Development

by Morris, 1963, 1968). The really objectionable feature was Marx's very one-sided, negative characterization of India's village institutions and customs (cf. *Capital*, vol. I, 1976T, 477–9).

Moreover, in his first 'Preface' to *Capital* (1867), Marx postulated that large-scale capitalist industrialization was *the only way forward*: 'The country that is more developed industrially only shows the less developed country the image of its future'; and 'when a society has got on the right track . . . it can neither leap over nor legislate away the hurdles posed by the successive phases of its normal development, although it can shorten and lessen the birth-pangs'.

However, if it was indeed necessary to undergo capitalist industrialization and proletarianization *en route* to socialism, then this posed an agonizing dilemma for Marx's disciples in peasant societies. They would have to welcome and support these processes as 'necessary' advances towards socialism, despite (1) all the attendant exploitation, expropriation, degradation, social disruption, concentration into squalid overcrowded cities, destitution and debilitating work regimes, so vividly publicized by Engels and Marx, among others; (2) Marx's warning, in his first 'Preface' to *Capital*, that the capitalist road would be even more arduous for later-industrializing countries than it had been for the pioneer; (3) the consequent conflict between their humanitarian pretensions and their economic prescriptions; and (4) the danger that such a dismal prospectus would attract little popular support, especially from the intended victims. In 1877 the dilemma was posed most poignantly by a leading Russian socialist, Nikolai Mikhailovsky (1842–1904):

> All this 'maiming of women and adolescents' still lies before us. Yet, from the standpoint of Marx's historical theory, we should not only not protest, as that would mean acting to our own detriment; we should even welcome it as a steep, but necessary step towards the temple of happiness. Such a contradiction, which in certain situations would rend the soul of a Russian disciple of Marx, must be hard to bear. His role is that of an onlooker, dispassionately . . . chronicling a double-edged progress in which he cannot participate. He cannot further the abhorrent side of the process, yet any activity conforming to his moral imperatives would only serve to prolong the agony. His ideal, if he's a disciple of Marx, includes a conjunction of labour and property, with cultivators possessing the means of cultivation. But, if he shares Marx's historico-philosophical views, he must welcome the separation of labour and property, the separation of producers from the means of production, as the first phase of an inevitable and ultimately benign process; i.e. he must welcome the subversion of his own ideal. (Translated from Mikhailovsky, 1897, 172)

In Mikhailovsky's view no *bona fide* socialist could honestly welcome or acquiesce in the prospective proletarianization of the peasantry. As he wrote in 1872,

> In Europe the labour question is a revolutionary one, since it demands a *transfer* of the means of work to the workers, expropriating the current owners. In Russia the labour question is a conservative one, merely entailing a *retention* of the means of work in labour's possession. . . . Even around Petersburg, a most Anglicized area, dotted

with factories, foundries and manors, villagers live on their own land, burn their own timber, eat home-made bread, wear clothes made by their own labour from their own sheep. Guarantee them their property and Russia's labour question is solved. . . . It will be said we cannot forever make do with wooden ploughs, the three-field system or antediluvian methods of making clothes. True. But there are alternative ways out of this difficulty. One, favoured by expediency, is simply to raise tariffs, break up the village communes and let industry spring up like mushrooms, English-style. But this would . . . expropriate labour. The alternative is obviously more difficult, but the simpler solution isn't always the right one. The alternative is to develop the existing, albeit primitive and crude, relations between labour and property. This cannot be achieved without broad State support, beginning with legislative consolidation of communal landownership. (Mikhailovsky, 1888, 102–3)

In reply, Marx wrote a swingeing disavowal of attempts 'to metamorphose my outline of the genesis of capitalism in Western Europe into a historico-philosophical theory of *la marche générale*, fatally incumbent on all peoples, whatever their historical circumstances':

By studying each evolution separately and then making comparisons, one can easily find the key to such phenomena, but one won't get there using the passe-partout of a historico-philosophical theory whose only virtue consists in being supra-historical. . . . To be able to make informed judgements on Russian economic development I have learned Russian and for years I have studied official and other publications on this subject. This is my conclusion: if Russia continues down the path pursued since 1861 [when formal dissolution of serfdom was begun], she will miss the finest opportunity history has ever offered a people and undergo all the vicissitudes of the capitalist regime. (Reprinted in Danielson, 1902T, 507–9)

Encouraged by the emergence of a Russian socialist movement which deferentially and attentively went along with his critique of Western capitalism, Marx undertook 'to write specially for Russia a brochure on the development potential of the village commune – a question of burning interest to Russian socialists' (Riazanov, 1924, 265). Indeed Engels, as Marx's main financial backer, was increasingly annoyed that the fascinating development problems of a peasant society (albeit one comprising nearly half Europe's peasants) were distracting Marx from the tiresome task of completing the later volumes of *Capital* (see Maenchen-Helfen and Nicolaievsky, 1976T, 395). Unfortunately Marx never completed his projected brochure. But when his daughter, Laura Lafargue, committed suicide in 1911, the Marxist scholar David Riazanov discovered she had been sitting on three very significant drafts: Marx's last and least-acknowledged major writings (early 1881), constituting his most considered and informed prospectus for a peasant society.

From Draft I:

Viewed historically, the only serious argument advanced as proof of the Russian peasant commune's decomposition is this: far back in history we encounter throughout Western Europe communal landownership of a more or less archaic type; with society's progress, it disappeared. Why should it escape such a fate only in Russia? I reply: because in Russia, thanks to a peculiar conjunction of circumstances, the village commune still exists nationwide and can shake off its primitive traits and directly develop as an element of collective production on a national scale. Russia is neither secluded from the modern world nor prey to a foreign conqueror. . . . Precisely because it coexists with capitalist production, it can assimilate its positive achievements without undergoing its terrible vicissitudes. . . . If the village communes had been placed in normal conditions of development when serfdom was abolished, and if the huge public debt incurred largely at peasant expense and the vast sums furnished via the state to the emerging, capitalistic 'new pillars of society' had been used to further develop the village commune, today nobody would contemplate the 'historical inevitability' of the commune's annihilation: everybody would see it as an element of the regeneration of Russian society and of superiority over countries enthralled by capitalism. . . .

There is yet to be written a history of the decomposition of the primitive communes. . . . So far we've had only the bare outlines. But research on this subject has advanced enough to let us affirm that the primitive communes were far more durable than Semitic, Roman and other societies, especially modern capitalist societies; and their disintegration was caused by . . . circumstances quite unlike those of the modern Russian commune. Histories of the primitive communes by bourgeois authors must be read guardedly: e.g. Sir Henry Maine, once a zealous adviser to the English government in its forcible demolition of India's communes, hypocritically tells us that all the government's benign efforts to support these communes were thwarted by the peaceful force of economic laws! Either way, this commune perished amid incessant internal and external warfare. It also perished by force when Germanic tribes conquered Italy, Spain, Gaul, etc. . . .

Russia is the only European country where the 'agricultural commune' has been preserved nationwide. . . . Communal landownership empowers it to directly and gradually transform individualistic, parcellized agriculture into collective agriculture, which Russian peasants already practise on unpartitioned meadows. The physical configuration of Russian farmland favours mechanization on a broad scale. The peasant's familiarity with co-operative setups will facilitate his transition from parcellized to communal farming. . . . If spokesmen for 'the new pillars of society' deny the possibility of such an evolution of the contemporary village commune, they should be asked whether Russia, like the West, has had to undergo a protracted incubation of mechanical production to arrive at machinery, steamers, railways, etc., and how they managed to introduce straight off all the exchange mechanisms (banks, joint-stock companies, etc.) whose development took centuries in the West.

One characteristic of Russia's 'agricultural commune' is a source of weakness, inauspicious for all its relationships: its isolation, the lack of connections between communes; the *localized microcosm* which isn't everywhere an innate characteristic of this form, but on which a more-or-less centralized despotism arises wherever it is encountered. . . . But nowadays this shortcoming is easily eliminated. One must simply create, in place of rural townships, governmental institutions and a peasant assembly elected by the communes as an administrative organ defending their interests. A historical circumstance very auspicious for preserving the 'agricultural commune' by further developing it is that it not only coexists with Western capitalism, allowing it to incorporate its fruits without submitting to its modus operandi, but it has also survived the era when capitalism was inviolable; in Western Europe and the USA capitalism is now at loggerheads with the toiling masses, with science, with the productive forces it engenders – i.e. in crises which will end in capitalism's annihilation and modern society's return to a higher form of the 'archaic' type of property and collective production. Of course, the commune's evolution should be gradual, initially placing it in normal conditions on its present basis. . . . But for collective labour to replace parcellized cultivation (the basis of private appropriation), two things are necessary: an economic need for such a change; and material conditions for its realization. The economic need will be felt by the 'village commune' once it is placed in normal conditions, i.e. once its oppression is lifted and it obtains a suitable amount of land to farm. Russian agriculture no longer merely requires land and its parcellized cultivator equipped with primitive implements – especially when oppression of the cultivator exhausts his soil. It now needs co-operative labour, organized on a broad scale. . . . But where to find the equipment, fertilizer, agronomic techniques, etc. necessary for collective labour? Herein lies the great advantage of Russia's 'village commune' over archaic communes: in Europe it alone has survived on a vast national scale, in a historical context where the concurrent existence of capitalist production grants it all the conditions for collective labour. . . . Russian society is duty-bound to grant the initial organizational, intellectual and material inputs to the 'village commune', at whose expense it has lived so long and wherein it must seek its 'regenerative spring'.

Since the so-called emancipation of the serfs, the state has placed the village commune in abnormal economic conditions, ceaselessly oppressing it by every available means. Weakened by taxation, the commune has become easy prey to merchants, landlords and usurers. This external oppression has unleashed within the commune an already present conflict of interests, exacerbating internal sources of decomposition. And, at peasant expense, the state has nurtured in a hothouse those branches of the Western capitalist system which, without enhancing agriculture's productive potential, are likely to expedite appropriation of its fruits by non-productive middlemen. It has thus helped to develop a new capitalist parasite, sucking the blood of an already anaemic commune; i.e. the state has aided a precocious development of the economic and technical means most likely to promote exploitation of the cultivator – Russia's main productive force – and to enrich 'the new pillars of society'. This conjuncture of destructive influences, unless strongly counteracted, must naturally lead to the village commune's demise. But why have these interests, including large-scale state-protected industries, seen advantage in the village commune's present plight? Why do they knowingly kill the goose which lays the golden eggs? Precisely because they consider 'present conditions' unsustainable, rendering the present methods of exploitation obsolete. Already the cultivator's poverty has fostered soil exhaustion. Good harvests alternate with lean years. The average for the past decade indicates an agricultural retrogression. . . . So there's no time to lose. Matters must come to a head. One must turn the prospering minority of peasants into a rural middle class and the majority into a proletariat. That is how 'the new pillars of society' portray the wounds inflicted on the commune as natural symptoms of decrepitude. . . . While they breed and torture the commune and impoverish its soil, the literary lackeys of 'the new pillars of society' ironically . . . claim that it is dying naturally and that it would be a kindness to curtail the agony. Here there is no theoretical problem to be resolved, merely an enemy to defeat. To save Russia's commune, a Russian Revolution is necessary. . . . If the revolution is opportune and concentrates its forces to ensure free development of the village commune, the latter will soon develop as the regenerative element of Russian society, conferring superiority over countries enthralled by capitalism. (Translated from Marx and Engels, 1935, 677–87)

Draft II adds:

In 'Capital' I have shown that the transformation of feudal into capitalist production originated in the expropriation of producers and, in particular, that 'the basis of this entire process is expropriation of the cultivator' (French edn, 315). 'This has been accomplished thoroughly in England alone. . . . The countries of Western Europe are following the same path' (ibid.). Thus I explicitly restricted this 'historical necessity' to 'the countries of Western Europe'. . . . The process I analysed replaced the scattered property of cultivators by the capitalistic property of a tiny minority . . . substituting one form of private property for another. How can this apply to Russia, where land has never been the cultivator's private property? The only conclusion one could legitimately draw from the West's evolution would be this: if her own capitalist production is to get established, Russia must begin by annihilating communal landownership and expropriating the peasantry, the broad popular masses. That's what Russian Liberals desire. . . . Of course, if capitalist production must triumph in Russia, then most peasants – most Russians – must become hired workers, expropriated by prior annihilation of communistic property. But, either way, Western precedent proves nothing here. . . . If Russia were secluded from the world, she would have to accomplish by her own forces the economic attainments which Western Europe achieved only by undergoing a long series of evolutions from primitive communes to its present position, and then I don't doubt the communes would be doomed to extinction as Russian society developed. But the Russian commune's position is utterly unlike that of the primitive Western commune. Russia is the only country in Europe where it has been preserved nationwide in a modern historical context, alongside a superior civilization, connected to a world market wherein capitalist production predominates. By assimilating capitalism's achievements, she can develop and improve her archaic village communes. . . . What threatens the Russian commune is not historical necessity, nor a theory, but oppression by the state and exploitation by intruding capitalists, nurtured at peasant expense by that state. (Translated from Marx and Engels, 1935, 687–92)

To the Liberal jurist Boris Chicherin's thesis that Russia's village commune had been a fiscal device ancillary to serfdom, not an autonomous institution, Marx had already replied in a letter to Nikolai Danielson in 1873:

> How this form of property originated in Russia is naturally a secondary question, not affecting this institution's importance. . . . Besides, every analogy contradicts Chicherin. How could it be that in Russia this institution was introduced as a purely fiscal measure, ancillary to serfdom, when everywhere else it emerged naturally and formed a necessary phase in the development of free peoples? (Reprinted in Rubel, 1947, 552)

Draft III adds:

> Primitive communes aren't uniform. They constitute a series of social formations, differing as to type, age and evolutionary phase. One type, commonly termed the agricultural commune, includes the Russian commune. Its Western counterpart is the Germanic commune. . . . One also finds 'village communes' in Asia . . . but everywhere these represent the newest type and, so to speak, the last word in archaic social organization. . . . So we must consider what characteristics distinguish the 'agricultural commune' from more ancient communes: (1) The 'agricultural commune' was the first union of free people not bound by blood. Other communes rest on consanguinity. . . . (2) In the agricultural commune house and yard are the cultivator's private property, whereas communal housing and living were the economic base of the ancient commune. . . . (3) Farmland is inalienable communal property, periodically repartitioned among the agricultural commune's members, so that each farms his allotment using his own resources and reaping his own harvest. In the more ancient commune work is performed communally and, excluding a portion reserved for seed, the communal product is distributed according to consumption needs.

> Obviously the *dualism* inherent in the agricultural commune's structure can be a source of strength. Freed from the strong, but constricting bonds of blood relationship, it has firm foundations in communal landownership and the corresponding social relations; yet the house and yard, as each family's exclusive domain, parcellized cultivation and private appropriation of the harvest foster an individualism incompatible with the more primitive commune's circumstances. No less obviously, this individualism can in time become a germ of decomposition. Not to mention external destructive influences, the commune contains undermining elements. Private property has intruded in the form of a house and yard, which could become the citadel for an assault on communal farmland. It has happened before. But the critical factor is parcellized cultivation as a source of private appropriation. It provides the soil for concentration of moveable assets, e.g. cattle, money, sometimes even slaves and serfs. This moveable property, not being under communal control, yet subject to fluctuations wherein cunning and chance play large roles, will press ever more heavily on the entire village economy. It is the solvent of primitive economic and social equality. It introduces heterogeneous elements, engendering within the commune conflicts of interests and passions liable to erode communal property – first, in cropland, then in

woods, pasture, wastes, etc., which, once converted into *communal annexes* to private property, will eventually succumb to it. The agricultural commune, as the final phase of the primitive communal formation, also represents a transition . . . from a society based on communal property to one based on private property. The latter obviously includes the series of societies based on slavery and serfdom.

But does this mean that the agricultural commune's historical path must inevitably lead to such an outcome? Not at all. Its innate dualism allows an alternative: either its element of private property will subdue its element of collectivism, or vice versa. All depends on the historical context. . . . Communal property in land offers Russia a natural base for communal appropriation, and its historical context – coexistence with capitalist production – grants it ready-made the material conditions for co-operative labour, organized on a broad scale. . . . Once placed on a normal footing in its present form, it can become the *direct point of departure* for the economic system towards which modern society is moving. . . . Russia would try in vain to escape its impasse by introducing English-style capitalistic tenancy, to which its social conditions are all opposed. The English have already tried this in India: they have merely succeeded in disrupting native agriculture, increasing the frequency and severity of famine years. (Translated from Marx and Engels, 1935, 692–6)

Marx's Russian socialist critics, the leading proponents of village communism, could not have asked for a greater or more authoritative *retreat* from the hard-nosed 'capitalist-roader' mentality of Marx's earlier, best-known writings – the writings which underlie the 'Marxist' orthodoxies elaborated by Engels, Kautsky, Plekhanov and Lenin. The West had obviously passed the point of no return, but by the same token there was indeed no historical or theoretical 'necessity' for capitalist industrialization elsewhere. As Marx clearly recognized, communal institutions and the growing scope for international trade, capital transfer and technology transfer would enable a peasant-based revolution and regime to lead a peasant society *directly* to a village-based communism, without first *forcing* that society at enormous and unnecessary cost to undergo the traumas and tribulations of large-scale, city-centred industrialization. Marx's new stance offered the most promising way out of the dismal dilemmas posed by his earlier writings on peasant societies and a more positive alternative to the grim thesis that socialists in peasant societies should be prepared to mark time for the century or more which it would take to proletarianize the peasantry and create costly, centralized, congested, polluted, seedy, satanic and corrupting industrial conurbations, as dubious 'prerequisites' for 'proletarian' socialism. Indeed, it was arguable that the latter course could just as well lead *away* from socialism and communism. By the 1880s it was conceivable that capitalism could enthral its proletariat indefinitely and/or give the proletariat a vested interest in the system, either of which could render the proletariat about as menacing to capitalism as battery hens are to factory farming. And Marx's Russian socialist critics saw that it was self-contradictory to suppose that large-scale industrialization, which progressively *expands* and *entrenches* social division of labour and hence multilateral exchange, the various roles of money, specialist intermediary/co-ordinating functions, hierarchy and inequality, could move societies nearer to the advent of a thoroughly egalitarian, moneyless, classless, stateless regime. Naturally Marx's literary executors, who remained staunch 'industrializers' and 'capitalist-roaders', were in no hurry to publish or even acknowledge the existence of manu-scripts which aligned Marx with Russia's proponents of village communism, against the 'literary lackeys' of capitalism. These manuscripts, 'discovered' in 1911, weren't published until 1924, when the fledgling Soviet regime was wooing the peasantry and flouting the 'Marxist' orthodoxy that any 'premature' bid to 'build socialism' in a peasant society would be doomed from the start. But note that, though the Soviet regime used these manuscripts to that end, the drafts provide no support for the kind of collectivization implemented under Stalin. The latter was a brutish external offensive *against* the peasantry, bloodily destroying Russia's autonomous village communes after their Indian summer of 1922–7, so as to render state control and exploitation of the peasantry more thorough and systematic. By contrast, Marx, like Stalin's major communist opponents, clearly envisaged that Russia's socialist revolution should lead to an evolutionary develop-ment pattern, *subservient* to the needs and aspirations of *self-determining* village communes. Marx rightly rested his hopes on the advantages an outward-looking communist state could obtain from international trade, capital transfer and technology transfer, not on the introversion and seclusion preferred in practice by Stalinist states.

In a 'Preface' to the 1882 Russian edition of *The Communist Manifesto*, Marx seemingly conceded that *direct* transition to socialism in Russia would *only* be possible 'if the Russian Revolution becomes the signal for a proletarian revolution in the West, so that both complement each other'. Actually this was an idea put forward by Engels, in 1875, in a vain attempt to patch up his growing divergence from Marx; and there is strong manuscript evidence that the 1882 'Preface' was written by Engels over Marx's signature, at a time when Marx was in mourning (his wife and a daughter had just died), in decline and past caring; Marx wrote nothing of any importance in 1882 and he died the following year (see Marx and Engels, 1952T, 282, 231, 241; Wada, 1981, 147, 144; Levine, 1975, 181). A proletarian revolution in the West could conceivably have aided communal village-based development in Russia (I have my doubts), but it would have been utterly impractical to have made the anticipated Russian Revolution *conditional* upon a *coinciding* proletarian revolution in the West, and Marx's writings did not do so.

However, like most writers on pre-revolutionary Russia (whatever their ideo-logical persuasion), Marx rather exaggerated the *economic* plight of Russia's peasantry and thus underestimated the potential for communal, village-based development. In fact, despite scant use of fertilizers and persistent alarmist talk of soil exhaustion, grain yields per sown hectare on peasant land in European Russia roughly *doubled* between the 1860s and 1911–13, equalling the concurrent population increase (1.5 per cent per annum) (Khromov, 1967, 338–40, 512; Antsiferov, 1930, 54–6):

	1860s	1870s	1880s	1891	1890s	1901–5	1911–13
Tons per hectare	0.44	0.47	0.51	0.40	0.59	0.77	0.86

The three main, mutually independent sources of information on Russia's peasant grain yields broadly corroborate one another. At most, there may be a case for a modest 7 per cent upward correction of these grain yield data (see Wheatcroft, 1974, 166–7 ff.). In addition, total cultivated area expanded from 58m. ha in 1861 to 98m. ha in 1911–13 (USSR, 1960T, 114, 199), enabling the grain output of European Russia (excluding Russian Poland) to rise from 20m. tons p.a. in 1864–6 to 37m. in 1886–90 and 57m. in 1906–10 (Kennard, 1913, 166–78), and steadily growing proportions of the cultivated area to be devoted to potatoes, flax, tobacco, sunflowers and sugar beet. Moreover, private landlords were steadily *losing* ground: of the land area they retained when serfdom was dissolved in the 1860s, they owned only 87 per cent by 1877, 76 per cent by 1887, 52 per cent by 1905 and a mere 41 per cent by 1916 (Chayanov, 1966T, 237); and only 27 per cent of the land they retained was cropland, as against 53 per cent for peasant holdings (Kaufman, 1918, 59). Moreover, the proportion of estate land leased out to peasant farmers apparently increased from one-third in 1886–90 to one-half in 1896–1900 (Pavlovsky, 1930, 191) and reached two-thirds by 1916 (Chayanov, 1966T, 237). So, not surprisingly, the peasantry was producing 88 per cent of Russia's grain output by 1909–13, including 78 per cent of Russia's *marketed* grain (estimates by Kondratiev and Nemchinov; Karcz, 1970, 273). This adds significance to the fact that, by the 1890s, per capita grain and potato output was *two to three times* higher in Russia than in Southern Europe, Japan, East Asia and the Indian subcontinent, areas where grain and potatoes also accounted for two-thirds to three-quarters of human calorie intake up to the 1930s or even beyond (see Statistical Appendix, Tables 8 and 11). The slightly lower importance of grain and potatoes in Southern Europe was entirely attributable to much higher alcohol consumption. Per capita consumption of alcoholic drinks (in terms of alcohol content) was as follows (Mulhall, 1898, 58, 634; Connor, 1971, 571–2):

Litres p.a.	Russia	France	Italy	Spain	Germany	Denmark
1891–5	2.7	15.9	8.7	7.7	10.0	11.4
1906–10	3.4	22.9	18.3	14.0	7.6	6.8

Litres p.a.	UK	Romania	Serbia	Greece	Austria-Hungary
1891–5	8.6	4.6	6.8	—	7.3
1906–10	9.7	—	—	13.9	—

South Europeans averaged over a litre of wine per day, causing widespread alcoholism, cirrhosis of the liver and infant deformity (see Ardagh, 1973, 432–5). Russian men went in for periodic drinking bouts, but this drinking pattern was less injurious to the body than the incessant daily imbibing of alcohol in Southern Europe (see Williams, 1914, 340). Moreover, contrary to common belief, Russia's considerable grain exports in the last decades of tsarism were not obtained by 'starving' the peasantry: grain exports quite consistently averaged only 10–13 per cent of Russia's grain and potato production in the periods 1883–99, 1900–8 and 1909–13 (see Mitchell, 1975, 246, 262, 340, 342; Timoshenko, 1932, 472, 524, 553). So even if one deducts grain exports, which actually increased peasant purchasing power, Russia's per capita grain and potato supplies were still comparatively high. And, unlike Southern Europe and Japan, Russia had a comparatively small non-agricultural population to feed (see Table 1). Overall, Russia's peasantry was consistently able to retain around three-quarters of its net output of grain and potatoes from the late 1880s to 1913 (see p. 119 and Gregory, 1980a, 147, 153, 157, 158).

Moreover, doctrinaire Liberal assertions that communal landownership tends to impede agricultural advance were misplaced. There is no evidence, to my knowledge, that peasant agriculture was any more 'parcellized' in Russia than in peasant Europe generally; indeed, it was well known that excessive fragmentation of holdings was more easily corrected under repartitional communal landownership than under permanent private possession. And as Europe's peasants generally could not afford expensive large-scale changes in agricultural technology and land use, any disincentive effects of communal landownership must have been negligible: Russian peasant grain yields per sown hectare were actually rising faster than those of Southern and Eastern Europe, where private property prevailed. Many historians have concluded, from the mere absence of steam threshers, tractors, heavy iron ploughs, expensive fertilizers, etc., that Russia's peasant agriculture was technically stagnant. But the doubling of European Russia's peasant grain yields between the 1860s and 1911–13 suggests the opposite. There actually occurred a steady diffusion of inexpensive, unexciting, mainly small-scale agricultural advances which were revolutionary in their cumulative impact, and which were accommodated without intolerable risk by pragmatic, uneducated, but not stupid smallholders: new seed strains; new or newish crops (especially potatoes, maize, beets, sunflowers and tobacco); improved livestock breeds; poultry and pig rearing; considerable specialization within cattle and sheep rearing; iron parts for wooden ploughs, carts, wheelbarrows, spades, forks, hoes and seed drills; and cheaper, more modern, more mass-produced scythes (often replacing the slower and more back-breaking sickle), horseshoes (increasing the productivity and durability of horses), harrows, galvanized iron buckets, storage jars and bottles, wheels, axles, nails, screws, bolts, wire fencing, roofing iron, bricks, cement, glass, fossil fuels, rope, sacking, etc. Russia's stock of agricultural equipment roughly *trebled* from 1890 to 1913 (Kahan, 1978, 300), and in the 1890s agriculture consumed more of Russia's booming iron output than the concurrent railway bonanza (Liashchenko, 1949T, 508). The increasing intensity, diversity and territorial extent of Russia's peasant agriculture was also related to the fact that, by the 1880s, the former serfs were mainly working for themselves. Moreover, by 1915 nearly one-third of Russia's population belonged to credit co-operatives, mainly in rural areas (Pavlovsky, 1930, 231–45).

It is also beyond doubt that Russia was comparatively well endowed with both cropland and pasture per agricultural inhabitant (see Table 6), and the doubling of Russia's cultivated area since 1913 proves that there were still huge reserves of arable land. Very little of the extension of cultivated area has depended on expensive irrigation, which was still confined to only 6 per cent of Soviet cropland in 1975, and this 6 per cent was mostly in Central Asia and Azerbaijan. On average, peasant allotments in European Russia in 1905 were two to three times bigger than farms in early twentieth-century Southern and Eastern Europe and three to ten times bigger than farms in mid-twentieth-century Japan, East Asia and India (see Table 7, last column). Thanks to communal landownership and ample reserves of arable, only 4.4 per cent of European Russia's peasant allotments were under 2.2 ha in 1877 and the proportion was still under 5 per cent in 1905 (Table 7). But in Southern and Eastern Europe one-third to two-thirds of all farms were until recently under 2 ha (Table 7), and this contrast was seldom offset by differences in yields per hectare (see Table 12). Moreover, in 1900 hired labourers made up only 5 per cent of Russia's agrarian workforce, easily the lowest proportion in pre-1914 Europe (see Table 4). The relatively Westernized Ukraine was an exception which proved the rule: here communal landownership was relatively rare (see Table 5) and arable reserves were running short (its cultivated area has only risen by one-fifth since 1913); so by 1905 about half its peasant allotments were under 5.5 ha (Table 7), although its yields per hectare weren't much above average (Table 12). But even here hired labourers made up only 3–4 per cent of the agrarian workforce (Table 4).

Russia was also comparatively well endowed with livestock, especially horses (see Table 13); and before the First World War, 86, 82 and 83 per cent of horses, cattle and pigs, respectively, belonged to the peasantry (Antsiferov, 1930, 87–8). As was normal in peasant Europe, peasant livestock were scrawny, undemanding beasts, appropriate to the smallholder's limited means and requirements. The powerful English carthorse would have been grossly underused relative to capital cost and upkeep.

Contrary to another common belief, Russia's gross tax burden was comparatively light in the years 1888–95. Gross tax revenues amounted to the following percentages of national income (Mulhall, 1896, 393, and 1898, 557; Oshima, 1965):

	Russia	Italy	Spain	Portugal	Greece
1888–90	7	22	12	14	—
1891–5	11	19	11	13	15

	Austria-Hungary	Germany	France	Japan
1888–90	10	10	14	15
1891–5	12	10	12	15

And to the following amounts per inhabitant (in pounds sterling p.a.):

	Russia	Italy	Spain	Portugal	Greece
1888–90	0.8	2.7	2.0	1.7	1.2
1891–5	1.0	2.7	1.7	1.8	1.8

	Austria-Hungary	Germany	France	Japan
1888–90	1.4	2.3	3.7	—
1891–5	2.0	2.5	3.7	—

As late as 1913, amid the prewar arms race, Russia's gross state revenues per capita amounted to only '12 rubles 78 kopeks, or 11.2% of gross national income', and in European Russia the peasant contribution was 10 rubles 54 kopeks per capita, so non-peasants must have made rather higher contributions than peasants (Preobrazhensky, 1979T, 35). The Soviet Finance Ministry also estimated that in 1913 the proportion of peasant income paid in taxes was close to the national average, enabling the peasantry to spend two-fifths of its income – far more than it paid in taxes – on manufactures (Sokolnikov, 1931T, 281, 283, 141). The burden of state spending was 'no more than about 13% of national income' in Russia during 1885–1913 (Milward and Saul, 1977, 385). Nowadays, even in capitalist states, public spending commonly exceeds 30 or 40 per cent of national income. Also the *composition* of Russia's state revenues reveals that the business community – the main beneficiary – paid disproportionately large, but fully justifiable, direct and indirect contributions (see Miller, 1926, ch. 7; Drage, 1904, 273; Seton-Watson, 1952, 121, 288). Like most of pre-1914 Europe, the Russian state increasingly relied on indirect taxes on consumer goods, which supposedly hit the poor hardest. But in Russia over two-thirds of these indirect tax revenues came from alcohol, sugar and tobacco, which were not prime necessities of life and which were consumed less in Russia than elsewhere in Europe (Mulhall, 1898, 557; Mitchell, 1975, 709–15); and these revenues grew more via rising consumption levels and elimination of middle-men (tax farmers) than via increased tax rates (Simms, 1977, 386–91). So the common assumption that Russia's peasants were being impoverished by excise duties on non-essentials is largely nonsensical.

Russia's peasants were also benefiting from the expansion of Russia's manufacturing output, which grew by approximately 5 per cent per annum during 1860–83 and 1883–1913 alike, allowing for small workshops as well as factory industry (Goldsmith, 1961, 471). Consumer goods industries contributed 78.5 per cent of factory output in 1887 and 70 per cent in 1913 (Table 15); about one-quarter of the output of Russia's producer goods industries was bought by the agricultural sector (see Liashchenko, 1949T, 508); food processing and textiles contributed two-thirds of the craft industries' output up to 1913 (Kaufman, 1962, 20); and Russia was not a major exporter of manufactures. So there must have been a commensurate growth of popular purchasing power, or industry would have been unable to sell its output. According to Gregory (1980b, 100), personal consumption expenditures rose 3.4 per cent per annum during 1885–1913 in constant 1913 rubles, but this probably understates the real rate of increase, given that this was a period of major technical change and cost reduction. Moreover, increasing popular expenditure on manufactures did not depress peasant consumption of food grains and potatoes, which rose 3.5 per cent per annum from 1885–89 to 1897–1901 and 3.7 per cent per annum from then to 1909–13 (Gregory, 1980a, 148).

Recognition of the comparatively light taxation and comparatively high, rising peasant production and consumption levels in pre-1914 Russia undermines the common assumption that the accumulation of peasant tax arrears was caused by excessive taxation and mounting impoverishment. In practice, the accumulation of arrears was a form of tax evasion or passive resistance, based on fully vindicated expectations that successive tsars and finance ministers would periodically remit taxes and cancel arrears and that endemic inflation would meanwhile reduce the real amount owed to the Treasury. Also fear of the emergent revolutionary movement and of possible peasant unrest made the state increasingly reluctant to exact full, punctual payment of taxes and arrears (cf. British India after the First World War). Mr Micawbers will always mistake problems of cash flow or insolvency for poverty, but in Russia all classes tended to live beyond their financial means, none more so than the wealthy landlord class, and decades of rampant inflation had further encouraged them to live on credit and postpone payments. Significantly, peasant tax arrears were greatest in the relatively prosperous, lightly populated Volga basin, and least in the relatively poor, thickly populated Ukrainian black earth region (see Drage, 1904, 115–16).

Furthermore, while insecure tenancy and burdensome rents were widespread in Europe (see Table 5), by 1906 Russia's peasants had become outright owners of their allotments, 78 per cent on a communal basis, 22 per cent on an individual family basis (Table 5); the land they rented merely supplemented the land they now owned. Up to 1905 nearly all Russia's peasant households were obliged to buy by instalments the land they had been allotted during the dissolution of serfdom, but the real burden of these so-called 'redemption payments' had been rapidly reduced by inflation (1860s to 1880s) and remissions (1880s and 1890s). 'Redemption payments' amounted to no more than 9 per cent of state revenue in the years 1886–97 and had fallen to only 4 per cent of state revenue by 1903 (Drage, 1904, 273; Seton-Watson, 1952, 121). Given that state revenue amounted to approximately 11 per cent of Russia's national income and that agriculture contributed over half Russia's national income, these 'redemption payments' must have amounted to less than 2 per cent of agricultural output by the 1890s.

In the meantime capitalist industrialization was also expanding opportunities for intensive horticulture, dairying, livestock rearing and industrial crops. It cut transport costs, broke local monopolies, squeezed middlemen's margins, cut the real cost of manufactures, spread new skills, broadened horizons and increased non-agricultural opportunities and the alternatives to helpless dependence on local landlords, employers and moneylenders, for those who were so dependent. Recognition that capitalist industrialization was conferring benefits as well as costs does not entail acceptance that industry must take the form of vast, inhuman barracks, concentrated in foul, congested conurbations. Light industries, which still make up the greater part of industrial output in consumer-oriented market economies (see Table 15), can be widely dispersed; conversely, the old concentrations of heavy industry have been in long-term decline. Industrialization has undermined the least efficient village industrial activities, but it has also provided new markets, new or cheaper inputs, new technologies, new products and new leases of life for industries which gain from proximity/responsiveness to peasant markets, direct access to agricultural raw materials, low overheads, low congestion costs, relatively unspoiled surroundings, etc. As foreseen by the likes of Kropotkin in the 1900s, electricity, new fuels and cheap overland transport have made location and scale of industry very flexible. In 1913, when Russia had become the world's fourth largest manufacturer, small and mainly rural workshops still provided one-half of Russia's industrial employment and one-third of its industrial output (Kaufman, 1962, 19). The common impression that Russian industry was heavily concentrated in large urban combines was a statistical illusion: official industrial censuses simply omitted the plethora of small workshops located in Russia's villages; yet census data have often been used as if they were comprehensive reflections of industrial structure (e.g. in Lenin, 1964T, 513–22).

Naturally it was widely believed that the advent of railways would accelerate the impoverishment of the peasantry (see Danielson, 1902T; Stepniak, 1888, part I; Marx and Engels, 1934T, 358–60). However, as shown on p. 12, Russia's peasantry was the *main* producer of grain for the market, while still increasing its own per capita consumption of grain (on Nemchinov's estimates even Russia's 'small and middle peasants' were marketing 15 per cent of their grain output before 1914). So the peasantry stood to gain from reduced marketing costs and access to wider markets: 'The immediate effect of the construction of railways was that they raised prices for agricultural produce on the spot of production, thus benefiting the farmers and encouraging agricultural progress' (Pavlovsky, 1930, 31). Agriculture stood to gain most from the 18,800 km of railway opened during 1851–75: 'primary trunk lines connecting the "wings" of European Russia (the Baltic area, the western region, the Black Sea and the Sea of Azov), as well as the central region around Moscow with the northwestern, western, southern and Volga regions' (Metzer, 1974, 535–6). Railways promoted interregional specialization along lines of comparative cost advantage and a more unified grain market, helping to even out interregional price differentials and the effects of local year-to-year harvest fluctuations (ibid., 536–43; White, 1975). Indeed, until 1897 grain was the main freight on Russia's railways (Liashchenko, 1949T, 515). Agriculture also benefited from the expanding fleet of steamboats on the 83,000 km of navigable inland waterway: 646 in 1863; 1824 in 1890; and 2539 in 1895 (ibid., 516; Drage, 1904, 216). The attendant fall in real retail food prices was bound to benefit urban and rural wage-earners much more than the rich, who spent most of their money on items other than food.

Moreover, despite persistent assertions that the 1860s extension and consolidation of Russia's village commune system could only restrict labour mobility, the number of 'internal passports' issued per year rose rapidly (Rashin, 1958, 327, 333):

1861–70	1871–80	1881–90	1891–1900	1901–10	1906–10
1.3m.	3.7m.	4.9m.	7.0m.	8.9m.	9.4m.

According to the 1897 population census, 11.3 million people lived in provinces other than the ones in which they were born and a further 6.5 million people lived in cities or districts other than the ones in which they were born; in all, 15 per cent of the population lived away from its native city or district (Leasure and Lewis, 1968, 377). On this showing Russian mobility was about one-half the very high US level, but probably above West European levels. In the century preceding 1913 around 5 million people colonized Siberia and around 20 million settled on the steppes. And contrary to Gerschenkron's unsound notion that Russia's industrialization was being retarded by alleged immobility of peasant labour, 'the number of so-called "long-term passports" issued to peasants leaving for extended labour in industry' rose from 59,200 per year during 1861–70 to 1,845,000 per year during 1891–1900 (Liashchenko, 1949T, 419), enabling Russia's industrial proletariat to expand comparatively fast: 2.4 per cent per annum during the 1860s to 1890s and 2.5 per cent per annum from then to 1913, when the number of factory and mining workers in European Russia reached 2.6 million (Rashin, 1958, 192). Besides long-term mobility, the number of passengers per year on Russia's railways rose from 21 million in 1871 to 37 million in 1882, 104 million in 1900 and 245 million in 1912 (Mitchell, 1975, 606).

These facts, far from invalidating Marx's case in favour of communal village-based development in Russia, indicate that its prospects were more favourable than he realized: communal village-based development was already making good headway alongside the large-scale capitalist sectors. So why did Russia experience massive peasant unrest from 1902 to 1922? Despite their improving and comparatively favourable economic position, most of Russia's peasants had good reason for deep discontent. Many resented being made to redeem land which they had regarded as their own communal or family property for centuries back, however modest the 'redemption payments'. And, adding insult to injury, in European Russia the peasantry had forfeited 4 per cent of the land it had held in usufruct up to the 1860s dissolution of serfdom (Zaionchkovsky, 1954, 206–7). However, this forfeit was soon more than offset by new acquisitions (see Antsiferov, 1930, 20). Also usury was by all accounts rife in rural Russia, although the comparatively low tax and rent burdens on Russia's peasants and the inalienability, egalitarian regime and comparative abundance of Russia's allotment land presumably meant that it was much less of a problem here than in most other peasant societies. More seriously, the Russian state's previous neglect of rural services had left the peasantry abysmally ignorant of even the most elementary principles of personal and domestic hygiene. So, despite comparatively plentiful food supplies, Russia suffered Europe's worst mortality and morbidity rates (see Tables 2 and 23).

Dr H. P. Kennard, a peripatetic physician who 'gained his knowledge of the Russian peasant from personal contact and living with him in villages in all parts of European Russia' (Kennard, 1907, ix), described a 'typical' Russian peasant dwelling thus: 'The wooden structure rises perhaps 8 feet . . . and encloses an area of 14 to 20 feet square.' On entering, 'we find . . . our feet enveloped beyond the ankles in farmyard slush. . . . Puddles of insanitary messes reflect a dull light, while from the same pools of filth rises an unutterable stench' (ibid., 23–6). The inner room is 'a steaming hole inexpressibly fouler than the one we have just left. . . . Looming through the stifling, sickly mist appears a large block of stone, taking up about a third of the tiny room. . . . This is the oven'. There is 'no chimney in the ordinary izba [hovel]', so 'the wretched inmates . . . wallow like pigs in this pestilential atmosphere, blended of the excretory putrescences exhaled from men and animals'. The oven 'besides acting the part of vapour and warmth producer, is used as a kitchener . . . and as a sort of open wardrobe, on which everything is laid to keep warm. Further, it is used as a public bed for the family . . . during the night and frequently during the long winter days – as many as can crowd on. . . . Pigs, lambs, lie where they may and are all covered with loathsome parasites. . . . Fresh air there is none' (ibid., 27–30): 'But in times of sickness the Russian izba becomes even more insupportable.' Attending victims of typhus and scurvy, 'all in a state of indescribable filth . . . their hair matted in hopeless entanglement . . . by the matter exuding from unsightly sores, I noticed batches of bloated flies tumbling over one another in their efforts to feed on the sores' (ibid., 35–8). Russian peasants 'frequent en masse the village vapour bath [sauna]', but afterwards 'again don their discarded, filthy sheepskins' (ibid., 75, 78).

To quote Ivan Bunin's *The Village* (1909): 'Epidemic diseases broke out in the villages: smallpox, typhus, scarlet fever, croup. But those maladies had existed uninterruptedly in the villages since time immemorial . . . and people had become so used to them that they made no more mention of them than they did of changes in the weather.' In winter 'little girls capered out of the houses straight from the stoves, wearing only their tiny chemises'. Young boys 'were racked by terrible coughs and returned home at evening in a state of fever . . . so chilled they could barely move their lips . . . and, after drinking, they would creep tearfully on to the oven. But even the mothers ignored the sick' (pt 3.4).

In my view, Russia's peasants were mainly victims of ignorance, disease, a harsh climate and state negligence, rather than narrowly economic circumstances. Data for 1924–6, when agriculture had almost regained pre-1914 levels of output, suggest that regional variations in net agricultural output per person dependent on agriculture were remarkably small for so large a country (see Table 9). And in a book on the legendary *Famine in Russia, 1891–1892*, Professor R. G. Robbins (1976, 2) admitted that the 1891 grain harvest was merely '26% below the norm' in a country which normally produced a surfeit of grain, whose other food crops were far less affected and whose railways had by then produced a unified grain market, capable of evening out the effects of the very localized 1891 crop failure. Moreover, 'the available evidence for 1891–92 seems to indicate that if starvation occurred, it was rather rare. . . . No deaths from starvation were listed' (ibid., 236): 'We possess fairly good data on mortality. . . . The big killers . . . were by all accounts cholera and typhus' (ibid., 170). Cholera claimed 'up to 300,000 lives in 1892', but it had 'also appeared when there were no great agricultural difficulties. Typhus was endemic to the Russian countryside, so its presence cannot be blamed on lack of food' (ibid.). Perversely, he persists in treating this disaster as if it was primarily a famine (see ibid., 4–6, 171). It is more credible that the poor 1891 grain harvest was responsible for an above-average slaughter of livestock (ibid., 173), with which Russia was well endowed (see Table 13). Russia's susceptibility to cholera (and other Asiatic diseases) is best explained by unhygienic housing and life-styles, extensive direct contact with Central Asia and Turkey, and state negligence. As cholera is a water-borne disease, its prevention is mainly a matter of public sanitation and domestic hygiene, especially in relation to waterways, water supplies and waste disposal. The cholera epidemics of 1829–33 (0.24 million deaths), 1847–55 (1.02 million deaths), 1866–72 (0.33 million deaths) and 1908–10 (0.14 million deaths) were apparently unconnected with so-called 'famines' (see Baroyan, 1968, 17; McGrew, 1965). Interestingly Dr J. D. Post, whose challenging doctoral thesis systematically compared evidence from many parts of early nineteenth-century Europe, also found that dearths did not regularly coincide with unusually high mortality and morbidity rates; instead the incidence of high mortality and morbidity rates was more closely related to housing conditions, life-styles, popular ignorance, state negligence and degree of contact with Asia (see Post, 1976). And it is pertinent that, thanks to concerted public health and education programmes, Asian states have greatly reduced mortality rates, despite persistently low per capita food supplies (see Tables 11 and 2: China, India and Pakistan). So, within broad limits, food supply and mortality can be mutually independent variables.

Nevertheless, the dissolution of serfdom, complementary reforms in the way Russia was administered, and the advent of railways and modern industry generated expectations and demands which were not (or could not be) adequately fulfilled, thus breeding violent and sometimes 'unreasonable' discontent. To maintain its power and prestige the tsarist regime repeatedly took calculated risks – and eventually lost. And although serfdom had been dissolved, peasants remained fourth-class citizens, denied civil equality with townspeople, segregated by a system

of social apartheid. Moreover, demand for education was outstripping the overdue expansion of educational opportunities, although by 1914 the facilities
weren't so bad: two-thirds of army recruits could read, over half Russia's industrial workers could read, and nearly half Russia's adults could read (see Table 3;
and Rashin, 1958, 582–601). Hence the escalation of political pamphleteering,
which presupposed a literate audience. None the less, Russia's mushrooming
radical intelligentsia remained outraged by the system's inequities and narrow-
minded restrictions. Pobedonostsev, the real power behind the throne from 1881
to 1905, actually 'evaluated the contradictions hidden in the depths of national
life far more soberly than did the liberals. He understood that, once the screws
were loosened, the pressure from below would tear off the social roof in its
entirety. . . . It wasn't his fault that the processes of history proved mightier
than the Byzantine system which he . . . defended so forcefully' (Trotsky,
1975T, 96). Ethnic minorities, in particular, were antagonized by his per-
secutions and heavy-handed discrimination. Moreover, the state and predatory
capitalism were increasingly perceived as violating and undermining the pseudo-
Christian, paternalistic value-system which they pretended to uphold, sowing disaffection even among would-be loyalists. The rather disreputable official church
was losing ground to untainted nonconformist movements numbering some 20
million Russian adherents by the 1900s, especially in rural areas (Lane, 1978, 26,
91–166). Although traditionally too other-worldly and secessionist to join political opposition movements, persecution was goading them into more active rejection of the tsar 'Antichrist' and the state: Tolstoyans, Dukhobori and Baptists
were most conspicuously active. All in all, it was very widely felt that tsarism
had forfeited any *right* to rule.

Meantime, due to profligacy, the fatal attractions of city life, feckless inability to
successfully employ wage-labour in competition with leaner and fitter peasant
farms, and loss of nerve when confronted by an increasingly assertive, self-
confident, literate, class-conscious and indomitable peasantry (see Mavor, 1925,
vol. 2, ch. 7; Perrie, 1976, ch. 11), Russia's former serfowners were relinquishing
their estates and hence their residual control of Russia's countryside. So social
control increasingly rested on the police and the army, bringing the peasantry into
more direct confrontation with the state and thus *politicizing* social relations to an
unprecedented degree. Railways, improved firearms, the telegraph and the
conscript army increased the repressive power of the state and the temptation to
resort to repression (14,000 people were executed during 1901–16, inclusive, as
against 94 during 1866–1900: Legget, 1981, 468). But once police or troops were
called in, peasant 'incidents' easily escalated into full-scale trials of strength –
particularly in ethnic-minority areas, where native officials were being replaced by
Russians who, as strangers, were more likely to act clumsily. From 1905 to 1917
most provinces were under 'emergency law' (sweeping police powers) or under
martial law, as tsarism was obviously sitting on a powder keg.

The revolutionary dissolution of Russia's old order bore significant resemblances to the dissolution of 'feudalism' in France, as described by Alexis de Tocqueville:

> In all centralized countries the rural districts lose their wealthy and enlightened inhabitants. . . . None remained but those gentry whose limited means compelled them to stay. . . . Being no longer in leadership positions, they had not the same interest as of old to attend to the village population. . . . The peasantry were no longer the gentry's subjects; the gentry were not yet the peasant's fellow citizens. . . . This gave rise to a sort of absenteeism of feeling. . . . Hence a gentleman residing on his estate . . . learned to look upon his tenants as debtors and rigorously exacted from them all that he could claim by law or by custom, which sometimes rendered the application of the last remnants of feudal rights harsher than it had been in feudal times. . . . About thirty or forty years before the Revolution, the scene began to change. . . . The breath of a new life pervades the mighty body, but only to complete its dissolution. Restless and agitated, all classes are straining to better their condition. . . . Roads, canals, manufactures and commerce are the chief objects of . . . a thousand schemes to augment the nation's wealth. . . . As this prosperity became more extensive, the community nevertheless became more unsettled and . . . hatred against all established institutions increased. . . . Discontent was greatest in precisely those areas which benefited most. . . . It most frequently happens that a people which had supported the most crushing laws, without protest and apparently as if unfelt, violently throws them off as the burden begins to be diminished . . . and experience has shown that the most dangerous moment for a bad government is usually that when it embarks on reform. Nothing short of political genius can save a sovereign who undertakes to relieve his subjects after a long period of oppression. Evils patiently endured so long as they seemed inevitable become intolerable once hope of escape can be entertained. The abuses removed seem to lay bare those that remain . . . the evil has decreased, but the perception of evil is more acute. Feudalism at its apogee did not inspire so much hostility as it did on the eve of its disappearance. . . . The King was the first to show how contemptuously it was possible to treat the oldest and apparently most established institutions . . . and hastened the Revolution as much by his innovations and energy as by his vices and indolence. (de Tocqueville, 1856T, 222–7, 312–29, 344–5)

The available statistical evidence indicates that, during the eight decades preceding the French Revolution, agricultural output rose by two-thirds, industrial output rose two- or threefold and foreign trade trebled, while population rose by only one-third (Crouzet, 1967).

Similar perspectives hold good for post-Famine Ireland. Output per head in Irish agriculture doubled and grain yields per hectare rose by half between the 1850s and the 1900s. By 1922 85 per cent of Irish farmers owned their farms and hired labourers made up only one-fifth of the agrarian workforce. One in three farms had less than 10 acres, but output per acre on these farms was by 1926–7 nearly double that on farms exceeding 30 acres. Yet the further the socioeconomic position of the Irish peasantry was raised by land reform, educational advance, intensification of agriculture and emigration of surplus population, the more class-conscious, assertive and uncompromising Irish hostility to British tutelage became (see Tables 3, 4, 5, 7, 11, 12; and Crotty, 1966, 67, 82–4, 118, 130).

Likewise the great groundswell of peasant radicalism in early twentieth-century Eastern Europe occurred as the socioeconomic position of most peasants was being strengthened in the course of protracted national-revolutionary struggles to establish independent, predominantly peasant nation-states and to expropriate landed nobilities (see Tables 4, 5, 7, 11, 23; and Tomasevich, 1955; Mitrany, 1930; Bell, 1977; Kieniewicz, 1969; Bizzell, 1926). Similarly, Dr Anne Waswo's major study of *Japanese Landlords* (1977, 4–6 ff.) found that, during the early twentieth-century upsurge in tenant unrest, 'Landlords lost the respect and obedience of their tenants less because they opposed progress than because they promoted it.'

Not every eruption of peasant unrest is explainable à la de Tocqueville. But the more impoverished and downtrodden the peasantry, and the more it is preoccupied by day-to-day, hand-to-mouth survival, the less it can engage in sustained, purposeful revolutionary activities. That is not to deny that it is often *politically expedient* to exaggerate the peasants' economic plight.

Engels on peasant societies

Ironically, while Marx was preparing to resist attempts 'to metamorphose my outline of the genesis of capitalism in Western Europe into a historico-philosophical theory of la marche générale, fatally incumbent on all peoples, whatever their historical circumstances', Engels was aiding and abetting that very metamorphosis, as can be seen most clearly in his essay on 'Social relations in Russia' (1875):

> The revolution sought by modern socialism is, in short, the proletariat's victory over the bourgeoisie and social reorganization by elimination of class distinctions. This needs both a proletariat to accomplish the revolution and a bourgeoisie in whose hands society's productive forces are sufficiently developed to permit a final elimination of class distinctions. Class distinctions are often absent in primitive societies and every people has passed through such a state. But it's unthinkable that we should restore such a state, since class distinctions necessarily arise as productive forces develop. Only at a definite high level of development of society's productive forces does it become possible to raise production sufficiently for elimination of class distinctions to become really progressive, to survive without engendering stagnation or decline in the mode of social production. . . .

> The mass of the Russian people – the peasantry – have in truth lived for centuries in a monotonous, timeless stupor, interrupted by sporadic fruitless revolts, engendering further suppression. . . . But the Russian government itself set 'history in motion' in 1861 by abolishing serfdom . . . in a self-defeating manner, sure to ruin most peasants

and drive them into an opposition movement. . . . Thus the peasantry as a whole has been placed in an utterly miserable, untenable position. . . . And, on top of land tax, interest payments and redemption payments to the State, the recent introduction of local government has added provincial and cantonal taxes. . . . Such a situation is as if tailor-made for usurers and, with the Russian's almost unequalled talent for petty trade . . . the usurer appears everywhere. Just before taxes are due, the kulak – often a prosperous peasant in the same village – offers ready cash to peasants who, needing cash at any price, must meekly accept the usurer's terms. This only leads to ever deeper insolvency. At harvest the grain dealer arrives; insolvency forces the peasant to sell some of the grain needed for his family's subsistence. The dealer spreads false rumours to depress prices . . . and often pays in over-priced goods, as the truck-system is highly developed in Russia. Thus Russia's large grain exports rest upon peasant starvation. . . . Nowhere is primitive capitalist parasitism so developed, extensive and all-ensnaring as in Russia. . . .

The Russian peasantry's communal property, discovered c. 1845 by Prussian State Councillor Haxthausen, was proclaimed to be something extraordinary. . . . Herzen, himself a Russian landowner . . . used this to represent the Russian peasantry as the true bearers of Socialism, born Communists, unlike the workers of the senile, decadent, European West, who would have to undergo the ordeal of acquiring Socialism artificially. . . . Communal landownership is in fact an institution found among all Indo-Germanic peoples at a low stage of development. . . . In western Europe, including Poland and Malorussia [the Ukraine], communal landownership at some point became a fetter and brake on agricultural development, so it was progressively eliminated. But in Great Russia [Russia proper] it has survived, proving that here agriculture and hence rural social conditions are still very undeveloped. . . . The Russian peasant lives and has his being only in his village commune; for him the outside world exists only inasmuch as it intrudes. . . . Such complete mutual isolation of village communities, creating identical rather than truly common interests, is the natural basis for *Oriental* despotism, and from India to Russia this form of society has always engendered and found its complement in Oriental despotism. . . . Further development of Russia in a bourgeois direction would gradually destroy communal property. . . . The more surely as, in Russia, communally owned land isn't communally cultivated . . . instead it's periodically repartitioned among heads of families, and each cultivates his own allotment. This makes possible great disparities in prosperity amongst commune members. Almost everywhere one finds rich peasants, sometimes millionaires, who practise usury and suck the peasants' blood. . . . The commutation of corvée dealt the severest blow to communal landownership. . . . The peasant was left scarcely sufficient, often insufficient, land to subsist on. Also woods were awarded to the nobility, so peasants must now pay for the firewood, wooden implements and building timber formerly obtained gratis. . . . Under such conditions and pressure of taxation and usury, communal landownership is a fetter, not a blessing. Peasants often run off, with or without their families, relinquishing their land. So in Russia communal landownership is clearly long past its heyday and apparently approaching disintegration. Yet the possibility of upgrading this social form undeniably exists, if it survives until circumstances are ripe and if it proves capable of developing individualistic into communal cultivation. . . . But this can only happen if, before communal property fully disintegrates, revolution triumphs in western Europe and creates for the Russian peasant the preconditions for such a transition.

The artel . . . is a form of association widespread in Russia, the simplest form of free co-operation. . . . Such artels are formed (1) for temporary enterprises . . . (2) by members of a trade . . . and (3) for permanent industrial ventures. They are established by the members signing a contract. If, as often happens, they cannot put up the necessary capital . . . the artel falls prey to a usurer who . . . thereafter pockets most of the labour product. Artels which collectively hire themselves out to an employer are even more exploited: They save him supervision costs and he advances food and shelter, fostering an abominable truck system. . . . There also exist artels employing non-members as wage-labour. So the artel is a spontaneous and hence very undeveloped cooperative, and as such neither peculiarly Russian nor even Slav. . . . True, its prevalence in Russia proves that Russians have a strong urge to associate, but not that this enables them to leap directly from the artel into socialism. For that the artel would have to become capable of development, to shed its primitive form (wherein it serves capital more than labour) and rise *at least* to the level of West European co-operatives. . . . The modern co-operative has at least proved it can profitably operate large-scale industry (spinning and weaving in Lancashire). So far, the artel is incapable of that and, unless it develops further, it will of necessity be destroyed by big industry. (cf. Marx and Engels, 1951T, 46–56, and 1952T, 204–15)

Engels evidently sided with the 'literary lackeys' of capitalism, whose views were roundly rebutted by Marx in 1881. Regarding the 'necessity' of capitalist industrialization, Engels summarized his views most trenchantly in three letters to Marx's 'anointed' Russian disciple, Nikolai Danielson:

I maintain that industrial production nowadays means *grande industrie*, steam, electricity, self-acting mules, power looms, finally machines that produce machinery. From the day Russia introduced railways, introduction of these modern means was a foregone conclusion. You *must* be able to repair your own locomotives, wagons, railways, and that can only be done cheaply if you are able to *construct* those things at home. . . . From the moment warfare became a branch of *grande industrie* (ironclad ships, rifled artillery . . . etc.), *la grande industrie* . . . became a political necessity. All these things cannot be had without highly developed metal manufacture. . . . This necessity of the transition . . . to the modern methods . . . once conceded, it becomes a secondary question whether the hothouse process of fostering the industrial revolution by protective or prohibitive duties was advantageous or even necessary. . . . This hothouse atmosphere renders the process acute. . . . It crams into twenty years a development which otherwise might have taken sixty or more years. But it does not affect the nature of the process. . . . One thing is certain: if Russia really required, and was determined to have, a *grande industrie* of her own, she could not have it at all except under *some* degree of protection, and . . . the question of protection is one of *degree* only, not of principle; the principle was unavoidable. Another thing is certain: if Russia required . . . a *grande industrie* of her own, she could have it in one form only: the *capitalistic form*. And along with that form, she was obliged to take over all the consequences which accompany capitalistic *grande industrie* in all other countries. . . . You complain of the slow increase of hands employed in the textile industry, when compared with the increase of . . . product. The same is taking place everywhere. . . . You complain that machine-made goods supersede the products of domestic industry and thus destroy a supplementary production without which the peasant cannot live. But we have here an absolutely necessary consequence of capitalistic *grande industrie*: the creation of the home market. . . . Russians had to decide whether *their own grande industrie* was to destroy their domestic manufacture, or whether *the import of English goods* was to accomplish this. *With* protection, the Russians effected it; *without* protection, the English. . . . But without domestic industry the peasantry cannot live. They are ruined *as peasants* . . . and until they, *as proletarians*, have settled down into new conditions of existence, they will furnish a very poor market for the newly arisen factories. Capitalist production is full of internal contradictions. . . . This tendency to destroy its own market at the same time as it creates it is one. . . . Another is the *impasse* to which it leads . . . sooner in a country *without* a foreign market, like Russia, than in countries . . . capable of competing on the open world market. (22 September 1892)

Now . . . do you see any possibility of the *grande industrie* being grafted on the peasants' commune in a form which would . . . make the development of that *grande industrie* possible and . . . raise the primitive commune to the rank of a social institution superior to anything the world has yet seen?. . . . It strikes me that such an evolution, which would have surpassed anything known in history, required other economical, political and intellectual conditions than were present. . . . If we in the West had been quicker in our economic development, if we had been able to upset the capitalistic regime some ten or twenty years ago, there might have been time yet for Russia to cut short the tendency of her own evolution towards capitalism. Unfortunately we are too slow. . . . For the rest I grant you that the circumstance of Russia being the last [European] country seized upon by capitalist *grande industrie*, and . . . with by far the largest *peasant* population . . . must render the *bouleversement* caused by this economic change more acute than it has been anywhere else. (14 July 1893)

No doubt the passage from primitive agrarian communism to capitalistic industrialism cannot take place without great dislocation of society, the disappearance of whole classes . . . and what enormous suffering and waste of human lives and productive forces that necessarily implies, we have seen – on a smaller scale – in Western Europe. But from that to the complete ruin of a great and highly gifted nation there is still a long way . . . after all, a population of more than 100 millions will finally furnish a very considerable home market for a very respectable *grande industrie* and, with you as elsewhere, things will end by finding their own level. . . . I would go further and say that no more in Russia than anywhere else would it have been possible to develop a higher social form out of primitive agrarian communes unless that higher form was *already in existence* in another country, to serve as a model. That form being, wherever it is historically possible, the necessary consequence of the capitalist form of production and the social dualistic antagonism created by it, it could not be developed directly out of the agrarian commune. . . . I am afraid that institution is doomed. But on the other hand, capitalism opens out new vistas and new hopes. Look at what it has done and is doing in the West. . . . There is no great historical evil without a compensating historical progress. Only the *modus operandi* is changed. *Que les destinées s'accomplissent.* (17 October 1893)

Engels reaffirmed these hard-nosed fatalistic views in 1894, adding that Russia's difficulties in servicing her ever-mounting external debts were pushing her towards industrial autarky and that 'the young Russian bourgeoisie has the State entirely in its power'. Hence Russia's 'transformation into a capitalistic-industrial nation, the proletarianization of a large part of the peasantry, and the breakup of the village community all progress at an ever faster rate' (see Marx and Engels, 1952T, 229–41).

Engels obviously took great pains over his gloomy prognoses for Europe's largest peasant society. Like Marx, he learned Russian and studied an impressive range of Russian socioeconomic literature; and most Soviet and Western historians of Russia have gone along with the main thrusts of his thesis, which were easily incorporated into the conventional wisdom of industrializers and capitalist-roaders. But his dismal portrayal of the plight of the Russian peasantry is contradicted by the international and intertemporal comparisons which I have already put forward. Perhaps if Russian capitalism had been permitted to develop *unchecked* for another century or more, his dire predictions *might* have begun to come true (I have my doubts). But on his own admission in 1875 and again in 1894, 'Russia is undoubtedly on the eve of a revolution . . . which, once precipitated by the capital's upper classes or even by the government, the peasantry can only carry beyond the constitutional phase.' Moreover, the Russian Revolution would in fact cut short Russia's evolution towards capitalism, unaided by any 'proletarian' revolution in the West. Furthermore, the actual contraction of peasantries in modern Europe and Asia has so far been slow enough to proceed mainly through intergenerational mobility, as horizons and non-agricultural opportunities have broadened, rather than through the ineluctable 'ruin' of agricultural smallholders; and even the size distribution of farms has remained remarkably stable during capitalist industrialization in peasant Europe and Japan (see Table 7). Engels merely steered 'Marxist' orthodoxy deeper into the gloomy, fatalistic impasse which Marx had belatedly endeavoured to avoid.

At bottom, Engels was enthralled by the Anglocentricity of classical political economy. Since Britain's pioneering, trend-setting Industrial Revolution had occurred in an agriculturally and commercially advanced, highly urbanized and proletarianized society in which private property, private contractual relations, rule of law, individualism and *laissez-faire* ostentatiously rewarded greed and good fortune and humiliatingly penalized frailty and misfortune, it was widely assumed that other states must follow suit: Britain seemed to show less developed countries the image of their own futures; British norms and institutions became universal desiderata; and the behavioural laws of British political economy were metamorphosed into universal laws of the wealth of nations and of human happiness. But it was unrealistic and unimaginative to suppose that there was a single ineluctable path of development, one road to socialism. Many nations could echo the closing punchline of Stepniak's masterpiece, *The Russian Peasantry* (1888): 'We are not European enough to successfully imitate a progress based on the fruition of individual interests.' Precisely because Britain was already highly urbanized, proletarianized, and agriculturally and commercially advanced *before* her Industrial Revolution, which was the only one never to be threatened by foreign competition, her experience has little relevance to the problems, needs, aspirations and capabilities of most later-developing countries.

Unfortunately, in *Anti-Dühring* (1878), *Socialism: Scientific and Utopian* (1882), *The Origin of the Family, Private Property and the State* (1884), countless letters and his posthumously published *Dialectics of Nature*, Engels brought further 'necessitarian' rigidities into 'Marxist' dialectics, historiography, jurisprudence, sociology, theory of the state and philosophy of science. He metamorphosed 'Marxism' into a closed, all-embracing, rigidly deterministic system of thought, which would culminate in the reductionist crudities of the rival 'Marxist' orthodoxies contending for supremacy in the world today. The numbing orthodoxies propagated by Engels and Karl Kautsky in Germany, Paul Lafargue in France and Georgy Plekhanov in Russia seemingly offered leftist intellectuals weighty excuses for burying their heads in books and statistics while capitalism ran its course (see Kolakowski, 1978, vol. 2, chs 2, 6, 14). 'Marxists in reality remained imprisoned by the conservative mood of the eighties, displaying an inability to take bold initiatives . . . shoving the revolution into the indefinite future and generally inclining to regard socialism as a task for centuries of evolution' (Trotsky, 1975T, 100).

In 'The peasant question in France and Germany' (1894) Engels belatedly gave his rather damning views on the peasantry a more hopeful, more realistic twist. He still regarded peasantries as 'hopelessly doomed', 'apathetic' and increasingly 'prejudiced' against his own brand of socialism. But, like Lenin, he perceived that the industrial-capitalist road to socialism would be better served by pressing for immediate protection and further development of 'small peasant' agriculture than by letting it go to 'ruin'. However, even on this line of argument, the interests of the peasant majority were to remain very subordinate to those of industry and the proletarian minority – a prospect unlikely to elicit much peasant support.

2 The case for village communism: from Herzen and Bakunin to Chayanov and Gandhi

This chapter reconsiders the case for communal, village-based development and answers the principal objections raised by the critics of 'populism'. My arguments draw upon Indian, Yugoslav, Polish, Taiwanese, South Korean, Japanese, Vietnamese, Danish, Irish and Tanzanian experience, but one must begin in pre-Stalinist Russia: nowhere else has village communism achieved such sway over the political culture of a great nation or enjoyed such favourable prospects. Indeed, village communism had a *sounder* basis in Russia's popular traditions, peasant aspirations, rural institutions and economic capabilities than did the large-scale, city-centred industrialization strategies forced upon it by regimes which could only proceed by wasteful and stultifying coercion and intimidation of a people whose technical backwardness, lack of capital, indiscipline, and dominant traditions and aspirations were fundamentally at odds with the treadmills imposed by successive harsh taskmasters.

Alexander Herzen (1812–70)

Herzen, a wealthy Russian landowner who from 1847 lived in exile in Western Europe, was to become one of Russia's most prolific and widely respected writers. His famous essay on 'The Russian People and Socialism' (1851) was seminal to the subsequent elaboration of village communism:

> Only when united in an association of free autonomous peoples can the Slav world finally commence its real historical existence. Its past can only be considered a period of incubation. . . . Russia remains an unfinished edifice wherein everything smells of fresh plaster . . . and nothing has been finalized. . . . The innocent, nonchalant Russian peasant has been gradually ensnared by seigneurial power and the Germanic bureaucracy . . . but has never accepted the legitimacy of seigneurial prerogatives,

the law-courts and the administration. . . . The peasant venerates not Tsar Nicholas, but an abstract popular myth, a Providential avenger, a symbol of Justice. . . . He only acknowledges rights and duties *vis-à-vis* communes and their members. Outside the commune he recognizes not duties, merely coercion. . . . The plebeian only respects institutions reflecting his own conceptions of Right and Justice. . . . Peasants rarely cheat one another . . . they know nothing of written contracts. . . . Under repartitional landholding problems of field-measurement are necessarily complex . . . yet they cope without complaint or litigation. The state and landlords relish chances to interfere, yet few arise. Petty disputes are soon settled by elders or the commune and all unconditionally accept their decisions. The same goes for their co-operatives (artels). These comprise hundreds of individuals from different communes who associate for a given period – say, a year – and agree to divide their remuneration according to work done. Police are denied the satisfaction of meddling in their accounts. Co-operatives normally assume responsibility for all their members. . . . The Russian peasant has no morality but what flows naturally, instinctively from his communism . . . the little he knows of the Gospels supports it. . . . Although severely mauled, the communal system has fortunately withstood state interference and survived to see the emergence of socialism in Europe. . . . The tsar hesitates. . . . He sees that freeing the peasant involves freeing the land, which would in turn inaugurate a social revolution proclaiming village communism. (Translated from Herzen, 1954–65, vol. 7, 273–300)

Herzen detailed some of the virtues of village communism in his essay 'On the Development of Revolutionary Ideas in Russia' (1851):

Responsible for all its members, it's autonomous in all that concerns its internal affairs. . . . Land belongs to the commune, not to individual members; each has an inviolable right to as much land as every other member. . . . He cannot and doesn't need to bequeath it. His son, on attaining manhood, has a claim to a portion of communal land even in his father's lifetime. . . . Conversely, when a family member dies, his portion reverts to the commune. The elderly often renounce their land in return for tax exemptions. A peasant temporarily absent from the commune doesn't forfeit his rights to land, which can only be withdrawn if he is banished by unanimous vote or by the government, a sanction used only in extreme cases. A peasant also loses his rights if, at his request, he is released from the communal union. Then he can take with him only his moveable assets; he is rarely allowed to sell or remove his home. Each landholder . . . has a voice in the commune's affairs. The village elder and his assistants are elected by general meetings. Disputes between communes and allocation of land and taxes are decided likewise. . . . Haxthausen is very mistaken in his claim that the elder administers the commune as a despot. He can act despotically only if the commune supports him. . . . Germanic and Celtic communes succumbed to two social concepts utterly opposed to communal life: feudalism and Roman law. Happily we, with our commune, present ourselves to an age when anti-communal civilization is facing the impossibility of extricating itself on its own terms from the contradictions between individual and social rights. It's said that, by perpetual repartition of the soil, communal life will find its natural limit through population growth.

However grave this objection might appear, . . . Russia still has ample land for the next century, during which the burning question of ownership and property will be resolved one way or the other. Many writers, including Haxthausen, assert that under impermanent possession agriculture doesn't improve. Maybe, but these amateurs forget that agricultural improvement under the Western system of possession leaves most people in wretchedness. For me, the enrichment of a few farmers and agriculture's progress as an art cannot be considered just recompense for the horrific plight of a hungry proletariat. (Translated from Herzen, 1954–65, vol. 7, 128–32)

During the 1850s Herzen emerged as one of Europe's outstanding campaigners for peasants' liberation. He was widely admired because he articulated widely shared hopes, fears and sympathies and appealed to man's better nature. His tract against *Russian Serfdom* (1853) drew parallels with the concurrent crusade against American slavery and warned that to liberate Russia's serfs without guaranteeing them enough land to cover their basic needs would result in 'a proletariat of 20 millions of men in a country already so ill-governed that the free . . . find no shelter against the arbitrary vexations of an arbitrary police. . . . The communal element . . . of Slavonic life would be utterly destroyed.' He knew some would 'rejoice in the formation of a proletariat, because they see in it the source of revolutionary expansion'. But 'the rustic labourer (*prolétaire*) is not, generally speaking, a revolutionist like the operatives of great cities. In those dense hives of monopolized industry . . . the working man becomes a revolutionist; not so in the solitude of the fields.' He knew 'the communal life of Russian villages . . . would ill satisfy the aspirations of later European theorists. . . . But who pulls down an unfinished house with the idea of rebuilding it on the same plan?' The village commune was the embryo of 'complete socialistic self-government' (Herzen, 1954–65, vol. 12, 7–25):

The idea of social revolution is European. That doesn't mean that the people most capable of its realization are those of the West. Christianity was crucified in Jerusalem. . . . It's only natural to ask whether Russia must repeat all Europe's phases of development. . . . Such a repetition seems to me utterly unnecessary. . . . A job done, a result obtained, is done and obtained for all who grasp it. . . . Every schoolchild discovers Euclid's propositions anew, but what a difference between Euclid's labours and our children's. Russia has had done with Europe's schoolroom. . . . Her people need not repeat Europe's forlorn labours or shed blood merely to reach Europe's semi-solutions, whose only importance is to have posed *other* questions and to have aroused *other* aspirations. . . . For Europeanized Russians, the real rediscovery of the Russian people dates from the 1830s. . . . The supposedly indifferent, apolitical Russian people were seen to be groping towards a new non-European form of social organization. Maybe, critics say, but it also approximates the organization of some Asiatic peoples, e.g. the Hindu village commune. . . . I wouldn't deny that Asiatic peoples possess some social institutions superior to those of the West. What holds back Asiatic peoples isn't the commune, but immobility, exclusivism, unreadiness to root out patriarchy. . . . Conversely, the Slavs are displaying great adaptability; their facility for assimilating arts, languages, customs, technologies, etc. is remarkable. They are acclimatizing as well in the Arctic as by the Black Sea. . . . All our education is decidedly cosmopolitan. . . . Education detaches our youths from an immoral soil . . . and opposes them to official Russia. . . . To conserve the commune, free the individual, extend communal and district self-government to the towns and the entire state, develop individual rights, and to sustain national unity and the indivisibility of the land – that is Russia's revolutionary assignment. . . . Russian imperialism will soon wither, decompose, confronted by a liberal Europe. . . . The Petersburg autocracy is not a principle, a dogma, but a force; and to remain so it must have a role. Policing and repression are insufficient; yet it lacks the materials and the courage to do more. (Translated from Herzen, 1954–66, vol. 12, 134–63)

Beware persistent misinformed or mischievous assertions that the development potential of Russia's communes was only 'discovered' thanks to an observant foreign visitor, Baron August von Haxthausen (1792–1866), who undertook a study-tour of Russia in 1843–4. Admittedly Haxthausen's magnum opus (3 vols, 1847–52; 2 vols, 1856T) publicized Russia's commune system internationally. But, not surprisingly, Russia's basic rural institution had already dominated the agrarian programme propounded by Colonel Pavel Pestel, executed for his leading role in the abortive *coup d'état* staged by radical Guards officers in December 1825, and Herzen readily acknowledged an ideological debt to this celebrated 'Decembrist' (see Venturi, 1966T, 5–9). Moreover, as was enthusiastically described by Haxthausen (1856T, vol. 2, 404–49), the major assignment of the Ministry of State Domains and Agriculture established by Count P. D. Kiselev in 1837–8 had been to increase Russia's taxable incomes, to render the incidence of rural taxation more equitable, to render the peasantry less vulnerable to extortionate officials and middlemen, to arrest the formation of an undesirable rural proletariat and to prepare the ground for a gradual dissolution of serfdom, by strengthening and extending communal institutions on the State Domains, which comprised about half Russia's peasants. Kiselev also reinforced the economic position of village communes by promoting peasant banks (140 by 1845), fire regulations and insurance (vital to a people with mainly wooden housing), state and communal granaries (insurance against crop failure), potato cultivation (successful despite initial popular hostility), horticulture, diffusion of new seed strains, stud farms, communal schools, agricultural prizes and exhibitions, land surveys and a gradual transition from poll tax to land tax (ibid.). Kiselev was 'capable of appreciating in part, at least, the magnificent institutions on which the commune is based' (Herzen, 1954–65, vol. 6, 26). The economic *soundness* of the stances taken by Herzen and Kiselev is supported by Soviet research findings that, as early as the 1840s and 1850s, peasants working for their own account were already contributing *three-quarters* of Russia's grain and potato production, most of the commercial livestock production and nearly all the commercial production of flax, hemp, sunflowers, fruit and vegetables, with a 'much higher' labour productivity than was obtained on the nobles' estates: 'It was precisely the fact that the peasant economy constituted an independent leading sector of commodity production which made emancipation of the peasants without land impossible' (Kovalchenko, 1967, 384–6). At this time Russia already had about as many fatstock per inhabitant as did the rest of Europe, *twice* as many horses per inhabitant (see Table 13), and a comparatively high per capita output of grain (figures below are in hectolitres and are taken from Mulhall, 1898, 7):

	Europe	Russia	Germany	Austria-Hungary	Greece
1831–40	5	7	$3\frac{1}{2}$	$4\frac{1}{2}$	2
1851–60	$5\frac{1}{4}$	7	$4\frac{1}{2}$	$5\frac{1}{2}$	$2\frac{1}{2}$

	Italy	France	Spain	Portugal	Denmark
1831–40	2	$5\frac{1}{4}$	$5\frac{1}{4}$	3	13
1851–60	$3\frac{1}{2}$	$5\frac{1}{4}$	5	3	15

Mulhall's data, the most comprehensive available to me, are broadly corroborated by other statisticians (e.g. Schnitzler, 1856–69, vol. 1, 643–9, vol. 4, 119–80; Vilson, 1869, 112; Tegoborski, 1855T, vol. 1, 141, 266 ff.). These other sources indicate a per capita grain output of 9 hl for Russia, instead of Mulhall's conservative estimate. On p. 195 Tegoborski reveals that grain contributed only 52 per cent of Russia's agricultural product, much less than is commonly assumed.

Under the aegis of Kiselev's nephew and disciple Nikolai Miliutin, the 1860s dissolution of Russian serfdom was accompanied by important extensions of Kiselev's enlightened reforms, further enhancing the economic position of Russia's village communes (see Lincoln, 1977, 40–61). Herzen's ideas can be seen as a logical, albeit revolutionary, extension of existing agrarian policies and institutions. But the tsarist regime naturally wasn't prepared to pursue this logic to its communist conclusion. Instead Russia's communal institutions and traditions were constrained within an increasingly irksome straitjacket – a clumsily repressive police state.

Westernizers naturally accused Herzen of having sold out to Slavophilism, an atavistic, paternalistic, theocratic ideology elaborated by Ivan Kireevsky (1806–56), Alexei Khomiakov (1804–60), Konstantin Aksakov (1817–60), Yuri Samarin (1819–76) and Fyodor Dostoevsky (1821–81). Like Herzen, the true Slavophiles opposed serfdom and the many forms of corruption, perceived Russia's communal and co-operative traditions as the basis for a more autonomous and humane social order, demanded freedom of expression, sought a *rapprochement* between the educated élite and the peasantry and wanted the Slavs to avoid the evils of proletarianization (see Christoff, 1961, 172–268). To quote Konstantin Aksakov *On Russia's Internal Affairs* (1855):

> The country's present state is one of internal cleavage concealed under a shameless lie
> . . . fertile soil for the riotous weed of flattery. . . . Despite its unlimited powers, the

government cannot cajole people into truth and honesty; that is impossible without a free public opinion. . . . Bribery and organized official plunder are so much part of the general atmosphere that not only dishonest people, but men who are decent, good and in their own way honest are often thieves too, with few exceptions. It's no longer a personal but a social sin . . . illustrating the immorality of the social situation and of the entire system. (cf. Walicki, 1975T, 252)

However, Slavophiles were in spirit as hostile to secular socialisms – including Herzen's brand of communism – as they were to capitalist, materialist and bureaucratic corruption. As Ivan Kireevsky summed up in 1847: 'There is only one thing I desire, namely that the principles of conduct preserved in the teachings of the Holy Orthodox Church should permeate the convictions of all sections of society' (Walicki, 1975T, 147). 'The social organization of ancient Russia must be prized particularly for the traces it bears of pure Christian principles. . . . It's not any inborn advantage of the Slavonic stock which fills us with hope for its future', for 'the character of the fruit depends not on the soil, but on the seed cast upon it' (ibid., 144). Slavophiles desired not that the autocracy and landlordism should be dissolved, but that they should live up to their Christian pretensions and to their paternal responsibilities towards the peasantry, whose duty would still be to 'Render unto Caesar the things which are Caesar's'.

Herzen accepted that

Slavophiles have a true sense of the people's living soul, a 'glimpse of the future', but . . . I've read with revulsion some articles in Slavophile reviews. . . . Yet it would be difficult to demolish them using the West as an example, when in any newspaper one can see Europe's terrible maladies. . . . In the natural simplicity of our village life, our unfixed economic and juridical concepts, our vague property laws, our lack of a petit-bourgeoisie, our powers of assimilation, we possess advantages over fully formed, spent-force nations. . . . Whether the village commune was of tribal origin or the state's creation, whether the land originally belonged to communes or to landlords and princes, whether serfdom strengthened the commune or not – all that should be investigated. But what matters for us is the present position. . . . Communal land-ownership, administration and elections are a groundwork on which a new social order can easily grow up. . . . Instead of petty political reforms, which we've outgrown, we face an enormous *economic* revolution: liberation of the peasantry. Our problems are so posed that they can be resolved by sociopolitical measures, without violent upheavals. . . . Oppressed by authority, injustice, censorship and contempt for the individual, we wish to speak fearlessly, to exchange ideas, to unmask abuses of which even the government is ashamed and which it will never stop without publicity. We wish to liberate peasants from the power of landlords. . . . I see from the seedlings what the harvest might be; I see in the Russian people's impoverished lives an unconscious fitness for the social ideal European thought has consciously reached. . . . Conversely, Western Europe, possessing so much, is miserly with its hard-won wealth; like every owner of private property, it's conservative. . . . So, proceeding from opposite principles to opposite ends, I meet up not with the

Slavophiles, but with some of their ideas. (Translated from Herzen, 1954–65, vol. 12, 423–36)

Critics of village communism have misconstrued Herzen's open letters 'To an old comrade' (1870) as evidence of a *crise de foi*, causing Herzen 'to abandon his "Russian socialist utopia" and to put his hopes in the Socialist International' (Walicki, 1975T, 594). In fact these letters to Bakunin retracted nothing, and strengthened Herzen's commitment to non-violent, non-coercive methods:

> Should one try to force the pace of an evident process? Certainly a midwife should reduce the travails of labour, but within limits which are hard to ascertain and dangerous to exceed. . . . Plainly, things cannot go on as before. The exclusive rule of capital and the absolute right of property are finished. . . . Yet they aren't conquerable by violence. . . . Violence can only destroy and lay waste. Social revolution by the [coercive] methods of Peter the Great won't advance beyond Babeuf's punitive levelling or Cabet's communist corvée. The new forms must accommodate everyone, every type of modern activity, all man's aspirations. Don't turn our world into a Sparta or a monastery. The approaching revolution should not strangle certain forces for the benefit of others. . . . Woe to the revolution so poor in spirit and artistic sense as to reduce all that has been achieved to a grey workshop. . . . It must save not only the things it values, but everything innocuous, distinctive and original. . . . Workers will establish the nucleus of the future economic order by forming a sort of 'state within a state', with its own organization and laws, without capitalists and proprietors. . . . 'Gradualism' holds no terrors for me. . . . A headlong advance can become stranded, like Napoleon in Moscow, and perish in the retreat. . . . Neither of us has changed his convictions, but . . . I don't believe in the old roads to revolution. I try to comprehend the march of mankind, past and present, to learn how to keep in step, without straggling or running so far ahead that people cannot keep up. . . . Our strength lies in the power of ideas, of truth, of debate, in historical trends. . . . For us there's only one voice and authority – that of reason and understanding. Reject them and we become defrocked priests of science, renegades to civilization. . . . Incomprehension cannot be overcome by force. . . . People can be liberated outwardly only in so far as they have been liberated inwardly. (Translated from Herzen, 1954–65, vol. 20, 575–93)

Nikolai Chernyshevsky (1828–89)

Chernyshevsky is widely regarded as co-author of the ideology of village communism (see Walicki, 1979T, 186–202; Lampert, 1965, 189–96; Woerlin, 1971, 192–226; Venturi, 1966T, 129–55; Kitching, 1982, 35–6). To set the record straight it should be noted that, by the time Chernyshevsky began to write on the subject, Herzen had completed his exposition of village communism and that Chernyshevsky added very little, although he undoubtedly encouraged the Russian intelligentsia to give serious consideration to the village commune as Russia's basic social institution, as a valuable impediment to capitalist expropriation and prolet-arianization of the peasantry, as a possible framework for agricultural and rural–industrial development, and as the potential basis for a socialist economy and society (see the 1903 French edition of his major writings on *La Possession communale du sol*). Unfortunately, in his assaults on liberalism, Chernyshevsky threw out the baby along with the bathwater. However much Herzen criticized liberal vacillation and humbug, there was never any doubt that he cherished the important liberal values – not just individual liberty, but political and cultural pluralism, tolerance, mutual respect, individual (including official) accountability, the rule of law, rights of information and redress, and rights of association and assembly. But when Cherny-shevsky attacked liberalism, he saw only casuistry and class interest. He did not see that liberal values transcend class and political affiliations and that, in the absence of liberal values, even the most radical regime could quickly degenerate into new forms of corruption and oppression. Chernyshevsky has nevertheless taken precedence over Herzen in the revolutionary pantheon because, unlike Herzen, he impressed both Marx and Lenin, and because his ponderous and pugnaciously plebeian mentality was more congenial to the emergent intelligentsia than were Herzen's finer sensibilities.

Mikhail Bakunin (1814–76)

Most of the major advocates of village communism have favoured a highly decentralized society: a confederation of self-administering communes. In this respect they were much influenced by Bakunin who, as early as 1849, had published a rousing manifesto for village communism, to be built on Russia's existing communal institutions and traditions (see Venturi, 1966T, 48–50, 59–60). More-over, after the death of Pierre-Joseph Proudhon (1809–65), Bakunin became Europe's leading proponent of decentralized/stateless socialism – an extension of his earlier village communism, shorn of its Russian ethnocentricity (see Bakunin, 1973T, 76–97, 213–17, 259–344). At bottom, Bakunin abhorred 'revolution by decree, which derives from the idea of the revolutionary State' (ibid., 193), and in 1872–3 he presciently described the major hazards of étatist socialism:

> State implies domination, and domination presupposes subjugation of the masses and hence their exploitation for the benefit of a governing minority. We don't accept, even as part of a revolutionary transition . . . so-called revolutionary dictatorship. . . . The Marxists profess quite contrary ideas. As befits good Germans, they are wor-shippers of state power and hence prophets of political and social discipline, champions of a social order established from the top downwards, albeit in the name of universal suffrage and sovereignty of the masses, for whom they reserve the honour of obeying their leaders. . . . Marx's reasoning ends in self-contradiction. . . . His revolution would consist of either violent or gradual expropriation of proprietors and

capitalists and appropriation of all land and capital by the state which, to be able to fulfil its great economic/political mission, would have to be very powerful and centralized. The state would administer and direct agriculture via salaried officials commanding armies of rural workers organized and disciplined accordingly. And, instead of the existing banks, it would establish one bank to finance all labour and national commerce. . . . For the proletariat, this would in reality be a barracks regime, where uniformed working men and women would . . . work and live to the beat of a drum. (Translated from Bakunin, 1895–1913, vol. 4, 344–5, 381–3)

As every state is by nature placed outside and above the people, it inevitably must force them to submit to alien rules and objectives. . . . The difference between revolutionary dictatorship and statism is superficial. Essentially both represent government of the majority by a minority in the name of the former's supposed stupidity and the latter's pretended intelligence. . . . If the proletariat is to become the ruling class, over whom is it to rule? There would still remain another class, subordinate to the new rulers. The country bumpkins, known not to enjoy favour among Marxists, would presumably be ruled by the urban factory proletariat. Likewise . . . the Slavs would find themselves in a subordinate relationship to a triumphant German proletariat. . . . The terms 'scientific socialist' and 'scientific socialism', constantly encountered in the speeches and writings of Lassalleans and Marxists, testify that their pseudo People's State would be nothing but despotic control of the people by a new, not very numerous aristocracy of actual and pseudo-scientists. The uneducated would be relieved of the cares of administration and lumped together in a subjugated herd. Marxists see this contradiction and, admitting that government by scientists will be a dictatorship despite its democratic façade, console themselves that this dictatorship will be temporary. They say its only concern will be to educate and elevate the people economically and politically, enough to rapidly render such a government unnecessary; and the state, having lost its political/coercive character, will evolve into a completely free organization of economic interests and communes. . . . They claim that only a dictatorship – their own, naturally – can establish popular freedom. We reply that dictatorships have no objective other than self-perpetuation, and that servitude is all they can generate and instil. . . . Freedom can only be created freely, by a rebellion of the whole population and voluntary organization of the toiling masses from the bottom upwards. . . . If science were allowed to dictate life's laws, millions of men would be ruled by mere hundreds of experts. . . . Give the expert power and he becomes the most insufferable tyrant. . . . We must respect scientists only on their merits. To maintain their integrity and standards they must be denied privileges. . . . It's said that science won't always be an exclusive preserve; it will become accessible to all. Perhaps, but that's a long way ahead. . . . Meanwhile who would knowingly entrust his fate to the priests of science? (Translated from Bakunin, 1961–81, vol. 3, 113–14, 147–50, 111–12)

Significantly, in *The Civil War in France* (1871) and in his prospectus for Russia, Marx retreated from his previous emphasis on the need for a 'proletarian dictatorship' and a strong, centralized state during transitions to socialism, and came to prefer voluntary confederation of self-administering communes. Unfortunately Engels's and 'Marxist' orthodoxy in practice retained statist and élitist conceptions whose inner logic would indeed lead to oppressive, corrupt and degenerate tyrannies, as foreseen by Herzen and Bakunin.

An economic rationale

So far the case for village communism hasn't been narrowly economic, but there was no lack of economic support for village-based development. As the influential tsarist Privy Councillor M. L. Tegoborski argued in his massive *Studies on the Productive Forces of Russia* (1852–4):

> Those modern economists who have constituted themselves the zealous champions of industrial interests are fond of setting forth the advantages which agriculture more or less directly derives from the progress of industry. . . . Granted that industry's progress exerts a favourable influence on that of agriculture, the influence is more or less local: what is true of a district is not always true of a whole country – especially if that country be a great state occupying a vast territory, composed of various provinces differing from each other as to their material interests. . . . In large states industry is never evenly distributed. . . . Close to centres of industrial activity agriculture may no doubt derive considerable advantages. . . . As facilities of communication increase, these advantages may become wider extended; but their extension is nevertheless limited and often shackled by local circumstances; and distant provinces . . . have no interest in the matter. Or rather their interests will suffer if manufacture be excessively protected at their expense; that is, if it obliges them to pay a high price for home-manufactured articles. . . . We do not intend by these observations to deprecate the advantages of manufactures. . . . A great country like Russia, containing so many resources . . . could not condemn herself to remain stationary in the development of her industry and refuse to profit by the new inventions, discoveries and improvements with which the human mind has enriched itself in every branch of manufacture. But it does not follow that we are bound to enter the lists without taking into consideration the *ensemble* of our social economy and to . . . risk all the inconveniences which over-excitement of industrial interests has produced in other countries. On the contrary, our duty is to profit by the experience of others. . . . Russia, not being in a position to equal or outstrip other countries in the career of manufacturing industry . . . should rather seek to stimulate those branches of industry which are best adapted to the situation in our eminently agricultural country and best combine with the industry of our villages; and, as a general rule, we should endeavour to protect those manufactures for which our own soil provides us with raw materials. . . . In according protection to our industries, we must not push it to the extreme of endeavouring to manufacture everything for ourselves. . . . By concentrating our energy and resources upon the branches of industry most appropriate to the country's wants and the means at its disposal, we obtain surer and more durable results. (Tegoborski, 1855T, 443–51)

Moreover, as the radical publicist Dmitri Pisarëv (1840–68) argued in an interest-ing *Essay on the History of Labour* (1863),

> Means of communication are most useful to society when they assist the development of small local centres. These counter the power of attraction of big centres and spread throughout the country the varied occupations previously concentrated in big cities. . . . So roads should first be built or improved between separate villages and between villages and nearby towns. . . . Most economists think otherwise. . . . Their attention is concentrated on international trade . . . and, having the most tender regard for merchants' profits, they are concerned with means of communication which would link up big centres or big centres with seaports. . . . Meanwhile peasants who have to transport produce from their villages to the nearest towns, often many miles away, must make do with horses and carts. Thus the most onerous part of the transportation still lies with the peasants, while the merchants obtain relief. But economists do not deign to consider the menial details of the peasants' dreary existence. Their statistics take no account of the numbers of peasant nags lamed or cart-wheels broken. . . . Yet it should be remembered that society's well-being depends more on the numbers of well-fed people and healthy horses working in the fields than on the annual income of some prominent merchants. (Pisarëv, 1955–6, vol. 2, 295–6)

Where long-distance communications are developed first, for the merchants' benefit, they merely accelerate the demise of rural industries and increase the peasants' 'hopeless dependence on the arbitrary despotism of traders' (ibid. 299). Moreover, 'the development of rational agriculture requires, besides dissemination of useful knowledge among the masses, a widespread variety of occupations and widespread formation of local centres where the produce garnered by local inhabitants could be processed, consumed and recycled as fertilizer' (ibid., 317). Rural transport development and dispersed industrialization would also aid rural co-operation, undermine the monopolistic position of rural middlemen, cut market-ing costs and raise peasant purchasing power (ibid., 291–4). Diversification of rural industries would allow 'one industry to use the apparently useless waste thrown out by others' (ibid., 302). 'Individual talents, inclinations and abilities would come into their own, enhancing Man's moral state, increasing output, improving quality and lowering prices' (ibid., 274). 'The more the peasantry prospers, the more workshops and stores will spring up in the villages' (ibid., 295):

> If a great city were to suck in most of the country's industrial forces, everyone would depend on that centre. Peasants would have to bring their produce to a distant market and buy from it the manufactures they need, as few would risk establishing factories outside the big centre. The rural population would engage only in agriculture and impair their soil by constantly despatching produce to be consumed in the big centre, whence it's unlikely to be recycled as fertilizer. . . . Meantime all kinds of abomi-nation arise in the big centre. The hungry flock there seeking work, but more often sink into utter destitution, physical debilitation and involuntary vice. (ibid., 274–5)

Furthermore, as influential works by Nikolai Danielson (1844–1918), Vasily Vorontsov (1847–1918) and Sergei Kravchinsky (alias Stepniak, 1851–95) argued at inordinate length, the capitalist road and large-scale, city-centred industrialization were bound to be even more arduous, onerous and fraught for a capital-deficient, technically backward, illiterate and unruly peasant society, with a comparatively limited domestic market for manufactures and even less ability to export manufactures in competition with established industrial powers, than it had been for more advanced Western economies. Like Marx, these writers therefore favoured further extension of existing communal and co-operative ownership, enterprise and institutions and a development pattern subservient to peasant needs, preferably under the aegis of a revolutionary socialist regime, although they were deeply divided on interim strategy. The pragmatic Dr Vorontsov was a leading promoter of peasant co-operatives, village industries, agricultural extension services, rural sanitation and village schools via existing local institutions, preparatory to a more far-reaching socialist revolution, whereas the more doctrinaire, bookish and pessimistic Danielson scorned interim 'palliatives', while the somewhat naïve Kravchinsky was sidetracked into revolutionary terrorism, which became a self-consuming and self-defeating end in itself. In fact the 'palliatives' promoted by Vorontsov contributed most to the revolution of rising aspirations which undermined tsarism.

Prince Pyotr Kropotkin (1842–1921)

For this eminent scientist, writer, explorer and libertarian,

> There is only one way in which Communism can be established equitably, only one way which satisfies our instincts of justice and is at the same time practical, namely the system already adopted by the agrarian communes of Europe. . . . Accustomed as we are . . . to see Government, legislation and magistracy everywhere around, we . . . believe . . . chaos would come about if authority were overthrown. . . . And with our eyes shut we pass by thousands of human groupings which form themselves freely, without any intervention of the law, and attain results infinitely superior to those achieved under government tutelage. . . . The people commit blunder upon blunder when they have to choose by ballot some hare-brained candidate who solicits the honour of representing them and takes it upon himself to know all, to do all and to organize all. But when they take it upon themselves to organize what they know, what touches them directly, they do it better than all the 'talking shops' put together. . . . A political revolution can be accomplished without shaking the foundations of industry, but a revolution wherein the people lay hand upon property will inevitably paralyse exchange and production. . . . To tide them over the period of stress they will demand . . . communization of supplies. . . . How are the necessary provisions to be obtained if the nation as a whole hasn't accepted Communism? . . . To those who put their trust in 'authority' the question will appear quite simple. They would

begin by establishing a strongly centralized Government, furnished with all the machinery of coercion. . . . It would divide the country into districts of supply and then *command* that a prescribed quantity of some particular foodstuff be . . . received on a given day by a specified official and stored in particular warehouses. Now we declare . . . not merely that such a solution is undesirable, but that it is wildly Utopian. . . . The country will withhold its produce and the towns will suffer want, even if recalcitrant peasants are guillotined. . . . And as capitalists will soon realize that, when people are shot down by those who call themselves revolutionists, the Revolution will become hateful in the eyes of the masses, they will support the champions of *order* – even though they are collectivists. . . . It will be 1793 all over again. . . . Let the town apply itself [instead] to manufacturing all that the peasant needs. . . . Then provisions would pour in from every side. The peasant would withhold only what he needed for his own use. (Kropotkin, 1906T, 82, 167, 117, 77, 78, 92–7)

His *Fields, Factories and Workshops* (1899) made an interesting case for small-scale, village-based industrialization:

In an immense number of trades it isn't the superiority of the *technical* organization of the trade in a factory nor economies realized on the prime motor which militates against small industry in favour of factories, but the more advantageous conditions of buying and selling . . . which are at the disposal of big concerns. Wherever this difficulty has been overcome . . . by means of association . . . the conditions of the workers or artisans have immediately improved; and . . . rapid progress has been realized in the technical aspects. . . . The sudden start made of late by factories in Russia did not prejudice the domestic industries. On the contrary, it gave a new impulse to their extension. . . . As to the cheapness of the products manufactured in the villages . . . it cannot be explained in full by exceedingly long hours of labour and starvation earnings, because overwork (12 to 16 hours daily) and very low wages are [equally] characteristic of Russian factories. . . . In fact, if we analyse modern industries, we discover that for some . . . cooperation of hundreds or even thousands of workers gathered at the same spot is really necessary. The great iron works and mining enterprises decidedly belong to that category; oceanic steamers cannot be built in villages. But many of our big enterprises are nothing but agglomerations under a common management of several distinct industries. . . . The manufacture being a strictly private enterprise, its owners find it advantageous to have all the branches of a given industry under their own management; they can thus cumulate the profits of successive transformations of the raw material. . . . But from a *technical* viewpoint the advantages of such an accumulation are trifling and often doubtful. Even so centralized an industry as the cottons does not suffer at all from division of production of one given sort of goods at its different stages between several separate factories: we see it at Manchester and its neighbouring towns. . . . As to those countless descriptions of goods which derive their value chiefly from the intervention of skilled labour, they can best be fabricated in smaller factories. . . . Even under present conditions the great Leviathan factories offer great inconveniences, as they cannot rapidly reform their machinery according to the constantly varying demands of consumers. . . . As for the new branches of industry . . . they must always start on a small scale and they can prosper in small towns as well as in big cities, if the smaller agglomerations are provided with institutions stimulating artistic taste and inventive genius. The progress of late in toy making, mathematical and optical instruments, furniture, small luxury articles, pottery and so on are instances in point. Art and science are no longer the monopoly of the great cities and further progress will be in scattering them over the country. . . . However, such a change also implies a thorough modification of our present education system. It implies a society composed of men and women, each of whom is able to work with his or her hands as well as his or her brain, and to do so in more directions than one. . . . Under the pretext of division of labour, we have sharply separated the brain worker from the manual worker. The masses of workmen . . . have been deprived even of the education of the small workshop, while their boys and girls are driven into a mine or a factory from the age of thirteen, and . . . soon forget the little they may have learned at school. As to the men of science, they despise manual labour. . . . 'The man of science', they say, 'must discover the laws of nature, the engineer must apply them, and the worker must execute in steel, wood, iron or stone the patterns devised by the engineer. He must work with machines invented for him, not by him.' . . . Yet manual workers – not men of science, nor trained engineers – invented or perfected the prime motors and all that mass of machinery which has revolutionized industry for the last hundred years. But since the great factory has been enthroned, the worker, depressed by the monotony of his work, invents no more. . . . To the division of society into brain-workers and manual workers we oppose the combination of both kinds of activity; and instead of 'technical education', which means maintenance of the present division between brain-work and manual work, we advocate the '*éducation intégrale*'. (Kropotkin, 1907 edn, 139, 167, 173–86)

Ironically, while the West has experienced a relative contraction of the dirty, old heavy industries and an exodus of industry and people from the old, congested conurbations, Marxist states have continued to base their industrial development on costly, dirty and old-fashioned heavy industries and conurbations – to their present detriment.

In 1917, after forty-one years' exile, 75-year-old Kropotkin received a hero's welcome back to Russia at the Finland Station. Though no longer an active politician, in 1919 he wrote a poignant appeal 'to the workers of Western Europe'

to prevail on their governments to abandon entirely the idea of armed intervention in Russia. . . . The evils inherent in a party dictatorship have been accentuated by the conditions of war in which this party maintains its power. . . . I owe it to you to say frankly that . . . this effort to build a communist republic on the basis of a strongly centralized State under the iron law of party dictatorship is bound to end in failure. We are learning in Russia how *not* to introduce communism. . . . The immense constructive work demanded by a social revolution cannot be accomplished by a central government, even if it had to guide it something more substantial than a few socialist and anarchist handbooks. It has the need of the knowledge, brains and voluntary collaboration of a host of local and specialized forces which alone can attack the diversity of economic problems in their local aspects. To reject this collaboration and turn everything over to the genius of party dictators is to destroy the independent centres of our life, the trade unions and local cooperative organizations, by changing them into bureaucratic organs of the party. . . . The revolution will advance in its own way . . . perpetrating horrors . . . annihilating human lives . . . destroying without regard for what it destroys and whither it goes. And we are powerless for the present to direct it into another channel, until such time as it will have played itself out. (Kropotkin, 1927, 252–8)

Kropotkin died in 1921: 'A procession five miles long followed his coffin through the streets of Moscow; it was the last great demonstration of the lovers of freedom against the Bolsheviks' (Woodcock, 1963, 205).

Victor Chernov (1873–1952) and Russia's Socialist Revolutionary Party

The November 1917 general election, held *after* the Bolsheviks had seized power in Russia's cities, was a landslide victory for the Socialist Revolutionaries (SRs), a broad socialist movement founded in 1901 by its leader Victor Chernov and committed to a highly decentralized village communism as the central plank in its political and socioeconomic programmes. With 58 per cent of the popular vote, the SRs won 410 of the 707 seats in the short-lived Constituent Assembly, as against only 175 for the Bolsheviks, 16 for the Mensheviks, 17 for the Constitutional Democrats and 86 for the 'strongly anti-Bolshevik' ethnic minority parties. Thus the results of the only freely contested elections Russia has ever had were as much a show of popular support for village communism and a rejection of authoritarianism as they were a 'crushing vote of no confidence' against Bolshevism (Carr, 1966, 120). These results belied Bolshevik claims that the peasantry lacked a clear political consciousness of where its class interests lay and Western claims that the Russians incline towards authoritarianism. Unlike the Soviet system, which denied due representation to the peasantry, the Constituent Assembly had a mandate to restructure and decentralize Russian society along village communist lines and to ensure that there was an orderly, egalitarian redistribution of land, rather than a free-for-all in which the strong would grab the lion's share and the weak would lose out. Sadly a group of opportunists on the 'left' of the SR Party connived at Lenin's suppression of the Constituent Assembly in January 1918, having accepted ministerial positions in Lenin's city-based Soviet regime. To make matters worse, these 'left SRs' failed to prevent Lenin from ceding millions of Russian and Ukrainian peasants to the German invaders, or from authorizing towns to seize peasant grain, or from initiating a terrible reign of repression, and were soon obliged to resign in disgrace. Thereupon Lenin seized the first opportunity to outlaw the entire SR movement, whose various attempts to overthrow the Bolsheviks unfortunately failed. The Bolsheviks were able to consolidate their dictatorship because their minority support was *concentrated* in Russian industrial, military and administrative centres, which they ruthlessly reorganized into siege economies based on rationing, requisitioning, regimentation and repression, and because they made much *greater* use of ex-tsarist personnel than did the peasant majority. It proved remarkably easy for officers and officials to transfer their allegiance to the new Bolshevik champions of order, centralization and repression, and the principal victims were much the same as before the Revolution: socialists, radical liberals, ethnic minorities, anarchists, religious nonconformists, unruly workers and recalcitrant peasants (see Pipes, 1957; Erickson, 1962, ch. 3; Zenkovsky, 1960). Conversely, SR support was scattered throughout rural Russia, ill-equipped and averse to brutally effective authoritarian chains of command of the sort established by Lenin's government and Trotsky's Red Army. Peasants widely resorted to guerrilla resistance to Bolshevism, but guerrilla warfare is normally more effective against foreign invasion than against domestic oppression (on the main peasant resistance, see Voline, 1975T, 541–711; Arshinov, 1974T; Malet, 1983; Radkey, 1976). Like Perrie (1976, 201–2), I am unconvinced by Radkey's earlier books, which endeavoured to caricature and discredit the SRs and their agrarian programme.

Chernov added little to the ideological armoury of village communism. Chernov's major achievements were in *mobilizing* a peasant-based mass movement, wedded to village communism; in *bridging* the chasm separating town and country; and in *persuading* the rural intelligentsia (teachers, doctors, nurses, local government personnel) to participate in peasant movements, much as urban *intelligenti* do in workers' movements (see Perrie, 1976).

Alexander Chayanov (1888–1939) and the 'Agrarniki'

By 1914 some 12,600 agronomists and surveyors were active among Russia's peasants (Yaney, 1971, 6) and Russia had published several thousand detailed, first-hand peasant studies. Furthermore, when Russia's massive peasant socialist movements were crushed and outlawed by the Bolshevik regime, thousands of agrarian socialists sought solace in rural development work for the Agriculture Ministry, local government and hundreds of model farms and agricultural research establishments, including the Scientific Research Institute on Agricultural Economics, near Moscow, which was directed by the former agricultural officer Professor Alexander Chayanov. In the authoritative judgement of the late Daniel Thorner, 1920s Russia contained the 'most fertile and sophisticated group of scholars then working in any country on peasant economy' (Thorner, 1966, xxiii).

The major synthesis of these peasant studies was Chayanov's textbook on *The Organization of Peasant Economy* (1925, 1966T), which has become the most widely debated and influential book of its kind (see Kitching, 1982, ch. 3; Harrison,

1974–5, 1976–7, 1977–8, 1979–80; Solomon, 1978; Shanin, 1972, 1973–4; Mitrany, 1951; Littlejohn, 1977; Patnaik, 1978–9; Myers, 1970; Wolf, 1966; Thorner, 1965, among others). Like Marx, Chayanov adhered to the clear conceptual distinction between capitalist production, using hired labour, and centuries-older 'simple commodity production', using self-employed or family labour. (Unfortunately Marxists often confuse capitalism with commodity production in general, although Marx made it plain that commodity production was already widespread in his epochs of 'slavery', 'serfdom' and 'feudalism'.) However, Marx perversely continued to use inappropriate *capitalist* categories in his conceptualization of *pre-capitalist* 'simple commodity production':

> What is the position of independent handicraftsmen or peasants who employ no labourers and therefore do not produce as capitalists? . . . The independent peasant or handicraftsman is split into two persons. As owner of means of production he is capitalist; as labourer he is his own wage-labourer. As capitalist he pays himself wages and draws profit on his capital; i.e. he exploits himself as wage-labourer and pays himself, in the surplus value, the tribute that labour owes to capital. Perhaps he also pays himself a third portion as landowner (rent). (Marx, 1969T, 467–8)

By contrast, Chayanov shared J. S. Mill's no-nonsense view that 'In the regime of peasant properties . . . the whole product belongs to a single owner, and the distinction of rent, profit and wages does not exist' (Mill, 1891, 178). Hence profit-maximizing or profit-oriented theories of capitalist economic behaviour, presupposing clearly distinguishable and quantifiable rent, interest, wages and profit, weren't legitimately applicable to enterprises based on self-employed or family labour, which in the early twentieth century still accounted for approximately 90 per cent of Russia's agrarian workforce, approximately 80 per cent of Eastern Europe's agrarian workforce and over 65 per cent of the agrarian workforce in Southern Europe, Eire and Asia (see Table 4; and Chayanov, 1966T, 112, 119, 225–8). In a capitalist enterprise based on hired labour, land and labour are the variable factors which the entrepreneur tries to combine in such a way as to maximize his returns on the capital at his disposal. On a family labour farm, in Chayanov's view, land, capital and outside earnings are the variable factors which the farmer tries to combine in the way that would most efficiently satisfy his family's consumption and savings requirements with the family labour at his disposal, which is in turn governed by the family's size and age structure and – at the margin – the subjective trade-off between additional family income and additional leisure. The fact that the family labour farm is simultaneously a family unit, a work unit, a consumption unit and a business unit enhances its resilience in competition with farms based on less motivated, less resourceful hired labour, which generally does only what it is told to do and thus engenders greater managerial costs and lead-swinging. For Chayanov, such considerations largely explained why family labour farms so often found it worthwhile to undertake activities which would have been unprofitable for capitalist farms (ibid., 237–9), why family labour farms were increasingly in the ascendancy (ibid., 28, 237), and why

> the ideal vehicle for agricultural production is neither the large-scale latifundium nor the individual peasant farm, but a . . . peasant family farm which would have deleted from its organizational plan all those branches of farming in which large-scale production is superior to small-scale production and which would have these organized in varying degrees of scale in co-operatives. (Chayanov *et al.*, 1922, 4)

Danish agriculture was the closest (albeit imperfect) Western approximation to Chayanov's ideal. Various factors enabled this small, vulnerable, mineral-deficient, not naturally fertile country with very little heavy industry to sustain Europe's highest long-run grain and potato output per inhabitant and to use this as the basis for intensive livestock rearing and, from the 1880s onward, co-operative dairying and bacon production: the establishment of compulsory schooling for children aged 6–14, following the 1814 Education Act; gradual dissolution of serfdom (1780s to 1860s); a growing preponderance of family labour farms; a proliferation of loan societies and semi-vocational peasant high schools (1850s to 1870s); very widespread, labour-intensive reclamation, drainage and marling of marginal land, especially after the loss of half its farmland to expansionist Germany in 1864; and widespread adoption of new crop rotations, seed strains, livestock breeds and farm tools (see Tables 11, 12, 14 and 15; Skrubbeltrang, 1953; Jensen, 1937). By the late 1920s the following countries had in various ways begun to emulate Denmark's commercially and socially successful agricultural system: Sweden (see Olsson, 1968; Holmström, n.d.); Finland (see Wuorinen, 1965, 181–6 ff., 263–70); Ireland (see Crotty, 1966); and much of Eastern Europe (see Mitrany, 1930, 373–414 ff.; Madgearu, 1930; Tiltman, 1934, 68–88; Tomasevich, 1955, 616 ff.; Trouton, 1952; Textor, 1923; Mitrany, 1951, 99, 113–14, 125–7, 241–3, 255; Rothschild, 1974, 331–3, 353–5). But Chayanov rightly expected Soviet Russia to go beyond mere emulation of Denmark. His *Journey of My Brother Alexei to the Land of Peasant Utopia* (1920) envisaged that Russia's peasant majority would eventually capture proportionate representation in the soviets, aided by splits within a narrowly based 'proletarian' dictatorship confronted by intractable peasant opposition to wholesale collectivization and state control. (He didn't foresee that Bolshevik hard-liners would defeat the moderates.) Having gained majority rule, the new peasant regime would establish a highly decentralized, pluralistic, egalitarian society, with far-reaching local accountability, a minimal state apparatus (responsible only for co-ordinating defence and heavy industry), an independent judiciary and a plurality of competing transport and communications co-operatives. Three-quarters of Russia's industry and commerce would be turned over to local co-operatives and the system of family labour farms would be further developed through comprehensive general and technical education, other services, electrification, equitable farm product prices and fully autonomous farmers' co-operatives. Limited private employment of hired labour would be permitted, just to keep the co-operatives on their toes, but private profit and unearned income would be heavily taxed, and private finance houses and joint stock companies would not be allowed. This system would gradually induce most townspeople to take up village life and, in 1984, Moscow would contain no more than 100,000 inhabitants.

Sadly, although Chayanov prudently published this prospectus under a pseudonym (Ivan Kremnev) and in the form of a Utopian novel set in 1984, and although he capitulated to Stalinist 'gigantomania' in 1929 (see Jasny, 1949, 27, 28, 242, 244), he and many like-minded associates perished in Soviet labour camps in the 1930s.

Mohandas Gandhi (1869–1948) and the fate of village India

Although best known for his revolutionary techniques of non-violent civil dis-obedience, his somewhat puritanical moral teachings and his crusade for Indian *swaraj* (self-rule), Gandhi also became a major proponent of village communism:

> Independence must begin at the bottom. Thus every village will be a republic or panchayat having full powers. It follows . . . that every village has to be self-sustained and capable of managing its affairs. . . . It will be trained and prepared to perish in the attempt to defend itself. . . . This does not exclude dependence on and willing help from neighbours or from the world. It will be a free and voluntary play of mutual forces . . . in which every man and woman knows what he or she wants and . . . knows that no one should want anything that others cannot have with equal labour. . . . In this structure composed of innumerable villages, there will be ever-widening, never-ascending circles. Life will not be a pyramid with the apex sustained by the bottom. . . . Let India live for this true picture, though never realizable in its completeness. We must have a picture of what we want, before we can have some-thing approaching it. . . . In this there is no room for machines that would displace human labour and concentrate power in a few hands. . . . Every machine that helps every individual has a place. (*Harijan*, 28 July 1946, 236)

> My idea of village Swaraj is that it is a complete republic, independent of its neigh-bours for its own vital wants, yet interdependent for many others in which dependence is a necessity. Thus every village's first concern will be to grow its own food crops and cotton for its cloth. It should have a reserve for its cattle, recreation and play ground for adults and children. Then if there is more land available, it will grow *useful* money crops, thus excluding ganja, tobacco, opium and the like. The village will maintain a village theatre, school and public hall. It will have its own waterworks ensuring clean water supply. . . . Education will be compulsory up to the final basic course. As far as possible every activity will be conducted on the co-operative

basis. There will be no castes such as we have today . . . and non-cooperation will be the sanction of the village community. There will be a compulsory service of village guards . . . selected by rotation from the register maintained by the village. The Government of the village will be conducted by the panchayat of five persons annually elected by the adult villagers, male and female. . . . To model such a village may be the work of a lifetime. (*Harijan*, 26 July 1942, 238)

Communism of the Soviet type, 'that is Communism which is imposed on a people, would be repugnant to India. I believe in non-violent Communism. . . . If Communism came without any violence, it would be most welcome' (*Harijan*, 13 February 1937, 6). Indeed, Gandhi had long maintained that 'real Swaraj will not come by the acquisition of authority by a few, but by the acquisition of the capacity by all to resist authority when abused' (*Young India*, 29 January 1925, 41). 'No mere transference of political power in India will satisfy my ambition, even though I hold such transference to be a vital necessity' (*Young India*, 3 September 1925, 304). 'Self-government means continuous effort to be independent of government control, whether it is foreign government or whether it is national' (*Young India*, 6 August 1925, 276). He developed similar doubts concerning state socialism: 'It is my firm conviction that if the State suppressed capitalism by violence, it will be caught in the evils of violence and will fail to develop non-violence. . . . The State represents violence in a concentrated and organized form. The individual has a soul, but as the State is a soulless machine, it can never be weaned from violence to which it owes its very existence' (*Modern Review*, October 1935). He voiced further misgivings in 1940:

> Nehru wants industrialization because he thinks that if it were socialized, it would be free from the evils of capitalism. My own view is that the evils are inherent in industrialism and no amount of socialization can eradicate them. . . . I do visualize electricity, shipbuilding, ironworks, machine-making and the like existing side by side with village crafts. But . . . I do not share the socialist belief that centralization of the production of the necessaries of life will conduce to the common welfare. (Ganguli, 1973, 321–3)

These misgivings were reinforced by his perception of the Soviet Union: 'As I look at Russia, where the apotheosis of industrialization has been reached, the life there does not appeal to me. . . . In modern terms, it is beneath human dignity to become a mere cog in the machine' (*Harijan*, 28 January 1939, 438).

In Gandhi's view, even if a humane person could somehow disregard the traumatic, dehumanizing, divisive and socially disruptive effects of the factory system, extreme division of labour, urbanization and primitive accumulation which were so powerfully publicized by Marx in *Capital* and by Engels in *The Condition of the Working Class in England*, large-scale urban industry would at best provide livelihoods for a tiny fraction of India's teeming millions for many decades to come: 'I am convinced that if India is to attain true freedom . . . then sooner or later the fact must be recognized that people will have to live in villages, not in towns. . . . You must not imagine that I am envisaging our village life as it is today. . . . They will not live in dirt and darkness as animals. Men and women will be free and able to hold their own. . . . Everyone will have to contribute his quota of manual labour' (letter to Nehru, 5 October 1945). 'The villagers are to be their own buyers. They will primarily consume what they produce, for they are 90% of the population. They will manufacture for the cities what the latter want. . . . This is no programme of preparing shoddy goods in the villages and forcing them on unwilling buyers' (*Harijan*, 13 April 1935, 68). So 'we have to concentrate *mainly* on the village being self-contained, manufacturing *mainly* for use. Provided this character of village industry is maintained, there would be no objection to villages using modern machines and tools' (*Harijan*, 29 August 1936, 226; my italics): 'If we could have electricity in every home, I should not mind villagers plying their implements and tools with the help of electricity. But then the village communities . . . would own power houses, just as they have their grazing pastures' (*Harijan*, 22 June 1935, 146). He acknowledged that 'Heavy industries will need to be centralized and nationalized. But they will occupy the least part of the vast national activity, which will be mainly in the villages' (Gandhi, 1948, item 4; cf. Gandhi, 1941, item 4). Indeed, as late as 1956, India's heavy industries produced under one-quarter of total industrial output (including crafts) and under 10 per cent of national income and employed under 5 per cent of India's workforce. In Gandhi's scheme of things, 'The proper function of cities is to serve as clearing houses for village products' (*Harijan*, 28 January 1939, 438). And in 1935 he assured his followers that 'if all the land that is available was properly utilized and made to yield up to its capacity, it would maintain the whole population. Only we have got to be industrious and make two blades of grass grow where one grows today' (Tendulkar, 1960–3, vol. 4, 24). India's grain yields per hectare were indeed about half those obtained in China, Vietnam and Korea at that time (see Table 12). Gandhi also attached great importance to sanitation and elementary education:

> A sense of . . . social sanitation is not a virtue among us. . . . I regard this defect as a great vice which is responsible for the disgraceful state of our villages and . . . sacred rivers and for the diseases that spring from insanitation. . . . The very high death rate among us . . . could be mitigated if the people were properly educated about health and hygiene. (Gandhi, 1941, items 6 and 10)

> It is difficult to get clean, drinkable water in village wells, tanks and streams. The approaches to an ordinary village are heaped with muck. . . . At present this rich manure, valued at lakhs of rupees, runs to waste every day, fouls the air and brings disease into the bargain. Village tanks are promiscuously used for bathing, washing clothes, drinking and cooking. . . . Many village tanks are also used by cattle. . . . Village sanitation is perhaps the most difficult task before the All-India Village Industries Association. . . . Attention to personal and corporate hygiene is the beginning of all education. (*Harijan*, 3 February 1935, 416)

Gandhi also repeatedly urged that education should be polytechnic, not narrowly academic, and that it should be expanded from the village upwards, not from the university downwards: 'India is not to be found in her cities. India is in her innumerable villages. . . . Forget them, and you forget India' (Tendulkar, 1960–3, vol. 4, 175–6, 186–92, and vol. 8, 164–6).

Finally, beware mischievous suggestions that Gandhi's techniques of non-cooperation and non-violent civil disobedience were designed to perpetuate popular passivity, in the interests of the Indian capitalists who financed the Independence movement: 'Gandhi's principal objective was to arouse a collective sense of wrong, to liberate the power of resistance of the masses. . . . This was to be a training in democracy and not merely a means of removing a temporary local grievance' (Ganguli, 1973, 225). Gandhi had nothing but contempt for spineless acquiescence: as he put it in 1930, 'The peace we seem to prize is mere makeshift and it is bought with the blood of starving millions. If critics could only realize the torture of their slow and lingering death . . . they would risk anarchy and worse in order to end the agony. . . . It is a sin to sit supine' (ibid., 401). In 1938 he added: 'In my opinion, non-violence is not passivity in any shape or form. . . . I have not yet come across a situation when I had to say I was helpless, that I had no remedy in terms of non-violence' (ibid., 399). Violent resistance invites repression and is more easily repressed than civil disobedience and non-cooperation, as illustrated most recently by events in Poland in the early 1980s. Recourse to violence normally favours the strong and the exploiter, against the weak and the exploited.

Significantly, Gandhi was influenced by 'an assiduous reading of Kropotkin' (Woodcock, 1963, 218), and Kropotkin's books were 'avidly read in India' (Ganguli, 1973, 72). Moreover, Gandhi's world-view was foreshadowed in Leo Tolstoy's anarchistic and anti-capitalist tract on *The Slavery of Our Time* (1900), and in Tolstoy's seminal 'educational' essays of 1862 (see Tolstoy, 1967T).

However, the extent to which Russian influences rivalled other influences on Gandhi is ultimately *less important* than the fact that he *shared* the view that village communism offered the most humane path of development for a backward peasant society and that, while rejecting *indiscriminate* Westernization, he judiciously advocated *selective utilization* of Western capital and know-how (Gandhi, 1959, vol. 1, lxvi).

The assassination of Gandhi by a religious bigot in 1948 deprived India's masses of their most effective tribune. However, the balance of power was already tipping in favour of the state, machine politicians, big business and Nehru's brand of social-ism. Gandhi's 'public life was not a triumphal procession' and 'he could command a mass following . . . only sporadically, in 1920–22, 1930–32 and 1940–42. The educated class . . . was inclined to discount his politics as romantic and his economics as unpractical' (Nanda, 1974, 64). Despite the mutual respect and affection between Gandhi and Nehru, his chosen successor, 'their philosophies of life never really converged' (ibid., 103). When Gandhi tried to settle their differences on village-based development, Nehru replied: 'A village, normally speaking, is backward intellectually and culturally and no progress can be made from a backward environment' (letter to Gandhi, 9 October 1945).

In the 1950s Nehru and India's Planning Commission repeatedly declared that large-scale industry, village industry and agriculture would be developed in tandem and that neglect of the village sector had been a major defect of Soviet industrialization. However, these pious declarations weren't reflected in the allocation of development resources. The village sector, with over 80 per cent of India's people, obtained only 15, 12 and 13 per cent of India's development outlays in 1951–5, 1956–61 and 1961–6, respectively (Chaudhuri, 1971, 53–4). Agriculture, which contributed half the national income, obtained only 1 per cent of the foreign aid to India during 1951–66 (ibid., 34, 168) and was allocated only 18 per cent of total investment in the 1956–61 Plan (Government of India, Planning Commission, 1958, 31). This Plan promised that by 1961 India would have 118,000 (industrial) engineers, but only 38,000 rural extension workers (ibid., 103, 159). Electrification, which absorbed 10 per cent of India's development outlays in the 1950s, was planned to benefit only 2.5 per cent of India's villages, but 100 per cent of towns with over 10,000 people (ibid., 82, 241). The village institutions (*panchayats*) fostered by Nehru's regime were to be allowed revenues amounting to under 4 per cent of total tax revenues or under 0.4 per cent of national income (ibid., 125, 137–8), and the expansion of education and medical care was heavily concentrated in the small urban sector (Lipton, 1978, ch. 11). Village and small-scale urban industries, which contributed three-quarters of India's industrial employment and half its industrial output, were allocated only 11.5 per cent of total industrial investment in the 1956–61 Plan; larger-scale consumer goods industries were allocated another 9 per cent of industrial investment; and the rest went into large-scale producer goods industries, whose output was planned to grow five or six times as fast as the output of agriculture and consumer goods industries (Government of India, Planning Commission, 1958, 255–7, 285, 76). In all, the share of investment allocated to rural development under Nehru was about as low as in Stalin's Russia, although rural development was far more crucial for India than it had been for Russia (Soviet agriculture received approximately 13 per cent of Soviet investment in 1928–53 and there was disinvestment in Soviet village industries, but Soviet investment in health, education and infrastructure was more equitably distributed). Thus the persistence of almost undiminished poverty in rural India under Nehru was partly attributable to the extent of the deviation from Gandhi's more realistic and humane economic priorities.

Nehru's lopsided development strategy 'used too much of the country's resources to build up a bureaucratically controlled industrial sector and a wide range of inefficient heavy industries' (Maddison, 1971, 89). The vaunted diminution in India's dependence on imported producer goods did little to raise consumption levels or to alleviate India's festering poverty, because (1) its import-substitutes were up to three times more expensive than foreign-made alternatives (Chaudhuri, 1971, 72); (2) India's producer goods industries were 'largely buyers of each other's products', few of which went into agriculture or village industry (ibid., 83; Government of India, Planning Commission, 1966, 13); and (3) as late as 1970 these industries provided employment for under 5 per cent of India's workforce. It is truly remarkable that, despite the deplorable lopsidedness of India's development strategy under Nehru, foodgrain and other crop production managed to grow 3.0 and 2.9 per cent per annum, respectively, from 1952–6 to 1961–5 (Swamy, 1973, 11, 17); and that in 1970 small-scale industries (including village industries) still accounted for 40 and 75 per cent of industrial output and employment, as against 46 and 75 per cent respectively in 1945–6 (Maddison, 1971, 62, 126). Admittedly, in both periods output per man-year was approximately five times higher in large-scale industries than in small-scale industries (ibid., 62, 128). But this had little to do with economies of scale: in the mid-1960s India's large-scale industries used over 100 times more capital per worker than the 'traditional' small-scale industries and fifteen times more capital per worker than the 'modern' small-scale industries (Shirokov, 1973T, 290, 273); and when capital was scarce and labour was over-abundant, there was little human or economic virtue in using more capital and less labour. Moreover, it is significant that Japanese manufacturing, whose efficiency isn't in doubt, averaged only fifteen persons per manufacturing establishment in 1978 and that the corresponding figure for Italy's successful export-oriented manu-facturing sector was only eight in 1971, showing that small scale is not in itself a barrier to manufacturing success (see Lorenz, 1982; Smith, 1982; Buxton, 1982). In 1963 74 per cent of Japanese manufacturing enterprises employed under eleven persons each (as against 93 per cent for manufacturing enterprises in India in 1961) and the branch distribution of small-scale manufacturing employment in Japan was very similar to India, but Japan's mini-manufacturers employed five times more capital per person and produced eight times more output per person than their Indian counterparts (see Shirokov, 1973T, 268–74 ff.). Similarly it is significant that Japanese farms averaged only 0.9 ha in the 1960s and yet produced four or five times more grain per hectare, and per farmer, than India's farms, which averaged 2.5 ha in 1961; that this was based on the use of very intensive, small-scale tech-nologies by well-educated farmers, for whom large-scale mechanization was utterly impractical; that by 1971 the average per capita income of Japanese farm households was only 4 per cent below that of non-agricultural wage-earning households, partly because 86 per cent of farm households also had non-agricultural incomes; and that there are 'virtually no hired labourers' in Japanese agriculture, as 'virtually all Japanese farms are family enterprises dependent on family labour' (see Tables 7 and 12; and O'Hagan, 1978, ch. 1; Sanderson, 1978). All these considerations support Gandhi's belief in the development potential of small-scale industry and peasant agriculture, as against the high-cost, large-scale, lopsided and spatially concentrated industrialization which has benefited village India so very little.

Village communism and the critics of 'populism'

Village communism was given the name 'populism' by its Russian opponents as a term of abuse, with connotations of demagogy and vapidity (see Pipes, 1964). Regrettably the name has stuck, enabling critics of village communism to lump it together with many other 'populist' ideologies with which it often has little in common (see, for example, Byres, 1979; Gellner and Ionescu, 1970; Lenin, 1960–70T, vol. 18, 163–9). Indeed, the term 'populism' has been more appropriately applied to European fascisms, Peronism and Nasserism. Moreover, in the course of Russia's post-revolutionary debates on development options the very diverse followers and associates of Alexander Chayanov and Nikolai Kondratiev were collectively branded 'neo-populists', subjected to 'show trials' on charges of 'neo-populism' (as though this were a crime) and sent to die in forced labour camps (see Jasny, 1972; Solomon, 1977). It is also regrettable that the notion that the earlier 'populists' had favoured a 'purely agricultural' society, doomed to low productivity and narrow horizons, whereas the more modern 'neo-populists' favoured a balanced and evolutionary symbiosis of peasant agriculture and (mainly light) industry, has been perpetuated by David Mitrany (1951, 49–50), Michael Lipton (1978, 130–8 ff.), Terry Byres (1979) and Gavin Kitching (1982), albeit with the best intentions. In most peasant societies a 'purely agricultural' Arcadia would only be attainable by the murderous methods of Pol Pot's Khmer Rouge – a cruel parody of village communism. From the outset all the influential advocates of village communism have in fact favoured various forms of rural industrialization – 'pure populists' are thin on the ground. And Gandhi, Kropotkin, Chernov, Chernyshevsky, Vorontsov and Danielson (among others) explicitly recognized that railways and several heavy industries could best be organized on a large scale albeit under some form of socialized ownership and control, as noted by Kitching (1982, 91, 150–1). Conversely, although Kondratiev and Lipton have been branded 'neo-populist' by their critics, they have rightly disavowed any such affiliation. One can believe in an agriculture-first industrialization strategy and in the Mitrany–Lipton 'urban bias' thesis *without* being a socialist, let alone an advocate of village communism; and an advocate of village communism can consider rural industrialization to be even more important than agricultural development (this seems to have been the position taken by Vorontsov, Kropotkin and Gandhi, although even Lipton wildly misrepresents their views – see Lipton, 1978, 137). Too often the terms 'populist' and 'neo-populist' have been used to caricature opponents, to obscure differences, to prejudge issues and, in Stalinist hands, to impute 'guilt by association'. In his withering critique 'Of neo-populist pipe-dreams' (1979, 223) Byres quite rightly complains that 'The cheap jibe of "Stalinism" has become, in some quarters, all-too-common a substitute for reasoned argument.' Unfortunately he sometimes uses the terms 'populist' and 'neo-populist' in exactly the same way.

It has been suggested that 'populist' objectives can only be realized through agricultural collectivization and in a relatively closed economy (Kitching, 1982, 137). Voluntary co-operation and association between essentially autonomous households are indeed central to village communism. But any form of imposed collectivization, which presupposes an apparatus of coercion, would be abhorrent. Anyway, having studied the history of agricultural collectivization in thirteen communist states and in six minority Soviet republics, it is very clear that the net economic gains have on the whole been *inversely related* to the amount of coercion employed (see Chapter 12). Imposed collectivization has often subjected peasantries to new forms of 'social apartheid' and 'second editions' of Russian serfdom, including regimented fieldwork, overseers, a system of 'workdays' or 'workpoints', the distinction between 'collective' fieldwork and private cultivation of household plots, invidious restrictions on the mobility of rural inhabitants and the formal practice of denying the peasantry many of the political, civil and economic rights accorded to townspeople. Moreover, as Marx so eloquently argued in 1881, communal village-based development should derive great benefit from the fruits of Western capitalist industrialization, from imported producer goods and technology, i.e. from a relatively open and outward-looking economic system. There is no case for creating secluded, introverted peasant ghettos, doomed to economic and mental stagnation. The more open the economy, the more it can concentrate on activities in which it has a comparative cost advantage. In typically capital- and mineral-deficient peasant societies short of large-scale industrial–organizational expertise and infrastructure, this means concentration on agriculture and/or relatively small-scale labour-intensive light industries and services. Peasant societies with rich mineral endowments obviously enjoy wider development options, although Iran, Mexico, Venezuela, Nigeria, Romania and Soviet Azerbaijan have discovered the perils of lopsided oil-based development.

Referring to the experience of Iran, Venezuela, Algeria, Nigeria and (implicitly) Mexico since they became major oil producers, Gavin Kitching has queried the ability of peasant farmers to successfully compete against the large-scale, low-cost farmers of North America (Kitching, 1982, 136–7). Unfortunately he has overlooked the impact of oil bonanzas on exchange rates. By boosting the value of 'petro-currencies', or by preventing them from depreciating sufficiently to offset domestic inflation, oil bonanzas have undoubtedly made it harder for most producers in relatively 'open' oil-rich peasant societies to compete with foreign producers. But the difficulty is not specific to peasant agriculture. It also affects capitalist farmers, manufacturers and oil-rich industrial economies like Britain and Norway, whose overvalued 'petro-currencies' exacerbated the impact of world recession on their hard-pressed manufacturers in 1979–82. This difficulty has no bearing on the intrinsic viability of manufacturing or peasant farming or capitalist farming, given appropriate exchange rates. And there is absolutely no doubt that peasant farmers can successfully compete with capitalist farmers in third markets: Danish, Irish, Finnish,

Russian, Bulgarian, Yugoslav and Thai peasants did so in the early twentieth century, and Polish, Yugoslav, Greek, Irish, Danish, Taiwanese, South Korean and Thai peasants have done so more recently, as can most easily be seen from the importance of foodstuffs among the exports of each of these countries whose agricultural production has been largely in peasant hands.

Following Lenin, Preobrazhensky and Stalin, Marxist industrializers have often argued that peasant societies must develop large-scale heavy industries *first*, as a *prerequisite* for successful rural development. If this were true, village communism would indeed be 'a blind alley' (Byres, 1979). However, successful development of small-scale peasant agriculture actually *preceded* the creation of substantial heavy-industrial sectors in nineteenth-century Denmark, Ireland, Finland, Russia and Japan, and in twentieth-century Taiwan, South Korea, Thailand and Bulgaria, to name only the most obvious examples. Indeed, successful agricultural development and village industries long preceded large-scale industrialization in Japan and in most European states (see Bairoch, 1973; Jones, 1968; Braun, 1967; Smith, 1969; Hayami, 1976, among others). Moreover, as even Maurice Dobb had to acknowledge, 'the traditional pattern of development for capitalist countries in the past was to develop first of all consumer goods industries, such as textiles or clothing or food processing, only switching over to a more rapid expansion of capital goods industries at a fairly advanced stage' (Dobb, 1963, 30, 13–14; cf. Table 15). In theory producer goods inputs from the urban sector can accelerate rural development, but in practice the rural sector has had to become quite prosperous before it can finance widespread mechanization and wide use of chemical fertilizers and pesticides; in communist states agriculture has usually had to finance much of its investment out of its own low 'squeezed' income, whereas the state has heavily subsidized industrial investment along with other inputs into industrial production. Having studied the composition of industrial output in a dozen communist states, it is clear that farm machinery, fertilizers, pesticides, farm building materials and energy for agricultural consumption have normally made up less than 20 per cent of heavy-industrial output, despite their continued insistence that it is necessary to develop heavy industry *first* in order to develop agriculture later. This impression is reinforced by the fact that they have normally channelled less than 20 per cent of gross investment into agriculture (see Table 10); the distribution of investment must roughly reflect the distribution of the investment goods in which this investment is embodied. In China during 1950–79 agriculture received only 11 per cent of all state investment (Ishikawa, 1983, 259), which suggests that agriculture received under 16 per cent of total investment. Indeed, farm machinery, fertilizers and pesticides have made up only 3–5 per cent of China's industrial output since 1965 (Xue, 1982T, 972). And in Yugoslavia, the communist state most favourably disposed towards peasant agriculture, only 10 per cent of gross industrial output went into agriculture in the 1960s (OECD, 1969, 361). *Faute de mieux* successful agricultural development has usually rested on new crops, seed selection, education, organizational reforms, labour-intensive land improvements (drainage, irrigation, terracing, marling, liming), commercial incentives, small village-made implements and accessories, and the use of manure and night-soil, rather than expensive producer goods inputs from the urban sector (cf. Bairoch, 1973; Hayami, 1976). Moreover, before he became an apologist for forced industrialization, Maurice Dobb saw deeper reasons why communist states make a fatal mistake in giving priority or preferential treatment to large-scale industrialization: 'in a decade or two, when revolutionary traditions have faded into legend, the industrial workers who have tasted the fruit of "original sin" will desire to continue the eating of it'; and 'When they have had their cake made for them by others under duress, to expect them to turn and share it with its makers might well be a little utopian'; indeed, 'Why should the working class, having become a ruling class for a season, alone fail to become exclusive, possessive and gild-like, as has every other nascent exploiting class in history?' (Dobb, 1928, 264). Village communism proposes no privileged sector or class, but merely that the villages be allowed their due share of resources, to use more or less as they see fit.

Critics of village-based development have naturally made political capital out of the 'failure' of President Nyerere's *ujamaa* programme in Tanzania (see, for example, Byres, 1979, 240; Kitching, 1982, 104–24, 139). However, it is debatable whether 1970s Tanzania really implemented village-based development. Strictly speaking, village-based development strategies presuppose a society in which villages and settled agricultural households have long constituted the basic social units. But when the *ujamaa* programme was launched, much of Tanzania's rural population still led an unsettled, very dispersed, often pastoral existence, and many of the 'villages' established by Nyerere's premature and increasingly coercive 'villagization' programme existed only on paper, as figments of the bureaucratic imagination (Kitching, 1982, 106–9). In 1970 agriculture employed 86 per cent of Tanzania's workforce. But out of 2.7 million shillings of 'development expenditure' and 2.3 million shillings of 'parastatal investment', the 1969–74 Plan assigned only 13.6 and 13.5 per cent, respectively, to agriculture (including forestry and fishing); nearly twice as much was to be spent on urban as on rural water and sanitation services; despite very widespread illiteracy, primary education was assigned only 4.4 per cent of development expenditure, as against 9.5 per cent for post-primary education and 30 per cent for mainly non-agricultural transport projects; police and prisons were assigned more development expenditure than was housing, and defence and national service were assigned more than health care; industry and power generation, with under 3 per cent of Tanzania's workforce, were assigned 53.6 per cent of parastatal investment; and despite the fanfare for village industry, the National Small-Scale Industries Corporation was assigned only 0.3 per cent of parastatal investment (Tanzania, 1969, vol. 2, 13–19). Similarly, the 1976–81 Plan assigned nearly twice as much investment and development expenditure to industry as to agriculture (Kitching, 1982, 105), or over thirty times more investment per person to industry than to agriculture. And 'almost all new ventures in manufacturing were large-scale, capital-intensive and heavily dependent on imports' (Von Freyhold, 1979, 100); in 1973 Tanzanian manufacturing averaged 146 employees per establishment (Tanzania, 1974–5, 74). Admittedly, approximately two-thirds of Tanzania's manufacturing output used agricultural raw materials (ibid.), but the direct benefits went to the urban-industrial sector, which also indirectly benefited from the disproportionately large share of agricultural investment allocated to producers of industrial crops outside the *ujamaa* 'villages' (Von Freyhold, 1979, 92–3). Tanzania actually pursued a large-scale, town-based industrialization programme which proved too ambitious for a country so short of capital, minerals and industrial–organizational skills (*Financial Times*, 7 July 1980, 19 January 1983); and the *ujamaa* programme was more cosmetic than real.

'Populist visions imply that peasant living standards can be raised and equality increased while at the same time maintaining peasant households as landholding and labour-disposing units. *Unfortunately, there is no historical or contemporary example of this combination*' (Kitching, 1982, 136; emphasis added): if the latter statement were true, my views and the economic case for village communism would indeed be 'rather flabby' (ibid., 140). But, with all due respect, there are quite a few countries in which increased peasant living standards, redistribution of income and land in favour of the rural poor, broader educational opportunities, weakening of class barriers and an increased preponderance of family labour farms are known to have gone hand-in-hand, under a wide variety of regimes. Besides pre-revolutionary Russia, post-1850s Ireland, modern Denmark and post-1945 Japan, on which pertinent information and references have already been provided, we should also consider the instructive and well-documented examples of Taiwan, South Korea, Yugoslavia and Poland.

Taiwan is very mountainous, mineral-deficient and five times more densely populated than mainland China. Until the mid-1950s over 60 per cent of the workforce worked in agriculture (Ho, 1978, 82; Griffin, 1976, 257). With only 0.15 ha of farmland per agricultural inhabitant in 1970 (see Table 6), agriculture has been based on tiny family labour farms (Tables 4 and 7). Like mainland China, Taiwan has a repressive one-party state which in effect prohibits strikes and collective bargaining; and again like the mainland, it obtained considerable foreign aid in the 1950s (US aid amounted to 7.8 per cent of Taiwan's GNP in 1951–60, but became negligible during the 1960s: Griffin, 1976, 260). But while Taiwan's population rose 3.8 per cent per annum in 1953–60 and 2.5 per cent per annum in 1960–78 (Table 1), its per capita GNP rose 3.4 per cent per annum in 1953–62 (Taiwan, 1978, 2) and 6.6 per cent per annum in 1960–78 (World Bank, 1980, 111). By 1978 Taiwan's per capita GNP was over six times that of mainland China (ibid.; *Financial Times*, 9 October 1981), whereas it had been only one and a half times that of mainland China in 1953 and 1957 (see Ban *et al.*, 1980, table 2; Bairoch, 1975, 193, 247. If Taiwan's per capita GDP was US $390 in 1970, and if

Taiwan's per capita GDP rose 4.9 per cent per annum during 1953–70 and 5.4 per cent per annum during 1957–70, then Taiwan's per capita GDP must have been approximately $170 in 1953 and approximately $195 in 1957, in 1970 US dollars. On Bairoch's data, expressed in 1970 US dollars, China's per capita GDP was approximately $110 in 1953, $130 in 1957 and $160 in 1970). By 1977 adult literacy was 82 per cent in Taiwan v. 66 per cent in China (*Financial Times*, 9 October 1981). Moreover, according to Fei *et al.* (1979, 66–9, 118, 122), during 1952–72 there were successive substantial reductions in the inequality of family income distribution in Taiwan as a whole, and within the rural sector (ibid., 55, 60, 122, 125). The 1949–53 land reforms expropriated most landholdings over 3 ha, more than halved the number of tenant farmers, nearly doubled the number of owner-farmers, reduced the rentiers' share of total farm income from 25 per cent in 1936–40 to 6 per cent in 1956–60 and democratized the hitherto landlord-controlled farmers' co-operatives (ibid., 40–5). Taiwan has successfully emphasized labour-intensive, capital-saving technologies and the production of labour-intensive industrial and agricultural consumer goods, in line with her comparative cost advantages, instead of pursuing high-cost self-reliance in capital-intensive producer goods (ibid., 24, 25, 28, 49, 50, 57, 70). In Taiwan 'industrialization had its roots in agriculture' and 'Linkages between agriculture and the rural-based food-processing industry led to a marked spatial dispersion of economic growth', providing 'substantial nonagricultural employment to farmers' (ibid., 25, 37). This and specialization in small-scale, labour-intensive crops has especially benefited the rural poor (ibid., 49, 50, 55–63). Widely dispersed, small-scale labour-intensive industrialization and horticulture transformed Taiwan's formerly chronic unemployment and underemployment into a labour shortage by the late 1960s, thus eliminating a major cause of poverty and causing an accelerating rise in real wages, which in turn has made it appropriate to gradually go in for more capital-intensive methods and industries since the 1970s (ibid., 32–5, 50, 67–71, 100, 116–17). This growth pattern helped to redistribute income (ibid., 64–71, 127) and to make approximately 90 per cent of Taiwan's growing output available for consumption in the 1950s (ibid., 29), while turning Taiwan into a capital-surplus economy by 1972 (ibid., 34). Conversely, top-heavy, capital-intensive industrialization tends to widen intersectional inequalities, to depress the share of output available for consumption and to exacerbate shortages of capital and consumer goods. Among the key components in Taiwan's success were mass education (ibid., 37), an ideology of 'land to the tiller' (ibid., 39–40), rural co-operatives (ibid., 23, 45–9), irrigation of over half Taiwan's cropland (ibid., 37), fair terms of trade for agriculture (ibid., 27), and reduced tax rates for low-income families (ibid., 253–4), all of which increased agricultural incentives and performance (ibid., 39–40, 28, 47). Data on the size distribution of Taiwan's farms greatly overstate rural inequalities: in 1967 family income on landholdings below 0.5 ha was only 8 per cent lower than on landholdings of 0.5–1.0 ha and only 35 per cent lower than on holdings of 1.0–2.0 ha (ibid., 58), as the smaller landholders specialized in more intensive horticulture and had larger non-agricultural incomes (ibid., 56–61). Also small family incomes normally pertained to small families (ibid., 257). Naturally Taiwan's critics deplore the existence of cheap 'sweated labour', as if this were something that poor countries could simply 'abolish'. In Taiwan, however, the share of wages in value added in manufacturing has been comparatively high: in the 1950s to 1960s it generally exceeded 50 per cent (ibid., 71). Also consider a simple calculation: if Taiwan's workforce generally receives as little as half the value of its product (a very pessimistic assumption), and if China's workforce generally receives as much as three-quarters of the value of its product (a very optimistic assumption), this would still leave Taiwan's workforce about four times 'better off' than China's workforce, if Taiwan's per capita GNP was over six times that of China in 1978. Furthermore, by 1970 Taiwan's daily agricultural wages were only 10 per cent below daily industrial wages (Griffin, 1976, 275), and during 1950–69 the net drain of capital from agriculture to other sectors amounted to under 2 per cent of agricultural output (ibid., 266).

The South Korean economy is often mentioned in the same breath as Taiwan, but South Korea's growth pattern has been much less dispersed, less balanced, less export-oriented, less able to reap the classic gains-from-trade, much more dependent on fickle foreign capital and much more vulnerable to political strife (1959–61, 1971–2, 1974, 1977–81). In 1972 farm households obtained only 18 per cent of their income from non-agricultural activities in South Korea (as against 55 per cent for Taiwan and 68 per cent for Japan), due to 'the heavy concentration of industry in Seoul, Inchon and Pusan'; and 'the costly results of this concentration' included excessive migration from rural areas into increasingly overcrowded cities (Hasan, 1976, 23, 55). During 1977–81 South Korea was severely destabilized by the mounting megalomania and brutality of dictator Pak Chung Hee (assassinated in 1979), by excessive and lopsided investment in costly mineral- and capital-intensive producer goods industries, and by the consequent shortages, unrest and runaway inflation, all of which increased South Korea's external indebtedness to US $37 billion by December 1982 (FT Surveys, 19 August 1983, 9 June 1980, 5 June 1981). Moreover, this mountainous mineral-deficient republic, with four times the population density of China, had a distinctly inauspicious start. From the outset it was a police state, heavily reliant on profiteers, former collaborators in Japanese barbarism, and US military and economic support, against widespread popular opposition from democrats, nationalists and radicals, few of whom belonged to the Korean Communist Party, which had only 4350 members in December 1945 (see McCormack and Gittings, 1977, 13–21, 27, 28, 45, 48; Halliday, 1981, 25, 27). The high-handed Soviet–American partition of Korea gave the South 69 per cent of Korea's inhabitants, but only 8 per cent of the considerable electricity industry, 15 per cent of the substantial metallurgical industry, 12 per cent of the advanced chemicals industry, a tiny fraction of Korea's mineral wealth, 69 per cent of her relatively neglected light industry and 63 per cent of her meagre agricultural production (Halliday, 1981, 24; Suh, 1978, ch. 8). Agriculture supported three-quarters of South Korea's population, two-thirds of whom were small tenants paying very onerous rents before the land reforms of 1947–50; and the Korean War of 1950–3 reduced South Korea's agricultural output and GNP by 27 and 16 per cent respectively, as well as causing over 1 million deaths and a commensurate influx of refugees from the heavily bombed North (Adelman and Robinson, 1978, 38–9). In 1956 industry (including mining) employed only 3 per cent of the workforce in South Korea, as against 27 per cent in the North (Kim, 1975, 188); and South Korea 'entered the sixties with one of the lowest income levels in the world' (Hasan, 1976, 28). Nevertheless, South Korea's economy grew 5 per cent per annum during 1954–8 and 3.5 per cent per annum in the turmoil of 1959–62 (ibid., 27), accelerating to over 10 per cent per annum during 1962–76 (Hasan and Rao, 1979, 16). The land reforms of 1947–50 'virtually eliminated tenancy, put a ceiling of three hectares on paddy holdings and established a structure of small owner-operated farms'; in 1974 94 per cent of farms were under 3 ha and accounted for 93 per cent of all farmland (ibid., 37). These reforms helped to foster intensive horticulture and the second highest average grain yields per hectare in Asia (ibid., 6, 206–8). Despite very rapid urban–industrial development, the nominal per capita incomes of farm households averaged 57, 80 and 91 per cent of the per capita incomes of urban wage- and salary-earning households in 1967, 1973 and 1976, respectively (ibid., 41), even though farm price support amounted to under 1 per cent of GNP (ibid., 350). Moreover, during 1964–70 income was more equally distributed among farm households than among non-agricultural households, and the income share of the poorest 20 per cent of farm households again increased significantly (Adelman and Robinson, 1978, table 5). Adult literacy rose from 30 per cent in 1953 to over 80 per cent in 1963 (ibid., 41) and 88 per cent of the farm population (excluding pre-school children) were literate by 1970 (Ban et al., 1980, table 134): 'All village children go to primary school; 80% go on to high school' (The Economist, 17 May 1980, 40). By 1976 91 per cent of rural households had electricity (Hasan and Rao, 1979, 43). By 1980 all had TV and average rural household income was approaching $3000 per annum, as against $800 per annum in 1970 (The Economist, 17 May 1980, 40). As in Taiwan, 'The distribution of the benefits of growth was more the result of the growth strategy than of fiscal intervention'; the 'forces of comparative advantage' induced mineral- and capital-deficient South Korea to concentrate on labour-intensive activities, 'which in turn directly benefited those at the lower end of the income scale' (Hasan and Rao, 1979, 37). During 1963–75 the active workforce expanded 3.7 per cent per annum, rather faster than the population of working age, while the consequent reductions in open and latent unemployment helped to raise average real wages 7 per cent per annum over the same period (ibid., 174, 33, 35). The emphasis on labour-intensive production of consumer goods also helped to avoid pressure on consumption levels: savings amounted to only 7 per cent of GNP in 1962–6, 15 per cent in 1967–71 and

19 per cent in 1972–5 (ibid., 29). Naturally the fact that South Korean remuneration and working conditions remained appallingly low by affluent Western standards has excited international condemnation (see McCormack and Gittings, 1977, 62–5, 136); but this predicament was largely unavoidable in an economy whose output per inhabitant was still seven to ten times less than that of Japan, West Germany, France, Benelux, Scandinavia and the USA in 1978 (World Bank, 1980, 111). 'Sweated labour' is not peculiar to the capitalist system. Because per capita output sets a real ceiling on the sustainable level of real remuneration, the latter must have been even lower in communist China, whose per capita output was about four times less than the South Korean level in 1978. But it would be dishonest to insinuate that economies at these levels of per capita output can develop without 'sweated labour'. Moreover, without in any way condoning the evils of dictatorship (right or left), it seems beyond doubt that South Korea has experienced a comparatively equal distribution of the fruits of economic growth (see Hasan and Rao, 1979, 36–41, 89, 205, 226–8; Adelman and Robinson, 1978, 38–47; Ahluwalia, 1976, 340–1).

Yugoslavia is a mountainous and largely infertile country, but until 1945 over 75 per cent of the population depended on agriculture, in which 97 per cent of farms were under 20 ha in 1931 (see Tables 1, 4, 7, 12; and Stipetić, 1975T, 9, 49, 152). Moreover, with Poland, Yugoslavia was the European country most devastated by the Second World War (Berend and Ranki, 1974T, 338–41), and as late as 1953 industry employed only 8 per cent of the workforce (OECD, 1969, 367). This was the background against which the land reforms of 1945–53 expropriated German and church properties, abolished the last vestiges of landlordism and largely eliminated rural landlessness; since 1953 there has been a ceiling of 10–15 ha on private landholdings, according to quality (Bergmann, 1975T, 134–7). By 1951 state farms and producer co-operatives had appropriated 36 per cent of all farmland (ibid., 136), but rural collectivization was decisively defeated by the same peasantry which had earlier defeated the Nazi–Fascist occupation of Yugoslavia. From 1954 until the 1970s 2.6 million privately owned farms averaging 4 ha in size accounted for over 80 per cent of all cropland, over 90 per cent of all livestock and over 75 per cent of agricultural output, although the best land was reserved for the highly privileged, large-scale, capital-intensive state sector, which ensured that urban food supplies would remain largely under state control and which until 1965 monopolized 90 per cent of farm machinery and 80 per cent of chemical fertilizer supplies (OECD, 1973, 8, 13, 28–30; Stipetić, 1975T, 107, 108, 124, 154, 155, and Franklin, 1969, 191). By 1972 'basic assets' per employee (excluding the value of land and forests) and 'social product' per employee were both markedly higher in the state sector of agriculture than in industry, despite very wasteful use of the resources lavished on state farms (Stipetić, 1975T, 63, 70–3). But in the early 1970s 20 per cent of Yugoslavia's cropland was 'unsuitable for cultivation', 25 per cent was 'threatened by erosion', 20 per cent was in need of 'calcification and humification', 20 per cent was 'flood-prone', only 2 per cent was irrigated and during 1948–70 under 10 per cent of Yugoslav investment had gone into agriculture, so it is hardly surprising that the 44 per cent of the workforce engaged in agriculture in 1971 produced only 20–22 per cent of national income (ibid., 11, 152, 156). Nevertheless, the average per capita incomes of private smallholdings rose 3.5-fold in real terms during 1954–72 and increased from 60 per cent of the average per capita income of non-agricultural households in 1953–4 to 74 per cent by 1965–6 (ibid., 135–6), partly because Yugoslavia's comparatively labour-intensive agriculture incurred comparatively low capital depreciation and production expenses (Lazarcik, 1974, 342) and partly because an increasing proportion of private farms had one or more occupants fully engaged in non-agricultural activities: 9 per cent in 1931, 32 per cent in 1955 and 43 per cent in 1969 (Stipetić, 1975T, 133). And by 1967–72 average household income on private farms under 2 ha was only one-third less than on private farms exceeding 8 ha, because the smaller farms had larger non-agricultural earnings and engaged in more intensive forms of agriculture (ibid., 135). Moreover, total Yugoslav food consumption rose 4.7 per cent per annum during 1947–72 (as against 1.6 per cent per annum during 1920–40); the average diet included steadily increasing proportions of fruit, vegetables and animal produce; and by 1971–2 per capita food consumption on private farms was only 10–20 per cent below the national average (ibid., 102, 106, 137). Net agricultural output increased 3.5 per cent per annum in Yugoslavia during 1950–72, as against 1.4 per cent per annum in the collectivized East European states (Lazarcik, 1974, 339). Furthermore, per capita housing space on private farms increased from 7.5 to 10.1 sq. metres during 1951–69 and the proportion of private farms with electricity rose from 18.5 to 72.9 per cent during 1951–66 (Stipetić, 1975T, 136, 134), while adult literacy reached 85 per cent by 1970 (World Bank, 1975, 53).

In interwar Poland agriculture accounted for '68% of the country's total production and . . . over 60% of the economically active population . . . 44% of all arable land was owned by big landlords, who represented only 0.6% of all farms. . . . 65% of all farms had less than 5 hectares . . . 54.3% of all farms had no horses' (Lipski, 1969T, 6–8). In 1934–8 Poland's grain yields were among the lowest in Europe (see Table 12). The Second World War killed 6 million Polish citizens (17 per cent of the 1938 population), destroyed one-third of Poland's fixed industrial and agricultural assets, wrecked her transport network, halved her horse population and reduced her cattle, pig and sheep populations by two-thirds in each case (Lipski, 1969T, 20; Bozyk, 1975T, 14). Nevertheless, by 1950–5 agricultural output per person engaged in agriculture was 168.6 per cent of the 1934–8 level in Poland, as against 107.6 per cent of the 1934–8 level in Yugoslavia and only 90.6 per cent of the 1934–8 level in the rest of Eastern Europe (excluding Albania); by 1966–70 it was 259.4 per cent of the 1934–8 level in Poland, 257.0 per cent of the 1934–8 level in Yugoslavia and only 201.6 per cent of the 1934–8 level in the collectivized states of Eastern Europe (see Lazarcik, 1974, 371). The superior performance of Polish agriculture was partly due to territorial changes: the territory recovered from Germany in 1945 was potentially more productive than the territory lost to the USSR, although the recovered territory was in appalling shape in 1945. But a major factor was Poland's retention of a preponderance of small peasant farms. Resettlement of the recovered territory and the land reforms of 1944–6 created 814,000 new farms averaging 5–8 ha each (according to region) and enlarged 254,000 existing farms by an average of 1.9 ha each; 65 per cent of the 6m. ha redistributed went to former labourers; landlords and Germans were expropriated without compensation; and Poland established a ceiling of 15 ha on the size of farm which could be created by private purchase thereafter (Lipski, 1969T, 12–13, 32; Dunman, 1975, 165). Much of the credit for these changes belongs to the Polish Peasant Party (PSL), then Poland's largest political party, and to its leader Stanislaw Mikolajczyk, who as Minister of Agriculture (1945–7) did much to defend peasant interests before he was forced to flee abroad (see Korbonski, 1965; Narkiewicz, 1976, 246–8, 269). Thenceforth, 'Over most of the country social divisions within the peasantry were minimal. . . . Few characteristics of class polarization could be found in the results of the survey conducted in 1957. . . . The land tax is progressive and taxation on the use of hired labour prohibitive' (Lewis, 1973, 49, 70). Private 'exploitation' of hired labourers and poor peasants by 'kulaks' all but disappeared (Kozlowski, 1977, 26). By 1960 3.5 million private farms, of which 96 per cent were below 15 ha, occupied 85 per cent of all farmland (including 85 per cent of all cropland) and produced 88 per cent of gross agricultural output (Lipski, 1969T, 32–4). Such stratification as did occur was based not on differentiation into capitalists and labourers, but on the favours and privileges bestowed on peasants who collaborated with the ruling party and its state agencies; in theory, these favours and privileges were supposed to 'draw' the peasantry 'towards socialism', but they also encouraged corruption and cynicism and, in the eyes of those who lived by their own 'honest toil', they helped to further discredit the ruling party, its 'socialism' and its overprivileged collaborators (see Lewis, 1973, 76–80; Kozlowski, 1977, 22; Narkiewicz, 1976, 266–8). At their peak in early 1956 producer co-operatives occupied 9 per cent of all farmland, but by the 1960s their share was under 2 per cent; collectivization was defeated by a peasantry which had been part of Europe's largest wartime Resistance movement (see Korbonski, 1965, 44–5, 119, 306–7; Narkiewicz, 1976, 240). By 1966 large state farms occupied 13.4 per cent of all farmland (mainly in the relatively fertile resettled territory), enjoyed five times more tractors and two or three times more fertilizer and lime per hectare than did private farms, but produced only 10.9 per cent of gross agricultural output (Lipski, 1969T, 36–8; Kostrowicki and Szczesny, 1972T, 29). As early as 1956 party leader Gomulka was complaining that output per hectare on Poland's pampered state farms was barely half that on private farms (Dunman, 1975, 169). During 1970–4, when state farms were still receiving over half Poland's agricultural investment, the additional output per additional material input on state farms was under half that for private farms (Kozlowski, 1977, 32). The superior performance of Poland's private farms has rightly raised misgivings about the gradual extension of the state farm system at the private sector's expense since 1956. This policy is based on a doctrinaire belief in agricultural economies of scale, which have yet to materialize. The belief that most of Poland's private farms are too small to be efficient seems to ignore the experience of countries like Japan, Taiwan and South Korea, where farms are over five times smaller than in Poland (see Table 7), and seems to have prevented Poland from reaping the full development potential of intensive small-scale horticulture and animal husbandry. Until 1968 Poland's vaunted farm machinery industry wilfully neglected the needs of small farms, which could have used more minitractors, power tillers, milking machines, etc.; after a policy change in 1968, such machines were taken up very rapidly (see Dunman, 1975, 178; Kozlowski, 1977, 23–7). But as late as 1965 horses provided 80 per cent of the tractive power on private farms, whereas machinery provided 80 per cent of the tractive power on state farms (Kostrowicki and Szczesny, 1972T, 29). The development of truck farming was also handicapped by the state's preference for slow and inflexible rail (rather than road) transport and by the sluggishness of state-controlled wholesaling and retailing networks, with far too few retail outlets (see Osmova and Faminsky, 1980, 86; Turcan, 1977; Samli, 1978). More generally, Polish agricultural development has been handicapped by the state's persistently lopsided emphasis on industries like steel, heavy engineering, coal, petrochemicals and shipbuilding, for whose products small peasant farmers have limited use (see Poland, 1976, 24–5; Bozyk, 1975T, 34–59). In the 1970s agriculture and food processing still provided 48 per cent of Poland's employment, 38 per cent of its national income and approximately 14 per cent of its exports (Wos and Grochowski, 1978, 93, 119; Comecon, 1979, 376); yet agriculture had received only 13 per cent of Polish investment during 1950–70 (Table 10) and food processing received only 9.5 per cent of Polish industrial investment during 1966–75 (Poland, 1976, 25). Nevertheless, real agricultural incomes officially rose approximately 3.5 per cent per annum during 1956–75 (Hardt, 1977, 828), partly because Poland's comparatively labour-intensive agriculture incurred comparatively low capital-depreciation and production expenses during 1950–68 (Lazarcik, 1974, 342) and partly because by 1970 one-third of all farm inhabitants and two-thirds of all farms also had non-agricultural incomes (Wos and Grochowski, 1978, 74, 100). As early as 1957 90 per cent of the economically active occupants of farms below 0.5 ha and 67 per cent of those on farms of 0.5–2 ha had non-agricultural livelihoods, and by 1967 rural living standards were only about 30 per cent below urban levels (Lewis, 1973, 50, 56). In 1970–4 disposable income per private farm was roughly double the average 'net' industrial wage (cf. Kozlowski, 1977, 29, with Poland, 1976, 54). Furthermore, by 1960 98 per cent of Polish adults were literate (Table 3); both urban and rural areas had 13.4 m² of housing space per inhabitant (Poland, 1976, 62); by 1968

83 per cent of private farms had electricity, as against 34 per cent in 1955 (Dunman, 1975, 178); and by 1966 the vast majority of private farms belonged to various marketing and credit co-operatives (Lipski, 1969T, 61, 66). In the 1970s Poland's per capita supplies of meat, milk, sugar, vegetables, potatoes and grain were each among the highest in Europe (see Tables 11 and 14; and Comecon, 1976T, 225–7). Poland's infamous 'meat shortages' in the 1970s were caused not by any overall deficiency on the production side, but by the above-mentioned inefficiencies in the state-controlled distribution network and by inflated demand. The latter was created by overinvestment and disproportionately rapid expansion in heavy industry, causing the expansion of money incomes to persistently outstrip Poland's more slowly expanding supplies of consumer goods, and by the maintenance of fixed and increasingly subsidized food prices in state shops (cf. Blazyca, 1980; Nuti, 1981): 'Owing to artificially low price levels, supply could not balance demand, especially for meat. Shortages, queues, frustration and discontent became a permanent feature of the market and everyday life' (Pelczynski, in Leslie, 1980). By 1980 the state was spending 25 per cent of its budget or 12 per cent of national income on subsidizing excess demand for food (*Financial Times*, 24 July 1981, 23). This diverted resources from more important uses, boosted food and fodder imports, aggravated Poland's external indebtedness and made it increasingly worthwhile for farmers to sell the state food purchased from state shops rather than food produced on their own farms, and to feed their animals on food purchased from state shops. To correct its deep-seated economic disequilibrium Poland needs to establish price structures which broadly reflect relative costs and scarcities; it must not allow megalomaniacal expansion of industrial investment, heavy industry and money incomes to far outstrip its production of consumer goods; it should take more of its farmland and its distribution network out of inefficient state hands; and, whatever the formal regime, the authorities and Poland's economic decision-makers will have to win the respect, confidence and co-operation of Poland's workers and peasants. Provided these exacting conditions are met, there is no obvious reason why small-scale peasant agriculture shouldn't successfully coexist with large-scale state industry for the foreseeable future (cf. Kozlowski, 1977; Bukharin, 1982T, 183–329). Fundamentally,

> Conditions exist for Polish agriculture, aside from covering its internal needs, to take upon itself the leading role among the countries of [Comecon] in the field of intensive, specialized and labour-consuming cultivation. This will necessitate changing traditional methods of cultivating rye and potatoes and concentrating on industrial cultivation, animal breeding and vegetable production. It would be advisable to localize new food-processing plants in agricultural regions so as to stimulate the development of specialized agriculture. (Polish Academy of Sciences, 1974T, 150)

Significantly, by the mid-1960s Poland, Yugoslavia, South Korea and Taiwan had *pre-tax* income distributions which were not much more unequal than those of the collectivized states which published comparable data (see Ahluwalia, 1976, 340–1; Adelman and Robinson, 1978, 46; Fei et al., 1979, 66):

Income share (%)	Taiwan		South Korea		Yugo-slavia
	1964	1968	1964	1970	1968
Bottom 20%	7.7	7.8	7	7	6.5
Bottom 40%	20.3	20.0	18	18	18.5
Top 20%	41.0	41.4	45	44	41.5

Income share (%)	Poland	Hungary	Bulgaria	GDR	Czecho-slovakia
	1964	1967	1964	1970	1964
Bottom 20%	9.8	8.5	9.8	10.4	12.0
Bottom 40%	23.4	24.0	25.0	26.2	27.6
Top 20%	36.0	33.5	35.0	30.7	31.0

Moreover, these data probably overstate the real contrasts in income distribution: the communist states had very *low* and *ungraduated* rates of income tax; low incomes were even more likely to be under-recorded in 'scattered' market economies than in 'concentrated' planned economies; there was even more reason to conceal very high incomes in communist states than in non-communist states; and the communist states were less open to independent investigation. Unfortunately we do not have directly comparable data for Russia, China, North Korea, Albania, Romania, or Cuba; but if they had been more equal, they would surely have publicized the relevant information, which should be comparatively easy to assemble in collectivized economies. However, using different measures of income inequality, Professor Peter Wiles has shown that the USSR was somewhat less equal than Poland, Hungary, Bulgaria and Czechoslovakia in the mid-1960s (see p. 161). This raises further doubts as to whether the ordeals of imposed collectivization were really worthwhile. If peasant living standards have been raised and equality increased while at the same time maintaining peasant households as landholding and labour-disposing units in Taiwan, South Korea, Yugoslavia and Poland, under regimes which were only weakly committed to village-based development, then this combination ought to be even more feasible in a society strongly committed to village-based development. QED.

The strongest grounds for doubting the viability of village-based development are military rather than economic. It is commonly believed that, in the modern world, an effective national defence must rest on a large heavy-industrial sector. However, there is reason to believe that village-based societies can survive under some form of decentralized defence, without the offensive capabilities of a conventional or nuclear military–industrial complex. It must depend on popular preparedness to resist foreign invasion by engaging in tenacious locally concerted guerrilla warfare and non-cooperation, as practised in Yugoslavia and Greece during the Second World War.

Yugoslavia has continued to rely on this form of defence, realizing that small states cannot realistically hope to defeat any future Soviet invasion by conventional means; that NATO's nuclear 'deterrents' have not deterred Soviet invasions of East Germany (1953), Hungary (1956), or Czechoslovakia (1968), although they have increased the risk of a 'preventive strike' against states holding nuclear weapons; that 'nuclear deterrence' is a kind of Maginot Line, which creates a false illusion of security and causes Europeans to neglect more usable forms of defence; that it is in any case a delusion to think that small states can seriously compete with the super-powers in the technology of mass destruction; and that nuclear powers are unlikely to use strategic nuclear weapons against territory which they might wish to occupy, or which poses no threat, or from which nuclear fall-out could be blown across their own territory. Yugoslavia's standing army of only 0.26 million men is backed up by 1 million reservists, and every settlement has an armoury and defence assignments. Admittedly, this 'People's Defence System' has not been put to the test since the 1940s, but one can take considerable reassurance from the way in which North Vietnam has humbled foreign predators in recent decades.

As described in Gérard Chaliand's first-hand report on *The Peasants of North Vietnam* (1969T, 13), 'The survival of North Vietnam has been made possible by a massive decentralization, a wholesale movement away from the towns and cities; this process has been facilitated by the communal traditions of village life' (cf. White, 1982, 11, 16): 'The basic social structure in Vietnam is the village commune. . . . Flanked with pools and hedged about with stout bamboos, the Vietnamese village forms a whole and enjoys a large measure of autonomy' (Chaliand, 1969T, 16). 'The reclaiming of land within the [Red River] delta probably lies at the root of the Vietnamese community, as collective efforts have always been needed to dam the river' (ibid., 17). 'Collective action endowed the villagers with a remarkable degree of security against natural or supernatural risks' (ibid., 23), and 'communal units served as a barrier to the formation of extra-communal groups' (ibid., 21). 'The common lands were the property of all villagers: any inhabitant who was of age was entitled to a plot, and in practice these common lands were cultivated just as pains-takingly as privately owned acres' (ibid., 23). Beginning in the 1860s Vietnamese resistance to French colonization persistently 'employed guerrilla tactics, harrying the colonial army and avoiding pitched battles. Vast subterranean galleries were dug beneath the villages, so that the defenders could hold out against siege', and 'a remarkable capacity was shown for lengthy resistance based entirely on the use of local forces, without support from the State' (ibid., 29). Village solidarity was most vividly demonstrated 'when political cadres working for the Vietminh hid in villages for years at a time without being informed on' (ibid., 23). In 1953, as the Vietminh finally triumphed over the French, North Vietnam began in earnest to redistribute large landholdings and farm equipment in favour of the poor (ibid., 35). By 1957 72 per cent of the rural population had directly benefited from redistributive measures; and, taking 1939 as a base-year, cultivated area had increased by 24 per cent, yields per hectare by 36 per cent, crop output by 68 per cent and per capita crop output by 43 per cent (ibid., 40–1). Although these achievements were marred by the use of repression against peasant resistance to land reform and by the usual excesses attributed to overzealous, vindictive and uncouth communist officials and tribunals (ibid., 41–2), the ruling party nevertheless began to collectivize agriculture in 1958, and by 1961 85 per cent of peasant households had joined farmers' co-operatives of various kinds (ibid., 43–4). According to Gordon (1981, 21), only 12 per cent had joined fully-fledged collective farms, while 74 per cent had joined transitional institutions. However, whereas in Russia collectivization wantonly destroyed the existing autonomous village communes, in North Vietnam

> The commune was regarded as the logical point of departure for the co-operative. The Workers' Party was wise enough not to attempt to set up giant co-operatives combining dozens of villages, a policy which would have shattered their cohesion and taken away their sense of group security. The elders were got rid of, the landowners dispossessed, the common lands converted into co-operative estates. But the right to run the village independently has survived in large measure. (Chaliand, 1969T, 58)

According to Gordon (1971, 73), by 1966 85 per cent of peasant households belonged to fully-fledged collective farms, which averaged only 108 households and 62 ha of farmland per farm, and a further 10 per cent belonged to transitional institutions. The parochialism of village life was transcended not by smashing valuable village institutions and traditions, but by means of the radio, the national press and above all by mass education: by 1967 all children aged 7–11 were receiving primary education, many villages also maintained nurseries; post-primary education paid particular attention to agricultural needs; and North Vietnam could boast 'a school and a competently staffed medical unit in every village' (Chaliand, 1969T, 45–9, 59). Moreover, according to White (1982, 13), in North Vietnam collectivization was carried out 'without physical coercion', unlike the preceding land reforms, and it was spread over three times as many years as in China. 'The paddy fields, which were divided into tiny plots before collectivization, now lie in long straight lines, with rationally determined boundaries. There are many more dikes and dikelets . . . and agricultural production has continued to rise despite the bombing', which the Americans began in earnest in 1965 (Chaliand, 1969T, 65–7). According to Poppinga (1975T, 212), rice output was about double the 1939 level during 1965–72. American bombing was countered by a remarkable dispersal and decentralization of power, resources and personnel: 'The surviving factories were broken into smaller units and evacuated into country areas' (Chaliand, 1969T, 57); the war brought 'tens of thousands of cadres from Hanoi and Haiphong back into the provinces and villages' (ibid., 64); and the villages again provided the crucial underground tunnels, communications systems, dugouts, communal solidarity and air-raid shelters, which so decisively contributed to North Vietnam's survival (see ibid., 67). For further details on the achievements of the dispersal and decentralization policy, see J. M. Van Dyke's major study of *North Vietnam's Strategy for Survival* (1972, especially chs 5–10).

The foregoing is in no way intended to suggest that North Vietnam could do no wrong. On the contrary, even if one must welcome the overthrow of Pol Pot's regime in Kampuchea, it is clear that recent treatment of South Vietnam virtually as a conquered country, harsh treatment of petty traders and certain ethnic minorities, the related exodus of 300,000 refugee 'boat people', overhasty and somewhat predatory collectivization of the fertile Mekong Delta (where private property and medium-scale commercial agriculture were most strongly established), and the seemingly entrenched military occupation of Laos and Kampuchea all contributed to a disastrous decline in the per capita GNP of reunified Vietnam (from $241 in 1976 to $153 in 1981, according to the IMF, of which Vietnam is a member); and this in turn contributed to the food riots of 1980 and 1981 and to the rapid escalation of Vietnam's external indebtedness and dependence on the USSR (on Vietnam's economic decline since 1976, see Donnell, 1980; White, 1982; Chanda, 1979; *Financial Times*, 1 September 1981, 26 March and 15 June 1982, 8 March 1983). However, the crucial point is that even a society as poor and seemingly defenceless as North Vietnam was able to withstand the military–industrial might of the USA mainly by relying on a very decentralized village-based defence strategy. Although Russia and China supplied some military aid, this was no match for the US weaponry deployed in Vietnam, and two US officials have estimated that foreign economic aid to North Vietnam totalled only $993m. during 1955–64 and $4306m. during 1965–75 (Theriot and Matheson, 1979, 568–9). Admittedly, the ruling party formally shared the urban–industrial goals of other Leninist parties (Kaye, 1962, 109–13; White, 1982, 24). However, at least until the reunification of Vietnam in 1975–6, economic and military exigencies made it necessary to concentrate on village-based development and defence strategies. North Vietnam lacked the industrial muscle to defeat Western imperialism by conventional means (Kaye, 1962, 106–13). As late as 1977 the 50 million inhabitants of reunified Vietnam included only 2.8 million workers and white-collar workers, of whom only 0.6 million were industrial workers (Comecon, 1979, 37, 39), and Vietnam's per capita industrial output was no more than half that of India (see Table 16). And the million-strong Vietnamese army is essentially a peasant army, which absorbs part of the Red River delta's surplus agricultural population (see Woollacott, 1980). That is why North Vietnam's survival rested mainly on its villages.

The limits of village communism

It would be dishonest to pretend that village communism is a golden road to perfect equality, freedom and harmony – these only exist in the realms of socialist make-believe, just as the conditions of perfect competition are only fulfilled in the realms of capitalist make-believe. Like other highly decentralized systems (e.g. Yugoslav self-management), village communism must *forgo* central state institutions strong enough to massively redistribute wealth from richer to poorer areas, as such a state could easily emasculate local autonomy and monopolize power for its own self-serving purposes. Instead, as in Yugoslavia, reductions in interregional inequality must depend on the (uncertain) willingness of richer areas to transfer resources to and absorb immigrants from poorer ones. One cannot secure the advantages of decentralization without forgoing the potential (albeit uncertain) redistributive advantages of centralization; one cannot have one's cake and eat it. Furthermore, like the Yugoslav system of self-management, village communism must also maintain a *market system* and hence a reasonably disciplined and confidence-inspiring *monetary system*, if it is to function and develop efficiently and autonomously. This in no way precludes decentralized or 'democratic' economic planning. But to be translated from fantasy into an operational reality, decentralized or 'democratic' economic planning still entails locally negotiated contractual relations between producers and communities, i.e. some sort of market system (call it what you will), and hence a common denominator or *unit of account*, i.e. some form of money. The alternative, a return to primitive barter, would soon cause any modern economy to seize up.

Unfortunately many socialists still equate market systems and commodity production with capitalism. But Marx rightly recognized that market systems and commodity production existed long *before* capitalism, and eminent market socialists like Oskar Lange and Lev Trotsky expected them to continue *after* capitalism (see pp. 107–9, 126–7, 176; and Lange, 1936–7). But, if it must retain a market system, decentralized village communism cannot completely eliminate inequality, disharmony and opportunities for profiteering, although it can avoid the far greater and more corrupting evils inherent in hierarchical and monopolistic state socialism, which were most powerfully portrayed in Trotsky's *The Revolution Betrayed* (1937).

3 The quicksands of Leninism: Vladimir Ulyanov

'Bolshevism took shape, developed and became steeled in long years of struggle against petit bourgeois revolutionism, which smacks of anarchism' (Lenin, 1968T, 17). Indeed, Lenin's perception of village communism as a 'petit bourgeois' red herring pervaded his first publication, *What the People's Friends Are* (1894). In Lenin's view, 'Belief in the peasant's communist instincts' had induced Russian socialists 'to set politics aside and "go among the people" . . . but practice soon convinced them of the naïvety of the idea'. Thereupon 'their entire activity was concentrated on a fight against the government, a fight waged by intelligenti alone', but still 'based on a theory that the people were ready for socialism and that, merely by seizing power, it would be possible to effect a social as well as a political revolution'. But this too was 'based on a purely mythical idea of the peasant economy as a special communal system: the myth dissolved when it came into contact with reality; and peasant socialism turned into radical-democratic representation of the petit bourgeois peasantry'. For Lenin, village communism was a vain desire to have one's cake and eat it: 'Our petit bourgeois knights wish to preserve the peasant's "tie" with the land, but not the serfdom which alone ensured this tie. . . . They want commodity economy without capitalism. . . . They don't understand the antagonistic character of our production relations, within the "peasantry" as within other social estates.' And 'instead of trying to bring this antagonism into the open . . . they dream of stopping the struggle by measures that would satisfy everybody, to achieve reconciliation'. He thought 'credit, migration, tax reform and transfer of all land to the peasants won't appreciably change anything, but must on the contrary strengthen and develop capitalist economy', as 'all these credits, improvements, banks and similar "progressive" measures will be accessible only to the individual who, possessing a properly run and established farm, has certain "savings"', i.e. to . . . an insignificant minority'. Moreover, 'the possible improvement in the position of a few individuals . . . can only be meagre and precarious on the general basis of capitalist relations'. As for 'socialization' of agriculture and village industries, this 'requires organization of production on a scale exceeding the confines of a single village'. Indeed, 'the organization of our "people's" handicraft industries furnishes an excellent illustration of the development of capitalism'. Since 'most handicraftsmen occupy a position in production that is not independent, but completely dependent', organizationally 'handicraft industry is pure capitalism; it differs from large-scale mechanized industry in being technically backward . . . and in its workers' retention of minute farms'. But 'don't imagine that exploitation and oppression is any less pronounced because relations of this sort are still poorly developed. . . . Quite the contrary. This only leads to cruder, serf-like forms of exploitation, whereby capital, as yet unable to subjugate the worker directly . . . enmeshes him in a net of usurious extortion' and 'robs him not only of surplus value, but much of his wages too'. Lenin regarded 'the work of our capitalism as progressive when it draws small, scattered markets into one nationwide market . . . when it shatters the subordination of working people to local blood-suckers and subordinates them to large-scale *capital*'. The latter 'is progressive compared with the former – despite all the horrors of oppression of labour . . . the brutalization and the maiming of women and children because it *awakens the worker's mind*, converts dumb, incoherent discontent into conscious protest, converts scattered, mindless revolt into organized class struggle to emancipate all working people'. Assuming it to be the common aspiration of socialists to 'organize large-scale production without employers, it is first necessary to abolish the commodity economy in favour of a communal, communist system under which production is regulated not by the market . . . but by the producers themselves, and the means of production are owned not by private individuals, but by society as a whole'. But 'a change from a private to a communal *form of appropriation* apparently requires that the *form of production* be changed *first*, that the separate, small-scale productive processes of petty producers be merged into a single productive process; i.e. it requires the very material conditions capitalism creates'. Socialists 'can expect to perform fruitful work only by shedding their illusions and seeking support in the actual, not the desired, development of Russia; in actual, not potential, socioeconomic relations. Their *theoretical* work must be directed towards concrete study of all forms of economic antagonism', highlighting their interconnections and sequential development, revealing antagonisms whose existence has been obscured by 'juridical peculiarities or established theoretical prejudice'. Socialists 'must present an integral picture of our realities as a specific system of production relations, show that exploitation and expropriation inhere in the system and reveal the way out of this system which is indicated by economic development'. Like Engels, Lenin rested his hopes on capitalist industrialization and Russia's tiny industrial proletariat because 'only the higher stage of capitalist development, large-scale machine industry, creates the material conditions and social forces necessary for . . . open political struggle towards *victorious communist revolution*' (cf. Lenin, 1960–70T, vol. 1, 277, 235–47, 206–18, 296, 300).

Actually, despite his laudable insistence that socialist ideologies ought to be rooted in 'concrete study' of 'actual, not potential, socioeconomic relations' and 'actual, not desired, development', Lenin's position was less realistic, less rooted in Russian realities, than the one he attacked. His perception of the Russian peasantry as an individualistic and disintegrating petite bourgeoisie is belied by the continuing vigour of rural Russia's communal institutions and egalitarian traditions. It could be argued that measures to develop peasant agriculture and village co-operatives would only benefit 'an insignificant minority' in a highly individualistic, proletarianized society, but *not* in one characterized by vigorous communal institutions and widespread communal ownership of comparatively abundant farmland. Moreover Russia's nascent proletariat was far too tiny and downtrodden to serve as a credible primary vehicle for socialism and it was utterly unrealistic to suppose that Russian socialists could mark time until capitalist industrialization had run its course. Finally, 'large-scale machine industry' would only be a prerequisite for 'socialism', if by 'socialism' one means a closed, yet highly mechanized economy, ignoring the potential gains from international trade and capital transfers and the greater cost-effectiveness of intensive, small-scale, co-operativized agriculture on the Danish pattern, which has been far more successful and far less dependent upon large-scale machinery inputs than the gigantic mechanized 'grain factories' favoured by Lenin.

But, seldom one to allow seemingly recalcitrant facts to stand in his way, Lenin resumed his offensive against village communism in 1895 by publishing a tirade on *The Economic Content of Populism*, which incidentally helped to establish the labels 'populism' and 'populist' as collective terms of abuse, useful for lumping together very disparate ideologies and movements – some of them not even remotely socialist. In Lenin's view 'the reality (small-scale production) which populists wish to raise to a higher level, bypassing capitalism, already contains capitalism and its class antagonisms'. Incipient capitalism 'is totally enmeshed in the feudal relations of former times: here there is no free contract, but a forced deal', for 'the producer is here tied to a particular place and a particular exploiter'. This 'worsens the conditions of the labouring peasant tenfold', as he 'suffers not only from capitalism, but from insufficient development of capitalism'. Contrary to common fears of proletarianization, Lenin baldly asserted that the footloose landless labourer was better off than the smallholder and dismissed the common 'prejudice' which attributed rural impoverishment to 'Malthusian' population pressure, rather than commercial pressures, class differentiation and primitive accumulation of capital. He emphasized that rural proletarianization 'doesn't reduce the domestic market, but *creates* it: commodity economy grows at both poles of the differentiating peasantry, both among the "proletarianized" peasantry, compelled to sell "free labour", and among the bourgeois peasantry, who raise the technical level of their farms . . . and develop their requirements'. The domestic market for capitalist industry was also being expanded by 'the circumstance that in capitalist society an enormous and ever-growing part is played by the [production of] means of production, the part of social product used for productive and not personal consumption, for consumption by capital and not people'. But, he concluded, 'it would be absolutely wrong to reject the whole populist programme indiscriminately', for 'Populism is reactionary' only 'inasmuch as it proposes measures that tie the peasant to the land and old modes of production . . . inasmuch as it wishes to retard the development of a money economy and inasmuch as it expects . . . a change of path to be brought about by ''society'' and members of the bureaucracy'. But populists also advocated communal self-government, free popular access to knowledge, and promotion of peasant agriculture and village industries via cheap credit, technical assistance, reform of marketing, etc., measures which 'will not retard, but accelerate Russia's economic development along the capitalist road, the establishment of a home market and the development of technology and machine industry. . . . The more resolute such reforms, the higher they raise the living standards of the working masses, the more sharply will the already fundamental social antagonism stand out.' Populists were erroneously approaching socioeconomic reform from an idealist standpoint, 'as if the failure to implement such reforms had no profound causes inherent in *production relations*, as if the obstacle lies only in grossness of feeling and the feeble ''light of reason'' . . . as if Russia were a tabula rasa'. It was 'naïve' to combat 'bourgeois theories . . . as though they are merely mistaken reasoning, rather than expressions of the interests of a powerful class which it is churlish to admonish and which can only be ''convinced'' by the imposing power of another class'. Marxists must 'seek the roots of social phenomena in production relations' and 'reduce them to particular class interests', so as to prevent class aspirations from 'being utilized for professorial arguments that *transcend* class' (cf. Lenin, 1960–70T, vol. 1, 445, 484–5, 470, 462–4, 480–2, 497–8, 502–6).

Lenin developed his themes at inordinate length in *The Development of Capitalism in Russia* (1899, revised 1908), a book still widely respected as 'the fullest, best-documented and best-argued examination of the evolution of capitalism out of feudalism in the literature of Marxism' (Harding, 1977, 107).

Chapter I initially argues that nascent capitalism creates its own market by promoting 'social division of labour' and 'the ruin of small producers', i.e. 'the conversion of the small producer into a wage-worker' who buys what he previously produced for himself (Lenin, 1964T, 37–42). This perspective, derived from Marx's analysis of British experience, is far less applicable to continental Europe, where conversion of small producers into wage-workers has occurred much more slowly and at later stages of development. But the chapter's central thesis runs as follows:

> According to the general law of capitalist production, constant capital grows faster than variable capital. . . . The department of social production producing means of production consequently has to grow faster than that producing articles of

consumption. For capitalism, therefore, growth of the home market is to a certain extent 'independent' of the growth of personal consumption and takes place mostly on account of productive consumption. (ibid., 54)

In fact, even in the manufacturing sector, large-scale capitalist production was growing mostly on account of consumer goods (see Table 15). Lenin had twisted one of Marx's sound observations (that the relatively small producer goods sector tends to grow faster than the relatively large consumer goods sector) into an unwarranted doctrine that large-scale capitalist production has to grow mostly on account of the production and productive consumption of producer goods. (In the 1920s, Lenin and his closest disciples drew the even more unwarranted conclusion that this required absolute priority for heavy industry, even though they well knew that heavy industry and production of producer goods were not in fact synonymous.)

Chapter II attempted to demonstrate that capitalism had already 'disintegrated' the peasantry into three mutually antagonistic classes: 'rich peasants', possessing more land than they could farm by their own family labour alone and so obliged to employ hired labourers; 'middle peasants', possessing about as much land as could be farmed by their own family labour; and landless or near-landless 'poor peasants', obliged to live mainly by hiring themselves out to others. But, since about 95 per cent of Russia's peasant allotments exceeded 2.2 ha, Lenin was loath to classify them according to size, even though farm size would normally have determined whether or not a peasant household could be self-reliant. Lenin even acknowledged that, in the distribution of Russia's allotment land, 'we see the greatest degree of equality' (ibid., 138). So it suited Lenin's argument to classify peasants according to their holdings of movable assets, particularly horses, and to ignore allotment land on the dubious assumption that 'horseless' and 'one-horse' farms weren't viable. Actually Lenin could not have been unaware that many farms used oxen instead of horses, that small farmers could advantageously pool workstock, and that dairy farmers and market gardeners had relatively little use for horses. Indeed, in Southern Europe, India and East Asia agriculture was largely 'horseless' (see Table 13). Yet in the final analysis Lenin's thesis that Russia's peasantry had 'disintegrated' into mutually antagonistic classes, with a preponderance of dependent labourers, flimsily rested on indications that in 1896–1900 29 per cent of peasant households were 'horseless' and 30 per cent had one horse apiece (Lenin, 1964T, 148–9 ff.). Lenin actually admitted one weakness in his argument: 'the number of horses employed in agriculture in Russia is abnormally high for the area cultivated' (ibid., 149). Russia had about *twice* as many horses per inhabitant as did Europe (see Table 13). In Russia 'horseless' households were the exception, whereas in Europe and Asia they were the rule. It is most likely that Russia's 'horseless' peasant households mainly comprised those which were 'peasant' by legal status, but non-agricultural by occupation. On Lenin's data Russia's population was only 77 per cent agricultural in 1897, while at least half Russia's industrial workforce was village-based and 55 per cent of Russia's 'working peasants' in varying degrees engaged in activities other than work on their own farms (ibid., 507, 528, 243). Since Lenin's thesis on class differentiation within the peasantry also took no account of countervailing 'levelling' tendencies, which had ensured that about 90 per cent of Russia's agricultural households still constituted a single class of essentially self-reliant family labour farms (as perceived by Chayanov, 1966T, 112), it was empirically and methodologically unsound. As Lenin admitted in moments of candour, 'in Russia the process of differentiation among the peasantry, abundantly confirmed in Russian Marxist literature, is in an initial stage . . . it hasn't yet given rise to the immediately noticeable type of big peasant, for example' (Lenin, 1976T, 98); and his 'erroneous' agrarian perspectives resulted from 'an *over-estimation* of the *degree* of capitalist development in Russian agriculture' (Lenin, 1977T, 72). Only if capitalism could have developed unchecked for another century or more could Lenin's thesis on peasant class differentiation just conceivably have been fulfilled.

Chapter III mainly examines 'the principal manifestation of agricultural capitalism – employment of hired labour', claiming that 'about one fifth of the peasants have already reached a position where their "chief occupation" is that of wage-labour for rich peasants and landlords' (Lenin, 1964T, 240, 244). However, more thorough Soviet research on pre-revolutionary Russia has confirmed that hired labour constituted only 5 per cent of the agrarian workforce in European Russia in 1900 (see Table 4), thereby invalidating Lenin's other claims that 'the capitalist system of landlord farming must be considered the predominant one at present in European Russia' and that wage-labour had undermined serfdom (Lenin, 1964T, 199, 210).

Chapter IV documents the increasing commercialization and diversification of Russian agriculture since the 1860s dissolution of serfdom, correctly emphasizing that food production had outstripped population growth (ibid., 256). But Lenin naturally exaggerated the contribution of capitalism to these advances, thus obscuring the dominant role of self-reliant peasant farms.

Chapters V and VI go on to exaggerate the role of capitalism in Russia's industrial development by treating as *capitalist* 'economic structures which Marx explicitly described as *pre-capitalist*' (Harding, 1977, 87).

Chapter VII, while rightly lamenting 'the unsatisfactory nature of our factory statistics', none the less misuses those statistics to greatly exaggerate the concentration of Russian industry (Lenin, 1964T, 513–22). Russian industry only *appears* to have been highly concentrated so long as one forgets the plethora of small-scale village industries and urban crafts, not covered by Russia's factory statistics. Moreover, using grossly inflated estimates and lumping together very disparate occupational groups, Lenin reached the ludicrous conclusion that 'proletarians and semi-proletarians' constituted 51 per cent of Russia's population, with 'proletarians' alone accounting for 17.5 per cent (ibid., 506–10). Lenin's impatient desire to suggest Russia's imminent 'ripeness' for 'proletarian' socialism evidently got the better of his veracity. The concluding chapter VIII is an extravagant hymn of praise to capitalism as a revolutionary economic and social force.

Lenin's *magnum opus* had been written mainly in Siberia, where he had been exiled in 1897 for his leading role in the St Petersburg labour movement during 1894–5. But in 1900 he left Russia to join the editorial board of *Iskra*, a prestigious new Russian Marxist journal published in Germany. This move brought Lenin to the centre of heated Marxist debate on the fate of peasant agriculture under capitalism. Lenin naturally sided with the 'Marxist' orthodoxy fashioned by Engels, Kautsky and Plekhanov. Lenin's *Capitalism and Agriculture* (1900) was a blow-by-blow defence of Kautsky's authoritative 'capitalist-roader' views on *The Agrarian Question* (1899), particularly the crucial chapters on economies of scale in agriculture:

> The superiority of large-scale farming doesn't lie only in the fact that there is less waste of cultivated area, a saving in livestock and implements, fuller utilization of implements, wider possibilities of employing machinery and more opportunities for obtaining credit; it also lies in the commercial superiority of large-scale production, its employment of scientifically-trained managers. . . . Large-scale farming utilizes workers' cooperation and division of labour to a larger extent. (Lenin, 1960–70T, 126–7)

Like Kautsky, Lenin conceded that 'there are branches of agriculture in which, as experts admit, small-scale production can compete with large-scale production', e.g. horticulture, viticulture, industrial crops. 'But these branches occupy a position quite subordinate to . . . grain production and animal husbandry. . . . Hence, "taking agriculture as a whole, those branches in which small-scale is superior to large-scale production needn't be taken into account, and it's quite permissible to say large-scale is decidedly superior to small-scale production"' (ibid., 120). Lenin also endorsed Kautsky's view that agriculture's potential economies of scale weren't fully realizable under capitalism, because once a country's land surface had been carved up into private properties, agricultural production units could only be enlarged by protracted, piecemeal acquisition and amalgamation of contiguous farms (see ibid., 134) and because the need to retain pools of cheap labour in the countryside 'compels big landowners to allot land to labourers', with the result that 'within the limits of the capitalist mode of production it's impossible to count on small-scale production being eliminated from agriculture entirely' (ibid., 136). Elsewhere Lenin had already endorsed Kautsky's view that the tenacity of small-scale peasant agriculture in competition with large-scale capitalist agriculture employing wage-labour was 'due not to technical superiority of small-scale production in agriculture, but to the fact that small peasants reduce the level of their requirements below that of wage-workers and tax their energies far more than the latter do' (Lenin, 1964T, 27). But, unlike Kautsky, who was evidently cognizant of Heinrich von Thünen's ideas on optimal farm size, Lenin took virtually no account of the countervailing *diseconomies* of scale in agriculture. As Kautsky well knew (1899, vol. 1, chs VI and VII), greater farm size entails 'greater loss of material' and 'greater deployment of effort, resources and time for transport of material and men'; 'the smaller a given holding, the easier it is to exploit it intensively with a given amount of capital', yet 'A smallholding cultivated intensively can constitute a larger enterprise than a bigger farm exploited extensively'; the self-employed naturally display 'greater care' – including greater resourcefulness, adaptability and personal responsibility – than the 'hired labourer', who is most likely to waste time and to require costly supervision; on most farms, including small estates, the cost of employing 'scientifically trained' managers can exceed the potential gains, yet in the absence of 'scientific' management the amateur 'gentleman farmer' is likely to be a less efficient farm manager than the peasant smallholder; and industrialization most rapidly expands demand for precisely those products which most readily lend themselves to small-scale production (fruit, vegetables, dairy produce, pig meat, poultry, eggs, industrial crops, etc.). Moreover, his prescient observation that 'the farms least affected by desertion of the countryside are those which employ the least wage-labour and rely on family labour' (ibid., ch. IX) implicitly conceded that family-labour farms would outlive wage-labour farms.

In 1903, the year in which Lenin's 'Bolshevik' movement effectively came into existence, Lenin wrote a pamphlet appealing directly *To the Rural Poor*: 'What we need today is not the unity of the village commune, but a union against the . . . rule of capital; a union of all rural labourers and poor peasants of different communes with the urban workers, to fight both landlords and rich peasants', since 'money has become the principal power' and 'Members of the same commune will now fight one another for money like wild beasts.' He wanted no truck with communes comprising both employers and employees: 'What we need is a voluntary union only of people who have realized that they must unite with the urban workers . . . a voluntary union consisting only of labourers and poor peasants to fight all those who live off the labour of others.' He postulated that once the peasantry as a whole had won redress against the landlord class and civil equality with the rest of society, class war would erupt *within* the peasantry: 'farm labourers', in alliance with the urban proletariat, would fight for complete socialization of agriculture, against the opposition of 'rich peasants' (Lenin, 1960–70T, vol. 6, 379, 417).

Actually there has been remarkably little evidence of class conflict *within* Russia's peasantry: official Soviet historiography admits that even during the great upsurge of peasant unrest in 1905–7 only 1.4 per cent of it was directed against so-called 'kulaks', compared with 75.4 per cent against landlords and 14.5 per cent against the authorities and security forces (USSR, 1960T, 181); and from 1917 the peasantry closed ranks against external interference, with the village commune more than ever before serving as the last bastion of peasant resistance to external oppression (see Lewin, 1968T, 26–7, 85–93, for an honest and scholarly Marxist account). Indeed, the fatal weakness in Lenin's agrarian programmes was that they always presupposed and depended on strong grassroots support from a rural proletariat which barely existed and repeatedly proved itself utterly unfit for the 'vanguard' and executive roles he expected it to perform (cf. Shanin, 1973–4). At bottom, that's why Lenin's party and regime never attracted much rural support (see Lewin, 1968T, chs 4 and 5) and would thus be fatally tempted to rely on more or less blatant intimidation and coercion to control the peasant majority.

In 1907 Lenin openly admitted that his writings had contributed to 'an *over-estimation* of the *degree* of capitalist development in Russian agriculture' (Lenin, 1977T, 72) and he now proposed a 'revised' agrarian programme for his party, postulating that rural Russia could develop along either 'the Prussian path' or 'the American path'. In the former, 'feudal landlord economy slowly evolves into bourgeois, Junker landlord economy, condemning the peasants to decades of most harrowing expropriation and bondage, while a minority of Grossbauern ['big peasants'] arises'. In the latter, 'there is no landlord economy, or it is broken up by revolution, which confiscates and splits up the feudal estates. In that case the peasant predominates, becomes the sole agent of agriculture and evolves into a capitalist farmer' (ibid., 25). Lenin favoured the latter path, believing that 'the greater the prosperity of the peasantry in general, the *more rapid* is the differentiation of the peasantry into antagonistic classes' (ibid., 27): 'The real "difficulty" lies in securing the victory of a *peasant* agrarian revolution in a country which, at least since 1861, has been developing along Junker-bourgeois lines' (ibid., 119). Curiously, using the 1905 land census 'to ascertain precisely the comparative size of peasant and landlord landholdings' (ibid., 8), Lenin classified 81 per cent of European Russia's peasant households as 'ruined peasants, crushed by feudal exploitation', even though he reckoned that the households in that category possessed on average 7.7 ha of farmland apiece! Actually Lenin's data indicate that Russia was developing along neither 'the Prussian path' nor 'the American path': by 1905 77 per cent of European Russia's peasant households owned farms exceeding 5.5 ha apiece, mostly on an egalitarian communal basis, while a steadily shrinking 'feudal latifundia' sector owned only 25 per cent of European Russia's farmland (ibid., 9–14). And although the state was trying to impose a transition from communal to private peasant land-ownership, only 11 per cent of European Russia's peasant landholdings were converted into enclosed private properties before the 1917 Revolution, which fostered a return to communal landownership (see Table 5). So, by his own criteria, Lenin's revised agrarian programme was no sounder than its predecessors. But it is of some interest, partly for its zany attitude to land nationalization: 'Nationalization makes it possible to tear down *all* the fences of landownership to the utmost degree, and to "clear" all the land for the new *economic system* suitable to the requirements of capitalism', and 'Nationalization of the land is not only the sole means for completely eliminating medievalism in agriculture, but also the best form of agrarian relationships conceivable under capitalism' (Lenin, 1977T, 104, 192). It also made clear where Lenin considered power should lie: 'Without a centralized peasant movement, without a centralized nation-wide political struggle of the peasantry led by a centralized proletariat, *there can be no* serious "revolutionary gains" worthy of "consolidation"'; so 'We should not "adapt" our programme to "local" democracy; we should not invent a rural "municipal socialism"' (ibid., 108, 193). Above all, it showed that Lenin had belatedly recognized that the peasantry was 'imbued with a far more spontaneous revolutionary spirit' and a more 'passionate desire to destroy the landlord regime and to immediately create a new system' than the more cautious, calculating industrial proletariat (ibid., 168); and that, in a peasant society, an astute 'proletarian' socialist movement should use this other more revolutionary force for its own ends (ibid., 191–4).

Nevertheless, Lenin continued to regard large-scale industrialization as the gateway to socialism: 'Capitalism in its imperialist stage reaches the threshold of the most complete socialization of production. In spite of themselves, the capitalists are dragged into a new social order transitional from complete free competition to complete socialization' (Lenin, 1948T, 32): 'Monopoly is the transition from capitalism to a higher system' (ibid., 108). He was most explicit in his *Impending Catastrophe and How to Combat It* (1917) and in his *State and Revolution* (1918):

> That capitalism in Russia has also become monopoly capitalism is sufficiently attested by the examples of Produgol [the coal cartel], Prodamet [the steel cartel], the Sugar Syndicate etc. The Sugar Syndicate is an object-lesson in the way monopoly capitalism develops into State-monopoly capitalism. . . . Socialism is merely the next step forward from State-capitalist monopoly. I.e. socialism is merely State-capitalist monopoly *which is made to serve the interests of the whole people* and has to that extent *ceased* to be capitalist monopoly. . . . The dialectics of history are such that the war, by extraordinarily expediting the transformation of monopoly capitalism into State-monopoly capitalism, has thereby extraordinarily advanced mankind towards socialism . . . not only because the horrors of war give rise to proletarian revolt – no revolt can bring about socialism unless the economic conditions for socialism are ripe – but also because State-monopoly capitalism is a complete *material* preparation for socialism, the *threshold* of socialism. . . . Universal labour conscription, introduced, regulated and directed by Soviets of Workers', Soldiers', and Peasants' Deputies, will *not yet* be socialism, but it will *no longer* be capitalism. It will be a tremendous *step towards* socialism. (cf. Lenin, 1972T, 9–12)

> Capitalist culture has *created* large-scale production, factories, railways, the postal service, telephones, etc., and *on this basis* the great majority of the functions of the old 'State power' have become so simplified and can be reduced to such exceedingly simple operations of registration, filing and checking that they can easily be performed by every literate person. . . . We, the workers, shall organize large-scale production on the basis of what capitalism has already created, relying on our experience as workers, establishing strict iron discipline backed by the State power of armed

workers. . . . Such a beginning, on the basis of large-scale production, will of itself lead to the gradual 'withering away' of all bureaucracy. (See Lenin, 1969T, 41, 46, 87, 89)

In fact Lenin was still wildly exaggerating the socioeconomic basis for 'proletarian' socialism in Russia. Russia's large-scale monopolistic enterprises and state institutions were still mere islands in an ocean of small fry – peasants, craftsmen and small middlemen (see Pethybridge, 1974, ch. 5). And it was dangerously naïve to suppose that, once established, a state strong enough to crush the bourgeoisie and to accomplish large-scale industrialization would in due course meekly and obligingly 'wither away'. Indeed, it was under Lenin – not Stalin – that the Soviet system first became a repressive police state: Russia's political police numbered approximately 250,000 in mid-1921, as against approximately 15,000 before the Revolution (Legget, 1981, 359); under Lenin some 200,000 people were formally executed by the Soviet regime, as against some 14,000 in the preceding half-century (ibid.); and Lenin's government re-established the practice of sending political opponents to forced labour and concentration camps (ibid., 176–81). Moreover, beware Lenin's ritualistic use of the phrase 'dictatorship of the proletariat': officially, 'workers' made up 41 and 43 per cent of party membership in 1921 and 1923, respectively, but only 10–20 per cent of these were in proletarian occupations and few of the latter held influential party posts (Schapiro, 1970, 238–42). As Lenin reminded the 1919 Party Congress, 'the Soviets, which by virtue of their programme are organs of government *by the working people*, are in fact organs of government *for the working people* by the advanced section of the proletariat', meaning the Communist Party (Lenin, 1975T, 127). There was little to stop the soviets becoming organs of government *against the working people*.

By usurping state power in the name of his narrowly 'proletarian' party in October 1917, by suppressing Russia's democratically elected Constituent Assembly in January 1918 (after his party had won only one-quarter of the 42 million votes counted), by reviving a political police in December 1917, by unleashing an uncontrollable 'Red Terror', by surrendering millions of Russian and Ukrainian peasants to the rapacious German army in early 1918, and by showing himself to be as unworthy as he was unwilling to really share power in a humane and broad-based coalition government, Lenin more than anybody else plunged Russia into a civil war in which at least 8 million people perished (several times greater than Russia's loss of life in the First World War: see Lorimer, 1946, ch. 3). The concurrent economic collapse was more a consequence than a cause of the Revolution: as late as 1916 gross industrial output was 21. 5 per cent above the 1913 level, industrial employment was up 12.6 per cent on 1913, railway freight turnover was up 58 per cent on 1913, and although grain and potato output was only 73 per cent of the 1909–13 level, 'with the complete cessation of exports the . . . decline in harvest should not have resulted in a food crisis' (Liashchenko, 1949T, 762–8).

By 1920, however, gross industrial output was only 13.8 per cent of the 1913 level, industrial employment was down 53 per cent on 1913, railway freight turnover was 30 per cent of the 1913 level and agricultural output was half the 1909–13 level (USSR, 1960T, 275). Suggestions that all would have been well if only the Russian Revolution had obtained aid from a 'proletarian revolution' in the West are escapist nonsense: the economic disruption caused by such an upheaval would have rendered the war-weary West totally incapable of furnishing enough aid to significantly affect the outcome. In any case, the 'genetic deformities' of the state Lenin established and the difficulties it confronted were largely of his own making (cf. pp. 79–81, 91–4).

4 The momentous industrialization debate: an introduction

Bolshevik victory in Russia's civil war had fateful implications not only for Russia, but for the one-third of mankind subjected to Stalinist regimes by the 1950s: the Soviet empire naturally came to dominate the Eurasian landmass; after 1922 the international communist movement was systematically 'Bolshevized', to use the official jargon; and the awesome 'triumphs' of Stalinism rather queered the pitch for more humane socialisms. As Orwell rightly observed in his 'Preface' to a Ukrainian edition of *Animal Farm* in 1947, 'destruction of the Soviet myth' was 'essential' for 'a revival of the socialist movement' (Crick, 1980, 309). But, contrary to what determinists tell us, Stalin's ascendancy wasn't the inevitable outcome of inescapable economic, ideological, or military imperatives. As late as April 1929 even Stalin acknowledged that there were less draconian alternatives to his *chosen* policies (Stalin, 1952–5T, vol. 12, 66–7).

By 1922 the Bolshevik leaders had consolidated their victory: by denying effective political representation to Russia's peasant majority (e.g. representation in the Supreme Soviet was weighted 5:1 in favour of the cities: see Carr, 1966, 136); by crushing peasant and proletarian defiance; by unanimously banning non-party and intra-party pressure groups; by completely banning strikes and independent trade unions; by transforming the official trade unions into state agencies for implementing party policy and for enforcing labour discipline; by steadily substituting appointment-from-above for election-from-below in all important posts; by 'purging' the party (one-fifth of the membership was expelled in 1921, but far more left in disgust: see Schapiro, 1970, 236–7); and by establishing a mixed economy in which large-scale industry, transport, foreign trade and finance remained state monopolies, and agriculture, small workshops and petty trade were to be dominated by family and co-operative ventures. Restrictions on land and capital markets and on private employment of hired labour would impede the making of private profits and capital gains, and each village would decide how its member households would hold village land (about 90 per cent chose communal tenure: see Lewin, 1968T, 85–93). Urban requisitioning of farm produce gave way to a single, stable, flat-rate tax on the gross output of every smallholding, to promote peasant confidence, renewed agricultural development and urban–rural 'exchange'. Economic concessions were coupled with political stringency, because 'a small minority, ruling by force in the teeth of proletarian and peasant opposition, can ill afford to saw away the only firm branch which supports it – a well disciplined organization' (Schapiro, 1970, 312).

All this made up Lenin's 'New Economic Policy' (NEP), which he launched in 1921 as a 'retreat into state capitalism' after it had become 'perfectly clear that we could not proceed with our direct socialist construction'. However, from the outset, Lenin insisted that this retreat was only a respite 'in order, eventually, to go over to the offensive' (Lenin, 1972T, 151–3). The hollowness of Lenin's commitment to NEP is demonstrated in Chapter 5.

The 1920s debate on Russia's unusually wide development options was also a power struggle to succeed Lenin, who died in January 1924. (By contrast, debates and development options in other fledgling communist regimes have usually been constrained by Soviet influence and/or the interventions of a final arbiter.) As the 1920s debate encompassed an exceptionally wide spectrum of industrialization strategies and so many crucial issues, it merits careful study by anyone interested in development problems and/or the considerations which have – for better or worse – decided the fate of one-third of mankind.

The debate revolved around choice of sectoral priorities: was it more urgent or advantageous to develop domestic capacity to make producer goods, especially machinery, than to expand agriculture and/or light industry, which more directly raise popular consumption levels and economic incentives? Answers to this question conditioned attitudes to import substitution, rural collectivization and the respective roles of market forces, external trade, mass mobilization and mandatory economic planning. Choice of sectoral priorities also affected requisite levels and methods of capital accumulation, town–country relations, forms of organization and remuneration, and choice of technologies.

In 1926, as the economy at last fully recovered from the ravages of civil war, the principal participants in the industrialization debate lined up as follows:

BUKHARIN   Balanced, mutually reinforcing, largely autarkic development of smallholder agriculture and light industries, propelled by rising consumption levels, by vertical integration of food and fibre production through co-operatives, and by providing positive economic incentives for both town and country, thereby gradually creating a domestic market for profitable self-financing heavy industries without straining town–country relations and without letting effective demand outstrip the supply of consumer goods.

TROTSKY, KRASIN, BAZAROV, SHANIN, SOKOLNIKOV AND KONDRATIEV Variously conceived 'least-cost' industrialization strategies, designed to maximize potential gains from international economic relations and specialization along lines of prospective long-run comparative cost advantage, to be achieved by dirigiste industrial planning, indicative agricultural planning, equitable urban–rural 'exchange', financial disciplines, positive economic incentives, progressive direct taxation and a buoyant, receptive, outward-looking society.

PREOBRAZHENSKY Forced, state-funded industrial development, with priority for heavy industries incorporating large-scale, capital-intensive 'American-style' methods, sustained by systematically squeezing: 'private capitalist profit'; an increasingly productive and state-dominated peasant agricultural sector; 'non-productive expenditure'; and every conceivable advantage obtainable from state-monopolized trade with capitalist countries.

STALIN Construction of virtually self-sufficient 'socialism in one country', based on forced development of new, integrated, large-scale, capital-intensive, import-substituting heavy industries, funded by a stringent cost-reducing and capital-accumulating 'regime of economy' within the state sector and by maintaining town–country terms of trade unfavourable to the peasantry.

These are mere silhouettes, snapshots taken at a single instant in an unfolding drama. To fully comprehend what was going on and its wider significance one must examine both how the protagonists worked out their prescriptions and the drama's denouement (Chapters 5–7).

The 1920s industrialization debate was further enlivened by a heady self-confidence, a temporary lifting of the Russian industrializer's characteristic inferiority complex *vis-à-vis* the West. And paradoxically, having monopolized political power, the Bolsheviks felt a pressing need to make people *feel* that this was *everyman*'s revolution. So 1920s Russia experienced an unprecedented eruption of creativity and experimentation in communist and Christian communal living, 'free love', pedagogy, popular festivities and, above all, building and the arts – constructivism, system-built workers' flats, new types of cities, graphics, Eisenstein's revolutionary films, mobile cinemas, imported movies and jazz bands, Shostakovich's iconoclasm in music, Isadora Duncan's iconoclasm in dance, Meyerhold's revolutionary theatre, Mayakovsky's 'superstar' poetry recitals to mass audiences, futuristic novels set in 1984, etc. Briefly, the sky was the limit.

5 Creeping socialism: Bukharin versus Lenin

Nikolai Bukharin (1888–1938) is most widely remembered for his Marxist analyses of Western capitalism, which were written during the First World War and profoundly influenced Lenin, but he also became the leading communist proponent of balanced economic growth and conciliatory policies towards agricultural smallholders and independent craftsmen. In his contributions to the best-selling *ABC of Communism* (1920) Bukharin wrote:

> Our Party's task . . . is to hasten . . . the formation of industrial (productive) unions, each of which shall enrol every worker and employee in each branch of industry. . . . Trade unions shall assume an ever-increasing share of industrial administration until the whole economy, from the bottom upwards, shall constitute a unity effectively controlled by industrial (productive) unions. (Section 98)

> Small producers must not be bludgeoned into socialism. We must do all we can to make it easy for them to undergo the necessary change. . . . Under capitalism, producers' co-operatives tended to degenerate into capitalist enterprises as they grew. . . . But now, as we can envelop them within a worker's State, such bodies can help to build socialism. (Section 97)

Following the adoption of NEP, Bukharin began to argue that the peasantry could become an active ally of the Communist Party, rather than a group to be 'neutralized' and 'led by the nose'. He told the 1923 Party Congress that 'the large industrial states are the cities of world economy and the colonies and semi-colonies are its countryside' and that the latter constituted 'a gigantic reservoir of revolutionary infantry' in the struggle against capitalist imperialism (Cohen, 1975, 149). Impressed by the eruption of radical peasant movements in 1920s Eastern Europe, he joined the new Soviet-sponsored Peasant International in October 1923 (Jackson, 1966, 69) and took an active interest in China's incipient peasant revolution (1924–7). His 'Theses on the peasant question', adopted by Comintern in 1925, emphasized that, as most human beings were peasants, 'the struggle for the peasantry' was crucial to the future of 'proletarian' socialism (no. 2); the First World War and its aftermath had induced 'a great widening of peasant ideological horizons' (no. 35); the advent of 'proletarian dictatorship' now permitted 'non-capitalist development of peasant economy' and colonial countries to 'bypass' capitalism (nos 25 and 27).

The 1927 edition of *The Road to Socialism and the Worker–Peasant Bloc* (1925), possibly Bukharin's most popular publication, argued that 'the struggle for sway over the peasantry is a class struggle between the proletariat and the bourgeoisie', and 'The proletariat can win this struggle in so far as it manages to develop its industries and trade apparatus, showing the peasant that the State sector is best able to satisfy his needs.' Failing that, 'the old regime can return by the back door'. Moreover, 'Our industry works primarily for the peasant market'; hence 'The faster peasant purchasing power grows, the faster industry will develop. Industrial accumulation will accelerate in as much as the peasantry prospers, purchases machinery and raises its organization and techniques.' Conversely, 'rural development is inconceivable without urban industrial development, as it needs products solely obtainable from our industries [implicitly assuming a closed economy]': 'To this end, we must further liberalize trade . . . even for the rural bourgeoisie.' The latter 'no longer endangers us, as we control the commanding heights, enabling us to provide urgent help to . . . peasant co-operatives, collective farms and consumer societies. Our wager is on ourselves, on the proletariat and the toiling peasantry, on the growth of State industry and rural co-operatives.' Though collective farms may seem 'the natural organizational form for "poor peasants", transition to such a system would entail the smashing of entrenched habits, so it's doubtful whether collective farms will attract the broad mass of "poor peasants"'. But 'The "middling", increasingly self-supporting peasantry, the vast majority, will associate in three basic types of agricultural co-operative (purchasing, marketing and credit co-operatives), as appropriate.' Likewise 'Strong, prosperous peasants will strive to form their own co-operatives, including credit institutions, and to make these their bastions.' So 'rural class struggle will only begin to die down after a very significant interval. Meantime we'll have a process of stratification . . . and "peaceful" struggle within the peasantry.' But 'despite the stratification process, the "middling" peasant will remain "the central figure in agriculture" . . . because stratification will be even slower under proletarian dictatorship than it was under capitalism', and because 'Inasmuch as the State can aid "poor" and "middling" peasants, we shall start a countervailing levelling trend' (translated from Bukharin, 1967, 247–316).

In a controversial article 'On NEP and our tasks' (1925), written at the height of his influence on Soviet policy, Bukharin argued that 'our State sector gradually strengthens itself by various means, including competition with the remnants of private capital and absorption of backward enterprises, normally *via the market*'.

Therefore, 'If private enterprise undercuts us, we must cut our costs still further. That is the form our class struggle now takes. Thus we shall approach a planned economy after years of economic warfare with the remnants of private capital.' Meantime 'we develop our adversary's forces as well as our own, so we must put him in a position where – like it or not – he simultaneously serves our cause'. That is, 'if the kulak is a depositor in our banks, he will not conquer us'. Bukharin emphasized that if the peasants were to develop their 'productive forces' and provide an expanding market for industrial products, they had to be allowed and encouraged to accumulate capital. However, 'the prosperous peasant and the prospering middle peasant are both *afraid to accumulate* . . . for fear of being branded *kulak*; if one buys a machine, one makes sure the communists aren't watching'. Moreover, 'the poor peasant complains that we stop him selling his labour to the prosperous peasant'. Therefore, 'We must remove a whole web of restrictions on prosperous peasants and hired labour' and 'urge peasants in every stratum: enrich yourselves, accumulate, develop your farms', because 'the prosperous farms have to be developed so that aid might be provided to middle and poor peasants', both through the employment and multiplier-effects and by using the consequent increase in state revenues and bank deposits to increase state and bank aid to peasant co-operatives and the rural poor. However, he warned that it would be pointless to urge peasants to 'accumulate' so long as the party spoke menacingly of 'a second revolution or forcible expropriation of the kulak', as 'people will simply be afraid to accumulate. . . . Class struggle in the villages won't suddenly die out. . . . On the contrary, it will soon increase. But to infer from this that there will be a "second" revolution is nonsense.' He urged the party to adopt a policy of rural détente and to act only 'through *economic* channels. . . . We have NEP in the town; we have NEP in urban–rural relations; but we still lack NEP within the village' (cf. Bukharin, 1982T, 189, 194, 196–200, 206).

Sadly, Bukharin's bold articulation of home truths merely hastened his vilification by the Party's hard left. But it is often the case that the measures, policies and institutions which can most effectively alleviate the plight of the rural poor will also benefit the prosperous, and to grudgingly reject such remedies on this account is both mean-spirited and a disservice to the poor.

Urban workers, 2 million of whom were unemployed in 1925–9, naturally feared the incipient 'rural bias' in Bukharin's economic thought. But, as he reassured the October 1927 Trades Union Congress in Moscow, 'By reason of our backwardness, we have a tremendous number of surplus workers in the villages and hence in the towns, seeing how redundant population . . . converges on the latter.' Therefore, 'so long as we fail to abolish unemployment in the villages, we shall fail to eliminate this evil in general. Certain "economists" . . . suggest we should extend our industry sufficiently to absorb the unemployed', but 'the extensions in question would have to be so great that no sane person could demand them'. Nor could unemployment be effectively alleviated by higher social insurance benefits, as 'this would cause yet more unemployed villagers to converge on the towns'. Instead he advocated 'measures making it possible to retain rural population on the land. If this problem is to be treated in a liberal way, steps must be taken towards industrializing agriculture', namely increased local processing of farm produce, increased industrial inputs into agriculture and increased specialization and intensification of farming (Bukharin, 1927).

Bukharin's 'Observations of an economist' (1928) incisively analysed the constraints on industrialization in a peasant society under an avowedly socialist regime. The human and economic costs of wilful disregard for these constraints under Stalinist regimes have been enormous. Note that Bukharin now emphasized 'supply-side' considerations rather than his earlier 'demand-side' arguments for basing industrialization on the peasant market, whose relative importance was being sharply reduced by the overriding priority given to heavy industry by the ascendant Stalinists.

The central arguments ran as follows: rural demand for industrial goods by now 'represents only a fifth or at most a quarter of the total'. As for the other three-quarters or four-fifths 'industry itself – as it develops at record tempi – simultaneously generates record demand for industrial goods, which cannot be met'. Claims that 'industry cannot keep pace with rural demand' are 'only superficially convincing. Careful analysis shows that industry "lags" behind itself' (Bukharin, 1967, 388). 'Almost half peasant income – and hence almost half rural demand – is derived from non-agricultural, mainly industry-related sources.' Hence 'it's absurd to conclude from the non-satisfaction of rural demand that industry is lagging behind agriculture'. On the contrary, 'we're producing too little grain', due to: '(1) the wide, increasing disparity between grain prices and industrial crop prices; (2) increased peasant income from non-agricultural sources; (3) insufficient taxation of kulak farms; (4) insufficient supplies of manufactures to the villages; and (5) the growth of kulak influence in the villages' (ibid., 385–7).

'Industrialization of the Soviet Union is imperative from every angle: development of productive forces, agriculture, socialism, firmer collaboration within the country, our weight in the world, defence, mass consumption, etc.'; but 'socialist industrialization must differ from capitalist. . . . It mustn't be parasitic on the village . . . but a means of reorganizing, expanding . . . and industrializing agriculture' (ibid., 390–1). But 'this presupposes the possibility of rapid real capital accumulation in agriculture'; and 'The law of accumulation presupposes the existence of another law on whose basis it acts', namely that 'if any branch of production fails to regularly recoup its production expenses plus an additional amount to finance expanded reproduction, it will stagnate or even regress. This law especially pertains to grain production' (ibid., 381–2, 387).

'To industrialize in actuality and not just on paper . . . one must assure not only the necessary funds, representing a claim on resources, but a commensurate supply of actual resources', as 'one cannot build a real factory with future bricks. . . .

A strange "money fetishism" prevails here: the assumption that all's possible if money's available.' But 'money's of no avail if . . . the time required for the production of a certain material exceeds the interval in which it's to be productively consumed' (ibid., 392): 'Excessive extension of capital expenditure (1) is unmatched by actual capital construction, (2) delays further advanced projects, (3) reacts unfavourably on other sectors, (4) aggravates shortages and (5) ultimately retards development . . . and destabilizes the monetary system.' He reminded his readers of 'the dangers of tying up too much capital in vast projects whose output cannot be realized for many years'; the 'faster turnover of light industry . . . permits the use of its capital to build up heavy industry [at a later date] in the context of light industrial development' (ibid., 394–5). 'Two separate phenomena have been confused': (1) 'the temporary lagging of productive capacity behind faster-growing demand', which 'simply indicates that society is advancing towards socialism' and that 'growth of demand is the driving force'; and (2) 'crisis-like disruptions', arising from 'failure to observe the preconditions of economic equilibrium', that is, from 'grave violations of basic economic proportions'. The latter, if continued, 'could engender a regrouping of classes unfavourable to the proletariat' and so 'upset the country's political stability' (ibid., 377–8).

Acceptance of Bukharin's stance would have entailed (1) paying fairer grain procurement prices to the peasantry and increasing supplies of home-produced or imported consumer manufactures, fertilizers and farm equipment to rural retail outlets, to entice peasants to grow and market more grain and thereby retain more labour on the land and reduce urban grain shortages and black-marketeering; (2) diverting resources from long-gestation capital construction projects in the heavy industrial sector, which were in any case creating and running up against acute supply-side bottlenecks, in order to enable the state sector to meet the higher grain procurement costs and the increased demands made upon light industries, without having to greatly increase urban retail food prices or greatly reduce urban supplies of consumer manufactures; and (3) fostering, as a long-term first priority, an expanding food and raw material base and peasant market for state-run light industries, which in turn would have slowly expanded the domestic market for profitable self-financing production of producer goods. The USSR's favourable farmland–population and livestock–population ratios (see Tables 6 and 13), its large reserves of unused cultivable land (cultivated area has nearly doubled since 1913) and the large backlog of educational, technical, sanitary and organizational advances which any enlightened regime could have introduced from abroad at comparatively low (but high-yielding) capital cost, meant that Bukharin's strategy was not only feasible, but could have paid off handsomely. Moreover, as proven by parts of Eastern Europe since 1945, rural collectivization can be effected gradually and harmoniously (see pp. 200–1).

The standard objection to Bukharin's relatively humane and cost-effective strategy is that it would not have reduced the military vulnerability of the beleaguered Soviet state, whereas Stalin's policies during 1928–41 decisively increased the military preparedness of the USSR. However, it can be replied that Stalin's policies in fact squandered millions of lives, decimated the Red Army, caused severe setbacks in agriculture and light industry, and greatly depleted Russia's vital human capital, inducing many Ukrainian and Belorussian towns and villages to initially welcome the Nazi invaders as 'liberators' in 1941; and, by encouraging Comintern and the German Communist Party to subvert the Weimar Republic in 1928–33, Stalin facilitated Hitler's ascent to power. Conversely, a Bukharinist regime could have counted on a much larger, more motivated, more competent and more cohesive workforce and army, and a more balanced economy, making more effective use of an admittedly smaller heavy industrial base. Russia would not have been torn asunder on the eve of the Nazi invasion, the Nazis would have been denied an easy walk-over in the Ukraine and Belorussia, and a Bukharinist Comintern would have rallied the German left in defence of the Weimar Republic against Nazism in 1930–3. However, in 1929–30 Bukharin and his closest collaborators, Prime Minister Rykov and trade union supremo Tomsky, were ousted by Stalinists and in 1938 they were executed on bogus charges of treason.

Bukharin's divergence from Lenin

As the Soviet industrialization debate was also a power struggle to succeed Lenin, and as the 'legitimacy' of the Soviet dictatorship came to rest on its formal adherence to Leninism, each of the very different contenders had to show that he (alone) was Lenin's 'true' disciple. So Bukharin and his camp followers argued that he was faithfully upholding Lenin's conception of NEP and, superficially, that might seem to have been true.

In introducing NEP, in March 1921, Lenin had contended that, 'Difficult as our position is in regard to resources, the needs of the middle peasantry must be satisfied. There are far more middle peasants now than before . . . the kulak's position has been undermined . . . the peasantry in general has acquired the status of middle peasant' (i.e. he now acknowledged the vast preponderance of largely self-sufficient family-labour farms which actually antedated the Russian Revolution, as shown in Chapters 1–3). 'Any Communist who thought the economic basis, the economic roots of small farming could be reshaped in three years was a dreamer. . . . The only way to solve this problem of the small farmer – to improve his mentality – is through the material basis, technical equipment', although this 'may take decades'. Also 'the vastness of our agricultural country, with its poor transport, boundless expanses, varied climate, diverse farming conditions etc., makes a certain freedom of exchange between local agriculture and local industry inevitable'. So 'the situation is this: we must satisfy the middle peasantry economically and go over to free exchange; otherwise it will be economically impossible, in view of the delay in the world revolution, to preserve the proletariat's rule in Russia. . . . The basic thing is to give the small farmer an incentive', to assure him that 'all his surplus produce will not be taken away from him and that he will only have to pay a tax, which should whenever possible be fixed in advance' (Lenin, 1975T, vol. 3, 513–20).

Moreover Lenin's article 'On co-operation', published in *Pravda* on 26–27 May 1923, argued that 'since political power is in the proletariat's hands, since this political power owns the means of production, our only remaining task is to organize the population into co-operatives', whereupon 'socialism . . . will achieve its aims automatically. . . . By adopting NEP we made a concession to the peasant as a trader . . . it's precisely for this reason (contrary to what some people think) that the co-operative movement is so important.' But 'State power over the large-scale means of production, political power in the proletariat's hands, the alliance of this proletariat with many millions of small and very small peasants, the assured proletarian leadership of the peasantry, etc. – isn't this all that's necessary to build a complete socialist society out of co-operatives alone . . . under NEP?' Co-operatives would offer a 'transition to the new system by the means that are the *simplest, easiest* and *most acceptable to the peasant*'. Thus 'NEP is an advance because it's adjustable to the level of the ordinary peasant.' But 'it will take a whole epoch to get the entire population into the work of co-operatives through NEP. At best we can achieve this in one or two decades.' To that end, 'economic, financial and banking privileges must be granted to co-operatives. . . . For, given social ownership of the means of production and the proletariat's class victory over the bourgeoisie, the system of civilized co-operators is the system of socialism.' Then 'Why were the plans of the old co-operators, from Robert Owen onwards, mere fantasy? Because they dreamed of peacefully remodelling modern society into socialism, without taking account of such fundamental tasks as class struggle, conquest of political power by the working class and overthrow of the exploiting class.' But, under NEP, 'the mere growth of co-operation . . . is identical with the growth of socialism. . . . Formerly we had to emphasize political struggle, revolution, winning political power, etc. Now the emphasis is shifting to peaceful organizational and "cultural" work.'

And in *Pravda* on 25 January 1923 Lenin quite rightly warned that 'in the final analysis our Republic's fate will depend on whether the peasant masses will stand by the working class'. Persistent refusal to give the peasantry their due would soon have fatal consequences for socialism in the USSR and for all concerned.

Bukharin quickly saw that, if NEP was to become a politically and economically viable and stable framework for industrialization and rural development *in tandem*, peasant agriculture and light industry would have to receive shares of investment and remuneration commensurate with their paramount importance in providing popular livelihoods. The peasantry couldn't be continually duped or fed on empty promises. Agriculture and light industry couldn't be expanded by injections of hot air. But Lenin, despite his pious homilies on the importance of satisfying the economic needs of the 'middle peasant', was still hooked on heavy industry. In *Pravda* on 19 September 1922 he declared that 'it is precisely that part of industry known as heavy industry which is the main basis of socialism'. And the closing paragraphs of his last major written work, 'Better fewer, but better', lapsed into the bravado of the advocates of forced industrialization:

> If we ensure that the working class retains its leadership over the peasantry, we shall be able, by practising maximum austerity in our state's economic life, to use every saving we make to develop our large-scale machine industry, electrification, hydraulic extraction of peat, the Volkov Power Project, etc. In this lies our only hope. Only by doing this shall we be able, figuratively speaking, to change over from the poor peasant nag . . . to the horse which the proletariat necessarily seeks – the horse of large-scale machine industry. . . . This is what, in my opinion, justifies the exceptional care and attention which must be given to Workers' and Peasants' Inspection. . . . And this justification is that only by thoroughly purging our governmental machine, by minimizing all that's non-essential therein, shall we be sure of being able to keep going . . . not on the level of a small-peasant country, not on the level of universal limitation, but on a level steadily advancing towards large-scale machine industry. (*Pravda*, 4 March 1923)

Bukharin's conception of NEP presupposed that increased prosperity would render the peasantry *more amenable* to socialism. But, in Lenin's view, the more peasants prospered, the *more capitalist* they would become. Furthermore, Bukharin quickly saw that if NEP was to 'deliver the goods' and realize its full potential, the Bolsheviks would have to overcome the deeply ingrained mistrust, contempt, condescension and class prejudice prevalent in their attitudes to the peasantry – after all, class prejudice against peasants is as objectionable as class prejudice against workers. But Lenin underwent no such change of heart. For Lenin, writing in 1920,

> small-scale production engenders capitalism and the bourgeoisie continuously, daily, hourly, spontaneously and on a mass scale. . . . Abolition of classes means, not merely ousting landowners and capitalists – that we accomplished with comparative ease; it also means abolishing small commodity producers. . . . They surround the proletariat on every side with a petit bourgeois atmosphere, which permeates and corrupts the proletariat and constantly causes among the proletariat relapses into petit bourgeois spinelessness, disunity, individualism and alternating moods of exaltation and dejection. The strictest centralization and discipline are required within the political party of the proletariat in order to counteract this. . . . Dictatorship of the proletariat means persistent struggle – bloody and bloodless, violent and peaceful, military and economic, educational and administrative – against the forces and traditions of the old society. . . . It's a thousand times easier to vanquish the centralized big bourgeoisie than to 'vanquish' millions upon millions of petty proprietors; however, through their ordinary, everyday, imperceptible, demoralizing activities, they produce the very results which the bourgeoisie need and which tend to restore the bourgeoisie. Whoever brings about even the slightest weakening of the iron discipline of the proletariat's party (especially during its dictatorship) is actually aiding the bourgeoisie against the proletariat. (Lenin, 1968T, 9, 10, 29, 30)

Lenin's involuntary retreat into NEP was not accompanied by any substantial change of attitude towards the peasantry as a class. Lenin's fullest exposition of NEP, the booklet entitled *The Tax in Kind* (1921), denounced 'the error of those who fail to see petit bourgeois conditions and the petit bourgeois element as the *principal* enemy of socialism'. In Lenin's view, 'Freedom to trade is capitalism; capitalism is profiteering'; and 'the economic basis of profiteering is both the small proprietors, who are exceptionally prevalent in Russia, and private capitalism, of which every petit bourgeois is an agent'. Moreover, 'the millions of tentacles of this petit bourgeois octopus intermittently encircle various sections of the proletariat', so that 'profiteering forces its way into every pore of our social and economic organism'. Hence 'Either we subordinate the petite bourgeoisie to our control . . . or they will overthrow Soviet power.' So 'We must revise and redraft all our laws on profiteering and declare . . . every direct or indirect, open or concealed evasion of state control, supervision and accounting to be a punishable offence (and indeed prosecuted with redoubled severity).' Lenin also revealed his lingering misgivings about peasant co-operatives: 'Small commodity producer co-operatives (and it is these, not worker co-operatives, that we are discussing as the predominant and typical form in a small-peasant country) inevitably give rise to petit bourgeois capitalist relations, facilitate their development, push small capitalists into the foreground and benefit them most.' Under NEP 'freedom and rights for co-operatives mean freedom and rights for capitalism' (Lenin, 1975T, vol. 3, 531, 532, 553, 545). And, in Lenin's opinion, ominously expressed in a letter to Stalin on 13 December 1922, 'Bukharin is acting as an advocate of the profiteer, the petit bourgeois and the upper stratum of the peasantry, in opposition to the industrial proletariat' (ibid., 664). This shows how far apart Lenin and Bukharin had grown.

Furthermore, Bukharin saw NEP and the co-operative road to socialism as an evolutionary process, whereas Lenin in November 1922 reaffirmed his view that 'We are now retreating . . . in order, after first retreating, to take a running start and make a greater leap forward', that is, 'in order to start a most stubborn offensive after our retreat' (ibid., 679). There is a world of difference between social change by *evolution*, as envisaged by Bukharin, and social change by *successive assaults*, interspersed by tactical retreats, as practised by Lenin, Stalin and Mao, among others. For Lenin (as for Stalin), NEP was merely a period of preparation for the next offensive, a respite enabling the Bolsheviks to concentrate on 'regrouping our forces' (ibid., 631). This rendered his pious disavowals of the use of force against the peasantry under NEP very conditional, if not entirely disingenuous, as he evidently hoped it would be possible to abandon NEP within one or two decades and, therefore, did not share Bukharin's redeeming concern to steer the Soviet regime towards social and economic strategies which would enable NEP to function as a stable, viable framework for industrialization, rural development and social reconciliation.

6 'Least-cost' industrialization strategies: from Bazarov and Krasin to Kondratiev and Trotsky

As the USSR emerged from the destruction and depravities of the civil war and 'war communism', many prominent Russian socialists began to formulate industrialization strategies which were intended to minimize the initial economic and human costs of industrialization, and to maximize the immediate pay-off. Beware defamatory tendencies to portray such strategies as 'betrayals' of socialism. Socialist revolutions necessarily raise popular expectations and, in the absence of real sustained increases in consumption levels, revolutionary *élan* easily dissolves into disillusionment and disaffection.

Vladimir Bazarov (1874–1937)

Bazarov was the most widely respected advocate of comprehensive economic planning under NEP. He had been a leading dissident Bolshevik theoretician in 1904–9, but sided with the Mensheviks in 1917–20. His book *On the Road to Socialism* (1919) explained: 'it seems absolutely incredible to us that a worker's party could before long use the new form of bourgeois system (State capitalism) to establish a genuine socialist planned economy. The only task accessible to it under existing conditions is . . . the conversion of a profit-making economy into a State rationing system' (pp. 21–2). However, the Bolshevik retreat into NEP induced him to join Gosplan (the State Planning Commission) in 1922.

Bazarov's 'Problems of planning the economy as a whole' (1923) explained that the restoration of a market system with a stable common denominator (money) and financial accounting, far from diminishing the scope for economic planning, alone made it feasible to work out and implement internally consistent, realistic, comprehensive economic plans whose fulfilment could be monitored and equitably rewarded. Without a stable common denominator, it would be very difficult to aggregate and compare the outputs of different enterprises and industries, and to make meaningful intertemporal comparisons. And prices which failed to reflect relative costs and scarcities would promote misallocation of resources. Plan and market are complementary, not mutually exclusive opposites.

Bazarov's essay 'On the methodology of perspective plan formulation' (1926) spelled out his basic approach. In appraising a 5-Year Plan 'usually only one criterion is considered – its correspondence to reality. That would suffice when applied to a scientific economic forecast . . . based exclusively on objective regularities and spontaneous economic trends.' But a 5-Year Plan is 'not merely a forecast, but also a directive . . . a teleological construct; not merely an assessment of objective feasibilities, but also a system of measures necessary to make the most of them. And if economic policy hasn't been directed as envisaged in the Plan, then discrepancies between that Plan and reality don't in themselves attest to methodological or empirical errors by its authors.' Empirical investigation and forecasting had to predominate in the agricultural sector, comprising millions of autonomous farms, but peasant agriculture could be 'influenced by planning directly inasmuch as State industry consumes farm produce and indirectly inasmuch as, through the wages fund, State sector operations determine the share of marketable produce consumed by factory and office workers'. By contrast, 'Teleological constructs predominate in the State sector.' An optimal Plan should meet three overall requirements: (1) 'the economy's movement from its initial position to its planned destination should be smooth, without stoppages, which in turn presupposes definite economic reserves'; (2) 'a continuous moving equilibrium', which presupposes 'internal consistency' or 'proportionality', in turn requiring 'as a separate task' the planning of intermediate stages and their sequential interrelations so as to increase the planner's ability to respond to the unplanned snags and disproportions which inevitably arise en route; (3) 'provided the first two requirements can be met, the selection of the shortest path to the planned destination. . . . Computation of the shortest or optimal path, given specified constraints, is a most difficult computational problem [the more so, the larger and the more diverse the economy].' 'Modern mathematics only offers solutions to the simplest cases [computerized mathematical programming was only a pipe-dream in 1926]. Anyway, our data are unavoidably incomplete and unreliable. . . . Meantime our search for optimality must resort to crude successive approximations.' Furthermore, 'our economic planning apparatus is comparatively expensive, due partly to inefficiency and inexperience, partly to our socioeconomic backwardness, whereas under capitalism such an apparatus and the attendant expenses are absent. . . . Therefore surpassing the growth rates attained by advanced capitalist states during their industrialization will be rather difficult and isn't, as many imagine, assured by the mere existence of a planned economy.' Soviet economic development would also be retarded by the 'disproportions and anomalies' bequeathed by the civil war, by the remote and inhospitable location of much of the USSR's mineral wealth and by the USSR's involuntary retreat into autarky, caused by its 'strained relations with the capitalist world'. However, in the long run, 'international division of labour' would be 'no less imperative' for the USSR than internal interregional specialization: 'Exceptions are permissible . . . only for defence reasons.' That apart, 'productive activities in which, due to natural conditions, production costs cannot foreseeably be reduced sufficiently for home-made products to cost us no less than comparable imports . . . should be omitted from the long-term Plan'. He also outlined a procedure for Plan formulation: all economic ends and means are kaleidoscopically interacting variables, but one has to start somewhere, so the 10- to 15-Year Plan should initially postulate – as very tentative working hypotheses or extrapolations – overall guidelines on the size and prospective growth of productive forces. These can be revised as the detailed implications for intermediate stages are worked out in 5-Year Plans and then in annual Control Figures, all of which have to be rendered internally consistent in advance via input–output balances for each sector and for the economy as a whole, making due allowance for foreign trade. Inasmuch as productivity should rise and production costs should fall faster in industry than in agriculture, internal consistency should require industry to expand faster than agriculture and to reduce its selling prices in line with falling production costs. Input–output balances should also permit projections of labour requirements, and hence projections for educational, urban population and housing requirements, culminating in overall revenue and expenditure balances. Furthermore, a 'paramount task' of the 5-Year Plan is to strike a viable balance between creation of new productive capacity, which won't come on stream for several years, and renovation of existing obsolescent capacity. Ideally one would limit outlays on obsolescent capacity to routine maintenance and repairs, allowing most investment to create new capacity. But in practice acute crises would arise from the time-lags between the immediate expansion of effective demand and the subsequent expansion of the output of finished goods. That is, 'the shortest path' requirement conflicts with the need for 'proportionality' and 'smoothness', so considerable stopgap investment must go into obsolescent existing capacity (as well as into new capacity) in the interests of balanced, crisis-free growth. (Beware disparaging references to the 'technocratic' approach to planning: the endeavour to establish a centrally planned economy of *any* kind necessarily poses inescapable 'technocratic' problems which have to be resolved if very costly and dangerous 'disproportions' and 'disequilibria' are to be avoided, however much you 'democratize' the planning process.)

Bazarov's 'Principles of plan formulation' (1928) put forward his most interesting ideas. Since the USSR was 'rich in latent potentialities, but poor in tangible capital', the most appropriate industrialization strategy would economize on capital by: (1) giving a high investment priority only to products (including *some* producer goods) which could readily be mass-produced for internal and external markets and offer the greatest scope for cost-reducing specialization, standardization, streamlining and automation, instead of dissipating scarce resources over a wide range of ventures which would yield costly inferior products and, 'having absorbed a huge aggregate of capital outlays, would drag out a sickly existence' and 'fetter Soviet development for years to come'; (2) purchasing other essential products from abroad and from foreign subsidiaries or joint ventures operating in the USSR; (3) restricting import substitution to those special-purpose defence requirements which wouldn't otherwise be catered for in a peacetime economy and to products like cotton and synthetic rubber, for which it was reasonable to expect to achieve mass production at internationally competitive prices within a decade; (4) promoting interregional specialization; (5) generating reliable comprehensive economic data, 'without which long-range planning lacks substance'; (6) assigning priority to projects promising the greatest increments in output per increment in capital input; (7) absorbing under-employed or seasonally idle peasant labour into labour-intensive industries and infra-structural construction projects, wherever and so long as this won't actually depress output per worker or per unit of capital employed; (8) electrification of towns and large villages to permit wide-ranging 'mechanization of crafts without transforming them into factory production' – thus obviating 'huge capital outlays' on construct-ing 'barrack-like' factories, high-rise buildings and crowded urban slums, 'the most glaring manifestations of the cultural barbarity produced by the crude technology of classical capitalism'; and (9) promoting state-supplied 'cooperative production among technologically renovated crafts' and a proliferation of vertically and horizontally integrated 'industrial–agricultural combines' as 'powerful centres of industrial culture in the heart of the countryside', thus reaping external economies on state and communal investment in rural infrastructure.

Sadly Bazarov was banished to the back of beyond in 1931 and died in detention in 1937. But his ideas were taken much further by a Gosplan economist, Leonid Sabsovich, in a book on *The USSR within Fifteen Years* (1929). He postulated that uni-versal electrification could enable the USSR to transform itself into a federation of col-lectivized low-density agro-industrial settlements, each containing 40,000 to 60,000 inhabitants, eliminating both 'the idiocy of rural life' and big-city congestion costs. Communal services (laundries, catering, baths, crèches, etc.) would broaden partici-pation in 'productive' employment and quickly recoup the initial cost. But although such ideas were all the rage in Russia in 1928–30 and could have been implemented more readily in Russia than anywhere else, they were anathematized in 1931 as manifestations of 'Chayanovism'; Stalin's Russia went in for urban sprawl, over-crowding and congestion instead (see Starr, 1978). However, these ideas resurfaced in Khrushchev's 'agrotown' proposals of 1950, in China's 'People's Communes' and in Bulgaria's 'Agrarian–Industrial Complexes' (see Wiedemann, 1980).

Leonid Krasin (1870–1926)

Before the Revolution, Krasin was both a senior Bolshevik Party organizer and a successful electrical engineer and business executive – good grounding for his future role as Soviet Trade Minister (1920–5) and leading Bolshevik advocate of accommodatory policies towards foreign capital:

> We're devoting attention to a huge international loan, without which it will be impossible to rebuild Russia quickly and economically. . . . In France, England and America there are thousands of cars, tractors . . . tools, scientific instruments, iron, steel etc. for which there is no market. . . . Europe is in the throes of an unprecedented crisis . . . and, without reconstruction of Russia, there's no possibility of attaining a healthy world economy. . . . European and American interests demand that this loan be placed on the agenda. (*Izvestiya*, 7 September 1921)

> Foreign concessionaires, granted certain large ventures in the Urals, Siberia, Donbas and the North Caucasus could quickly plunge into these areas with hundreds of trainloads of food, clothing . . . and necessary components and scarce equipment, and could supply the requisite administrators and technical personnel. (*Pravda*, 6 August 1921)

Accusations that Krasin advocated an 'open door' policy, an imperialist 'scramble for Russia', were unwarranted. Partly to maintain his own internal and external bargaining position, he staunchly defended his ministry's monopoly of foreign trade as a means of safeguarding Soviet industry and sovereignty, of rationing imports, of stabilizing the currency and of inducing foreign firms to establish subsidiaries and joint ventures in the USSR. But Krasin overestimated the business acumen of Western capitalist interests, who seized very few of the opportunities for profitable trade and investment in the USSR under NEP, despite the existence of massive excess capacity in many Western industries in the 1920s. However, while it lasted, Krasin's strategy did attract significant support from Medvediev and Shlyapnikov, co-leaders of the Soviet 'Worker's Opposition'. Medvediev warned that:

> To conclude that we could extract enough capital to develop our extinct industry by taxation would be self-delusion. To flatter ourselves that we could raise this capital by penny-pinching would add another delusion. . . . The government should take energetic steps to raise the necessary means by internal and external State loans and by granting concessions. . . . Great material sacrifices to international capital which is prepared to build up our industry would be a lesser evil than the condition into which we may drift in the next few years. ('Letter to Baku', 1924)

Grigory Sokolnikov (1888–1939)

As Soviet Minister of Finance (1921–6), Sokolnikov initially supported Krasin's bid to rebuild the economy via foreign mining and lumbering concessions, joint manufacturing ventures and technical reconstruction contracts. But, after the failure of Soviet–Western negotiations at Genoa in 1922, snowballing hyperinflation obliged him to put the Soviet house in order by restoring financial discipline: strict accounting, self-finance and bank supervision in industry; credit- and import-rationing; centralized 'Treasury control' over all state expenditure; and progressive taxation of incomes and luxury expenditure. He also assigned financial priority to export-oriented mineral, agricultural and timber production, transport, electrification and primary processing industries, rather than to costly new steps towards manufacturing more complex products, which could be more cheaply and quickly imported. By 1926 he had successfully established a stable, confidence-inspiring currency, a return to cash transactions, a buoyant and increasingly efficient economy, an expanding state revenue base and, to encourage greater peasant participation in Soviet affairs, the budgetary autonomy of rural local government. He scorned notions of the state as universal provider, warning that financial open-handedness would foster indiscriminate profligacy and massive waste of scarce resources, not careful consideration of socialist priorities. Unfortunately his outspoken hostility to Stalinism led to successive demotions from 1926 onwards, imprisonment in 1937 and death in a labour camp in 1939.

As Finance Minister, Sokolnikov had been zealously supported by Lev Shanin, head of the State Bank. Shanin's essay on 'The economic nature of our goods shortage' (1925) deplored illusions that shortages can be overcome 'by developing industry to the utmost'. He attributed current shortages to overhasty, premature expansion of heavy industries, which by their very nature couldn't satisfy the additional effective demand created by their expansion. By 1925–6 'almost twice as much capital' was being invested in heavy industry as in light industry, whereas heavy industry ought to be developed 'only on the basis of light industry', so that the additional effective consumer demand generated by heavy-industrial development can be met. Only when consumer goods output began to meet consumer demand would relatively painless and non-inflationary heavy-industrial development become possible. Furthermore, considering the greater cost effectiveness of basing light-industrial development on cheap imported equipment rather than costly and inferior import-substitutes, 'our economic strategy should involve, first, export of agricultural commodities and, secondly, investment in branches serving those exports' – the requisite investments being minute compared with those 'required by immediate, full-scale development of heavy industry' (cf. Spulber, 1964T, 205–11).

Shanin's *Problems of Economic Strategy* (1926) added that 'preference should be given to agriculture', because its expansion requires relatively small 'investment per unit of output', because it 'throws goods upon the market much faster than industry' and 'the scope for achieving an economic upsurge via agricultural exports – i.e. in the cheapest way possible – is our economy's greatest asset'. But such a strategy would only be feasible inasmuch as agriculture could be assured export markets, and in some branches of agriculture 'exports are only possible on the basis of preliminary industrial processing': sugar beet (sugar refining), potatoes (alcohol distilling), fruit and vegetables (canning and bottling), animal rearing (bacon factories, refrigeration). However, each unit of capital input 'activates eight times more labour in agriculture than in industry and so, given similar rates of labour utilization, yields much greater accumulation in agriculture than in industry'. Moreover, 'the lower consumption levels in agriculture reinforce the accumulative effect of agricultural investment'. So resources currently earmarked for industry would, if passed through agriculture first, advance industry 'more tellingly' later on than if they were to be poured directly into industry. The initial retardation of industry would be 'made up with interest in subsequent years', and both sectors would gain, although agriculture would gain more than industry: 'Simultaneously, we should develop industries which, though not based on agricultural raw materials, are nevertheless important exporters (oil, manganese, platinum etc., and the rubber, match and timber industries).' Any industry in which there was no comparative cost advantage merited low priority, unless: (1) it was an infant industry in which there was every reason to expect the USSR to become internationally competitive before long, in which case 'tutelary protectionism is unquestionably rational'; (2) high Soviet production costs were caused 'not by an uneconomic set-up within that industry', but by the high cost of home-produced inputs, in which case it would be preferable to import those inputs from lower-cost foreign producers; and (3) defence interests dictated otherwise. Paradoxically, self-restraint in industrial development would result in greater supplies of industrial goods by releasing for export resources which could purchase considerably more abroad than they could at home (cf. Spulber, 1964T, 212–20).

Shanin evidently shared Preobrazhensky's and Trotsky's belief that Soviet manufactures were costing two or three times as much as similar, but superior quality, imports and that this favoured far greater reliance on imports than the ascendant Stalinists were willing to accept. However, Shanin somewhat overstated his case. Bazarov pointed out that, if heavy manufacturing were to be completely neglected in favour of agriculture, light processing and extractive industries, then when it eventually became heavy manufacturing's turn for rapid development, the already existing metallurgical and engineering industries would have to be started afresh – at unnecessarily great expense. Moreover, when pushed to extremes, an agriculture-first strategy could self-defeatingly result in terms of trade even more unfavourable to agriculture than those already prevailing and thus discourage peasants from expanding their marketable surpluses. Agriculture stood to gain from a light industry-first strategy, which would improve agriculture's terms of trade and boost the village industry sector (see Erlich, 1960, 64–5).

Nikolai Kondratiev (1892–1930s)

Kondratiev's international fame rests on his studies of the fifty- to sixty-year 'long waves' or 'Kondratiev cycles' which he (among others) had observed in the Western economy. But the 'long waves hypothesis' actually played only 'a minor role' in establishing this gifted young economist's great influence in 1920s Russia (Jasny, 1972, 158). The idea that after the First World War, the West would merely experience a transient cyclical downswing, and not 'the death agonies of capitalism', was quite incredible and unacceptable to many Marxists until they were confounded by the 1948–73 upswing (Marx himself tended to treat every crisis as terminal). Moreover, Kondratiev's 'long waves' were tainted by association with Trotsky, who put forward a similar hypothesis in 1921–2 (see Trotsky, 1945T, 176–211). In fact Kondratiev was primarily an agronomist who first gained prominence as Deputy Minister of Food in the provisional government of Russia in mid-1917. As founder/director of his own economics institute in Moscow from 1920 until it was suppressed by the Stalinists in 1928, and as a leading 'Treasury adviser' in the mid-1920s, he championed independent smallholder agriculture, pricing and agricultural procurement policies favourable to the peasantry, rural extension services and the virtues of indicative planning. In 1924, with the 'Chayanovist' N. P. Makarov, he published an indicative 5-Year Plan for agriculture which was largely fulfilled by 1929 (see Jasny, 1972, 163–8).

Kondratiev perceived that NEP offered three ways of achieving greater economies of scale, marketable surpluses and innovation in peasant agriculture: (1) vertical integration and inter-farm co-operation, supported by rural extension services and cheap credit, as championed by Chayanov and Bukharin in their separate ways; (2) farm amalgamation (horizontal integration), as advocated by the champions of collectivization; and (3) a so-called 'wager on the strong', meaning policies favourable to successful farmers, which would accelerate rural class differentiation, rural specialization and private piecemeal amalgamation of farms. In 1927 Kondratiev declared that, 'if the State disposed of fully adequate means of assistance for poorer households', it could improve their position without detriment to agricultural productivity, but 'the State does not at present dispose of adequate resources' (see Carr and Davies, 1974, 22); hence he favoured the third option, in order to enable the State to concentrate its very limited resources in light industry and infrastructural projects, which offered both quick returns and incentives to farmers to expand their marketable surpluses.

As a trenchant critic of Russia's first 5-Year Plan (see Kondratiev, 1927), he was imprisoned in 1929 and tried for 'treason' before his final disappearance in 1931.

Trotsky v. 'Trotskyism': Lev Bronstein (1879–1940)

Eminent socialist theoreticians have usually established their reputations as critics of capitalism, in the fallacious belief that by demonstrating the evils and deficiencies of capitalism they are by the same token demonstrating the superiority of their generally vague conceptions of future socialist systems. It is much easier to criticize capitalism than to devise viable socialist alternatives and systems of checks and balances strong enough to prevent socialist degeneration into new forms of oppression and exploitation, yet not so strong as to effectively block socialist reconstruction of society. To his credit Trotsky's major writings were part of an unending quest for a foolproof socialist system, whereas his writings on capitalism were incidental to that quest.

Unfortunately Trotsky's socialism is enveloped in myth. Self-styled 'Trotskyists' have appropriated the radical mystique of 'Trotskyism' for a motley assortment of sectarian and pseudo-proletarian movements and ideologies, transforming Trotsky into a bogeyman in the eyes of 'Reds under the beds' conservatives. In the power struggle to succeed Lenin, Trotsky was shrewdly misrepresented as a 'super-industrializer' who would recklessly force the pace of industrialization and collectivization, given a chance; and Western historians (including Isaac Deutscher) have usually argued that Trotsky did take such a stance. However, although he undeniably advocated ruthless and brutal policies during the Russian civil war and shared responsibility for the attendant atrocities, in times of peace he consistently advocated relatively sober, circumspect and humane policies. And as he correctly informed the Comintern Executive in 1926, 'The theory of "Trotskyism" was artificially manufactured – against my will, against my convictions, against my real views' (Trotsky, 1980T, 174). The policies usually labelled 'Trotskyist' were actually propounded by Preobrazhensky (see Chapter 7). Trotsky repeatedly disavowed and was acutely *embarrassed* by Preobrazhensky's harsh proposals (see Day, 1977). Until 1928 Preobrazhensky supported Trotsky's courageous opposition to Stalin. But so did many others who disagreed with Trotsky's policy prescriptions, for they shared Trotsky's fear that Stalin posed a threat to one and all.

Trotsky was an independent-minded latecomer to Lenin's Bolshevik Party. Indeed, when Russia's labour movement split in 1903, Trotsky naturally sided with the more educated, cosmopolitan and 'broad church' Mensheviks against Lenin:

> Lenin's methods lead to this: first the Party organization substitutes itself for the Party as a whole; then the Central Committee substitutes itself for the organization; and finally a 'dictator' substitutes himself for the Central Committee. . . . The new regime's tasks will be too complex to be solved other than by competition between various methods of economic construction. . . . The working class will undoubtedly include quite a few political invalids . . . and much ballast of obsolescent ideas, which it will have to jettison. . . . But this intricate task cannot be solved by exalting above the proletariat a few well-chosen people . . . or someone with the power to liquidate and to downgrade. (Trotsky, 1904, 54, 105)

After playing a leading role in the Russian Revolution of 1905, Trotsky also reached the conclusion that 'Urban Russia was too narrow a base' and that, in the next revolutionary upsurge, there would have to be 'revolutionary cooperation with the army' and 'formation of Peasant Soviets to take charge of the agrarian revolution'

(Deutscher, 1954, 149). In his *Results and Perspectives* (1906) Trotsky argued that the acute contradictions in Russian society would only be resolved by an 'uninter-rupted' passage from 'bourgeois-democratic' revolution against tsarism to socialist revolution against capitalism and that the socialist proletariat's chances of success would depend 'not on the level attained by the productive forces, but on relations in the class struggle, international circumstances and subjective factors'. Thus the pro-letariat was already more in the ascendant in backward Russia than in economically advanced America. Attempts to make proletarian revolution conditional on full 'maturity' of productive capacity, class differentiation and proletarian consciousness under capitalism were 'hopeless formalism', deformations of Marx's 'historically relative' scriptures into 'supra-historical dogma'. The *sufficient* 'prerequisites for socialism' were that: (1) 'the development of productive forces has reached the stage where large enterprises are more productive than small ones', a precondition which had already fostered large-scale capitalist production for two centuries; (2) 'the proletariat should be sufficiently numerous to overcome the resistance of bourgeois counter-revolution', a matter for subjective rather than arithmetical assessment, as the proletariat's spatial concentration and indispensable role in capitalist economies conferred power out of all proportion to its numbers and the ambiguity and ambivalence of worker-peasants, the petite bourgeoisie and the lumpenproletariat precluded precise classification and enumeration; and (3) the proletariat 'should be conscious of its objective interests'. The survival of a Russian proletarian revolution would depend on successful conciliation of the peasantry. Since the revolutionary regime 'would gain nothing economically from expropriation of smallholdings', which would moreover evoke 'tremendous resistance', it should limit itself to ratifying revolutionary changes (expropriations) effected by the peasants them-selves, to 'dissolution of the standing army into a popular militia', to abolishing church imposts and to 'shifting the entire burden of taxation on to the rich'. Thus, in 'the most difficult period', the maintenance of the revolutionary regime would be in the peasant interest. Prohibition of private employment of farm labourers would be counterproductive until such time as the proletarian regime could provide enough alternative employment on collective farms, to be organized on state land and remnants of the old estates – *not* on peasant land. Eventually the expansion of collective agriculture 'will render small capitalist farming impossible [for want of employable labour] while still leaving room for subsistence or semi-subsistence holdings, whose forcible expropriation in no way enters the socialist proletariat's plans'. However, the new regime would only survive 'by overstepping the limits of its democratic programme', as the necessary urban and rural protective labour legis-lation, unemployment relief and strike assistance would evoke retaliatory boycotts, lock-outs, tax strikes, etc. from industrial and agricultural employers, forcing the new regime into remedial expropriations and the reorganization of production 'on a socialist basis' – thereby further antagonizing urban and rural capitalists. Moreover, a proletarian revolution in Russia would precipitate crises in France, Russia's chief creditor, and in Poland thereby embroiling Austria and Prussia. Thus 'the fate of the whole Russian Revolution' would become linked with 'the fate of socialist revolution in Europe' and, 'Without direct State support from Europe's proletariat, Russia's working class won't be able to remain in power.' Quite understandably, Trotsky overestimated the political interdependence of Europe and Russia and failed to foresee that Russia's deeply divided proletarian socialist movement would be dwarfed by the peasant-oriented Socialist Revolutionary Party, which would not meekly accept 'proletarian' claims to a monopoly of political power. But he rightly recognized the decisive importance of the peasantry in determining the fortunes of socialism in Russia and, like Marx and the Russian advocates of village communism, he foresaw that Russia's *peasant* society could become the *first* society to attain a socialist system. In 1906–9 Trotsky also took it for granted that Russia's industrialization should be based on agrarian measures to expand peasant demand for manufactures (see Trotsky, 1922, ch. 3), foreshadowing his stance in the 1920s industrialization debate.

In 1917, despite his earlier misgivings, Trotsky joined forces with Lenin and organized the Bolshevik *coup d'état* of October–November 1917. After bungling Soviet peace negotiations with Germany in early 1918, Trotsky assembled and led a Red Army of 5 million men, which was used mainly to crush the widespread peasant opposition to Bolshevism and to smash popular secessionist movements in the Ukraine, Georgia, Armenia, Azerbaijan, the Volga–Urals region and Central Asia. In 1920 generalissimo Trotsky was also the leading advocate of the Bolshevik Party policy known as 'militarization of labour' (see Trotsky, 1961T, ch. 8). But paradoxically, in a famous letter to the Party's Central Committee in February 1920, Trotsky took a circumspect and conciliatory line on town–country relations: urban requisitioning of peasant surpluses and the massive exodus from Russia's ravaged cities were together promoting village autarky, slaughter of livestock and black-marketeering; overall, current Bolshevik policy was lowering agricultural output, atomizing the proletariat and threatening to completely disorganize economic life; and the downward spiral should be arrested by shifting from arbitrary surplus appropriation to a stable and moderate agricultural levy (proportionate to output) and by establishing fair exchange of industrial for agricultural products. Trotsky thus became a leading advocate of NEP.

Trotsky cogently explained his growing commitment to NEP at the 1922 Congress of Comintern: After 1917, Russia 'found herself squeezed by economic blockade' and 'confronted by the task of rebuilding her economy by her own organizational and technical resources during the indefinite period required to prepare Europe's proletariat for conquest of power'. Strictly, 'expropriation of the bourgeoisie is justified only insofar as the proletarian State can organize exploitation of enterprises on new bases'. But, 'under pressure of Civil War, we had to complete nationalization'. Greater economic caution would have been 'political folly'. However, 'having liquidated the market and the credit system, each factory resembled a telephone whose wires had been cut'. By indulging in non-market methods of economic management, 'we risked completely losing control over what was necessary and what was not, what was profitable and what was not'. Hence 'the need – even after wholesale nationalization – to permit individual lines or groups of lines to retain their economic independence, to adjust themselves to other enterprises on which they depend or which they serve'. So 'we shall have to engage in large-scale transitional operations through the market over many years'. However, since economic recovery would be slower in industry than in agriculture, 'State industry will be unable to supply the peasant with an equivalent product' and 'marketed peasant surpluses will provide a basis for private capitalist accumulation', as 'market relations have a logic of their own, whatever goals we may have in restoring them'. But this would at least ensure that 'available resources are directed where they are most needed – into branches producing goods for personal or productive consumption by workers and peasants. . . . Only after gaining success in agriculture and light industry can real impetus be given to engineering, metallurgy, coal, oil' (for a fuller translation, see Trotsky, 1953T, 220–74).

The New Course (1923) is best known as Trotsky's seminal critique of Soviet 'bureaucratic degeneracy', which he (naïvely) thought could be remedied by increasing 'intra-Party democracy' and by promoting more 'proletarians' into bureaucratic posts, while retaining a one-party police state. But it also deepened his commitment to NEP: 'The proletarian State must aid the peasantry (inasmuch as its means permit) by instituting credits and agronomic assistance. . . . It must furnish the countryside with farm implements and machines at accessible prices', as well as 'artificial fertilizers and household goods'. To pay for all this, 'industry must yield profits'. Industry's costs should be reduced 'through systematic planned organization . . . in conformity with agricultural development . . . not by suppressing the market, but on the basis of the market'. Under capitalism 'crisis is the natural . . . way of regulating the economy, of realizing harmony between different branches and between supply and demand. But in our Soviet economy . . . crises cannot be accepted as normal. . . . Crisis annihilates or disperses part of the State's possessions and some of this falls into the hands of middlemen.' The peasant economy 'is conditioned by the market, which develops spontaneously. The State can and should act upon it, push it forward, but cannot canalize it according to a unitary plan.' So 'success in economic organization will largely depend on how far we succeed, through precise knowledge of market conditions and correct economic forecasts, in harmonizing State industry with agriculture in accordance with a plan' (see Trotsky, 1965T, 109–12, 83–5).

In 1925 Trotsky was 'relieved' of his military responsibilities: 'I yielded . . . without a fight . . . as I was thereby wresting from my opponents their weapon of insinuation concerning my military intentions.' Besides, 'Economic problems were of prime importance' and, since 1920, 'had absorbed my time and attention'. So 'I took a rest from politics' and 'tried to relate my new work not only to current economic problems, but to the fundamental problems of socialism'. Above all, he aimed to challenge (Stalin's) 'stolid national approach to economic questions, "independence" through self-contained isolation' (see Trotsky, 1975T, ch. 42). His conclusions were published in *Pravda* in September 1926: 'The dynamic equilibrium of the Soviet economy should by no means be approached as that of a closed self-sufficient entity'; it should increasingly be maintained by imports and exports: 'The more we are drawn into the international division of labour, the more openly and directly are . . . the price and quality of our goods made to depend on corresponding elements in the world market.' Soviet involvement in world trade was 'already sufficiently voluminous to oblige us at every step to compare our wares with those of foreign origin'. Assignments to foreign travel should become more frequent, as 'we must acquaint our trust-managers, factory-directors, best technical students, foremen, mechanics and specialists with foreign industry'. The economic advantages of socialism – the elimination of 'parasitic' classes, institutions and practices; the removal of private property impediments to optimal, centrally planned resource allocation, standardization and specialization; and the reduced amplitude, if not the elimination, of exogenous cyclical fluctuations – would be 'immensely enhanced by the possibilities afforded by the world market', which would permit ever-increasing 'access to the achievements of technology'. Pre-revolutionary Russia's factory industry imported almost two-thirds of its plant and equipment, so 'it will hardly be economically advantageous for us to produce more than two-fifths or at most one-half of our own machinery' in the foreseeable future: 'If we attempt to readjust . . . in one leap to the production of new machinery, we will either disturb the necessary proportions between the different branches of the economy and between basic and working capital within each branch, or, if we preserve those proportions, we will greatly retard economic expansion.' Moreover, 'Every foreign product that can fill a gap in our economic system – raw material, intermediate goods and consumer goods – can under certain conditions accelerate our reconstruction.' Of course, importation of luxuries 'can only retard our development'. But timely importation of consumer goods which 'serve to restore necessary market equilibrium and fill gaps in the peasant or proletarian budget can only accelerate economic progress'. The benign influence of foreign trade would be 'the greater, the more extensive the credit opportunities it acquires on the world market'. The 'dialectics of history involve capitalism assuming temporarily the role of creditor to socialism'. A situation had arisen wherein 'we, as a business entity, are within limits interested in an improvement of the conditions in capitalist countries', as 'Our present order rests not only on the struggle of socialism against capitalism, but also, within limits, on cooperation between socialism and capitalism.' Of course, 'loans, concessions and greater dependence on exports and imports involve dangers. So we mustn't go too far.' But 'there is a greater, opposite danger. It consists in delaying our economic progress.' Besides, 'the more diverse our international economic relations, the harder it will be for our enemies to disrupt them', and the more resilient and resourceful the Soviet economy would become (cf. Trotsky, 1926T, chs 8–12).

Within a month the Stalinists expelled Trotsky from the Politburo, but this enabled him to speak out more freely. As he told the Comintern Executive on 9 December 1926, 'when you review the technical equipment of our factories, you see the crystallized dependence of Russia . . . on world industry'. During 'the last decade we have made practically no renewal of our industrial fixed capital', so 'anyone who thinks that within the next few years we shall be able to produce all our equipment, or a large part of this equipment, with our own forces is a dreamer'. Industrialization 'means not a lessening, but a growth of our connections with the outside world'. And 'if we attempt to ignore the division of labour in world industry', if 'we are to make everything ourselves, this will unavoidably mean a slowing down of the rate of our economic development', amounting to 'a refusal to exploit the world market to fill the gaps in our technology'. So 'to industrialize our country we must import machines from abroad and the peasant must export grain'. But 'the machines are in the hands of the world bourgeoisie, which is also the purchaser of our grain'. So during the 'whole series of decades that are necessary for the complete building of socialism', the USSR must knowingly 'fall into a certain dependence upon and struggle with' the encircling capitalist world (*Inprecor*, 6 January 1927).

Trotsky thus showed himself to be a truly internationalist disciple of Marx, rejecting the economic nationalism preached by many self-styled 'Marxists' and anti-imperialists.

In *The Real Situation in Russia* (1928T, 31) Trotsky argued that 'By introducing NEP . . . we created a certain place for capitalist relations in our country, and for a prolonged period ahead we must recognize them as inevitable.' The 'direct fault of the Stalin group' was its suppression of information and dissent, 'creating everywhere and in everything an official appearance of success'; this and Stalin's political 'zig-zags' engendered popular disbelief, distrust, disorientation and passivity (ibid., 32–4). The soviets were being reduced to mere appendages of the executive organs (ibid., 99) and the autonomy of the minority Soviet republics was being nullified (ibid., 102–10). Shopfloor workers made up only 37 per cent of the party's membership, under 16 per cent of the membership of party committees, and only 12–13 per cent of trade union officials, whose remote dealings with factory directors had atrophied rank-and-file participation (ibid., 112–13, 49–51). For Russia's workers, Trotsky proposed: raising of real wages in line with productivity growth; higher minimum wages; proper redeployment of workers displaced by 'rationalization of production'; higher and more comprehensive 'social insurance' charges and benefits; imposition of greater housing obligations on state industries; promotion of workers' co-operatives; equality of access to education and housing; genuine collective bargaining, though still without a right to strike in the state sector; work norms based on the average, not the outstanding, worker; higher mandatory allocations to health care, safety and improvement of working conditions, with stiff penalties for non-compliance; upgrading of women's and adolescents' jobs; special protection for seasonal, casual and farm workers; genuine autonomy, elections, debate, publicity, mass participation and accountability in trade union affairs; and publication of comprehensive labour statistics (ibid., 52–8, 69). Most of these demands have also been part of the stock-in-trade of liberal social-democrats, the crucial difference being that Trotsky still believed in a one-party polity and prohibition of strikes in the state sector (ibid., 58, 188), thereby renouncing the weapons most likely to secure his demands – political pluralism and the right to strike. For agriculture, Trotsky advocated: a reallocation of land, state credit, taxation and machinery supplies in favour of co-operatives and landless or near-landless rural households; exclusion of 'kulaks' from rural Soviets and co-operatives; subordination of traditional village communes and peasant land committees to the (unpopular) rural soviets; statutory protection for farm labourers; encouragement of agro-industrial integration and autonomous producer co-operatives, free from external 'bureaucratic regulation', as and when adequate supplies of appropriate equipment became available; and accommodation of the state's pricing and procurement policies to the requirements of 'poor' and 'middle' peasants (ibid., 68–73). Excessive *disparities* between agricultural and industrial prices, between wholesale and retail prices, between domestic and world prices, and between prices in different branches of rural economy and in different regions and seasons, could only enrich profiteers at state and popular expense (ibid., 27). On average, in real terms, the peasants were receiving one and a quarter times the pre-1914 price for their produce, but were paying two and a half times the pre-1914 price for manufactures (ibid., 29). But, given the chronic shortage of consumer goods, 'bureaucratic lowering of wholesale prices' wouldn't benefit the consumer – it would merely benefit the retailer at industry's expense. The real remedy was to alleviate the shortages and cut costs by assigning priority to light industry; yet the output of light industry was actually planned to grow more slowly than effective demand, because of the priority accorded to heavy industry (ibid., 78–81). Furthermore, ungraduated taxation of farm incomes and growing reliance on indirect taxes on consumer goods were burdening the rural poor more than the prosperous (ibid., 28–9). So he justly demanded a shift to progressive income taxation, with exemptions for the poorest 40–50 per cent of peasant households, stiffer taxation of 'excess profits' and lower sales of state-monopolized alcoholic drinks (ibid., 92, 69, 71, 91). He also demanded strict financial discipline in the state sector and more effective use of foreign trade, foreign credit, foreign concessions and foreign technical assistance to increase revenues and the pay-off on existing expenditures (ibid., 90–2). However, Trotsky still proposed no credible means of wresting such desirable changes from a polity which he rightly believed to be increasingly degenerate, self-serving and unresponsive to pressures 'from below'.

Trotsky was banished to Kazakhstan in 1928 and deported to Turkey in 1929, only to be hounded to France in 1933, to Norway in 1935 and to Mexico in 1937, but he remained Stalin's most formidable adversary and critic until he was murdered by one of Stalin's thugs in 1940. Sadly, despite his intellectually impressive advocacy of market socialism and 'least-cost' industrialization, Trotsky failed to draw people like Bukharin, Premier Rykov, Sokolnikov, Bazarov and Kondratiev into a politically effective 'moderate' opposition to Stalin. Since they actually put forward realistic and humane socialist alternatives to Stalinism, I conclude that they failed not as development strategists, but as politicians; they most conspicuously failed to co-operate sufficiently in their separate struggles against the ascendant Stalinist faction, which therefore managed to play them off against one another.

7 Socialist forced industrialization strategies: Preobrazhensky, Feldman and Stalin

Evgeny Preobrazhensky (1886–1937), economic guru of the Bolshevik Party's strident 'left opposition' to the more conciliatory and 'consumerist' facets of NEP, has remained one of the world's most noted proponents of forced industrialization in a peasant society under a socialist regime. His *Prospects of NEP* (1921) argued that the mixed economy established by the fledgling 'proletarian dictatorship' was only a battleground on which resurgent private enterprise would prepare for an 'inevitable' showdown with the state sector, whose expansion would have to be funded mainly through progressively increasing 'deductions from the income of the petit bourgeois encirclement'. He favoured six main sources of 'accumulation' for the socialized sector: progressive taxation of capitalist incomes; profits from the state monopoly of foreign trade; the profits of state industry; new currency emissions, proportionate to economic expansion; imported venture capital, on which the pay-off to the state sector would amply exceed the 'extortionate interest rates' charged by foreign capitalists; and imported human capital, or 'proletarian colonization' of Russia by millions of Europe's unemployed workers. The faster this mixed economy developed, the sooner the 'inevitable' showdown would ensue.

In *From NEP to Socialism* (1922) Preobrazhensky envisaged that large advances in peasant agriculture could be achieved through contractual state loans which would be repayable in kind and which would thus mortgage or bind smallholders to the state for several years ahead, preparatory to their ('inevitable') eventual 'mass conversion to co-operation'. Taken in isolation, this may seem feasible enough. However, he blithely presumed that the state could *both* obtain the wherewithal to make massive loans to the peasantry and rapidly expand state industry by bleeding the (mainly agricultural) private sector and by attracting foreign capital, overlooking the likelihood that his proposed 'deductions' from private sector income would have adverse repercussions on agricultural output/investment and on foreign investment in Russia.

Preobrazhensky's influential 'Economic notes' (1925–7) observed that when social revolution and the attendant disruption, destruction and capital depreciation occur in an industrializing peasant society, output and productive capacity fall further in industry than in agriculture, industrial labour productivity falls further than industrial wages, industrial recovery requires greater replacement investment than does agricultural recovery, and yet the attendant reduction or erosion of real levels of rent and personal taxation benefits the peasantry more than the urban–industrial sector. These differentials cause industrial output to lag behind the recovery of agriculture and effective demand for manufactures; and the consequent shortages and faster increases in industrial than agricultural prices discourage peasant production of marketable surpluses, thereby exacerbating urban shortages. Hence, in his view, the key constraint on post-revolutionary economic development is deficient industrial capacity, not deficient effective demand. So industrial capacity and output must now be expanded faster than agricultural output and consumer demand, and industrial capital accumulation must be pushed high enough to ensure that the productive capacity of the capacity-creating producer goods industries can expand fastest of all, 'at the expense of the economy as a whole'. He ignored objections that faster expansion of heavy industry could only generate additional unrequited demand for consumer goods and exacerbate already acute shortages, which would in turn jeopardize fragile town–country relations. He conceded that 'We need proportionate development of both heavy and light industry', but only to assert that proportionality requires faster expansion of heavy industry.

His most controversial book, *The New Economics* (1926), explained how and why he thought a socialist regime in a mixed, largely agrarian economy must force the expansion of state sector producer goods industries at peasant expense – a process for which he appropriated the term 'primitive socialist accumulation', paraphrasing Marx's conception of the role of rapacious 'primitive' or 'preliminary' accumulation of capital at popular expense in the emergence of Western capitalism. Essentially Preobrazhensky's 'law of primitive socialist accumulation' postulated that: the more backward an economy is at the start of its transition to 'socialist organization of production', the less state sector accumulation can be 'nourished by the surplus product of workers in socialist industry' and the more it must depend upon appropriation of 'surplus product' generated outside the state sector; conversely, the more developed the economy at the outset, the more it should rely on accumulation within the state sector, thereby reducing its parasitic reliance on sources of accumulation outside the state sector (Preobrazhensky, 1965T, 124). In fact the USSR's state sector was only able to become heavily reliant on accumulation at peasant expense because the USSR inherited a comparatively *productive* peasant sector (see Table 11). Communist regimes in much poorer societies later discovered that, the *less* productive the agrarian sector is at the outset, the *more* perilous it is for the state sector to rely on accumulation at peasant expense, and the *more* it must rely on its own internal accumulation. So Preobrazhensky's law ought to be stood on its head. None the less, he avowed that the task of the socialist state 'consists, not in taking from petit bourgeois producers less than capitalism took, but in taking more', as he amazingly expected peasant income to *treble*, even while unprecedented amounts of peasant income were being 'siphoned off' by the state and industry (ibid., 89, 254). So far as I know, he never even tried to explain how this trebling of peasant income could be reconciled with his proposals for a massive state squeeze of peasant income, although these were both recurring themes in his readily available writings. However, like Chayanov, Preobrazhensky favoured a piece-meal/functional approach to socialization of agriculture, spearheaded by rural electrification projects, by leasing 'State tractors on a mass scale among poor peasants' who would provide ploughing and harvesting services to smallholders, by dairying collectives and by using state credit to mortgage smallholders and their future surpluses to the state (ibid., 222, 238, 173, 181). Yet, as a small industrial sector faced over 100 million peasants, the resource flow into agriculture could only 'become a broad river' when 'primitive socialist accumulation' became no longer necessary; meantime the contrast between meagre agricultural and massive industrial investment was bound to excite peasant resentment against the 'proletarian' dictatorship, which was both 'prisoner' and 'prison warder' to the peasantry and whose immediate task was to further subjugate the peasantry (ibid., 237, 40, 161): 'The proletariat's collective economy must either develop rapidly or perish. There's no third way' (ibid., 219).

The New Economics favoured sixteen channels of 'primitive socialist accumulation': (1) progressive taxation of peasant incomes and capitalist profits; (2) semi-compulsory state bond sales; (3) capital imports, which enhance socialist more than capitalist accumulation; (4) increased emission of paper money, whose inflationary repercussions would usefully diminish popular purchasing power and consumption; (5) discriminatory transport tariffs, favouring state and co-operative enterprises at the expense of private users; (6) exorbitant interest charges on state loans to private borrowers, as against interest-free loans to state and co-operative enterprises; (7) exclusion of private intermediaries ('leeches') from state sector business; (8) state profits from procurement of peasant produce at low prices for resale on urban and export markets at much higher prices; (9) monopolistic pricing of exports which enjoy a seller's market (e.g. gold, furs); (10) use of the state's monopoly of foreign trade to restrict domestic access to imports, to increase state profits on the resale of imports to domestic users and to increase the profits of state industries, whose product prices were already 'on average twice as high as the prices of the same goods abroad'; (11) use of the monopolistic position of state industries on the domestic market to increase profits at the consumer's expense; (12) the 'frightful poverty inflicted by war and revolution' had accustomed the worker to reduced wages, and it would be legitimate to continue 'wage restriction in the interests of socialist accumulation'; (13) use of the state monopoly of foreign trade to drive hard bargains with foreign trade partners, especially producers of primary products; (14) restriction of the leasing of state enterprises and natural resources to foreign concessionaires, as the latter tend to appropriate most of the 'surplus value' their activities create and to circumvent the state's foreign trade 'cordon'; (15) austerity and restriction of 'non-productive' services; and (16) optimization of the potential gains from importing producer goods from reliable, low-cost foreign producers, while at the same time assigning first priority to 'State production of the means of production' (ibid., 89–138, 38, 250–2, 195, 238, 166, 186–7). Willingness to optimize gains from importing producer goods was an important difference between Preobrazhensky and Stalin. Note also that Preobrazhensky's conception of 'primitive socialist accumulation' presupposed continued growth of a market economy and a private sector; 'if accumulation at the private sector's expense entails a balance of values exchanged in favour of the State sector, this balance will be the greater . . . the greater the volume of exchange' (ibid., 144–5). However, Preobrazhensky's strategy differed fundamentally from 'primitive capitalist accumulation' in that the latter was directed towards mass production of cheap textiles, processed foods and other consumer goods, which necessarily reduced living costs and raised popular consumption levels and accelerated agricultural development, and not towards producer goods which are largely consumed by industry itself (especially by heavy industry); and he presupposed impossible feats from a peasantry which stood to gain very little and to lose a great deal from his proposed strategy of 'primitive socialist accumulation'. Indeed, his strategy was bound to undermine the town–country and market relations which he deemed essential to its fulfilment.

Finally, Preobrazhensky's 'Economic equilibrium in the Soviet system' (1927) presented the fatal inconsistencies in his proposed strategy as a set of dialectical 'contradictions', to be resolved by a non-existent *deus ex machina*: aid from 'other socialist countries' (see Preobrazhensky, 1979T, 195–7, 200–3, 207–12, 224–30ff.). This was a virtual admission of his own bankruptcy, and in 1929–30 he capitulated to Stalinism. However, his subsequent misgivings led to his execution in 1937.

G. Feldman's essay 'On the theory of economic growth-rates' (1928), resurrected by Evsei Domar (1957, 223–61), has conferred respectability on the priority assigned to heavy industries in communist states. Using abstract tautological reasoning and certain 'simplifying assumptions' – an autarkic economy; constant technical coefficients and prices; mutually independent producer goods and consumer goods industries; no timelags; no capital depreciation; no bottlenecks; no time preference; no service sector; no transfer payments; and capital scarcity as the only operative constraint on economic growth – Feldman seemingly demonstrated that the higher the proportion of gross investment channelled into production of producer goods, the higher that economy's long-run growth and investment potential; and that such an acceleration of economic growth and investment could be achieved *without* depressing popular consumption (only the latter's rate of increase would be affected): 'Feldman's model contains an important truth: a closed economy without well-developed metal, machinery and subsidiary industries . . . is unable to produce a sizeable quantity of capital goods and thus to invest a high fraction of its income, however high its potential saving propensity may be' (Domar, 1957, 236).

However, the 'simplifying assumptions' of abstract economic models tend to simply leave out too many crucial mundane and/or non-quantifiable considerations. By assuming a closed economy, Feldman 'simply' evaded comparative cost considerations, the advantages of importing superior, readily available plant and equipment from established, lower-cost foreign producers in exchange for primary commodity or light-industrial exports, instead of endeavouring at great cost and delay to become self-sufficient in producer goods. True, some economies may be too backward to produce significant exportable surpluses, but then they will be even less able to produce investible surpluses large enough to develop heavy industries. By neglecting capital depreciation, Feldman conveniently overlooked the mundane probability that the initial productive capacity of a backward economy's equipment-producing industries will be barely sufficient to meet routine replacement requirements in existing industries, transport and agriculture, so that autarkic attempts at forced expansion of heavy industries are bound to run down other sectors, thereby squeezing popular consumption. And once one takes into account actual sectoral interdependence, human and material supply bottlenecks and the comparatively long gestation periods of investment in heavy industries, there is little to commend Feldman's thesis.

Man of steel: Jozef Djugashvili (1879–1953)

Stalin's importance as a development strategist derives from his regime's decisive and unparalleled impact on development patterns in the USSR, East Asia and 1950s Eastern Europe, on the political culture of communist parties everywhere, on the fortunes of socialist movements in the West, on widely held conceptions of forced industrialization and development planning, and on the course of world history since the 1930s. Yet his own seemingly coherent rationalizations of his policies are not widely known. Indeed, he is often portrayed as a dullard, so incapable of independent thought that he merely borrowed Bukharin's ideas in 1924–7, during his witch-hunt against 'Trotskyism', and then appropriated the 'Trotskyist' programme in order to ditch Bukharin and steal a march on the disarrayed 'Trotskyists'. Such interpretations misrepresent the platforms adopted by the major protagonists and fail to explain how a supposed dullard could so successfully upstage his adversaries. Actually Stalin had formulated a development strategy of his own by 1926, although until 1929 he found it expedient to play down his fundamental divergence from Bukharin, and the policies which unfolded thereafter were corollaries of the course he adopted in 1925–6. Stalin displayed a frighteningly *literal* belief in his own ideology and demonology, and ruthless logic (or fanaticism) in translating them into practical policy. He never adopted Trotsky's programme.

Before the mid-1920s, Stalin contributed little to Bolshevik economic debate (see Stalin, 1952–5T, vols 1–5). But, as an able machine politician and party spokesman on nationalities policy, the Soviet regime soon gave him posts conferring wide control of Party and state appointments 'from above', and in 1922 he was made General Secretary to the party's Central Committee – a position which Stalin's ever-astute exercise of patronage soon elevated to the status of party boss.

In 1924, in 'The Party's tasks in the countryside', he began to warn that Russia's peasantry was 'no longer the old peasantry, downtrodden and terrified lest they lose their land. . . . It's a new, free and active class which has already forgotten the landlords and is now concerned to receive cheap commodities and to sell its grain at the highest possible price.' The peasantry 'finds our price policy irksome and wishes to weaken or even get rid of the levers by which this policy is operated and without which our industry could not advance'. This 'new rural struggle against Soviet price policy is inspired by kulaks, profiteers and other anti-Soviet elements'. Hence 'our task is to isolate kulaks and profiteers'. In this, 'we must remember the peasant's natural mistrust of townspeople' (Stalin, 1952–5T, vol. 6, 328–32).

Following Lenin's death in 1924, the bravado of Stalin's *Foundations of Leninism* gave Bolsheviks a much-needed tonic, a new sense of mission and pride in the USSR's (involuntary) self-reliance. Hitherto Bolsheviks had deemed socialism in a single, isolated country 'impossible, on the assumption that it would require combined action by proletarians of . . . at least a majority of advanced countries to achieve victory over the bourgeoisie'. Actually the 'uneven, spasmodic development of capitalist countries under . . . imperialism, the development of catastrophic contradictions within imperialism leading to inevitable wars, and the growth of the revolutionary movement in all countries' all lead 'not only to the possibility, but also the necessity of proletarian victory in single countries'. But 'establishment of proletarian power in one country doesn't yet mean that a complete victory for socialism has been ensured'. For that, 'victorious revolution in at least several countries is needed. Therefore development and support of revolution in other countries is an essential task'. Hence 'the whole point is to retain power, consolidate it, make it invincible'.

In 1925 Stalin began to fashion the rhetoric of 'socialism in one country' into a development strategy. Denouncing proposals 'to reduce our army to the level of a militia', he demanded expansion and re-equipment of the armed forces: 'The most dangerous thing in our political practice is the attempt to regard the victorious proletarian country as something passive, only capable of marking time until assistance comes from victorious proletarians in other countries.' He claimed that 'growth of the metal industry is the basis of industrial and economic growth . . . for neither light industry, nor transport, nor the fuel industry, nor electrification nor agriculture can be put on their feet unless the metal industry is powerfully developed' (Stalin, 1952–5T, vol. 7, 11–14, 17, 132).

Stalin told the December 1925 Party Congress: 'we must make every effort to make our country an economically self-reliant, independent country . . . a centre of attraction for all other countries which gradually drop out of capitalism and enter the channel of socialist economy.' That would entail 'utmost expansion of our industry', but without 'converting our country into an appendage of the world capitalist system'. His explicit priorities were to develop large-scale state industry 'at all costs'; fuel industries, ahead of demand; metallurgical industries, sufficient to meet internal demand; skilled labour; and new railway capacity. Meantime agriculture could fend for itself (see ibid., 306, 322–4). And from 1926 onwards most industrial investment did go into heavy industry (see pp. 100, 145).

In 1926 Stalin warned that 'the land of proletarian dictatorship cannot remain economically independent if it doesn't produce the instruments and means of production in its own country'. Hence 'industrialization is to be understood above all as development of heavy industry, especially machine-building', and 'the question of accumulation for industrial development, socialist accumulation, has become one of primary importance'. He emphasized the following sources of 'socialist accumulation': (1) the reduction in rental, interest and royalty charges on industry and the state, consequent upon Soviet annulment of capitalist property and debts in 1917–18; (2) the profits of state industry and banks; (3) the state monopoly of foreign trade; (4) taxation; (5) public borrowing; (6) retail price reductions, to 'minimize the seepage of surpluses from accumulation into capitalists' pockets'; (7) 'It's necessary . . . to reduce and simplify our State and cooperative apparatus. . . . The inflated establishments and unparalleled extravagance of our administrative agencies have become a byword'; (8) as 'Communists sometimes don't scruple to intrude like pigs into the State's vegetable garden and snatch what they can, or to display their generosity at the State's expense', it was necessary 'to make life impossible for thieves and pilferers of the people's wealth'; (9) a crackdown on absenteeism, which was costing industry 'hundreds of thousands of man-days'; and (10) mass participation in an industrial economy-drive, based on shopfloor 'production conferences' (Stalin, 1952–5T, vol. 8, 126–34).

Stalin's progress report to the December 1927 Party Congress acknowledged that Gosplan's projected 5 per cent annual increase in farm output during 1928–32 was insufficient 'for maintaining in future the necessary equilibrium between agriculture and our nationalized industry', whose output was planned to grow 15 per cent per annum during 1928–32: 'What's the way out for agriculture? Perhaps to slow down our industrial development . . .? Never! That would be most reactionary. . . . Nationalized industry must and will develop at an accelerated rate. That's the guarantee of our advance towards socialism' and of the eventual industrialization of agriculture. 'The way out is to convert small, scattered peasant farms into large, amalgamated farms based on . . . collective cultivation of land on the basis of new, higher techniques' (Stalin, 1952–5T, vol. 10, 307–13). It was time to 'systematically eliminate' capitalists from agriculture and crafts (ibid., 306): 'The

kulak must be defeated by economic measures, in conformity with Soviet law. . . .
This does not, of course, preclude certain administrative measures against kulaks'
(ibid., 319, alluding to Article 107 of the RSFSR Criminal Code – the legal basis
for Stalin's imminent reign of terror against rural 'speculators'). Indeed, 'the fact
that we're developing production of means of production faster than light industry
predetermines that there will be a goods shortage in the country during the next
few years. But we cannot . . . cut down heavy industry to develop light industry
. . . if we want to push forward industrialization to the utmost'. Rather than
concede that his policy of forcing heavy industry at the expense of other sectors was
severely exacerbating shortages and hence 'the extremely slow reduction of industrial production costs', Stalin blamed 'the enormous resistance of the apparatus'
(ibid., 317–19). And, preparatory to his revival of the siege conditions of 1918–20,
he warned that the latest 'crisis of world capitalism' was 'fraught with new wars'.

Stalin's final solution

By 1928 the sectoral imbalance of Soviet economic strategy was causing disruptive
urban 'grain shortages'; urban grain supplies were not keeping pace with the rapid
growth of urban demand, although there were good harvests and per capita food
consumption remained rather higher in the towns than in the villages (see Jasny,
1949, 750–1, 777–8). But, rather than offer the peasants fairer terms of trade to
induce them to produce larger marketable surpluses of grain, Stalin and his hench-
men inflicted 'emergency measures' on an increasingly disaffected peasantry. In
Stalin's own words, they resorted to 'allocation of grain delivery quotas to separate
farms, posting interception squads on district boundaries' and 'compulsory allocation of loan subscription quotas'. Above all, 'Article 107 yielded splendid results'
(Stalin, 1952–5T, vol. 11, 21, 5). Realizing that the Party's rural support was so
thin that he would depend on village thugs and pariahs to implement his
'emergency measures', Stalin even decreed that '25% of the grain surpluses confiscated by law from speculators and kulak speculating elements should be turned over
to poor peasants' (ibid., 20).

Stalin evidently understood that his chosen methods and priorities could only
make the peasantry increasingly introverted and non-compliant unless they were
fully and forcibly subordinated to an externally imposed and controlled production
regime. But Stalin still had to justify his policies to the party: he was not yet
sufficiently powerful to bludgeon the party into complete insensibility. Stalin's 'On
the grain front', published in *Pravda* on 2 June 1928, argued that industry, towns
and areas producing industrial crops were rapidly expanding, causing a rapid
expansion of demand for grain: 'But production of marketable grain is increasing at
a disastrously slow rate. . . . The reason is primarily the structural change brought
about by the October Revolution, the passage from large-scale landlord and kulak

farming . . . to small- and middle-peasant farming.' He quoted some estimates provided by V. Nemchinov:

	Grain production (P)				Grain sold to towns (S)				(S) as % of (P)	
	'Prewar'		1926–7		'Prewar'		1926–7		'Prewar'	1926–7
	(million tons)	(% of total)	(million tons)	(% of total)	(million tons)	(% of total)	(million tons)	(% of total)	(%)	(%)
Landlords	9.8	12.0	—	—	4.6	21.6	—	—	47.0	—
Peasants	72.2	88.0	76.6	98.3	16.8	78.4	9.7	94.0	23.3	12.7
Collective and state farms	—	—	1.3	1.7	—	—	0.6	6.0	—	47.2
Total	82.0	100	77.9	100	21.4	100	10.3	100	26.0	13.3

Large-scale farming could produce 'the maximum quantity of marketable grain'. Conversely, 'the weakness of small-peasant farming lies in the fact that it lacks or almost lacks such opportunities'. Hence 'the amount of marketable grain is half what it was prewar, although gross output has reached prewar levels', and the 'way out lies, above all, in passing from small, backward, scattered peasant farms to united, socially-managed, large farms . . . capable of producing the maximum amount of marketable grain': collective farms in populous areas and gigantic state farms in sparsely populated areas (Stalin, 1952–5T, vol. 11, 86–96).

In July 1928 Stalin acknowledged the real reason why the peasantry was consuming more of its own grain, instead of selling it to the urban sector: the peasantry 'not only pays the State the usual taxes, direct and indirect; it also *overpays* . . . for manufactures and is more or less *underpaid* . . . for agricultural produce. . . . This is an additional tax levied on the peasant for promoting industry . . . a kind of "tribute"'. But he declared the peasantry 'capable of bearing this burden' because, as indicated by Nemchinov's estimates, Russia's peasants had somewhat strengthened their economic position since 1914. Moreover, it was necessary to satisfy not only the peasants' personal needs, but also their need for producer goods: 'But the more we advance, the greater will be the resistance of capitalist elements and the sharper the class struggle.' So 'the Soviet government, whose strength will steadily increase, will pursue a policy of isolating, demoralizing and crushing the resistance of exploiters' (ibid., 167–70, 178–9). Yet, on his own admission, the Soviet government was itself the major 'exploiter'.

In October 1928 Stalin warned that 'there are people in our Party who are striving, perhaps unconsciously, to adapt socialist construction to the tastes and requirements of the "Soviet" bourgeoisie' and that 'victory of the Right deviation in our Party would mean the development of conditions necessary for a restoration of capitalism'. Moreover, 'since small-scale production predominates in our country and *engenders* capitalism and a bourgeoisie continuously and on a massive scale, particularly under NEP, we have conditions which make a restoration of capitalism possible' (ibid., 234–6). Thereupon, on their own initiative and authorization, Stalin's stalwarts again resorted to grain requisitioning, enforced by Article 107. Furthermore, paramilitary deployment of 340,000 rural Party members, 284,000 members of 'poor peasant' committees and about as many urban volunteers, employing a brutally effective combination of Article 107, punitive requisitioning, foreclosure, distraint and sharply discriminatory income taxes (exceeding 100 per cent of income on prosperous farms), increased the proportion of peasant households enrolled in collective farms to 7.6 per cent by 1 September 1929, to 20 per cent by 30 December 1929 and to 53 per cent by 1 March 1930 (USSR, 1977T, vol. 2, 202–10). In *Pravda* on 7 November 1929 Stalin proclaimed that 'All the objections raised by science against the possibility and expediency of organizing large grain factories of 40,000 to 50,000 hectares each have collapsed. . . . Large grain factories don't take root in capitalist countries. But ours is a socialist country.' Under capitalism 'large grain factories cannot be organized without buying up numerous plots of land and paying absolute ground rent, which can only burden production with colossal expenses'. But 'in our country neither absolute ground rent nor sale and purchase of land exist'. Under capitalism 'large grain farms aim at maximum profit or at least profit equal to the so-called average rate. . . . In our country . . . as State undertakings . . . they can limit themselves to a minimum profit and sometimes manage without any profit.' Finally, 'under capitalism large grain farms don't enjoy special credit or tax privileges, whereas under the Soviet system, designed to support the socialist sector, such privileges exist'. According to Stalin, 'The decisive new feature of the present collective farm movement is that peasants are joining . . . not in separate groups, as before, but by whole villages.' Now 'even the blind can see that the middle peasant has turned towards the collective farm'. Thus the 'last hope for restoration of capitalism is collapsing', which 'explains the desperate efforts of capitalist elements in our country to rouse all the forces of the old world against advancing socialism. . . . We can now accomplish and even exceed what was considered fantasy several years ago' (Stalin, 1952–5T, vol. 12, 135–41). And in *Pravda* on 29 December 1929 he assailed 'bourgeois' claims that there were few economies of scale in agriculture and that, because the smallholder 'is ready to bear any privation if only he can hold on to his little plot', he displays extraordinary perseverance. Such claims 'merely eulogise and strengthen the capitalist system, which ruins the vast masses of small peasants'. According to Stalin, decisive economies of scale were available not only to 'developed collective farms with machinery and tractors at their disposal, but also collective farms in their primary stage . . . based on simple pooling of peasant tools', which would enable 'peasants to till neglected and virgin soil'. Certainly 'it used to be thought that . . . there was in Russia no more free land suitable for cultivation', but he rightly pointed out that 'scores of millions of hectares of free land were and are available'. So 'after accelerated development of the collective farm movement, peasants can combine their labour . . . plough virgin soil, utilize neglected land, obtain machines and tractors and thereby double or even treble labour productivity', thus reducing the gaping disparity between urban and rural purchasing power. However, he drew the unwarranted conclusion that 'Today we have an adequate material base from which to strike the kulaks, break their resistance, eliminate them as a class and replace their output', and that kulaks couldn't be permitted to join collective farms as 'they are sworn enemies of the collective farm movement'. But he admitted that 'There are bound to be elements of class struggle within collective farms. . . . It would be a mistake to imagine that members of collective farms are already socialists. No, much has to be done to remould the peasant collective farmer' (ibid., 160–6, 170–7).

The effects of 'dekulakization' can be construed from official Soviet sources: 'As of 1928, there were more than 1m. kulak farms. . . . In two years around 600,000 kulak farms were expropriated and more than 240,000 kulak families were deported. . . . At the end of 1932 there remained approximately 60,000 kulak farms' (USSR, 1977T, 208–15). This presumably left at least 5 million people, including Russia's best farmers, either without a livelihood or languishing in 'corrective labour' camps.

In *Pravda* on 2 March 1930 Stalin admitted that his impromptu, insidious campaigns were causing widespread fear and confusion as to how far peasant property was to be collectivized. Fearing that the attendant conflict and bloodshed would jeopardize the coming agricultural season, he signalled a truce, disingenuously blaming all 'excesses' on local officials who had become 'dizzy with success' (Stalin, 1952–5T, vol. 12, 197–205). But within a month he added: 'People who talk of retreat fail to understand . . . the laws of an offensive.' Offensives only succeed when you don't confine yourself 'to advancing headlong, but endeavour simultaneously to consolidate captured positions, regroup your forces . . . and bring up reserves' (ibid., 221). The summertime proportion of peasant households enrolled in state and collective farms was indeed allowed to slip back to 24 per cent in 1930. But successive off-season offensives and systematic monopolization of all workstock and tractors by state farms and state-controlled machine tractor stations (MTS) raised it thus: 1931, 53 per cent; 1932, 62 per cent; 1933, 64 per cent; 1934, 71 per cent; 1935, 83 per cent; and 1936, 90 per cent. 'The bastions of proletarian dictatorship in the village were state farms and MTSs. Through them the Soviet state organized production and exercised leadership over collective farms': e.g. their 'political sections', established in 1933, quickly 'purged' 47 per cent of collective farm managers, 34 per cent of storesmen and 24 per cent of accountants and clerks (USSR, 1977T, vol. 2, 215–16). Above all, despite severe agricultural setbacks, the MTSs enforced increasingly onerous farm deliveries to the state:

Output (million tons p.a.)	Grain	Potatoes	Milk	Meat	Grain and potatoes per inhabitant (grain equivalent)	Notes
1926–8	74.8	42.5	29.3(a)	4.6	570 kg	(a) 1924–8
1931	69.5	44.8	23.4	3.9	496 kg	
1932	69.6	43.1	20.6	2.8	485 kg	
1933	68.4	49.3	19.2	2.3	478–90 kg	
1934–9	72.4	53.3	21.2	3.4	500–15 kg	
Deliveries (million tons p.a.)						
1928	11.7(b)	1.1	1.9	0.7	—	(b) 1925–9
1931–3	21.3	5.7	1.7(c)	2.1(c)	—	(c) 1928–32
1933–7	27.5	6.3	4.3	1.1	—	
1938–40	32.1	6.0	5.6	2.2	—	

However, these widely used data from official post-Stalin Soviet publications cast doubt on Western assertions that approximately 5 million Soviet peasants perished from starvation in 1932–4 (the allegations are summarized in Dalrymple, 1963). The data indicate that the USSR still enjoyed *comparatively high* per capita supplies of basic foods (see Table 11) and that retained rural food supplies per rural inhabitant were never less than double the levels for Southern Europe, India and East Asia at that time. Moreover, in 1928 the USSR still enjoyed comparatively favourable livestock–population ratios (see Table 13), and 1930s livestock data indicate that, when forced to choose between feeding people and feeding livestock, the peasantry put people first:

	Horses	Cattle	Sheep	Goats	Pigs
January 1928	32.1m.	60.1m.	97.3m.	9.7m.	22.0m.
January 1934	15.4m.	33.5m.	32.9m.	3.6m.	11.5m.
January 1939	17.2m.	53.5m.	69.9m.	11.0m.	25.2m.

If 97 million livestock survived in 1934, I find it hard to believe allegations that 'ordinary' Soviet peasants let millions of their compatriots starve to death and/or resort to cannibalism rather than share their reduced food supplies. 'Witnesses' who allege that dead bodies were left lying in the streets diminish their own credibility, as bodies would surely have been removed – if only to reduce the public health risks. Moreover, some Western visitors who checked out rumours of starvation found them to be false (see, for instance, Eddy, 1934, xiv; Webb and Webb, 1936, vol. 1, 259–60). But this is not to exonerate Stalin. Official Soviet population statistics reveal that the USSR's population rose by roughly 15 million less than was to be expected between 1932 and 1939, considering the apparently stable officially reported rates of 'natural increase':

Population	Annual increment	Annual rate of 'natural increase'
1926 147.0m.	1924–6 3.1m.	1924–9, 2.2%
1932 165.7m.	1926–32 3.1m.	
1939 170.6m.	1932–9 0.8m.	1938, 2.0% 1939, 1.9%

In 1936 the official population projection for 1937 was 180.7 million, indicating a continuing annual increment of 3 million people per annum since 1932 (Conquest, 1971, 708). If so, and if mass starvation seems implausible, the large 'population deficit' revealed by the 1939 census must be largely attributed to the events of 1937–8, when a further 6–9 million people were sent to diseased 'corrective labour' camps in remote inhospitable regions, joining the 5 million people incarcerated in such camps before 1937 (ibid., 454, 700–9). This helps to explain the continuing high incidence of major diseases, especially malaria (see Table 23). Persistent Soviet silence on the precise reasons why approximately 15 million people were missing by 1939 reinforces my worst suspicions. Incidentally, this 'population deficit' was additional to the 'deficit' of approximately 28 million people incurred during 1914–26 (Lorimer, 1946, 41) and the 20 million killed in the 1940s, sometimes in equally suspicious circumstances.

'Proletarian cultural revolution' becomes betrayal of the peasantry

Contrary to what some writers on Soviet Russia would have us believe, it was far from easy for the ascendant Stalinists to mobilize strong support for hard-line 'proletarian' socialism in an industrializing peasant society whose peasantry still had strong village communist traditions and whose socialist intelligentsia had been nurtured on very tenacious traditions of sympathy and concern for the peasantry. Even those socialists whose main faith was in the industrial working class often refused to 'turn against' the peasantry and opposed Stalin's most draconian proposals; this was a major reason why Bukharinist and other 'least-cost' industrialization strategies won widespread and articulate support, even in Bolshevik circles. However, China's more recent Proletarian Cultural Revolution has helped to promote a major reappraisal of the means by which the Stalinists actively mobilized hard-line 'proletarian' support, ruthlessly ousted the old 'soft-line' intelligentsia, and rapidly replaced it with a much larger and more compliant 'Soviet intelligentsia', drawn partly from the proletariat and the peasantry (see Fitzpatrick, 1978, 1979; Bailes, 1978). The processes involved, which can only be given the briefest mention here, were soon to be repeated in Eastern Europe, China and North Korea; and they do help to explain how Stalinist regimes managed to fully subjugate and actively mobilize support in peasant societies whose peasants and intelligenti were (I believe) mostly hostile to Stalinism.

In mid-1928 Stalin sponsored a major 'show trial' of three German and fifty Soviet engineers on bogus charges of 'treason' and 'wrecking', for which eleven defendants received death sentences and thirty-eight received prison sentences (Bailes, 1978, 74–94). The attendant barrage of party propaganda inaugurated the USSR's Proletarian Cultural Revolution, directed against the 'soft' intelligentsia. As he urged the 2-million-strong Communist Youth League to shake up Soviet society, Stalin announced that 'There are no fortresses that workers, Bolsheviks, cannot conquer. . . . Bureaucracy is one of the worst enemies of our progress. . . . The Communist bureaucrat is the most dangerous.' Stalin admitted that 'by rousing the fury of the masses against bureaucratic distortions in our organizations we sometimes have to tread on the toes of comrades who have past services to their credit', but 'for present blunders and bureaucracy it is quite in order to give them a good drubbing. . . . Mass criticism from below, control from below, is needed. . . . The working class cannot become the real master of this country if it doesn't succeed in overcoming its lack of culture, in creating its own intelligentsia' (see Stalin, 1952–5T, vol. 11, 57–66, 74–82). Uncouth 'Red Directors' and ruthless 'trouble-shooters' rapidly superseded more sedate 'bourgeois specialists'. Thousands of (scarce) engineers were imprisoned. Mandatory output targets and work norms were repeatedly raised. 'Comradely' harassment of 'dilatory' personnel knew no bounds. New industrial ventures proliferated wildly. Financial discipline went by the board. Nominal wages, investment, employment, the total wage bill and inflation soared, and the consequent shortages caused physical rationing to supersede trade. Many thousands of urban workers with no agricultural experience were sent into the countryside, supposedly to galvanize the transition to collective agriculture. The Communist Youth mounted a quasi-military literacy campaign which degenerated into a literally rapacious purge of the predominantly female teaching profession. Most churches and mosques were desecrated, their clergy were often arrested, and lay believers – especially children – were persecuted (until 1935 children were legally 'answerable' for their parents). Many thousands of 'dissidents' (mainly socialists) were sent to penal labour camps. Charlatans gate-crashed the august Academies of Science, which suffered hundred of arrests. And pseudo-proletarians claimed hegemony over the media and the arts.

Professor Sheila Fitzpatrick (1979) has argued that the workers and peasants who actually *made* the Russian Revolution primarily aspired to upward social mobility via a vastly expanded state-financed system of general and vocational education and rapid expansion of urban and especially white-collar employment, the very things that Stalin was abundantly providing (see table on p. 125).

During 1926–39 23 million peasants moved into the urban sector, 'proletarian' representation among higher education students rose from 25 per cent in 1928 to 51 per cent in 1932 (before receding to 34 per cent in 1938), and the 1939 Party

	Blue-collar employment	White-collar employment	Graduate employment	Other 'specialist' employment	Literacy among 9–49 year-olds (%)
1928	8.7m.	2.7m.	0.23m.	0.28m.	58
1940	23.7m.	10.2m.	0.91m.	1.49m.	87
1955	36.8m.	13.5m.	2.18m.	2.95m.	98

Source: USSR, 1977, 55, 461, 477.

Congress quite plausibly boasted that 'The Soviet intelligentsia is yesterday's workers and peasants and sons of workers and peasants promoted to command positions' (Stalin's massive purges had created considerable scope for promotion). Fitzpatrick concludes that, for those promoted to command positions, 'industrialization was an heroic achievement – their own, Stalin's and that of Soviet power – and their promotion, linked to the industrialization drive, was a fulfilment of the promises of the revolution' (see Fitzpatrick, 1979, 188, 235, 239, 254).

However, while Professor Fitzpatrick has helped to explain how Stalinism mobilized a thrusting 'proletarian' minority, her devil's advocacy takes no account of the attendant misery and loss of life, which to a large extent cancelled out the gains. Indeed, many millions of 'proletarians' and peasants, including many who had been promoted to 'command positions', were also among the prime victims of Stalinism. She also ignores the fact that, in the November 1917 elections to the Constituent Assembly, only a small minority of votes had been cast in favour of the upward social mobility offered by the city-oriented Bolshevik Party, whereas there had been a clear majority for parties emphasizing village-based development (see pp. 43, 81). These election results suggest that, at the height of the 1917 Revolution, most peasants sought to improve their position *as peasants*, rather than to rise out of the peasantry; for them, Stalinism was a betrayal of the promises of the Revolution. Moreover, even in narrowly economic terms, Stalinist achievements scarcely began to offset the costs – including alternatives forgone and foreclosed. Admittedly, there was an impressive expansion of heavy industry, comparable to that achieved by interwar Japan and Italy (see Table 16). But agriculture and light industry, which still contributed the *greater part* of national output and employment and which directly affected the material welfare of the peasant majority, either *stagnated* or *contracted* (see Tables 11–14 and 16). That is why the Soviet economy grew only 2.3–2.8 per cent per annum during 1913–38, more slowly than the less favourably endowed economies of Japan, Bulgaria and Greece (see Table 17). The notion that Stalinist Russia achieved spectacular rates of economic growth is no more than a potent myth. Stalin only avoided *total* disaster because Russia's rich mineral and agricultural endowments enabled most of his subjects to survive his regime's rapacity and prodigality.

However, no 'bourgeois' critique of Stalin's regime can rival the poignancy of Trotsky's last major work, *The Revolution Betrayed* (1937). He acknowledged that by 1935 Soviet output of coal, iron and oil was '3 to $3\frac{1}{2}$ times' the 1913 level (ibid., 7). But Soviet industry was characterized by 'extremely high production costs', poor quality and finish, limited assortment, 'lack of skill', 'clumsy' design, frequent breakdowns, inordinate repair expenses, inadequate maintenance and 'very low' utilization of equipment (ibid., 11–13). Roads and housing were dilapidated (ibid., 14) and 'most workers huddle in communal dwellings whose equipment and upkeep are considerably worse than barracks' (ibid., 127). Premature collectiviz-ation of agriculture had caused 'not only extermination of over half the livestock', but 'complete indifference' of collective farmers towards 'socialized property and the results of their labour' and 'extremely low productivity of labour in collective farms' (ibid., 73–4). 'The destruction of people by hunger, cold and repression is unfortunately less accurately tabulated than the slaughter of livestock, but it also mounts up to millions', due to 'the blind, violent, gambling methods' employed (ibid., 40). Trotsky remained a staunchly pragmatic advocate of market socialism, because prices 'will serve the socialist cause better, the more honestly they begin to express real economic relations'. Stalin's 'obedient professors' had managed to create an entire theory that Soviet prices had 'an exclusively planning or directive character', but 'forgot to explain how you can "guide" a price without knowing real costs and how you can estimate real costs if all prices express the will of a bureaucracy' (ibid., 75). Deprived of international convertibility, the value of Soviet money had become entirely arbitrary, thus imparting a 'shut-in' character to the Soviet economy, limiting gains from trade and specialization, substituting 'fictitious for real magnitudes', depriving the Soviet economy of 'the necessary instrument for objectively measuring its successes and failures', weakening any 'correspondence between individual labour and individual wages', and causing 'a decline of personal interest, . . . productivity, and . . . quality of goods' (ibid., 68–72). Simultaneously 'local ruling groups seize the chance to escape their isolation by allowing the upper stratum of workers to participate in their privileges' and to obtain 'twenty to thirty times the earnings of lower category workers'; in inequality of remuneration the USSR had 'far surpassed the capitalist countries' (ibid., 125). Most important, Trotsky finally acknowledged that his more humane market socialism could only be secured through a liberal 'Soviet democracy', with free debate, 'genuine freedom of elections', revitalized trade unions and 'freedom of Soviet parties' (ibid., 289). He hoped that 'further development of the USSR' would eventually engender 'a clash between the . . . people and the bureaucratic oligarchy' (ibid., 287). 'Improvement of the material situation of the workers does not reconcile them to the authorities; on the contrary, by increasing their self-respect and freeing their thought for general political problems, it prepares the way for open conflict with the bureaucracy' (ibid., 285). However, 'the present state of production is . . . adequate to give significant privileges to a minority and to convert inequality into a whip for spurring on the majority'. Deliberate imbalance of supply and effective demand for consumer goods (caused by assigning priority to producer goods) was crucial to the role played by inequality and bureaucratic prerogatives: 'When queues are very long, it is necessary to appoint a policeman to keep order. Such is the starting-point of the power of Soviet bureaucracy. It "knows" who is to get something and who has to wait' (ibid., 112–13). Naturally bureaucratic degeneracy would afflict 'proletarian' regimes 'everywhere', but 'the poorer the society issuing from a revolution . . . the cruder would be the forms assumed by bureaucratism' (ibid., 55). The 'ignorant', 'rude' and 'pretentious' Soviet bureaucracy could manage the rough work of borrowing, imitating, transplanting and grafting advanced capitalist techniques. It could 'build gigantic factories to a ready-made Western pattern by bureaucratic command', albeit 'at triple the normal cost'. However, 'the further you go, the more the economy runs into the problem of quality. . . . Soviet products seem branded with the grey label of indifference. In a nationalized economy, quality demands a democracy of producers and consumers, freedom of criticism and initiative – conditions incompatible with a totalitarian regime of fear, flattery and lies' (ibid., 275–6).

Ultimately, Stalin's apologists fall back on the influential thesis that his industrialization strategy was *indispensable* to Soviet military security. If so, there was no realistic alternative to Stalinism. However, as indicated on p. 91, it can be argued that the Stalinist strategy increased the military vulnerability of the USSR, above all by squandering manpower on an unprecedented scale and by antagonizing, disrupting and demoralizing large sections of Soviet society (especially the peasantry and the armed forces). By mid-1941 Soviet heavy-industrial capacity certainly looked impressive on paper, but within six months of the Nazi invasion *over half* that industrial capacity had been lost (see Nove, 1972, 270–1). Ironically the USSR nevertheless went on to win the war with a drastically reduced industrial base. The temporary political concessions which revived wartime social unity and morale proved to be much more important than the size of the Soviet heavy-industrial base.

8 The Chinese road to Stalinism

The regime established by Mao Tse-tung in 1949 was heir to a civilization which, although it was backward by contemporary Western standards, already possessed markedly higher educational, organizational, technological, commercial, agricultural and industrial capabilities than the rest of mainland Asia, excluding Russia and Korea (see Perkins, 1975, 3–17; Eckstein, 1977, 14; T. Rawski, 1980, 2, 6, 7). By 1900 some 30–45 per cent of Chinese men knew how to read and write, printing and popular literature were developing well, the Chinese were accustomed to written contracts and government through the written word, and formal educational attainment had become the main basis of official recruitment and upward mobility (E. Rawski, 1979). By 1949 China had 'over 200 higher educational institutions, 4000 secondary and 289,000 primary schools, with a total of 24,000,000 students and pupils' (Qi Wen, 1979T, 167). And already by 1955 China had 600,000 engineers and scientists (Oldham, 1973, 85), nearly ten times as many as India. The technological fecundity of China's ancient civilization has been exhaustively documented by Needham (1954–83).

By 1949 China had 82,500 km of highway, as well as 400,000 km of navigable waterway (Qi Wen, 1979T, 138–40). These roads and rivers and the fertility of the great river basins, in which most of China's inhabitants lived, made it possible for China's farmers to market 30–40 per cent of their produce (Perkins, 1969, 114) and to sustain as many as ten cities with over 500,000 inhabitants apiece and thirty cities with over 100,000 inhabitants apiece, long before the communists came to power: 'Ever since the latter half of the eighth century, the influence of money had been increasingly felt', especially along the 80,000-km navigable length of the Yangtze River and its tributaries. By 1600 the commutation of labour services was virtually complete and long-distance trade was well organized. Interregional and local trade involved grain, salt, fish, drugs, timber, hardware, pottery, cloth and luxury goods: 'This growing internal trade stimulated industries and crafts and made possible regional specialization in commercial crops' (Ho, 1959, 196–202).

Contrary to the Wittfogel view of *Oriental Despotism* (1957), China's agriculture did not depend on a strong state to maintain the irrigation, flood-control and canal systems, as these systems were 'for the most part . . . locally conceived and managed through smaller-scale group effort' (Murphey, 1977, 159). Indeed, China's irrigated area reached an unprecedented 26m. ha during 1924–33 (Perkins, 1969, 64): 'China even at its nadir was able to cope with its basic economic and organizational needs. . . . The political landscape was disintegrating, which is what foreigners saw', but 'regional and local continuity in management kept much of the functionally beneficial aspects of the system going. . . . To see the rise of regionalism after 1850 as a symptom or cause of general deterioration may well be missing the point' (Murphey, 1977, 128, 156). China's intensive agricultural systems necessarily engendered considerable local co-operation and self-discipline (see Myers, 1975, 267–77; E. Rawski, 1979, 153).

As Chinese farms were not much larger than Japanese farms (see Table 7), only approximately 15 per cent of farmwork was performed by hired labour (see Table 4). According to Mao, even China's so-called 'landlords' owned only 11.5 ha per 'landlord' household in 1934 (Bergmann, 1975T, 185), or slightly *less* than the average peasant household in pre-revolutionary Russia. Tenancy and hence 'landlordism' predominated only in parts of southern China, notably Szechuan and Kwangtung; elsewhere owner-occupancy prevailed (see Table 5; and Perkins, 1969, 91; Tawney, 1932, 63–8). Moreover, 'The agricultural wage-workers of China . . . do not form a distinct class. . . . Whatever her rural problems may be, they are not complicated by the existence of a landless proletariat', and 'Attempts to apply to the land system of China analogies drawn from the history of the West are commonly based upon misconceptions of both' (Tawney, 1932, 34, 64).

By 1931–7 China's grain yields per hectare were at least double the Indian level (see Table 12) and China's per capita grain and potato output was at least 70 per cent above the Indian level (see Table 11). The spread of war and revolution caused a fall in China's per capita grain and potato output during 1938–50, but it regained the 1931–7 level as early as 1952 (Shen, 1951, 378–82; Evans, 1978, 69; Aziz, 1978, 20):

	1931–7	1952	1953	1954	1955
Kg per capita	273	275	267	266	287

	1956	1957	1961–5	1966–9	1970–5
Kg per capita	294	292	260	287	297

Suggestions that Shen's data for 1931–7 should be revised downwards are unconvincing, if only because a downward revision would (implausibly) imply that

China's per capita grain and potato output increased between 1931–7 and 1952–5, despite the cataclysmic intervening events. Moreover, the recent Howe–Walker estimate of grain and potato output in 1930s China is 20 per cent higher than Shen's (Howe, 1978, 72).

Data for 1952 – the year in which per capita grain and potato output regained its prewar level – indicate that interregional variations in China's per capita agricultural output were remarkably small. If we discount industrialized Kiangsu (Shanghai), agricultural output per inhabitant was at least 91 per cent of the national average in all but six provinces: Honan, Shansi, Anhwei, Fukien, Szechuan and Yunan, which were respectively 82, 83, 67, 85, 80 and 75 per cent of the national average (Lardy, 1978, 12). However, if one considers *industrial* as well as agricultural output, 1950s China appears to have had comparatively large interregional disparities in output per inhabitant, because Chinese *industry* was – and has remained – very unevenly distributed (see Lardy, 1978, 12, and 1980, 160–4).

Although 70–80 per cent of China's inhabitants were more or less dependent on agriculture up to the 1960s, communist China inherited a considerable industrial base: 'By 1949 industry accounted for roughly 30% of gross national output' (Qi Wen, 1979T, 104). Industrial output had expanded 9 per cent per annum during 1912–36 and 4.5 per cent per annum during 1936–42 (Chang, 1967, 68), and as late as 1949 consumer goods made up over 70 per cent of gross industrial output (Qi Wen, 1979T, 102). Contrary to common belief, imports and factory industry did not expand at the expense of China's handicraft industries. Up to the 1950s the output and workforce of the handicraft industries on the whole continued to expand and to benefit from the new inputs, services, methods and markets provided by the very much smaller 'modern' sector (see Hou, 1965, 166–87; Kang Chao, 1975; Liu and Yeh, 1965, 66–9, 86–9). The damage inflicted on Chinese industry during 1938–50 was ephemeral: by 1952 China's industrial output was '22% higher than the highest prewar level' (Qi Wen, 1979T, 104). Between 1936 and 1952 China's iron and steel output trebled and its output of coal, electricity and cement roughly doubled, while cotton yarn output rose 30 per cent, with the result that in 1952 China's outputs of cotton yarn, pig iron and coal approximated those attained by Japan in 1936 (Perkins, 1975, 120).

Furthermore, 22,900 km of railway (two-fifths of China's present network) were built before 1949 and 17,000 km of railway were in use even in 1949 (Leung, 1980, 94). By 1936 railways had connected up China's major cities (see Murphey, 1977, map on p. 111) and 'opened up a larger and more regular market for the grain surpluses of central China' (Perkins, 1969, 167). By 1952 79 per cent of China's freight traffic was transported by rail, as against 13 per cent by road and 8 per cent by water (Leung, 1980, 112). As China's farmers marketed 30–40 per cent of their produce before 1937 (Perkins, 1969, 114), and as rail transport was considerably cheaper than the alternatives (Liang, 1981, 80), these railways must have saved China's farmers considerable expense; and the consequent evening-out in interregional price differentials and in local year-to-year fluctuations must have benefited wage-earners. Ironically, although these railways were mainly built and administered by foreign capital for private profit and for penetration of the Chinese market, they were 'barely profitable enough to pay the [5–6 per cent] interest on the loans with which they had been built' (Hou, 1965, 212–13); imports always amounted to under 10 per cent of China's GDP (Perkins, 1975, 27, 121); and as late as 1931 over three-quarters of the foreign capital invested in China was confined to Shanghai and Manchuria (Murphey, 1977, 126). Moreover, 'a great deal of the Chinese reluctance to buy foreign goods or to adopt foreign business methods or technology was entirely rational', as on the whole 'Chinese goods and methods were equal or superior and prices as low or lower', the chief exceptions being kerosene, cigarettes and, to a limited extent, certain types of imported yarn (ibid., 122). Crude nationalist and communist attempts to blame China's ills on foreign capitalist penetration were essentially fallacious: 'In China the semicolonial system was never as effective as the nationalist or Marxist argument implied. . . . The treaty port Chinese remained a resented and feeble minority, divorced from . . . the traditional order' (ibid., 225). On balance, the very peripheral foreign penetration 'probably strengthened China economically', bringing in new investment and technologies, cutting internal transport costs, introducing hitherto unavailable crops and products, broadening China's export capabilities and markets, creating new employment and training a new pool of modern industrial personnel and technicians (ibid., 125–6).

So beware assertions that China's great civilization was falling apart prior to the communist take-over: the rapid recovery of 1950–2 reveals that the inheritance was essentially intact. Also beware romantic notions that China's Communist Party was swept to power by a tidal wave of active popular support (Qi Wen, 1979T, 67; Domes, 1973T, 12, 47):

	1927	1937	1945	1950	1953
Party membership	57,900	80,000	1.2m.	4.5m.	6.1m.
% of population	0.012	0.016	0.23	0.82	1.05

On their own reckoning the communist-led troops numbered only 100,000 in 1937, 1.2 million in mid-1946 and 4 million in mid-1949 (Domes, 1973T, 12; Pichon Loh, 1965, 9). These astonishingly small forces only had to fill the void created by the snowballing disintegration of the remarkably corrupt, repressive, treacherous and faction-ridden nationalist dictatorship, which eventually discredited itself in almost every possible way, promoted monetary collapse (hyperinflation) and antagonized millions of its initial supporters, especially within the army (see Pichon Loh, 1965, 1, 9, 24, 27–34, 107).

The revolutionary strategy of Chinese communism owed rather more to Stalin than is commonly realized. In his 'The prospects of the revolution in China' (1926)

Stalin affirmed that 'China's national bourgeoisie is extremely weak', so 'the role of initiator and guide of the Chinese revolution, the role of leader of the Chinese peasantry, must inevitably fall to the Chinese proletariat and its party'. Formerly, 'revolutions usually began with a popular uprising, for the most part unarmed. . . . In China, armed revolution is fighting armed counter-revolution. . . . Therein lies the special significance of the revolutionary army in China.' Hence 'Communists must in every way intensify political work in the army and ensure that it becomes a genuine and exemplary vehicle of the ideas of the Chinese revolution.' In Stalin's view, 'China's future revolutionary government will generally resemble . . . a democratic dictatorship of the proletariat and the peasantry', although 'it will be first and foremost an anti-imperialist government. It will be a government transitional to a non-capitalist or, more exactly, a socialist development of China.' Hence he was 'in favour of the Chinese Communist Party taking part in China's future revolutionary government', as a step towards the establishment of proletarian 'hegemony' in China. 'Soviets – specifically peasant Soviets – could only be organized if China were at the peak of a peasant movement which was smashing the old order and building a new power.' He recognized that 'there are Kuomintangists and even Chinese Communists who consider it impossible to unleash revolution in the countryside, fearing that . . . it would disrupt the anti-imperialist front'. However, 'immediate satisfaction of the most urgent peasant demands is an essential condition for the victory of the Chinese Revolution'. He thought it was 'high time to break down this inertness and "neutrality" towards the peasantry'. But 'What means must Chinese revolutionaries adopt to rouse China's vast peasant masses to revolution? . . . The first way is to form and infiltrate peasant committees . . . vested with sufficient authority to realize peasant demands.' However, 'Anyone who thinks that some tens of thousands of Chinese revolutionaries can cover this ocean of peasants is mistaken. . . . The second way is to influence the peasantry through the apparatus of the new people's revolutionary government . . . in the newly liberated provinces', either 'by expropriating landlord's land or by reducing taxation and rents – according to circumstances. The third way is to influence the peasantry through the revolutionary army . . . the force which first penetrates new provinces.' It would depend 'primarily on the revolutionary army's behaviour, its attitude towards peasants and landlords, its readiness to aid peasants, what the peasant attitude to the new government will be' (cf. Stalin, 1952–5T, vol. 8, 373–90).

Stalin undoubtedly overestimated China's immediate revolutionary potential and the strength of the Kuomintang's radical wing, which was largely annihilated along with China's Communist Party during 1927–33. But the usual suggestions that Stalin saw the Chinese Revolution as a narrowly urban/proletarian struggle are patently untrue. On the other hand, Mao's hagiographers have generally underestimated the role of industrial areas in the Chinese Revolution. In many Chinese towns communists fostered legal front organizations and illegal underground activities in the 1930s and 1940s, repeatedly sabotaged Kuomintang supply lines and ultimately helped to deliver China's strategic cities and railways into communist hands. And Soviet historians have quite rightly emphasized that, when Mao's Yenan base was overrun by Kuomintang forces in 1947, driving Mao into hiding in a remote village in north Shansi, the centre of gravity of the Chinese Revolution shifted to semi-industrial Manchuria, which was by then largely communist-controlled (under Kao Kang and Lin Piao) and able to field by far the largest and best-equipped communist-led armies in China. It was from Manchuria that Lin Piao (not the beleaguered Mao Tse-tung) launched the decisive communist offensives of mid-1947 and 1948 (see Borisov, 1977T, 41, 45, 168–78, 181–2). The common allegations that Russia removed a large part of Manchuria's mainly Japanese-built industrial capacity, to recoup part of the cost of driving over 1 million Japanese out of Manchuria in 1945, are contradicted by Soviet claims that by 1948 Manchuria was producing 67 per cent more than it did under the Japanese (ibid., 212), that 'The restoration of industry and agriculture in Manchuria did much to sustain the People's Republic of China in the restoration period which followed its establishment', and that 'Large metallurgical, engineering, chemical, ordnance and other factories built or reconstructed in Manchuria with Soviet aid and with the active participation of Soviet specialists became the nucleus of the PRC's heavy industry' (ibid., 265). It must be admitted that the Soviet account of Soviet policy in Manchuria best explains Manchuria's roles in the civil war and in China's postwar recovery and broadly parallels Soviet policy in North Korea in the same period (see Kim, 1975, 168–72; Kuark, 1963a; Halliday, 1981, 25).

Once established in power, Mao fostered an all-pervasive cult of the leader and a one-party polity in which intra-party and non-party opposition to the leader would be crushed. According to 'cautious estimates', no less than 5 million people perished during the agrarian reforms of 1950–3 (Domes, 1973T, 38). Kao Kang, Manchuria's Party leader from 1945 to 1953, died in prison in 1955 (Borisov, 1977T, 38). During 1958–62, as a result of Mao's recklessly overambitious Great Leap Forward, some 20 million Chinese apparently perished and some 20 million workers were 'rusticated'; and in 1980 the General Secretary of China's Communist Party acknowledged that, as a result of Mao's Proletarian Cultural Revolution and its 'radical' aftermath (1966–76), about 1 million Chinese had perished and about 30 million had been persecuted (Short, 1982, 154–66): 'Every county and town has forced labour brigades, every province prison farms and factories. Vast labour camps have been built in . . . Heilongjiang and in Qinhai', and 'violence to prisoners is much more widespread than in the Soviet labour camp system'. Indeed, 'the secret police in China are much more hated than the KGB', because 'China has more political prisoners than Russia' and, 'where political struggles have pitted children against parents, husbands against wives . . . no one can be certain where the consequences of a political error will end' (ibid., 115–17).

Mao's barnstorming rhetoric and mass mobilization stratagems were prefigured, not in the staid bureaucratic orthodoxies of Stalin's last years, but in Stalin's Proletarian Cultural Revolution (see Fitzpatrick, 1978; Stalin, 1952–5T, vols 8–13). Stalin's writings continued to enjoy wide official circulation in China for two decades after their fall from official favour in the Soviet bloc; communist China 'can pride itself . . . on its faithfulness to the letter as well as the spirit of Stalinism' (Leys, 1978T, 203–4). China's infamous fulminations against 'Khrushchev's phoney communism' (1964) condemned, not Khrushchev's retention of an essentially Stalinist system, but his 'revisionist' rejection of Stalin's most reckless and inhuman excesses (see *Peking Review*, 17 July 1964, 21–6; Mao Tse-tung, 1974T, 99, 115, 181). Mao's Proletarian Cultural Revolution, like Stalin's before it, was ostensibly directed against the bureaucracy and its 'deformations' of the 'proletarian' dictatorship, but 'objectively' served to crush intra- and non-party opposition to the leader, to oust the old intelligentsia (especially within the party), and to further curtail the very limited ideological pluralism and rational exchange of views which had somehow survived hitherto. But it culminated in military repression and an even more bureaucratic and corrupt dictatorship (see Evans, 1978, 27–30, 39, 86–90, 118–19, for a trenchant Trotskyist critique; Short, 1982, for a trenchant liberal critique): 'Maoist bureaucracy today has thirty hierarchical classes, each with specific privileges and prerogatives' and 'Maoist civil servants insist on being given the exact titles, functions and positions', as 'no sacrifice is too great to keep the classes, castes and hierarchies strictly separate' (Leys, 1978T, 113–14). In 1973 China's top administrators and industrial managers were still paid ten to twenty times more than lower-grade urban workers and clerks (Eckstein, 1977, 300; Howe, 1978, 178; Leys, 1978T, 117; Short, 1982, 84–5). But 'the salary is of course only a minor consideration compared to all the other advantages deriving from power and influence: the possibility of going abroad, of sending one's children to university, of finding comfortable jobs for relatives, of getting goods in times of scarcity' (Leys, 1978T, 117). Above all, 'shortages in the countryside are compounded by the corruption of local officials. Commune and county leaders embezzle relief supplies. When ration vouchers to buy bicycles or sewing machines arrive at a production brigade, the Party secretary hands them out to his cronies; even if you have money, it's no use unless you have friends in the right place' (Short, in the *Listener*, 15 April 1982, 12).

Mao's peasant background *did not* lead him to give a high priority to rural development. As early as 1949 he announced that China's peasant masses were no longer his prime concern:

> From 1927 to the present the centre of gravity of our work has been in the villages, gathering strength in the villages, using the villages to surround and then take the cities. The period for this method of work has now ended. . . . The centre of gravity of the Party's work has shifted from the village to the city. . . . Under no circumstances should the village be ignored and only the city be given attention. . . . Nevertheless, the centre of gravity of the work of the Party and the army must be in the

cities. . . . China's modern industry, though the value of its output amounts to only about 10% of the output of the national economy, is extremely concentrated; the largest and most important part of its capital is concentrated in the hands of the imperialists and their lackeys, the Chinese bureaucrat-capitalists. Confiscation of this bureaucrat-capital and its transfer to the people's republic led by the proletariat will enable the people's republic to control the economic lifelines of the country and the State-owned economy to become the leading sector of the entire national economy. (Mao Tse-tung, 1961–5T, vol. 4, 363, 367)

To reinforce 'proletarian' hegemony the 1954 Constitution weighted representation in the National People's Congress 8:1 *against* the peasantry (Domes, 1973T, 27), and communist China's lopsided priorities have been reflected in the sectoral distribution of investment (Klatt, 1979, 732):

% of total investment	Agriculture	Light industry	Heavy industry	Other
1952	13.7	9.0	31.8	45.5
1957	8.7	8.7	49.2	33.4
1978	10.7	5.4	54.1	29.8

These data indicate that industry received over 100 times more investment per employee than agriculture in 1957 and over forty times more investment per employee than agriculture in 1978. During 1950–79 heavy industry received 51 per cent of total state investment, light industry received 6 per cent and agriculture received 11 per cent (Ishikawa, 1983, 259); by 1957 state investment made up 66 per cent of total investment (Eckstein, 1977, 188). During 1952–72 China's engineering output grew 62-fold, ferrous metallurgy 16-fold, chemicals 35-fold and petroleum 76-fold, but her output of staple textiles and processed foods rose less than 3-fold (T. Rawski, 1979, 47), and by 1975 rural industries were contributing under 5 per cent of rural employment and only 10–15 per cent of industrial output (ibid., 65). Electricity output had risen 15-fold, but in 1974 only 14 per cent was consumed by rural areas (Howe, 1978, 87). By the late 1970s 'the rural 80% of the population received only 20% of national income' (Gray and Gray, 1983, 168), indicating an urban–rural disparity of 16:1. It is inconceivable that such a wide disparity was greatly reduced by transfer payments, when in 1978 the state budget amounted to under 20 per cent of national income (see Klatt, 1979, 732) and the terms of trade were persistently *adverse* to agriculture (Klatt, 1983, 34–6).

Mao's hagiographers have sometimes misconstrued his famous speech 'On the ten great relationships' (1956) as a radical departure from the Stalinist strategy of unbalanced growth, based on heavy industry. The speech did indeed flirt with the Bukharinist ideas which had briefly regained favour in Russia and Eastern Europe following Stalin's death, but it added: 'Does this mean that heavy industry is no longer the leading sector? No, it is still the leading sector. Are we no longer to emphasize heavy industry? If the question is posed in this way, the reply is that the emphasis in investment is still to be on heavy industry' (Mao Tse-tung, 1974T, 63). Denied their due share of investment, proportionate to their contribution to popular livelihoods, agriculture and light industry were to remain lagging sectors. The vast, unwieldy, party-controlled people's communes established in 1958 were poor substitutes for the real autonomy and the major share of investment which the rural sector required if it was really to develop in tandem with the towns. Like Stalin, Mao did not significantly increase his country's per capita output of grain and potatoes, which contributed 78 per cent of Chinese calorie intake in the 1960s (see Tables 11 and 8).

In 1953–7, when Russia provided China with a great deal of industrial equipment and technological know-how (see Cheng, 1976, 128–9, 155), China's industrial output roughly doubled (Liu and Yeh, 1965, 148–50). But after 1957, despite its initial advantages, China's economic growth was comparatively slow (Sinha, 1974, 35–6; Weisskopf, 1980, 48; Taiwan, 1978; FAO Yearbooks, various issues):

Output growth (% p.a.)	China	Taiwan	South Korea	India
Industry, 1957–70	6.0	17.8	16.0	6.2
Agriculture, 1952–70	1.7	3.8	4.2	2.5
People per square kilometre, 1975	87	449	352	182

Output growth (% p.a.)	Pakistan	Indonesia	Philippines
Industry, 1957–70	9.8	(6.7)	5.5
Agriculture, 1952–70	2.8	2.2	3.2
People per square kilometre, 1975	87	69	142

(Contrary to common belief, in 1970 China had more farmland per farm inhabitant than Taiwan, South Korea and Indonesia – see Table 6.) Many Sinologists cite much higher Chinese growth-rate statistics. However, as in other communist states, the accounting conventions employed in Chinese gross output calculations involve a great deal of double-counting of intermediate products, whose importance has greatly increased over time. My scepticism is reinforced by the following consideration: if Taiwan's per capita GNP was one and a half times that of mainland China in 1953 and 1957 and six times that of mainland China by 1978, and if Taiwan's per capita GNP rose approximately 5.5 per cent per annum during 1953–78, as indicated in Chapter 2, then China's per capita GNP must have risen by roughly 0.0 per cent per annum during 1953–78; output merely kept pace with population growth, which averaged 2 per cent per annum in the same period (see Table 1). Admittedly, Mao ensured that some of the additional resources generated by China's economy were used to greatly reduce her mortality and illiteracy rates, but here too China's achievements were exceeded – with far less upheaval – by right-wing Taiwan and South Korea (see Tables 2 and 3).

Under Mao China managed to feed a population which rose 2 per cent per annum (Table 1) and to provide work for a rural workforce which expanded from approximately 243 million in 1957 to approximately 342 million in 1975 (1.9 per cent p.a.). These feats were based on rural collectivization; increased irrigation, flood control and terracing of hillsides; a shift towards more labour-intensive crops; a lengthening of the 'average' farmer's working year (from some 159 days p.a. in 1957 to 250 days p.a. in 1975); intensified use of organic and inorganic fertilizers, double-cropping, intercropping and transplanting; some mechanization of milling, pumping and traction; and an expansion of forestry, fish-farming, rural industry and rural transport (T. Rawski, 1979, 35, 75–118). However, the pace of technical advance was too slow to avert the onset of diminishing returns: output per man-day in Chinese agriculture fell from approximately 1.46 yuan in 1957 to between 0.94 and 1.24 yuan in 1975, at 1957 prices; and total factor productivity in Chinese agriculture fell 26–36 per cent over the same period (ibid., 119–20). Whether we take the 1930s or the 1950s as a base, grain output per hectare and per inhabitant rose more slowly in China than in heavily populated Taiwan, Korea (both halves), India, Pakistan, Indonesia and the Philippines (see Tables 11 and 12; and Sinha, 1974, 36). Machinery, chemical fertilizer, electricity and cement inputs into Chinese agriculture grew 21–24 per cent per annum during 1957–8 (T. Rawski, 1979, 82), but these percentage increases impress only because the starting-points were so low; 'in 1978 fewer than one rural labourer in fifteen could operate machinery of any kind' (Short, 1982, 101). China's irrigated area reached 47.4m. ha in 1975, as against 26.5m. ha in 1929–33 (T. Rawski, 1979, 111); but this increase merely matched the intervening population increase, and in 1980 it was 'stated that, "due to failure to link up projects and to poor management", the water utilization rate was under 50%' (Gray and Gray, 1983, 167). According to Mao's successors, compulsory state appropriation of 30–40 per cent of China's farm produce and the unwieldy bureaucratic structure of the oversized people's communes prior to the decentralizing reforms of 1978–83 fostered inertia, apathy, waste, corruption and local autarky, and discouraged initiative, innovation, proper accounting, individual and group responsibility, honesty, promotion of able young farmers, demotion of ageing party hacks, efficient use of capital and labour and quality control (ibid., 168–74). Officially this is why, since 1978, the sale of farm produce has been liberalized while agricultural responsibilities have been devolved to the lowest possible levels. However, such moves also help to undermine the Maoist power base in the people's communes, which had created over 10 million administrative posts (Klatt, 1983, 28).

Besides stimulating sustainable increases in agricultural labour productivity, the crucial problem confronting Mao's successors will be how to absorb most of the future increase in China's workforce into non-agricultural employments (including rural industries). Having expanded 2.4 per cent per annum in 1957–75, China's workforce will expand approximately 2.7 per cent per annum up to 1990, due to

138   Communism and Development

births which have already taken place; and already in 1979 the urban workforce of 100 million included 13–20 million unemployed (White, 1983, 259; *The Economist*, 29 December 1979, 22; *Financial Times*, 10 November 1981). Unfortunately, most of China's mineral wealth lies offshore and in the remote, sparsely populated western interior, where development costs are high and infrastructure, expertise and equipment are very deficient (see *FT* Surveys, 1 May 1980, 29 August and 23 December 1981). The late-1970s hope that China's economy would be buoyed up by an oil export bonanza has evaporated. China is too populous to get by on windfalls, and in 1981 the Energy Bureau of China's State Economic Commission revealed that China is already in the grip of a long-term energy crisis, caused by excessive energy consumption in its bloated heavy-industrial sector. China's energy production grew 8.5 per cent per annum during 1957–80, but by 1978 her energy consumption per unit of output was four times the Third World average, four times the Western average and over double the Comecon average, even on the relatively generous World Bank estimate of China's per capita GDP (*FT* Survey, 14 December 1981, iv; World Bank, 1980, 111, 122–3). As a sop to Maoist megalomania, the September 1982 Party Congress pledged a 7.2 per cent annual rate of economic growth and a doubling of China's steel output between 1982 and 2000; but any attempt to honour these pledges will court disaster (*FT* Survey, 23 November 1982, ii). Sober calculations indicate that, even if Western-assisted offshore oil development proceeds smoothly and fruitfully, China's overall energy position will get considerably tighter up to 1990 (*FT* Energy Review, 27 October 1982). This in turn means that China's capacity to pay for imported capital, equipment and know-how will remain severely constrained and that how much other countries will be able to sell to China will ultimately depend on how far they are willing to buy Chinese manufactures, rather than the minerals which China will need for its own consumption in the continuing struggle to feed and employ its ever-expanding population.

Frankly, there is no easy or very promising way out of communist China's substantially self-inflicted difficulties. A return to the lopsided Maoist emphasis on high-cost, mineral-intensive heavy industries would only exacerbate its existing resource bottlenecks. There are prudential as well as ideological constraints on China's recent tolerance of private enterprise. Conversely, there are tight constraints on how much the state can efficiently undertake, even under socialism. Foreign investment could bring considerable benefits to coastal China, as it has done in the past, but the interior will as always have to rely on its own resources. Even if foreigners were to invest as much as US $30,000m. in China by 1990, this would amount to little more than $20 per person. So the least fraught way forward could be to promote a further groundswell of really autonomous co-operatives, especially in light industry and in the rural sector.

Where labour is plentiful and capital is scarce, the productivity of capital matters even more than the productivity of labour; and in 1973 industrial co-operatives produced 14 per cent of China's gross industrial output using just 3 per cent of her fixed industrial assets, indicating that gross output per unit of fixed capital was 5.2 times higher in industrial co-operatives than in state industry, which held 97 per cent of China's fixed industrial assets (Chang, 1975, 6). Yet in 1978–9 China's state industries employed over seven times as many persons per enterprise as did the industrial co-operatives (Lockett, 1983, table 7.1). Having swallowed nearly half China's total investment during 1950–79, China's state industries have provided jobs for only 7 per cent of its workforce. Moreover, each million yuan of fixed investment has provided only 94 jobs in heavy industry, as against 257 jobs in textiles, 800 jobs in small-scale village industries, and 800–1000 jobs in the commercial and service sectors; and it takes an average of 5 years 7 months to recoup capital outlays in heavy industry, whereas it takes only 22 months in light industry (*FT Survey*, 19 October 1983, v; White, 1983, 267). Furthermore, investment in light industry is generally seven times more profitable and engenders four times less energy consumption than equivalent investment in heavy industry (Short, 1982, 395). In sum, China should try to cut its losses through further retrenchment in the inefficient heavy industries and further diversion of resources into smaller-scale, light-industrial co-operatives, which would further enhance incentives and promote fuller utilization of scarce capital and energy.

Unfortunately there are dangers that, in mobilizing support for a proliferation of co-operatives and an influx of foreign capital, Mao's successors will arouse and perhaps fall victim to unrealistically high expectations. The benefits from foreign investment will be very localized. It will be hard to avoid disaffection among those who fail to get on the gravy train, and this is bound to be exploited by discomfited hard-liners, by the powerful heavy-industry lobby and by the poorly equipped armed forces (On military discontent, see *Financial Times*, 4 February 1982, 23 June 1981). However, as the outbreak of famine in Hopei and Hupei in 1980 made clear, 'the tightness of grain supplies and the uncertainties of China's monsoon climate leave less room for manoeuvre than had been hoped' (Gray and Gray, 1983, 167): 'The level of grain consumption per head is by far the most important indicator of human welfare in China', yet 'average grain consumption per head of rural population probably fell from 258 kilograms (unhusked) in 1955–57 to 252 in 1978–79' (Walker, 1982, 575, 588). The room for manoeuvre is further restricted by inequalities within the rural sector: 'The richest provinces . . . have more than twice the average per capita rural income of the poorest province' and 'The 10 million peasants around Beijing and Shanghai have an average distributed collective income which is two to two-and-a-half times the national average', or three to four times the average for the poorest province (Vermeer, 1982, 20–2). 'In the agriculturally favoured areas, income from collective work can be two to three times as high as in the poorer parts of the country', and in the late 1970s 'on the outskirts of large cities per capita incomes of 200–300 yuan were earned, whilst some counties in poorer areas . . . had incomes of about 30 yuan' (Klatt, 1983, 30, 32). In 1978 distributed collective income in the rural sector averaged 75 yuan per capita, but 'about one third of China's production teams had an average distributed collective income below 50 yuan per capita, of which 16.5% were below 40 yuan'; in 1979 distributed rural collective income in the rural sector averaged 84 yuan per capita, but for 27 per cent of China's production teams it was below 50 yuan per capita; and income differentials within people's communes and within production teams ranged up to 3:1 (Vermeer, 1982, 17–20, 30). In 1980 per capita personal income from collective work averaged 83.4 yuan in the rural sector, as against 427 yuan – five times as much – in the state sector (Ishikawa, 1983, table 4).

With so many Chinese peasants still living precariously close to the margins of subsistence, any future social convulsion or retreat from the recent emphasis on agriculture and light industry could again imperil millions of lives. However, the present policy of penalizing couples who have more than one child is not an appropriate remedy: the heaviest penalties will fall on those families who are least able to pay; the children in those families will suffer through no fault of their own; in the longer term the policy could produce a very high proportion of elderly people in the total population; this ageing population could constitute a far heavier burden for China than it does for the comparatively rich Western states; and the policy is obviously conducive to bribery, extortion and agonizing parental choices. Moreover, China is less densely populated than most of its South and East Asian neighbours (see p. 136) and its population growth has been somewhat slower than that of most other Asian states (see Appendix, Table 1). It is with respect to output growth, not population growth, that China compares unfavourably with its South and East Asian neighbours (see p. 136 and Table 11). Therefore, instead of pursuing invidious population policies, China would do better to liberalize and decentralize its economy sufficiently to sustain higher output growth, especially in agriculture and light industry. Those who spurn output growth in favour of 'distributive justice' seem to forget that, without output growth, there will be little to distribute.

9 Further lessons from
forced industrialization:
Russia, China and Eastern Europe

This chapter further examines the rationale, results and institutional requirements of the Stalinist industrialization strategy, which was adopted with remarkably few modifications in most of the communist states established during 1945–53, and highlights the integral roles played by education, health care, housing, transport, indirect taxation and income inequalities in the pursuit of Stalinist goals.

The command economy

Institutionally, comprehensive mandatory central planning requires an effective hierarchical chain of command through which production and investment decisions can be grasped, transmitted downwards, monitored and enforced in disaggregated form at intermediate and plant levels. Except in Hungary and Yugoslavia, which have abandoned comprehensive mandatory central planning since 1968 and 1965, respectively, communist states have on the whole met this requirement by subordinating each major industry and enterprise to a branch-related Economic Ministry or one of its subdivisions or agencies. Unfortunately this operationally necessary separation of hierarchies and responsibilities has bred 'suboptimization': each Economic Ministry and enterprise, in attempting to enhance or sustain its own performance rating and remuneration according to designated criteria (principally output targets), has tended to pull the economy as a whole away from optimal resource allocation. Thus each Economic Ministry has naturally tried to minimize its enterprises' dependence on (unreliable) inputs from enterprises subject to other ministries and each enterprise has naturally tried to minimize its dependence on (unreliable) inputs from enterprises outside its control. Conversely, the paramount concern of each enterprise and Economic Ministry has naturally been to fulfil its most remunerative main assignments, rather than subsidiary obligations to others, as rewards for the former have necessarily outweighed penalties for underfulfilment of the latter; and the more ambitious the main assignments, the stronger the pull towards high-cost ministerial and enterprise autarky (e.g. in the 1950s Industrial Ministries and railways tended to develop their own dependable but high-cost energy sources, thereby delaying the change-over from widely available solid fuels to cheaper and more efficient oil and gas). That is, the command economy has fostered vertical links and hierarchies rather than the horizontal inter-enterprise links and the gains from trade and specialization fostered by market economies. And enterprises operating under regional chains of command, e.g. in minority Soviet republics and in the separate provinces of China, have naturally tended to foster another form of 'suboptimization': regional autarky, impeding interregional specialization. Indeed, subdivision of command economies by region rather than by branch won't eliminate 'suboptimization', but will merely promote it in a different form, as Mao and Khrushchev discovered when they 'regionalized' their respective command economies in 1957–8.

A vaunted advantage of comprehensive central planning is that it should permit high-level *ex ante* co-ordination of production and investment decisions. 'What actually exists, as in any centrally administered economy, is an endless number of plans, constantly evolving, which are coordinated *ex post*'; and 'Unification of these innumerable plans into a single national plan, supposedly coherent, takes place rarely' (Zaleski, 1980T, 484). As the command economy develops greater complexity (by 1953 the USSR had 9490 monitored plan indices and over 20 million listed product types), many powers formally vested in high-level agencies are 'actually exercised by much lower echelons' (ibid., 485–6). So central planning is not as comprehensive and coherent as it appears. Even in the most centralized heavy industries Soviet plant managers have always been expected to display initiative: to experiment with new products and processes before practice becomes standardized; to bid for resources; to negotiate contracts; to decide which of the many mutually inconsistent orders from above should be fulfilled and in what sequence; and to decide their own input mix. Under Stalin there was 'contempt for any manager afraid to break the law and risk punishment in order to better carry out his duties', and 'Many directors regarded themselves as absolute "bosses" of their own plants' and as 'feudal lords outside Soviet law' (Granick, 1951, 191–9). Heavily shielded from financial disciplines and customers' grievances, managers naturally learned how to falsify their production and sales records with impunity, how to fob their customers off with junk and how to hoard hidden reserves of productive capacity in order to cope with importunate orders from above (Berliner, 1957, chs 6–10). Moreover, 'Awareness of a common interest in plan fulfilment often generates within the enterprise a "family relationship" in which party secretary, chief accountant and other control officials facilitate or overlook the transgressions of an enterprising director' (ibid., 319, 212, 324). Furthermore, as late as 1950 unplanned private enterprise contributed approximately 22 per cent of Soviet national income (the proportion has been still higher in most other communist states) and 'the second economy is a kind of spontaneous surrogate economic reform that imparts a necessary modicum of flexibility and responsiveness to a formal set up that is too often paralysing in its rigidity' (Grossman, 1977).

However, the degree to which planned economies conform to prescribed patterns shouldn't be the main measure of their success or failure. Generally the most useful functions of economic planning have been to generate relatively comprehensive economic information, to highlight the critical bottlenecks and hence the most urgent economic tasks, and to promote a producers' consensus on immediate and long-term priorities – or what the French call *concertation*. (I wouldn't deny that such advantages can be obtained without undergoing the rigours of authoritarian state socialism; they have been obtained under indicative planning in a pluralistic capitalist democracy since the mid-1950s – see Siebel, 1975; Bauchet, 1970; Martin, 1964. The tendency to equate economic planning with unacceptable forms of socialism has been one of the misfortunes of the English-speaking world in recent decades.) The benefits of *concertation* mainly arise from the interaction of central, intermediate and plant-level decision-makers during the perpetual process of plan formulation and readjustment. So the effectiveness of economic planning partly depends on how *freely* decision-makers can express their views and demands and on the efficiency of the feedback and readjustment mechanisms. Unfortunately the conditions under which Stalinist planning agencies have operated haven't always been conducive to an accumulation of competence.

Stalinist 5-Year Plans have also been used to mobilize the masses by dangling before them the carrot of imminent abundance, the Promised Land of 'proletarian' socialism. But the priority given to producer goods industries has normally expanded consumer demand faster than the supply of consumer goods, thereby aggravating shortages and inflationary pressures, and building up popular disillusionment and demoralization.

But, for all its shortcomings, the command economy may be the only way in which a Stalinist industrialization strategy and all-pervasive Party control can be sustained over long periods; and, once established, the requisite bureaucratic apparatus has a great capacity for self-perpetuation, for defending its sectional interests and prerogatives, for reasserting itself through thick and thin. Admittedly, until the late 1950s, Stalinist hegemony in the international Communist movement largely precluded alternative systems and strategies. Subsequently there was greater leeway in principle, but by then the basic moulds had set and they have proven remarkably durable and resistant to fundamental reform, even in Kadar's Hungary (see Jeffries, 1981, especially chs 1 and 8).

The problems of centralized economic planning and co-ordination have been greatly complicated by the inevitable proliferation of plants, processes, products and product specifications and the equally inevitable growth of economic interdependence as large-scale industrialization proceeds, despite a common presumption that such problems should become less intractable in the later stages of industrialization. And although electronic and mathematical advances have helped to streamline some aspects of the planning process, Party and state bureaucracies have been understandably reluctant to have their power and prerogatives usurped either by computers and computer specialists or by decentralized market forces, despite wide recognition that central planning and co-ordinating agencies are chronically congested and overloaded and that measures to decentralize decision-making, to make prices more accurately reflect relative costs and scarcities, and to increase the role of profitability criteria and market forces would increase overall and microeconomic efficiency and the pressure on enterprises to produce products that people actually want (see Nove, 1980; Höhmann et al., 1975, chs 1–12 and 17; Feuchtwang and Hussain, 1983).

Inefficient growth patterns

In the West, since the early nineteenth century, economic growth has been achieved largely by qualitative changes in and increasingly efficient use of resource inputs; increased resource inputs have accounted for only about one-fifth of total economic growth thereby avoiding severe pressure on popular consumption levels (see Kuznets, 1966, 490–7). By contrast, at least until the early 1960s, nearly all the communist states – including Russia and China – expanded their economies mainly by 'mobilizing' ever-increasing resource inputs on a scale conducive to inefficient resource utilization and severe pressure on popular consumption levels (see Wilczynski, 1972, 20–39; Fallenbuchl, 1970). In general, communist states have annually reinvested some 25–35 per cent of national income, or over double the proportions pertaining to the corresponding stages in Western capitalist industrialization.

To illustrate: from 1928 to 1958 (excluding the war years, 1941–5) the Soviet economy expanded 5 per cent per annum, at 1937 factor costs; but fixed capital stock expanded 8 per cent per annum, total workforce 2.3 per cent per annum and energy consumption 10 per cent per annum (Bergson and Kuznets, 1963, 6; Campbell, 1980, 10). Truncated population growth (0.6 per cent p.a.) was offset by increasing the 'productive' proportion of adults aged 15–64 from 57 per cent in 1928 to 70 per cent in 1937 and 72 per cent in 1950, and by lengthening the average working year – traditional holidays (over 100 days p.a. before 1917) were largely suppressed, and in agriculture the average working year rose from 120 to 185 days per annum (Wilber, 1969, 35). Household expenditure fell from 80 per cent of GNP in 1928 to 53 per cent by 1937, 49 per cent by 1940 and only 46 per cent by 1950 (Bergson, 1961, 237).

Moreover, except in Bulgaria, Cuba and Mongolia, communist industrialization has been based mainly on metallurgical, heavy engineering, fuel and power industries (see Table 15), whose products are largely consumed as inputs into further industrial output – mainly in heavy industry (see Chenery and Watanabe, 1958, 493). Conversely, except in a few mineral export economies, capitalist industrialization has been based on mass production of consumer goods, entailing increased popular consumption of manufactures from the outset (see Table 15; and Hoffman, 1958T, appendices; Dobb, 1963, 13, 14, 30).

To illustrate: in the USSR during 1928–55 heavy industries received 34 per cent of gross investment, as against only 5 per cent for light industries and 12 per cent for agriculture (USSR, 1977, 436); so while industrial output rose by an impressive 9 per cent per annum (Nove, 1959, 40–1), the share of metallurgy and engineering in the output of factory industry jumped from 19 per cent in 1928 to 45 per cent in 1937 and 65 per cent in 1955 (Table 15), the share of all heavy industries in gross industrial output jumped from 39.5 per cent in 1928 to 61 per cent in 1940 and 70.5 per cent in 1955 (USSR, 1977, 171), and yet per capita output of food and textiles – the staple consumer goods – fell by over 20 per cent in the 1930s and popular consumption never regained 1928 or 1913 levels until about 1958 (see Tables 11, 14(b) and 16; and Chapman, 1963, 38–9).

Even in China, where the need to raise popular consumption levels has been far greater than in Russia, the per capita output of staple foods and textiles has hardly increased under communist rule, because there too the main efforts have gone into building costly, inefficient, capital-intensive heavy industries whose products are mostly consumed by other heavy industries (see Tables 11, 16, 15 and Chapter 8).

Furthermore, the most readily available data on the effectiveness of investment in the 1950s and 1960s in Russia, China and Eastern Europe indicate that all three areas experienced very adverse trends in the amount of investment required to produce a given increment in output (see Wilczynski, 1972, 36; Fallenbuchl, 1970, 474; Ishikawa, 1983, 257–8).

Backward and forward linkages: the Hirschman fallacy

Professor C. K. Wilber, a leading 'Hirschman school' advocate of 'unbalanced growth', has argued that Stalinism 'pursued a "shock" strategy of bottlenecks successively created and resolved', thus identifying and attracting resources into those activities which would yield the highest cumulative economic pay-off: 'The industries that are bottlenecks will have a high social marginal product and thus should receive large investment allocations' (see Wilber, 1969, 87–9). Like Hirschman (1958, 106–7), he quotes evidence from Chenery and Watanabe (1958) on industrial interdependence in the USA, Japan, Italy and Norway as evidence that the industries 'pushed' by Stalinist regimes – fuel, metallurgy, electricity, chemicals and machine building – exhibit comparatively strong 'backward linkages' (bought-in inputs, stimulating suppliers) and 'forward linkages' (production of goods used by other industries). Likewise an authority on Chinese industrialization claims that 'it is the industrial sector – and especially engineering, chemicals, metallurgy, mining and other branches of the producer goods sector – whose output is essential to the transformation of society's production possibilities', to be accomplished by 'basic industries having a myriad of interindustrial links' (T. Rawski, 1979, 45–6). This certainly echoes Marxist–Leninist precepts. However, Chenery and Watanabe (1958, 493) actually estimated industrial interdependence to be as seen in the table below:

Purchased material inputs as percentages of output ('backward linkages'):

1 Grain milling	89	11 Chemicals	60	20 Electricity	27		
2 Textiles	69	Vehicles	60	21 Fishing	24		
Clothing	69	13 Shipbuilding	58	22 Coalmining	23		
4 Leather goods	66	14 Paper	57	23 Metal mining	21		
Iron and steel	66	15 Machinery	51	24 Services	19		
6 Petroleum products	65	Rubber products	51	25 Other mining	17		
7 Coal products	63	17 Printing and		26 Commerce	16		
8 Food processing	61	publishing	49	27 Oil and gas	15		
Timber products	61	18 Transport	31				
Non-ferrous metals	61	Agriculture	31				

Percentages of output consumed as inputs into other industries ('forward linkages'):

1 Oil and gas	97	11 Electricity	59	19 Fishing	36		
2 Metal mining	93	12 Textiles	57	20 Services	34		
3 Coalmining	87	13 Other mining	52	21 Machinery	28		
4 Non-ferrous metals	81	14 Rubber products	48	22 Transport	26		
5 Paper products	78	15 Printing and		23 Vehicles	20		
Iron and steel	78	publishing	46	24 Commerce	17		
7 Agriculture	72	16 Grain milling	42	25 Food processing	15		
8 Chemicals	69	17 Timber products	38	26 Shipbuilding	14		
9 Petroleum products	68	18 Leather goods	37	27 Clothing	12		
10 Coal products	67						

These data suggest that consumer goods industries generate stronger 'backward linkages' than do producer goods industries, that extractive industries exhibit the largest 'forward linkages' and that engineering scores unimpressively on both counts. Moreover, 'backward linkages are much more clear-cut in their stimulating effects than forward linkages', because 'whilst backward linkage creates demand, forward linkage depends upon the existence or anticipation of demand' (Wilber, 1969, 88), so the communist states presumably would have reaped greater and more dependable 'linkages' by emphasizing consumer goods rather than producer goods industries – and engineering least of all. That would also have reacted more positively on consumption levels, work incentives, morale, health, employment potential, town–country relations, capital scarcity, price stability and net economic growth. Moreover, 'backward linkages' from consumer goods industries go largely into agriculture, where they benefit more people than heavy industry does.

'Gigantomania'

By the mid-1970s Soviet and East European industry employed, on average, about *ten times* as many people per enterprise as did industry under 'monopoly capitalism' (World Bank, 1979, 200; Lorenz, 1982):

USSR	Hungary	Romania	East Germany	Yugoslavia	Bulgaria
712	1070	1480	297	531	520

USA	Canada	Japan	West Germany	Britain	Italy
53*	58/53*	15*	149/80*	87/66*	8*

Belgium	Switzerland	Sweden	Spain	Brazil	South Korea
35	15*	68	14*	54	49

* Employees per 'industrial establishment'.

In China, in 1978, state industries employed 887 people per enterprise and industrial co-operatives employed 78 people per enterprise, on average (Feuchtwang and Hussain, 1983, 183). In 1975 China's vaunted rural industries provided under 5 per cent of rural employment and only 10–15 per cent of industrial output (T. Rawski, 1979, 51–5, 43, 62–5). Indeed, the share of small workshops in China's manufacturing output had declined from 76 per cent in 1933 to 25 per cent in 1957, on constant definitions and at 1933 and 1952 prices (Liu and Yeh, 1965, 66).

To see why the Stalinist bias towards bigness came about one must examine Soviet experience. In the first place, for Lenin, 'handicraft industry is pure capitalism' (see Chapter 3) and Leninist regimes have therefore regarded it with ideological disfavour. In 1929–33 Russia's craft industries were largely absorbed into state industry (Kaufman, 1962, 2, 3, 19–21, 71):

	Employment (full-time equivalent)			Share of industrial output (%)		
	1913	1928	1933	1913	1928	1933
State industry	2.86m.	3.1m.	9.4m.	66	71	92
Craft industries*	2.95m.	2.4m.	0.4m.	34	29	8

* Three-quarters of employment and two-thirds of output was rural in 1913.

'Indeed, much of what appears to be growth . . . is often a statistical mirage: as productive capacity is transferred from scattered workshops to a single large establishment . . . formerly unrecorded output suddenly enters statistical annals.' In the USSR 'this illusion of growth was magnified by . . . publishing only large-scale output for the years in which the small-scale sector was being rapidly absorbed'. During 1913–33, 36 and 39 per cent of the growth of production and employment in large-scale (state) industry 'can be attributed to absorption of the small-scale sector'. Even rural co-operatives foundered on the Stalinist practice of pre-empting scarce resources for state industry (Kaufman, 1962, xv, 7, 42). This helps to explain how light industry appeared to boom in 1929–33, while popular consumption levels actually fell; how the rural sector forfeited valuable sources of income, capital, consumer goods and farm tools, along with important stimuli to entrepreneurship, skill acquisition and rural specialization; and how rural collectivization contributed to urban 'primitive socialist accumulation' at peasant expense in 1929–33, despite the setbacks in Soviet agriculture.

Fortunately China and Eastern Europe made greater use of village industries, and Brezhnev allowed village industries to produce about 5 per cent of Soviet industrial output and to employ 0.8 million people by 1975, although these modifications fall far short of the protracted positive role of rural 'proto-industrialization' in European and Japanese capitalist industrialization (see Mendels, 1972; Jones, 1968; Braun, 1967; Rosovsky and Ohkawa, 1961; Smith, 1969; Mokyr, 1974; Dawson, 1896).

Stalinist 'gigantomania' is also bound up with problems of industrial management, training and labour absorption. The massive expansion of Soviet industrial, construction and transport employment from 5.8 million in 1928 to 16 million in 1940 (see USSR, 1957, 251, present territory) mainly recruited inexperienced, un-skilled and undisciplined peasant labour and greatly overshot Plan targets and formal training provisions. Only about one-quarter of new industrial recruits received formal industrial training, so most had to make do with informal on-the-job instruction, provided on a scale analogous to the absorption of several million immigrants from peasant Europe into American industry in 1881–1914 (Granick, 1967, 108–9). In *Pravda* on 29 December 1934 Stalin presented the problem thus:

> We confronted a dilemma: either . . . to postpone the production and mass utiliz-ation of machines, for ten years, until technically trained people are turned out by the schools; or to proceed directly to the construction and mass-utilization of machines, so that in the very process of building and utilizing machines people would be taught technique and trained cadres would be turned out. We chose the second alternative. We proceeded openly and consciously to the inevitable outlays and over-expenditures attendant upon a shortage of adequately trained people. . . . True, in the process we destroyed many machines. But . . . we won the most important thing – time – and we created the most precious thing – cadres.

In fact 'there is no reason to assume that Soviet planners faced an either/or choice. . . . A less precipitous infusion of unskilled labour into industry would not only have reduced the wastage of scarce equipment, but would have made it easier for seasoned workers to tutor new recruits' (Erlich, 1967, 251–2). None the less, with US precedents in mind, Stalin's regime chose to purpose-build giant, vertically integrated, highly autarkic enterprises, designed to concentrate on long production runs of narrow ranges of rugged, standardized products, to use single-purpose equipment and unskilled labour and to reap large economies of scale – including savings on design, tooling-up, maintenance, training, materials handling, inventory, production scheduling, transport, management and planning costs: 'Soviet conversion to flow-type production with raw labour represented a major program of on-the-job training. Large numbers of peasant youth could be brought into immediate contact with machinery and given a rudimentary education in its use' (Granick, 1962, 155). However, many of the supposed advantages of the preferred form of industrial organization proved to be illusory or misconstrued. The internal supervisory, training and co-ordinating requirements of giant 'American-style' enterprises were *more* – not less – formidable than those of smaller enterprises. Reduced need for craft skills was offset by increased need for educated, disciplined workers, 'able to function within a relatively sophisticated production organization', and raw peasant youths did not adapt to this any more readily than to smaller forms of industrial organization (Granick, 1967, 87–9). Moreover, for best effect, giant enterprises need to operate in a sea of small firms which can furnish the flexibility, custom-made products and services which mass producers don't efficiently provide for themselves. Narrow product ranges do not satisfy the increasingly variegated needs of the users of producer goods (let alone consumer goods) in a developing economy. However, inasmuch as Soviet enterprises broadened their product ranges, they failed to reap the economies of mass production for which they had been built, often at exorbitant costs. To pay off, continuous flow production also demands stringent quality control, tight work schedules and stable technical norms, all of which are unsustainable in enterprises dependent upon raw peasant labour in an economy undergoing major technical changes. And inasmuch as 'sink-or-swim' methods of training wreck or even temporarily immobilize scarce equipment, it becomes advisable to divert resources from new projects into more formal training on existing installations, so as to spread the available expertise less thinly (see Granick, 1967, 112–21).

China's predominantly peasant workforce increased from approximately 280 million in 1957 to 420 million in 1975 (2.3 per cent p.a.). Although state-sector industry, construction and transport absorbed only one-quarter of the increase, this nevertheless means that they trebled their workforce by absorbing 36 million additional employees – an even more formidable task than that undertaken by Soviet industry, construction and transport (see T. Rawski, 1979, 35, 37).

Stalinist regimes also rapidly absorbed millions of peasants into proletarian occupations in Eastern Europe. Connor (1977) has assembled statistical sampling data on the percentage of the population who had 'risen' out of the peasantry:

	Czecho-slovakia (1967)	Hungary (1973)	Poland (1972)	Bulgaria (1967)	Romania (1970)	Yugoslavia (1960)
Peasant to worker	50%	49%	34%	50%	(41%)	26%
Peasant to non-manual	21%	11%	10%	10%	(14%)	11%

Factor proportions

In theory, Stalinism favoured capital- rather than labour-intensive methods, especially in priority industries. It underpriced capital goods, heavily subsidized heavy industries, renounced 'capitalist' interest charges on capital (both in selecting and in funding investment projects), subordinated cost and profitability considerations to a paramount imperative to fulfil overambitious physical output targets, measured production costs in terms of labour input, fostered cults around inappropriate capital-intensive US technologies, indiscriminately extolled capital intensity, lavished publicity and resources on gigantic long-gestation projects (encouraging 'inflation' of investment proposals and 'gigantomania'), repeatedly initiated too many new projects instead of extending or completing existing ventures (thus further pinning down capital in long-gestation projects) and engendered powerful forces of inertia ('steel-eating' interests, bureaucratic inertia in the ministerial/ planning system). Vast amounts of capital were indeed squandered by Stalinist regimes. Yet in the USSR the ratio of net capital stock to GNP remained remarkably stable (Moorsteen and Powell, 1966, 367). The relative scarcity of capital couldn't be abolished by socialist fiat, even with depressed consumption levels. Nor could the relative scarcity of venture capital be greatly alleviated by the emergence of an enlarged industrial base in the later 1930s, as the burden of routine replacement investment increased correspondingly. So, whether by design or by default, shortage of capital could only result in capital rationing, however crude. The outcome was severest on light industry, agriculture, housing and services. But even inherently capital-intensive heavy industries had to skimp or choose capital-saving, labour-intensive methods wherever feasible – notably in materials handling, repair and maintenance provisions, tooling, assembly, fitting, quality control and clerical support (see Granick, 1967, ch. 6). And while capital-intensive 'imported' technologies were concentrated in key processes for maximum pay-off, ancillary activities and construction were left to poorly equipped, lower-grade workers (e.g. women and 'raw recruits' from the peasantry) or to forced labour. The latter was concentrated in new mining/manufacturing sites in remote, inhospitable regions, where Stalin's penal labour camps averaged some 8 million inmates from 1936 to 1950 (Conquest, 1971, 472, 482, 710). Also the utilization of rapidly proliferating industrial installations was stepped up via additional labour inputs: the shift-coefficient of Soviet industry (total workforce ÷ workforce in the main shift) was raised from 1.3 (pre-1914) to 1.55 in 1930 and 1.73 in 1932, whence it slowly declined to 1.55 in 1959 (Spulber, 1964T, 500; Wilber, 1969, 96); flexible rostering kept key installations working six or seven days per week, incidentally diminishing their working lives and problems of obsolescence (Granick, 1962, 151, and 1967, 101); manning levels 'must have been increased by something like a third or more per machine' in 1929–32, thus providing assistance in feeding and removing work from machines and useful stand-ins for the principal operatives (ibid., 105–6); and installations were kept in service far longer than would have been profitable under a capitalist regime, in effect substituting additional energy consumption and repair work for replacement investment. However, this last practice was a mixed blessing, as energy supplies were strained until the 1950s and it also meant that approximately one-third of Soviet machine tools were laid up in repair shops and about one-third of mechanized production time was lost awaiting repairs in some branches.

Overall, even if one excludes transport, construction and forced labour, Soviet industrial employment expanded from 3.8 million in 1928 to 11 million in 1940 and 18.5 million in 1956, or 6 per cent per annum (USSR, 1957, 251, present territory). This was two-thirds as fast as industrial output growth, indicating rather modest growth of output per employee. And high investment rates substituted capital, not so much for labour as for industrial efficiency (cf. Granick, 1967, 174). Indeed, inputs were generally increased faster than an immature industrial system could have been expected to efficiently use them, and lopsided emphasis on output growth crowded out cost considerations (including human costs).

Moreover, it is doubtful whether any command economy has yet devised resource-conserving mechanisms anywhere near as effective as the commercial/financial disciplines inherent in relatively open market economies. For example, command economies generally use about twice as much energy per inhabitant as do market economies with comparable per capita GNPs (see Table 20), and twice as much energy per unit of GDP as either the Third World or the West (Table 19). This is not to be complacent about energy consumption in market economies, but merely to note that command economies are twice as inefficient.

Towards economic and technological self-reliance?

The value of imports into Russia fell from approximately 12 per cent of national income pre-1914 to under 5 per cent of national income under Stalin. Imported producer goods made up 12–14 per cent of Soviet investment in 1929–32, but under 3 per cent thereafter, and foreign credits made up only 3 per cent of Soviet investment at their peak in 1928–32 (Holzman, 1963; Baykov, 1946; Turpin, 1977).

Likewise China's imports have amounted to only 2–4 per cent of its national income since 1950 and the share of imported capital goods in Chinese investment fell from approximately 40 per cent in the 1950s to approximately 10 per cent in the 1970s (Eckstein, 1977, 235; Feuchtwang and Hussain, 1983, 300).

Normally industrialization increases trade dependence and the potential gains from trade and specialization. However, as late as 1974 the USSR accounted for only 3 per cent of world trade (as against 21 per cent of world industrial production); Eastern Europe accounted for only 5 per cent of world trade (as against 9 per cent of world industrial production); and other communist states accounted for only 2 per cent of world trade, as against 5 per cent of world industrial production (Wilczynski, 1977, 207). So, relatively speaking, the communist states must have greatly lost out on potential gains from international trade and specialization along lines of comparative cost advantage – mainly to their domestic consumer's disadvantage, although industry also suffers from overdependence on limited assortments of high-cost, inferior-quality, home-produced goods and equipment.

The autarkic, import-substituting policies of industrializing communist states are commonly defended on the grounds that, in the long run, they promote greater national independence, learning-by-doing, industrial technological capabilities and self-reliance. In fact nearly all the communist states have become increasingly dependent on heavily subsidized Soviet fuels, raw materials, equipment, technical aid and credit; on preferential access to 'soft' Soviet markets for their relatively inferior and unmarketable manufactures; and on Western technology and finance (see Table 21). However, their much publicized financial dependence on the West shouldn't be allowed to obscure their even greater economic dependence on the USSR. Thus even when direct financial and technical aid are excluded from the reckoning, the annual Soviet subsidy to Eastern Europe rose from about $8 billion in 1968 to about $20 billion in 1981; the annual Soviet subsidy to Cuba has exceeded one-quarter of Cuba's national income in recent years; communist Indo-China – or 'Greater Vietnam' – is so dependent on Soviet aid in so many ways that it would be hard to obtain a meaningful overall estimate; and even supposedly more non-aligned states like Romania and North Korea have remained strikingly dependent on 'soft' trade with the Soviet bloc. The USSR was able to sustain autarkic industrial growth internally and in its dependencies until 1978, thanks mainly to its vast mineral wealth, the 'captive' condition of its long-suffering consumers (260 million people by 1978), the soaring prices fetched by its primary exports to hard currency markets (oil and, intermittently, precious metals) and the indulgence of Western financial institutions and governments. But recent crises in Comecon, compounded by the inevitable tapering-off in Russia's mineral bonanza and the drying up of Western credit lines, portend an era of greater austerity and disaffection.

The apparent dichotomy or trade-off between self-reliant learning-by-doing and importation of readymade foreign technologies, plant and equipment is deceptive. In practice, they are complementary (not either/or) options, and technological choices have usually been restricted by the institutional seclusion of command economies and by the way hard currency is rationed. Moreover, Japanese and communist experience suggests that the demonstration effects of imported Western equipment, products, personnel and blueprints stimulate and accelerate the learning processes inherent in indigenous technological efforts, and that successful assimilation of Western methods has rested on creative adaptation: rethinking, redesign, remachining, retooling and repairs. The two reopenings of Japan (1854 and 1945) were fundamental to her subsequent industrial and technical virtuosity; there's every indication that the outward-looking openness of Taiwan and South Korea since the 1950s is also paying off; the most open communist states (Yugoslavia, Hungary and East Germany) have become the most successful communist exporters of manufactures to 'hard' Western markets; and, technologically, the most dynamic Soviet and Chinese industries have been those with preferential access to foreign technologies and equipment (see Sutton, 1968–72; Rawski, 1980; T. Rawski, 1979, 47–59). Conversely, the share of manufactures in China's exports and in Comecon exports to industrialized capitalist states has been rather inferior to the corresponding shares for more open, concurrently industrializing capitalist states such as India, South Korea, Spain, Portugal, Italy, Greece and – above all – Japan (see Table 22). All this tends to confirm the truism that by fostering or perpetuating economic, cultural and scientific introversion, seclusion and inertia, autarkic import-substituting policies normally retard an economy's technological performance and its capacity for self-reliance. The economic penalties are the greater: the smaller and the less diverse the economy; the smaller the number of competing firms in each industry; the more restricted the competition between domestic producers; and the broader the scope for capitalist or socialist abuse of monopolistic power. Lasting economic independence is really only attainable – at a price – in vast, naturally diverse, mineral-rich economies like Russia, China and the USA. Small states can best escape overdependence on economic superpowers not by pursuing national–autarkic delusions, but by fostering economic relations with each other and with as many different states as possible.

Furthermore, Soviet performance in industrial technology refutes simplistic beliefs that massive investment, mass production of competent pure and applied scientists, and lavish expenditure on technological research and development are passports to industrial technological success. Naturally 'scientific socialism' has exalted science and technology. Officially, Soviet R & D expenditure amounted to 0.63 per cent of national income in 1935 (as against 0.38 per cent in the USA) and 3.25 per cent of national income in the 1960s (as against 3 per cent in the USA, 2 per cent in North-west Europe and 1.5 per cent in Japan). The Soviet 'scientific' workforce grew from 10,200 in 1914 to 55,000 in 1934, 354,000 in 1960 and 770,000 in 1968 (one-quarter of the world total). By 1942 the USSR had 1421 R & D institutes (see Leontief, 1945; Hutchings, 1971). As in the USA, the main direct benefits have accrued to the military–industrial complex, enabling each superpower to produce approximately one-third of the world's military exports in recent years. But, unlike US experience, potential technical 'spin-off' from Soviet military and space programmes has been severely restricted by the forces of inertia inherent in command economies (see Campbell, 1972). Successful new civilian technologies have mainly emerged out of the spontaneous processes of 'natural selection' inherent in the cut and thrust of relatively open market economies, whereas economic planning in secluded command economies has had to be based almost wholly on well-known technologies – yesterday's already obsolescent technologies (cf. Sutton, 1968–72, vol. 3, 361–2).

Rates of technological advance have also been unimpressive in China's civilian heavy industries, in which investment and technological personnel have been concentrated at the expense of low-priority sectors. As in the USSR, élite Academies of Sciences took charge of advanced research, science strategy was set by a State Scientific and Technological Commission, applied sciences were funded and organized by the relevant industrial ministries, and graduates have been subject to direction of labour 'from above', although in practice this has caused massive misdirection of labour (see Oldham, 1973, 83–6; Howe, 1978, 28). Moreover, in the 1950s Russia supplied over 10,000 technical personnel, trained over 38,000 Chinese technical personnel in Russia, provided over 21,000 sets of scientific and technical documents and sponsored 156 large Soviet-designed enterprises in China, including 63 engineering works, 24 power stations, 21 metallurgical complexes, 27 mining enterprises, 5 chemical plants, 2 oilfields, and plants producing aircraft, tractors and motor vehicles, as well as 135 ancillary plants (Cheng, 1976, 128–9, 155). And yet in the late 1970s China's mechanical engineering was still based on 1950s technologies; China's coal industry was in much the same technological state as the Russians left it in 1960; China was still plagued by lack of roads and motor transport; and in the oil industry, China's second largest and second most capital-intensive industry, 'most current Chinese equipment and technology date from the mid-to-late 1950s' (see Hardy, 1978, 10, 24, 32, 33, 36, 40, 77, 141).

Unfortunately, unless central planners can fairly accurately anticipate technological trends five to ten years ahead and promptly incorporate their clairvoyance into disaggregated and easily monitorable entrepreneurial assignments, innovation and diffusion of new technologies must remain incidental and sometimes detrimental to plan fulfilment and to personal and collective remuneration. Therefore, most major technological changes in command economies have taken the form of recurrent, belated, party-inspired campaigns to 'catch up with and surpass' established Western practice, as perceived by remote and often capricious dictators, who have proven alarmingly susceptible to charlatans and cheap 'something-for-nothing' panaceas. However, such campaigns have to concentrate on *selected* 'leading links' or 'structure-determining tasks' or 'seminal processes', so they cannot match the ever-pervasive pressure to innovate and to diffuse new technologies found in market economies. Indeed, command economies are perpetually 'catching up', hanging on to the technological coat-tails of capitalism.

Broadly, it seems that recent rates of technological advance have been inversely related to the numbers of scientists and engineers in each major region (Wilczynski, 1974, 78; Oldham, 1973, 85; Maddison, 1971, 100):

1965:		Western	Eastern	1967:	1968:
USSR	USA	Europe	Europe	China	India
4.8m.	3.5m.	2.0m.	1.4m.	2.4m.	0.5m.

And Japan, which until recently devoted comparatively small proportions of GNP to R & D, has achieved the most outstanding industrial technological performance. An economy's industrial technological performance is much more influenced by the openness, responsiveness and efficiency of the system – including its ability to commercialize other countries' discoveries and inventions – than by the number of scientists and engineers at its disposal or the scale of its own R & D programmes.

Education

Stalinist educational achievements have been impressive, but scarcely more so than the advances achieved in interwar Bulgaria, Poland, Romania, Greece, Italy, Japan, Taiwan, Cuba, the Philippines and Thailand or post-1947 India, Turkey and South Korea – under capitalist regimes (see Table 3). Certain features of the Stalinist educational achievement stand out. (1) Many millions of the principal 'beneficiaries' have subsequently wasted away in prisons and penal labour camps, so they might as well have remained uneducated. (2) It created remarkably monolithic, comprehensive and 'polytechnical' education systems, embodying broad modern curricula and 'active discrimination' in favour of the offspring of party and state officials, key 'productive' personnel and loyal 'proletarians'. (3) There has been a strong bias towards the sciences in higher education. Out of 4.1 million Soviet students graduating in 1928–59, 27 per cent majored in engineering and another 30 per cent in other sciences, as against 9 and 13 per cent, respectively, in the USA in the same period. Vocational schooling and higher technological education and research have been provided mainly by specialized institutions funded and administered by industrial rather than general education ministries, to ensure (supposedly) that such activities are geared to the needs of those Industrial Ministries and that recipients pass directly into employment in the corresponding industries for specific periods. However, it is much easier to predetermine demand for 'front-line' personnel (e.g. engineers and physicians) than for support personnel (e.g. technicians and secretaries), so many 'front-liners' end up performing tasks which could be performed more efficiently by assistants if enough were provided. (4) Far more males than females have obtained a higher education, despite much higher female than male academic attainments among 16- and 17-year-olds, partly because education is so lopsidedly geared to traditionally male occupations (see Vasilieva, 1976T, 72–7).

Strumilin (1962T) estimated that the education embodied in the Soviet workforce was enhancing Soviet material product per man-year by 16 per cent by 1940, by 21 per cent by 1950 and by 23 per cent by 1960, and that the average economic return on fixed capital invested in education and culture had increased from 52 per cent per annum in 1940 to 131 per cent per annum in 1950 and 144 per cent per annum in 1960, indicating that this was a very profitable form of public investment.

Except for a disastrous lapse in China during Mao's Proletarian Cultural Revolution and its aftermath (1967–75), the Soviet education system has been quite faithfully reproduced in the other longstanding communist states, resources permitting (see King, 1980; Price, 1977; Yang and Chee, 1963). However, the Chinese still pay school fees (see Short, 1982, 88).

Health care

Returns on educational investment have been greatly enhanced by impressive advances in public health and longevity (see Table 2). But note that Soviet mortality rates were freakishly low in the 1950s to 1970s, as Stalin and Hitler had ensured that at least 25 million people who would 'normally' have entered retirement age in those years didn't.

Despite comparatively favourable per capita provision of hospital beds and physicians, the USSR has kept the proportion of its national income spent on health care at one-third below the corresponding proportions in most industrialized capitalist states: (1) by forcing all medical and paramedical personnel into one state-controlled union, enabling the state to break the professional autonomy and restrictive practices characteristic of medical professions under capitalism; (2) by reducing health service pay to 79 per cent of the average wage by 1931, to 77 per cent of it by 1940 and to 73 per cent of it by 1960, or by 42 per cent in real terms during 1928–40 (see Kaser, 1976, 91); (3) by heavy reliance on narrow, rarely updated ranges of poor-quality, state-manufactured drugs, eye-glasses, dressings and instruments, subject to very irregular supply, along with a virtual absence of many of the mechanical and electronic aids taken for granted by Western medicine (see Knaus, 1981); (4) by tolerating comparatively spartan, crowded hospitals of grim, rarely updated design; (5) by relying mainly on half-trained medical orderlies ('feldshers', forerunners of China's 'barefoot doctors') in rural areas. However, as my colleague Dr Ryan has shown, Soviet health policies also fostered wasteful and self-perpetuating overspecialization, underprovision of family/general physicians (only one-fifth of all physicians), reluctance to serve in rural postings, monolithic Health Ministries, stultifying orthodoxies and inertia, low job satisfaction and esprit de corps, prodigal use of expensively trained physicians in non-medical capacities and a mania for hospitalization. The proportion of Soviet citizens hospitalized per annum rose from 11 per cent in 1950 to 22 per cent in 1974. The value of Russia's vaunted health care has also been diminished by chronic urban overcrowding, insanitary water supplies, bad plumbing, and abysmal personal and toiletry hygiene, and the conditions in Soviet labour camps. Morbidity remained high through the 1930s (Table 23), and in 1974 Soviet hospitals were still using 7.7 per cent of their beds to treat infectious diseases (as against 0.7 per cent for England) and 8.8 per cent of their beds to treat consumptives. Gastro-intestinal diseases remain endemic, and since the 1950s alcoholism has become a major social disease (see Connor, 1972, chs 4 and 5).

As with education, the Soviet health care system has been quite closely copied in other communist states, resources permitting, although it should be noted that in 1974 state health insurance still covered under one-quarter of China's population (see Rifkin and Paterson, 1974; Kaser, 1976).

'Unproductive services'

Industrialization has generally increased substantially the proportion of the work-force engaged in tertiary/service occupations, unless it was already high at the outset (e.g. in Holland and Greece), and in the USSR it rose from 11 per cent in 1926 to 18 per cent in 1940, 20 per cent in 1950 and 24 per cent in 1964 (Ofer, 1973, 187). It is commonly assumed that communist states must be abnormally burdened by inflated bureaucracies. However, the proportions of the workforce in service occupations (excluding transport), in public administration alone and in clerical/administrative posts within industry were each roughly 40 per cent smaller in the USSR, in 1959, than they were in capitalist economies with similar per capita GNPs, despite the Soviet state's wider functions and comparatively large education and health services (ibid., 26–9, 32, 33, 42, 151, 157). Since Soviet office, communications and service industry technology has remained strikingly inferior to Western counterparts, one must look to less flattering explanations for the smallness of the service sector: (1) like certain classical economists, Stalinist economics has simple-mindedly regarded most service and administrative occupations as 'unproductive' activities, whose expansion should be minimized, even though their expansion has palpably underpinned the attainment of unprecedentedly high productivity levels in the so-called 'productive' sectors of the most advanced capitalist economies – those with the largest service sectors. Stalinism has also persistently pilloried and reinforced popular hostility to commercial and financial intermediaries as actual or potential 'profiteers', 'speculators', 'blood-suckers' and 'parasites', further encouraging fallacious notions that such people are intrinsically unproductive and that private enterprise must be gradually excluded from the service sector. However, the ensuing state systems of distribution and finance established by Stalinist regimes have been overcentralized, understaffed and extremely un-responsive to user requirements; crucial links between service sector remuneration and user satisfaction have been largely eliminated. The costs of underprovision of services have been borne partly by industrial users, but mainly by ordinary long-suffering consumers, who have to devote inordinate proportions of their lives to waiting and to tiresome shopping around and queuing for basic goods and services in badly managed and stocked retail outlets. (2) As communist states allocate com-paratively low proportions of GNP to popular consumption, effective per capita demand for consumer goods and services should be lower than it is in capitalist economies with similar per capita GNPs. (3) Low regard for service occupations under Stalinism has been reflected in their low-ranking rates of pay. This is the main reason why all but the top-ranking service occupations have been left to women, who formed two-thirds of Russia's service sector workforce by 1959. Not only have more Soviet women taken jobs, they have also performed more laborious housework than women in comparable capitalist economies, as Soviet women receive comparatively little in the way of labour-saving appliances, external services and help from men. Women's 'emancipation' has added to their burdens, without seriously challenging male dominance and 'prerogatives'.

In 1965 the percentages of the workforce in service occupations were similarly small in the other Comecon states (Comecon, 1979, 441–3):

USSR	Romania	Bulgaria	Poland	Hungary	Czecho-slovakia	East Germany	Mongolia
24.6	13.2	16.0	17.7	23.1	25.3	28.5	21.7

In China the proportion of the workforce in service occupations (still excluding transport) has been kept below 10 per cent, at least until 1975 (T. Rawski, 1979, 34, 156).

Housing

The USSR's urban population expanded by 30 million in 1926–39 and by 25 million in 1940–56, and 25 million Soviet citizens were rendered homeless by the Second World War, on official Soviet estimations. This indicates that at least 80 million people had to be newly housed in just thirty years (1926–56), posing a hous-ing challenge of unprecedented magnitude. Nevertheless, residential construction was limited to approximately 17 per cent of gross investment during 1929–55 (USSR, 1977, 436), with the result that per capita urban housing space failed to regain pre-1929 levels until the 1960s and in 1974 was still under half the West European average (Chapman, 1963, 239; George and Manning, 1980, 134–46):

USSR:	1913	1928	1932	1937	1940	1944
Square metres:	7	5.8	4.9	4.6	4.5	3.9

USSR:	1950	1955	1958	1974	Western Europe 1974
Square metres:	5.0	5.1	5.5	8.0	20

In the 1970s one-fifth of urban (let alone rural) housing lacked running water and one-half lacked piped gas or central heating (George and Manning, 1980, 147), as one can still see for oneself in towns around Moscow; indeed, some suburbs are virtually shanty towns, little better than Brazilian *favelas*, but exposed to a much harsher climate. Most urban families – especially young couples – still lack self-contained accommodation (ibid.). But urban overcrowding increased the efficacy of preferential access to low-rent publicly owned housing as a means of promoting sociopolitical conformity, 'company loyalty', discriminatory remuneration, political jobbery and immigration into otherwise unpopular areas (e.g. Siberia), thereby rendering more overt 'direction of labour' relatively unimportant (see Balinsky, 1961, 17–23; Dimaio, 1974, 6).

Very similar housing policies and problems prevailed in 1950s and 1960s Eastern Europe and in Mao's China (see Donnison, 1967, 49–54, 113–49; Howe, 1978, 172–3). Under Mao, China's urban housing space fell from 4.5m.² to 3.6m.² per person (Short, 1982, 81).

Transport and problems of food distribution

During 1929–55 transport investment was limited to approximately 15 per cent of total Soviet investment (USSR, 1977, 436), mainly by achieving extraordinarily intensive utilization of a sparingly expanded railway network; and the intensity of railway utilization has increased even further since 1955. Official Soviet sources referring to present Soviet territory give the following data:

	Railways (km)	Average haul (km)	Rail freight turnover (ton-km)	(% of all freight)	Rail passenger traffic (man-km)	(% of all travel)
1913	72,000	500	76 milliard	61	30 milliard	93
1928	76,900	600	93 milliard	78	25 milliard	90
1940	106,100	700	420 milliard	85	100 milliard	92
1955	120,700	750	971 milliard	83	141 milliard	83
1976	138,500	900	3295 milliard	61	315 milliard	40

By 1960 there was similarly heavy reliance on railways to transport freight in other communist states (Osmova and Faminsky, 1980, 86):

% of all freight:								
China	Mongolia	Romania	Bulgaria	Poland	Hungary	Czecho-slovakia	GDR	USSR
79	93	83	63	64	85	79	69	80

Unfortunately a heavy reliance on very heavily loaded railway networks has also had drawbacks. In 1955 the USSR still had less paved road than Britain – an area ninety-two times smaller than the USSR – and China has even less. This has helped to perpetuate rural isolation and 'the idiocy of rural life', impairing the development of truck farming, rural retailing and rural incentives to expand marketable surpluses of farm produce. The relative sluggishness of distribution by rail has tied up unnecessarily large amounts of capital as goods-in-transit and as inventories, and has caused vast amounts of perishable produce to spoil during or awaiting transportation. The food supply problems of the communist states are often blamed on the much exaggerated deficiencies of collectivized agriculture, but this is barking up the wrong tree: the generally accepted agricultural data indicate that, except in China and Indo-China, per capita food production in the communist states has been comparatively high (see Tables 11, 13, 14). On the supply side the major problem has been that so much of the food produced fails to reach the intended consumers or becomes inedible. Officially, 'nearly 20% of the annual Soviet harvest is wasted' (Financial Times, 15 December 1983, 3).

'Some are more equal than others'

Although the (exaggerated) anti-egalitarian tendencies within NEP were a pretext for Stalin's 'revolution from above', Soviet income differentials became wider under Stalinism than they had been under NEP, whose mixed economy fostered countervailing forces which constrained the evident abuse of monopolistic political and economic power (Wiles, 1975, 33; McAuley, 1979, 222):

Ratio of top decile to bottom decile of the earnings of all workers and employees							
	1928	1934	1946	1957	1964		1966
USSR:	3.8	4.2	7.2	4.9	3.3	UK:	2.9 (after tax)

At its peak Stalinism represented the consolidation and unconstrained abuse of monopolistic political and economic power. Even in the late 1960s, when Stalinism was supposedly in retreat, top industrial earnings remained ten to twenty times as high as average industrial earnings not only in Russia, but also in Eastern Europe

Europe and in China (see Lane, 1976, 178; Eckstein, 1977, 300). And it seems per capita family incomes were only slightly more equally distributed in Comecon than in Britain or Sweden (Wiles, 1974, 1975):

Ratio of top decile to bottom decile of per capita family incomes[*]

USSR	Poland	Czecho-slovakia	Hungary	Bulgaria	UK	Sweden
1966	1967	1965	1967	1963–5	1969	1971
3.7	3.1	3.1	3.0	2.7	3.9	3.6

[*] After tax and omitting unrealized capital gains and undistributed profits.

In theory, the communist states have paid 'each according to his work' (not 'according to his need' – that's supposed to come later). In fact irregular supplies have turned piecework into a lottery, skill differentials have only in part accounted for the much larger earnings differentials, and the multiplicity of 'skill scales' (the USSR had 1900 by 1955) and the residual nature of collective farm incomes have rendered 'equal pay for equal work' utterly unrealizable.

There has been *minimal* reliance on progressive direct taxation in the communist states. Once a state has socialized large-scale trade, finance and means of production, it can no longer finance itself by progressive taxation of large 'capitalist' incomes, as the remaining recipients of large incomes are the political and administrative élites and their associates in the security forces, the media, state sector management and in the sciences. The outcomes of umpteen thoroughgoing 'state socialist' revolutions have belied expectations that the new power-holders would tax away their hard-won spoils or that their hitherto vociferously egalitarian subordinates would bite the hands that feed them. Moreover, as no thoroughgoing 'state socialist' revolution has ever submitted its hard-won 'conquests' to the vagaries of freely contested elections and referendums, there has been no need to curry electoral favour by promoting equitable taxation. The communist states have financed very high public expenditure largely by what they euphemistically call 'socialist accumulation' or 'state appropriation of surplus value created by industry and agriculture' – in effect, by heavy and regressive indirect taxation of consumers and/or producers of food, drinks, clothing, footwear, tobacco, household fuels and consumer durables. In the USSR, state revenue from these easily adjustable quasi-taxes rose from 22 per cent of the gross value of retail sales in 1928–9 to 62 per cent in 1934–7 and 74 per cent in 1947–9; or from 27 per cent of the net value of retail sales in 1928–9 to 161 per cent in 1934–7 and 294 per cent in 1947–9 (Holzman, 1955, 142). They contributed one-third of state revenue in 1928–9, two-thirds in 1933–9 and three-fifths in 1947–50; by 1936 over one-half originated in the food trade (excluding drinks), mainly via underpayment of farmers for their deliveries to state procurement agencies, which then resold farm produce at a handsome profit. Such revenues were cheap to collect, hard to evade, easily disguised and least detrimental to the earners of high incomes. Overall, the proportion of household incomes paid to the state rose from approximately 30 per cent in the late 1920s to 60 per cent in 1935–7 and approximately 65 per cent in 1947–52 (ibid., 8, 63–8, 144–6, 217–22, 253). This helps to explain the erosion of real wages and the fall in consumption levels under Stalin (ibid., 168):

Average retail prices	1928	1933	1936	1940	1951	1952
State and co-operative stores	100	400	700	1000	2035	1925
Food markets	100	1500	700	1800	2810	3100
Average nominal wages	100	233	406	579	1128	1140

As for the Soviet peasantry, per capita income in cash and kind fell from about two-thirds of the urban level in 1928 to one-third of the (depressed) urban level in 1953 (Chapman, 1963, 240; Bronson and Kreuger, 1971, 229). Recent suggestions that peasants could compensate for their abysmally underpriced deliveries to state agencies by selling additional surpluses at inflated prices at urban food markets are pie-in-the-sky, as most farms were fairly remote from big towns and relatively few could have produced substantial surpluses additional to their deliveries to state agencies.

Other industrializing communist states haven't squeezed peasant incomes so severely, either because such a squeeze was deemed unnecessary (in relatively advanced Czechoslovakia and East Germany) or because they were basing their industrialization mainly on light industries (Bulgaria and Cuba) or because peasant incomes couldn't safely be squeezed much lower than they already were (the rest, especially China and North Vietnam). Inasmuch as they couldn't or wouldn't finance industrialization by squeezing peasant incomes, they financed it by holding down and/or indirectly taxing urban wages – above all in China, where average nominal wages were virtually static from 1957 to 1975, despite considerable growth in industrial output per man (Lardy, 1978, 175).

Other communist states have succeeded in controlling and disguising inflation more adroitly than did 1930s Russia: (1) by pursuing more cautious agrarian policies, thereby avoiding such severe agricultural setbacks; (2) by copying from the outset the much tougher wage controls and financial disciplines established in the USSR from 1947 (no country has had tougher wage and financial controls than China since 1957); and (3) by fudging official retail price indices (e.g. many goods are simply unavailable at their official price, others are withdrawn from sale to be reintroduced as higher-priced 'new' products, and subsidized goods are over-represented in official price indices).

Officially the USSR 'abolished' unemployment in 1930, so unemployment insurance was also abolished. In fact industrial labour turnover exceeded 100 per cent per annum in 1930–5 (Holzman, 1955, 32) and 20 per cent per annum in 1955–70, so 'frictional' unemployment must have remained considerable; in the latter period workers 'between jobs' remained so for one or two months at a time on average (see Powell, 1977, 269–72).

There has also been considerable 'frictional' unemployment in East European states, as any economy would seize up without it (see Koszegi, 1978), and China had approximately 10 per cent urban unemployment or 10 million unemployed workers in 1979, as against 20 per cent of urban unemployment in 1957 (see p. 138). Underprovision of unemployment relief obliges workers to take more or less whatever work they are offered, and job security is conditional on docile conformity.

All in all, it is by no means certain that the existing neo-Stalinist regimes can satisfactorily resolve the deep-seated economic, social and political problems and 'contradictions' of Russia, China and Eastern Europe, although they are certainly capable of preventing anyone else from doing so. Ultimately one must ask whether this kind of 'socialism' is really worth having, considering the attendant upheavals, loss of life, oppression and economic costs; and it is sobering to remember that the combined loss of life under Lenin, Stalin and Mao probably exceeded that for which the Nazis were responsible, and that these regimes depended on millions of dedicated accomplices.

10 The Cuba syndrome

For many socialists, Castro's Cuba represents an exciting radical alternative to the stale orthodoxies of Marxism–Leninism. Relying heavily on sources sympathetic to the Cuban experiment, this chapter will try to explain why the results have been so disappointing. Before Castro and Guevara wrested power from General Batista's murderous regime in 1958–9, Cuba's per capita national income was around 50 per cent *above* the average for Latin America and 'Only Venezuela and Argentina, of the larger Latin American countries, had a higher average income' (Seers, 1964, 18). But by 1970 Cuba's per capita GDP was approximately 2 per cent *below* the average for Latin America and her relative decline continued in the 1970s (*UN Economic Bulletin for Latin America*, 1967, 108; Warren, 1980, 230; Bairoch, 1975, 193, 247; Wynia, 1978, 326; World Bank, 1980, 110–11):

Current US dollars per capita	Latin America	Cuba	El Salvador	Guatemala	Peru
GDP, 1950	247	372	148	166	121
GNP, 1959–61	350	500*	321	269	198
GDP, 1970	540	530	295	350	435
GNP, 1974	937	640	410	580	740
GNP, 1978	1362	810	660	910	740

Current US dollars per capita	Columbia	Brazil	Mexico	Argentina
GDP, 1950	201	208	211	496
GNP, 1959–61	253	267	348	551
GDP, 1970	315	365	660	1055
GNP, 1974	500	920	1090	1520
GNP, 1978	850	1570	1290	1910

* 1957: Seers, 1974, 264.

National income comparisons aren't infallible. But as Bill Warren showed in his Marxist analysis of capitalist *Imperialism* (1980, 224–31), they do broadly reflect differences in levels of development and material welfare; and other development indicators corroborate the view that 1950s Cuba was among the more developed Third World states. By 1950 78 per cent of Cuban adults were literate – a proportion which, in Latin America, was exceeded only in Chile, Costa Rica, Uruguay and my native Argentina (Furtado, 1970, 48). In the 1950s Cuba's average life expectancy was sixty years, Cuba had over half as many physicians per inhabitant as did Western Europe, and Cuba's mortality rate was almost as low as it can go (see Table 2). Half Cuba's population was urban (Zeitlin and Scheer, 1963, 15) and only about 39 per cent depended on agriculture (Table 1). Cuba's famous sugar industry 'was probably the most modern in the region, despite its heavy reliance on labour-intensive methods' (Mintz, 1977–8, 483). But by 1954 agriculture and sugar-refining respectively contributed only 23 and 11 per cent of national income (Newman, 1965, 34–5), and by 1958 sugar cane was contributing only 36.5 per cent of agricultural output (Thomas, 1971, 1154). In 1953 58 per cent of Cubans had electricity (Griffiths and Griffiths, 1979, 121). Cuba had over 17,000 km of railway and led Latin America in the provision of electricity, railways, roads, bus services, radios, TVs and telephones (Thomas, 1971, 1161–3; Goldenberg, 1965, 120–1). Cuba was one of the few American nations which no longer had to contend with a problematic Indian minority, as 'the Spanish had completely obliterated Cuba's indigenous pre-Columbian population' (MacEwan, 1981, 11), and Cuba's underprivileged black and mulatto minority (26 per cent of the population) was largely urban and, by US and Caribbean standards, comparatively well assimilated (see Wolf, 1973, 252–4; Thomas, 1971, 1551).

MacEwan's Marxist analysis of *Revolution and Economic Development in Cuba* (1981, 12) claims that 63.6 per cent of the Cubans engaged in agriculture in 1953 were wage-labourers. But the 1953 census was taken at a time of year when many thousands of small own-account farmers used to take supplementary employment for just one to three months annually to earn extra cash and expedite the sugar harvest; according to the more thorough agricultural census of 1946, only 27 per cent of Cuba's farms employed any wage-labour, Cuban farms averaged 57 ha in size, only 20 per cent were under 5 ha, and only 2 per cent were under 1 ha; Cuban censuses tended to double or treble count 'workers employed on more than one farm'; and 'The 1953 Census . . . appears to have provided a perniciously "sound" statistical base to foster over-simplistic views concerning the agrarian class-structure', especially 'the erroneous view that . . . there was a "landless agricultural proletariat" . . . some 500,000 strong' (Pollitt, 1976–7, 167–72; Domínguez, 1978, 432). Moreover, the smaller farms specialized in intensive cultivation of fruit, vegetables, tobacco and coffee (Bergmann, 1975T, 225), and by 1953 income per family outside Havana was only 22 per cent below that within Havana (Griffiths and Griffiths, 1979, 58).

Cuba's sugar planters were criticized for not cultivating all the land at their disposal. But land had to be held in reserve to meet the large fluctuations in foreign demand for Cuban sugar, as Castro's regime would soon discover.

Yet the perception of Cuba's major problems was undoubtedly inflamed by being, like Mexico, 'so far from God and so close to the United States' and by the way thick-skinned imperialistic nations heavy-handedly meddle in the internal affairs of weaker nations. On the other hand, Cuba's main exports did enjoy preferential access to the protected US market and Cuba's consumers enjoyed almost unimpeded access to US products (MacEwan, 1981, 14–15). And, despite the xenophobic belief that the relationship prevented Cuban diversification away from US-dominated sugar production, the opposite occurred: by the 1950s the book value of US investment in Cuban agriculture and sugar-processing was under half the 1929 level; the proportion of Cuban sugar produced by US-owned mills fell from 62.5 per cent in 1927 to 43.0 per cent in 1953 and 36.7 per cent in 1958; by 1957 US-owned plantations accounted for only 40 per cent of cane output; and by 1958 74 per cent of US direct investment in Cuba was in industries other than sugar (MacEwan, 1981, 13; Domínguez, 1978, 67–8; Newman, 1965, 1, 54). Xenophobes needed reminding that, for US investors, Cuban sugar was an increasingly unattractive proposition and that erection of high protective tariffs against US products would have helped local monopolists to line their own pockets by raising their prices and profits at the Cuban consumer's expense, while limiting the choice and quality of goods on offer (this is often the main motive behind protectionist demands). In fact the openness of Cuba's economy induced the bourgeoisie to 'ally itself with American manufacturing interests, creating industries which used American equipment, raw materials, technology and a cheap native labour force' (Guevara, 1968T, 351). And 'With US supplies close at hand, the Cuban economy operated with limited stocks, a far from negligible advantage' (Furtado, 1970, 242). By 1958 US firms in Cuba employed 160,000 workers (98 per cent Cuban) and contributed nearly 20 per cent of Cuba's tax revenues, which amounted to approximately 18 per cent of national income (Thomas, 1971, 1172; Newman, 1965, 1, 35, 42). In the mid-1950s sugar cane and sugar refining together provided only 17–19 per cent of national income, livestock products rivalled sugar as the principal component of agricultural output and Cuba was producing 70 per cent of the food it consumed (Oshima, 1961; Newman, 1965, 34–5; Thomas, 1971, 1554). Cuba had become the world's third largest producer of nickel and it had three oil refineries which processed Venezuelan crude for Cuban consumption and for export to the USA and other Caribbean states (Guevara, 1968T, 97, 143). Cuba was also the world's third largest producer of manganese and a major producer of chrome, cobalt and copper; its first steelmill was completed in 1958 (it has low-grade iron ore); there was a booming drinks industry (beer and rum); it had five papermills (two based on bagasse) and 'a rather advanced chemical sector' (notably sulphur, sulphuric acid, pharmaceuticals and rubber goods); the famous tobacco and cigar industry was still prospering; and Cuba also had important textile, footwear, canning, dairy, vegetable oil and flour industries (see Table 15; Thomas, 1971, 1158–71). Despite valuable US participation in industry, transport, communications and banking, Cuba's public indebtedness to foreigners amounted to a mere 2.7 per cent of its GNP in 1955 (Newman, 1965, 43), and repatriated profits and interest payments absorbed only 6 per cent of Cuba's foreign currency earnings (Seers, 1964, 19).

'Cuba had a comparatively highly developed working class movement', and by 1954 over half the workforce was affiliated to the powerful Cuban Federation of Workers (MacEwan, 1981, 150, 25). Real wages jumped over 20 per cent in 1946–50 and again in 1951–7, thus raising the wage share of domestic national income above 60 per cent during 1949–57 (Domínguez, 1978, 74–5). Under Batista Cuba legally established an 8-hour day, a 44-hour week (with pay for 48 hours), four national holidays with pay, an additional month of holiday with pay, nine days of paid sick leave, twelve weeks' maternity leave for women, security from dismissal without (difficult) legal proof of just cause, and indexation of some wages to living costs; in 1952–8 Batista 'ran Cuba by means of an alliance with organized labour' and 'underwrote the vast number of restrictive practices, limitations on mechanization and bans on dismissals'; and the unions effectively vetoed mechanization of cane cutting and planting, thereby perpetuating the wide seasonal and cyclical fluctuations in employment on the sugar plantations (Thomas, 1971, 1144, 1173; Domínguez, 1978, 87–91). As in Argentina under Perón (1946–55), the trade unions and the urban proletariat were the popular power base of a corrupt corporatist/neo-fascist regime (see Wolf, 1973, 265; Thomas, 1971, 1174–9; Domínguez, 1978, ch. 3). This helps to explain why Cuba's Marxist party, the PSP, had shrunk to only 12,000 members by 1954 and why the working class and the PSP played 'little direct role' in Castro's rise to power (MacEwan, 1981, 25–6, 29, 50, 128; Wolf, 1973, 265–9).

The foregoing in no way condones the evils of dictatorship, but merely helps to place Cuba's problems in context. 'Bourgeois historians' readily concur with Guevara's estimate that, in a total workforce of 2.33 million, roughly 300,000 (13 per cent) were 'unemployed' and 'another 300,000 underemployed' (Guevara, 1968T, 99, 191). These unincorporated workers were largely excluded from the benefits enjoyed by organized labour (Thomas, 1971, 1175). However, it would be dishonest not to mention that the unemployment figures included the 50,000–60,000 'young men who annually reached the age of work', most of whom would eventually find full-time jobs; that 'Many nominally unemployed sugar workers also had small plots of land which enabled them to grow something between harvests'; that the size of the fluctuations in sugar employment were largely due to the strength of opposition to mechanization; and that this opposition partly arose because seasonal sugar employment provided extra cash for many thousands of farm households (Thomas, 1971, 1175, 1144; Pollitt, 1976–7, 169–72). Moreover, as

Castro's regime would soon discover the hard way, the tasks of employing, feeding, clothing, educating and housing Cuba's population were not helped by the fact that it was growing over 2 per cent per annum, whilst 36 per cent of Cubans were under 15 years old (Castro, 1972T, 379). This partly explains why most Cubans – like most Latin Americans – still lived in slums, shacks and shanty towns (ibid., 30), and why 1.25 million out of 7 million Cubans were still illiterate in 1959 (Guevara, 1968T, 163). 'Bourgeois historians' can also accept Guevara's view that the revolution triumphed essentially because 'The dictatorship created the necessary ferment' and, 'Once the conflict broke out, the regime's repressive measures and its brutality, far from diminishing popular resistance, increased it. The demoralization and shamelessness of the military caste facilitated the task' (Guevara, 1969T, 163). Batista became so brutal that the USA imposed an arms embargo on Cuba in 1958 and, for the military, that was the last straw: many soldiers deserted and Batista fled abroad.

Castro's regime began with considerable advantages: 'The swiftness of his victory and the involvement of so few Cubans . . . left much of the old political power structure intact' (Wynia, 1978, 265). 'Cuba was among the richer nations of Latin America', yet 'capital did not flee' and the 'negligible physical destruction' and 'minimal disruption of economic activity' permitted a euphoric economic boom in 1959–61 (MacEwan, 1981, 83, 32). The land reforms of 1959 and 1963, which expropriated nearly all properties exceeding 402 ha and 67 ha, respectively, and entitled every existing own-account farmer to at least 27 ha, encountered little resistance, as 'only a small percentage of landowners had land taken away from them' (ibid., 39–73). Moreover, 'Because of the predominant part which had been played by the latifundia in agricultural production and the enormous size of the sugar plantations organized along capitalist lines, it was relatively easy to convert this type of rural property into state farms and cooperatives' (Guevara, 1968T, 353). And even Castro's critics believe that his regime reduced unemployment, rural inequality and adult illiteracy. By 1974 income per family outside Havana was only 17 per cent below the Havana level, as against 22 per cent in 1953 (Domínguez, 1978, 228); and the pay scales established in 1963–5 marked some progress towards greater equality among wage- and salary-earners (see table at the top of p. 169, showing pesos earned per month, compiled from Mesa-Lago, 1968, 94–101, and Ritter, 1974). Even so, ministers still paid themselves salaries of 700 pesos per month, or seven to nine times more than most workers (see Sweezy and Huberman, 1969, 118). However, 'By the early 1970s egalitarianism was losing out' and 'The rationing system, which had once been an instrument for equality, now became a method to benefit the élite with goods provided by new trading partners.' Indeed, one could be forgiven for thinking that the 1970s rationing system was designed to promote party patronage, factory favouritism, corruption, black-marketeering and docile conformity (see Domínguez, 1978, 229; Mesa-Lago, 1978, 45–7).

Grades	Executive and technical staff (1963)	Agricultural labour (1965)	Non-agricultural workers (1963)	Percentage distribution of non-agricultural workers (1964)
1	303	64	85	20.9
2	351	72	99	30.8
3	408	84	115	20.6
4	478	97	134	10.6
5	560	112	157	10.2
6	660	131	185	4.3
7	778	154	218	1.9
8	938	—	264	0.7

Initially many of Castro's potential opponents were reassured by the fact that he and his Movement of 26 July had never been Marxist or part of a Marxist organization, had been vociferously anti-communist in 1957–9, had studiously avoided any commitment to socialism and had kept Marxist fellow-travellers in very subordinate roles; it was not until 1960–61 that US knee-jerk over-reaction against Cuba's radical nationalism drove Castro into an explicitly socialist course, into closer ties with Cuba's Marxist party and into the arms of the USSR (see Zeitlin and Scheer, 1963, 108–22; Domínguez, 1978, 129–30, 142–9). But, even then, Cuba was in a strong position to profit from the experience of thirteen existing communist regimes most of whom immediately offered generous material and organizational aid (Guevara, 1968T, 173, 203).

However, Cuba's economic performance after 1961 was distinctly unimpressive. Official Cuban data indicate that the sectoral composition of GMP changed remarkably little (MacEwan, 1981, 234–5):

% of total GMP	Agriculture, forestry and fishing	Industry	Construction
1962–4	22.5	68.1	9.4
1970–4	18.8	69.4	11.8

Changes in the product structure of factory industry were also small (see Table 15). Indeed, diversification was so bungled that sugar was still contributing 42 per cent of agricultural output in 1970 and 13 per cent of industrial output in 1972 (Darusenkov, 1974, 46, 69). In the absence of major changes in the composition of output, trends in the published per capita output of Cuba's principal products should reflect trends in overall output per inhabitant (Comecon, 1976T, 1979; UN and FAO Yearbooks, various issues):

Kg per capita	Sugar	Grain	Potatoes	Tobacco	Meat	Milk
1952–6	859	67	16	6	34	121
1969–71	744	46	9	4	32	78
1976–8	699	57	10	5	29	108

Per capita output	1958	1965	1970	1975	1978
Nickel ore (kg)	2.7	3.5	4.3	4.0	3.8
Chrome ore (kg)	4.0	1.9	0.9	1.4	1.0
Cloth (m²)	15	12	9	16	16
Leather shoes (pairs)	2	2	2	2	2
Paper (kg)	5	6	4	7	7
Beer (l)	18	13	12	27	26
Cigarettes (units)	1500	2200	2400	1700	1800
Cigars (units)	94	84	32	41	?

Moreover, according to the World Bank (1980, 111, 123), Cuba's per capita GNP declined 1.2 per cent per annum on average in real terms during 1960–78, and by 1978 Cuba was using 1.6 times more energy per unit of GDP than either the Third World or the West, whereas in 1960 Cuba's energy consumption per unit of GDP had been about average. Castro's regime has only avoided complete economic collapse thanks to Soviet aid. Although the USSR is a major producer of sugar and nickel, it has faithfully purchased most of Cuba's sugar at prices far above those obtainable on Western markets and since 1973 it has done the same for Cuban nickel, while supplying nearly all Cuba's primary energy needs at prices far below those obtainable on Western markets (one reason for Cuba's comparatively inefficient use of energy). Soviet trade subsidies and direct financial aid to Cuba amounted to approximately US $13 billion during 1961–78, and by 1978 annual Soviet assistance was running at approximately US $2.9 billion or one-quarter of Cuba's GNP (Theriot and Matheson, 1979, 553–60). And that was before the 1979 jump in international oil prices and further falls in international sugar prices further increased the real levels of oil and sugar subsidy (see *Financial Times*, 3 September 1981, 2 June 1982). Sadly, Cuba has become far more humiliatingly and obsequiously dependent on the USSR than it ever was on the USA. 'He who pays the piper calls the tune.' Cuba also depended on hundreds of millions of dollars in aid from Eastern Europe and China in the 1960s (Guevara, 1968T, 173, 192–4), and by 1982 Cuba had incurred a $3.84 billion debt to the West (*Financial Times*, 18 March 1983). Thus Cuba has not shown Latin America a promising way out of the vexations of dependent development.

Cuba's dismal economic record has not stemmed from high-minded disdain for the frenetic pursuit of economic growth. As Minister for Industrialization, Guevara had acknowledged that – on his ministry's calculations – Cuba's per capita national income in 1958 already comfortably exceeded the average for 'all the Americas', yet he none the less pledged that Cuba's per capita income would double in ten years; that Cuba's economy would grow 10 per cent per annum in the 1960s; and that Cuba would leap into the age of electronics and automation (Guevara, 1968T, 167, 352, 107, 172, 197). In 1967 Castro declared that '30% of the available GNP must be invested . . . to develop the economy at a rate of no less than 5% of gross per capita product annually' (Castro, 1972T, 380). And the 1976–80 Plan aimed to expand Cuba's economy 6 per cent per annum (Castro, 1976). So what went wrong?

(1) As Castro informed the very overdue First Congress of the Cuban Communist Party in December 1975, 'From the very beginning the Cuban Revolution did not take advantage of the rich experience of other peoples that had undertaken the construction of socialism' (Castro, 1976, 2).

(2) 'State structures were not set up according to a master plan of which the inner workings had been thoroughly studied. . . . Last minute decisions carried out suddenly, without any previous study, were characteristic of our work' (Guevara, 1968T, 222); 'The first steps as a revolutionary state, as well as the early period of our formation as a government, were strongly coloured by the fundamentals of guerrilla tactics as a type of state administration'; and 'Spreading across the whole complex structure of society, the fields of action of "administrative guerrillas" often came into open conflict, resulting in continuous friction, orders and counter-orders' (ibid., 220). Yet in 1960 Guevara had urged that 'the militias should be, in the populous centres, the tool which unifies the people . . . an opportunity to live together, joined and made equal by a uniform' (ibid., 119); and he was partly responsible for the militarization of Cuban society. The 300,000-strong army became 'as involved in execution of domestic policy as in the nation's defences. Its officers . . . staffed government agencies and played a direct role in the mobilization of the Cuban workforce. No organization has been more loyal to Castro or more useful to the establishment of his effective control' (Wynia, 1978, 274). After 1967, 'The army also ran the machinery sector of public enterprises and military officers were placed in administrative positions on many State farms' (MacEwan, 1981, 143); and the state farms were worked by 'organized brigades with military discipline' (Castro, 1972T, 382). By 1975 Cuba had two to three times more soldiers per inhabitant than any other Latin American state except Chile (which was roughly on a par with Cuba), and its military expenditures were Latin America's highest per capita and as a proportion of GNP (Wynia, 1978, 327–8). However, since Latin American soldiers aren't noted for competence in civil or economic administration, and since Guevara's writings make it clear that Castro's army was not short of charlatans, the exceptionally extensive and direct military control of Cuban society was probably counterproductive.

(3) 'We have tried to act upon nature subjectively, as if our direct contact with it would accomplish what we were after'; thus 'we did not investigate what we had, what we could spend. . . . The plan was a manifestation of absolute subjectivism. . . . It was all decisions made from the top' (Guevara, 1968T, 260–1). The Junta

Central de Planificación 'did not fulfil its task of direction, and could not', because 'it lacked sufficient authority over other bodies' and 'It was not set up to give correct orders on the foundations of a given system; neither did it have adequate controls or the help of an overall plan' (ibid., 222). 'Instead of embarking on diversification by degrees, we attempted too much at once. The sugar cane areas were reduced', even before more rewarding alternatives could be developed, 'because a fetishistic idea connected sugar with our dependence on imperialism and with the misery in rural areas, without analysing the real causes'. However, premature departure from sugar caused 'a general decline in agricultural production'. With hindsight, 'Diversification on a smaller scale could have been achieved by utilizing the reserves . . . existing in the resources assigned to various traditional types of cultivation' and by introducing 'more modern and complex technologies requiring a longer period of assimilation'. Once these changes bore fruit 'in the traditional fields, particularly in those related to exports, it would have been practicable to transfer resources . . . to areas of diversification without prejudice to the former' (ibid., 353–4). Until the 1970s Cuba's economy 'lacked the central rationale of either a price system or an overall development plan. . . . Managers of factories and farms ceased to keep accounts, or even to know their costs of production' (Seers, 1974, 266). However, Guevara was a fast learner and in 1962–3 he cogently urged the need for thorough book-keeping, proper inventory control and cost accounting, reliable national statistics, remuneration according to work done, monetary discipline and a price structure reflecting relative costs and scarcities, as the essential foundations for price stability and effective production incentives, forward-planning, cost control and monitoring of enterprise performance and remuneration (see Guevara, 1968T, 199–201, 250–5). He also urged the need to conceive annual plans as components of a long-range plan and to 'tailor our general plan of investments . . . to commitments already signed with friendly countries' (ibid., 193). Unfortunately in 1965 Guevara was diverted into foolhardy foreign adventures and during 1965–70 the compulsive meddler Fidel Castro personally took charge of economic policy on an *ad hoc* basis, downgraded economic planning, 'seriously neglected' economic calculation and entrusted successive mobilization campaigns to 'loyal fidelistas' responsible only to the Prime Minister – and he later had the gall to insinuate that his dead comrade Guevara was somehow to blame for the ensuing chaos (see Mesa-Lago, 1978, 31; Castro, 1976). Indeed, Castro has persistently bitten off more than he can chew: by 1980 he was simultaneously Prime Minister, party leader, Commander-in-Chief, Interior Minister, Health Minister and Culture Minister. He is in many ways reminiscent of Mussolini, with his multiplicity of offices and titles, his interfering personalistic style of government, his machismo, his militarism, his military adventures in Africa, his anti-Western rhetoric, his regimentation of labour, his monolithic polity and his iron fist.

(4) On Guevara's testimony the 'peasant' who joined Castro's army typically

'came from the section of this social class which . . . wanted land for himself, for his children, to manage it, sell it and get rich' (Wolf, 1973, 270–1), hardly an ideal popular basis for the future socialist course. 'The best among us felt deeply the need for . . . an overturning of the social system', but 'they always had to drag behind them the weight of those who came to the struggle out of nothing but a hunger for adventure or in the hope of winning not only laurels but economic advantage' (Guevara, 1969T, 161). Others 'joined the Revolution without any clear under-standing of its significance . . . waiting to see which way the wind would blow' (ibid., 168). Moreover, as late as May 1958 relations with the towns were 'charac-terized by lack of understanding on the part of the urban movement's leadership of our importance as the vanguard of the Revolution and of Fidel's stature as its leader' (ibid., 185). This speaks volumes about the degree of urban support for Castro's forces, which only numbered 'between 1000 and 3000 troops during the entire campaign' (Unseem, 1977–8, 102). Furthermore, 'During two years of warfare Fidel did not hold a single political rally in his zone of operations' (Debray, 1968T, 53), and 'The combat did not bring forth working-class leaders, nor did it contri-bute to the organizational strength of the working class' (MacEwan, 1981, 29, 50). Indeed, 'Only a very small percentage of the Cuban people had the opportunity to learn the invaluable lessons of initiative, innovation and self-reliance which come from participation'; and 'the relationship between government and people con-tinued to be a paternalistic one, with Fidel Castro increasingly playing the crucial role' (Sweezy and Huberman, 1969, 202, 204). Castro has been both midwife and Godfather to the Cuban Revolution, and his one-party polity is unashamedly élitist. As Guevara acknowledged in 1965, 'The Party is a vanguard organization. . . . The Party is a minority. . . . Our aspiration is that the Party become a mass one, but only when the masses reach the level of the vanguard' (Guevara, 1968T, 397). The Party has 'never left the control of Castro and his close associates' (Wynia, 1978, 275), and no Party Congress was held until 1975. The Soviet-style organs of Poder Popular established in 1976 were rubber-stamp institutions, as they promptly demonstrated when they obtained the support of 97.7 per cent of the electorate in February 1976 and when 92 per cent of the delegates elected to the First National Assembly were Party members, with executive power still remaining virtually a Castro monopoly (ibid., 276). Thus few Cubans can feel that this is their revol-ution, embodying their aspirations.

(5) Non-whites have remained an underprivileged, under-represented minority (see Domínguez, 1978, 225–7, 521–6). And despite the fanfare for women's emancipation, the proportion of women employed outside the home only increased from 15 per cent in 1958 to 24 per cent in 1973 (MacEwan, 1981, 80), because the work they were offered was still rather menial (e.g. cane cutting), because there was little for the extra income to buy (see ibid.), because child-minding facilities were a low priority (ibid.) and because Castro has pandered to Cuban machismo (Thomas, 1971, 1485).

(6) In the 1960s 'Failure to take account of remuneration according to work done markedly increased the excess currency in circulation against a background of shortages in goods and services', and this 'stimulated absenteeism and caused disciplinary problems with labour' (Castro, 1976, 2). 'A family's consumption level came to depend partly on whether its members had between them the time and stamina needed for queuing, which penalized the elderly and those with children', and 'queuing led to absenteeism and production difficulties, which in turn aggravated shortages' and 'impaired the appeal to moral incentives' (Seers, 1974, 267). As early as 1962 Guevara was complaining that 'Absenteeism is a defect of national importance' (Guevara, 1968T, 201). In 1963 a survey of 136 state farms found that 'employees only worked from 4.5 to 5 hours daily, but were paid for 8 hours'; tractor drivers worked only 19–21 days per month; and the vice-chairman of Cuba's National Institute of Agrarian Reform acknowledged that rural unemployment was being concealed by allowing state farms to employ two or three men to do the work of one (MacEwan, 1981, 54–5). In 1970 the rate of tractor utilization was only 25 per cent and, at the height of the sugar harvest, the rate of absenteeism among agricultural workers was 29 per cent (see ibid., 132, 145). During 1968–9 31 per cent of working time was lost in the food industry, 16 per cent was lost in other light industries, 25 per cent was lost in mining and metallurgy, and 22 per cent was lost in other heavy industries (Risquet, 1970, 4). And in 1967 Castro complained that Cuba was plagued by 'loafers' and 'parasites' (Castro, 1972T, 388). However, for many proletarians, becoming the nominal ruling class meant at the very least getting more pay for less work (MacEwan, 1981, 54–5, 145), so perhaps Castro's complaints were misplaced.

(7) 'Again and again, unrealistically high targets have been set, promises have been made which could not be kept, hopes have been raised only to be disappointed' (Sweezy and Huberman, 1969, 205). But so far disaffection has assumed non-violent forms: besides the absenteeism, over 550,000 Cubans 'voted with their feet' by emigrating during 1960–72 and a further 125,000 emigrated in 1980 (Domínguez, 1978, 140; *Financial Times*, 2 June 1982). Emigration alleviated unemployment, which as mentioned amounted to approximately 600,000 before the revolution, and it defused discontent. But it also represented a net loss of human capital, nurtured at Cuban expense, and helped to perpetuate an unfavourable age structure: in 1967, 38 per cent and 7 per cent of Cubans were under 15 and over 60 years old, respectively, as against 36 and 7 per cent in 1953 (Castro, 1972T, 377–9). However, a Soviet source has indicated that the population aged 15–64 increased *much more* than total employment (Darusenkov, 1974, 88):

	1953	1958	1970	1972
Population aged 15–64	3.51m.	3.93m.	4.95m.	5.15m.
Total employment	2.06m.	2.20m.	2.36m.	2.44m.

This casts considerable doubt on Cuba's achievement on the employment front.

(8) Private agriculture, which has persistently produced a disproportionately large share of Cuba's marketed agricultural output, has slowly but surely lost ground to the relatively unproductive state sector of agriculture, because private land can pass by inheritance from parents to children but can only be sold to the state, and not every farmer's son wants to be a farmer when he grows up (see Sweezy and Huberman, 1969, 113–24; MacEwan, 1981, 196–7). And, despite claims that agriculture was assigned 30–40 per cent of state investment in 1962–6, in 1970 the rate of utilization of tractors was only 25 per cent, and only 2 per cent of cane cutting was performed by machine, thereby perpetuating huge fluctuations in sugar employment (MacEwan, 1981, 111, 132, 137).

(9) Cuba also encountered a major technical hitch: before 1959 Cuban producers could request identical replacement parts and equipment from the USA 'and next day they arrived by ferryboat direct from Miami'. After 1959, Cuban producers were 75–80 per cent supplied by 'countries which are two months away and which operate under a plan of their own . . . with different technology, equipment and raw material'. Indeed, existing Cuban equipment was based on US, not Soviet, weights and measures and specifications (Guevara, 1968T, 261). Moreover, although Cuba 'acquired a great number of factories' from Comecon, it 'found that in many of these plants the technical efficiency was insufficient when measured by international standards', making it hard for them to hold their own in international markets, 'and that the net result of the substitution of imports was very limited, because the necessary raw materials were not nationally produced' (ibid., 355).

The most radical change in recent years has been the 1982 law offering foreign investors a 49 per cent stake in Cuban joint ventures: 'Cuba is promoting its foreign investment law as vigorously as a capitalist country. Great emphasis is being placed on Cuba's strike-free record (strikers are imprisoned), cheap labour (the average monthly wage is 168 pesos – $215), unhindered repatriation of profits and low taxes' (*Financial Times*, 2 June 1982). But it seems this law will be applied mainly to peripheral activities like tourism and offshore oil-exploration (*Financial Times*, 21 April 1982), so it won't go to the heart of Cuba's problems. And Cuba's recently published economic guidelines still attach greater importance to further increases in co-operation and integration with Comecon (*Financial Times*, 9 September 1982). Sadly there is little reason to doubt that Cuba's foreseeable future will be as dismal as her recent past, especially as she is due to start repaying her debts to the USSR in 1986.

11 Yugoslavia and the vicissitudes of market socialism

In principle, collective ownership and control of the means of production ought to go hand in hand with some form of 'producers' democracy' and a market economy in which prices are allowed to broadly reflect relative costs and scarcities and so enable spontaneous market forces to promote an increasingly efficient use of resources to produce goods and services which consumers really want. However, until Yugoslavia and Hungary actually took major steps towards market socialism in the 1960s, the intellectually distinguished exponents of various forms of market socialism seemed to be championing a politically hopeless cause. Bazarov, Kondratiev, Trotsky and their closest associates were prematurely dispatched to the socialist Valhalla, signalling that Stalin's regime would have no truck with market socialism, and in the West Oskar Lange and Frederick Taylor epitomized the way in which 'mainstream economists escape reality by retreating into mathematical abstractions and an artificial world of formulae' (Nove, 1983, 60, 119–20). In Poland, in 1956–8, the same Professor Lange and his distinguished Polish disciples tried to steer their country towards market socialism and decentralized workers' control of the means of production, but their reforms were easily emasculated by Poland's neo-Stalinists, who naturally refused to relinquish their bureaucratic prerogatives (see Brzezinski, 1967, ch. 14; Pelczynski, in Leslie, 1980, chs 13–14). When Hungarian Premier Imre Nagy attempted to liberalize his country's economic and political system in 1956, with broad peasant and proletarian support, he merely precipitated a 'fraternal' military occupation of Hungary by Soviet troops, who crushed Hungary's incipient *socialist* revolution as brutally as Russian troops had previously crushed the Hungarian nationalist revolution of 1848–9 (see Lomax, 1976, on the *socialist* nature of the popular unrest in 1956). During the Soviet occupation over 15,000 Hungarians were wounded (2000 fatally), over 2000 Hungarian revolutionaries were executed and over 15,000 were imprisoned

(Molnar, 1971T, 240, 249). Determined to avoid Nagy's 'mistakes', the Czecho-slovak Communist Party attempted a much more cautious and controlled liberaliz-ation of the Czechoslovak economy and cultural life during 1963–8; indeed, it went to extraordinary lengths to reassure its nervous 'allies' that liberalization would not be allowed to jeopardize either the Party's so-called 'leading role' in every domain or Czechoslovakia's adherence to the Warsaw Pact (see Golan, 1971, 1973; Skilling, 1976; Kýn, 1975; Sik, 1967T, 1971T, 1972T). But the Soviet Politburo perceived that any genuine liberalization of Czechoslovakia's economic and cultural life would ultimately become incompatible with the Party's monopoly of power and decision-making; that the party was in fact unleashing forces which it couldn't hope to control for long; and that, in these circumstances, Czechoslovakia's continued allegiance to the Warsaw Pact could not be assured, despite the undoubted popu-larity of the Party's new leaders and the strength of pro-Russian sentiments in the past (not least because the West had betrayed Czechoslovakia in 1938). So the Soviet Politburo again demonstrated its understanding of 'proletarian international-ism', by sending 1 million troops into Czechoslovakia to emasculate the com-munist-led reform movement of 1963–8.

However, since the 1960s Yugoslavia and Hungary have made sufficient progress towards market socialism to prove beyond doubt that it really is a practical prop-osition, while at the same time highlighting major problems which remain to be solved.

The Yugoslav road to market socialism and workers' self-management

Many considerations have favoured a gradual transition to market socialism and towards a system of workers' self-management in Yugoslavia. (1) A small develop-ing economy with a comparatively narrow internal market and resource base is bound to be heavily dependent on international trade and, therefore, heavily exposed to the discipline of international market forces, including the constant pressure to use imported fuels and raw materials more and more efficiently and to produce products whose quality and cost are internationally acceptable. (2) Although Yugoslavia's communist regime initially adopted a Stalinist strategy emphasizing heavy industries, the inherent costs of such a strategy were com-pounded by the lack of an appropriate mineral resource base (apart from non-ferrous metals). (3) The power and prowess of Tito's Partisan movement, which numbered 1 million members by 1945 and liberated many parts of Yugoslavia, gave Tito's dictatorship more freedom of manoeuvre than that of any other East European state after 1945 (see Johnson, 1962, 173). (4) When Yugoslavia was 'excommunicated' by the other communist states in 1948 (for getting too big for its boots), it became vulnerably dependent on trade with and economic and military aid from the capital-ist West, which has always preferred clients who conduct their business on a

178   Communism and Development

commercial footing. And although Yugoslavia resumed economic relations with the Soviet bloc after Stalin's death (to reduce its dependence on the West and regain its freedom of manoeuvre), it preserved its independence by cultivating relations with a wide variety of states. (5) In 1961 Yugoslavia's population of 18.5 million included 7.8 million Serbs, 4.3 million Croats, 1.6 million Slovenes, 1.1 million Macedonians, 1.0 million Bosnian Muslims, 0.9 million Albanian Muslims, 0.5 million Montenegrins, 0.5 million Hungarians and 0.2 million Turks; and, according to the 1953 census, 41 per cent of the population was Eastern Orthodox, 32 per cent was Roman Catholic, 13 per cent Muslim and 13 per cent atheist or agnostic. Therefore, a centralized federation controlled by the largest ethnic group, as in the USSR, was really out of the question in communist Yugoslavia; indeed, most of the 1.7 million Yugoslav citizens killed in the 1940s perished as a result of ethnic and religious strife between Yugoslavia's mutually antagonistic nationalities, especially between Serbs and Croats (see Singleton, 1976, chs 6 and 14; Pavlowitch, 1971, 107–87). This has made it exceptionally desirable to devolve power to regional and local institutions (including enterprises), as the framework through which the nations of the Yugoslav federation can best hope to attain a modicum of co-operation. But, as regionalization was also liable to strengthen the centrifugal tendencies of Yugoslav society, there was considerable support for a gradual devolution of power to the lowest possible level, as the framework most likely to preserve Yugoslavia's territorial integrity. (6) Thoroughgoing decentralization also promised to make Yugoslavia less susceptible to Soviet take-over, whether by invasion or Soviet-backed coup: 'There would be no ready-made State apparatus for the Russians to take over, and no bureaucracy at the local economic or political level which was accustomed to carrying out orders from the centre. Partisan-type resistance could thus survive' (Granick, 1975, 333; cf. p. 67). (7) Marshal Tito, who remained the aloof yet charismatic strongman of Yugoslavia from 1945 until his death in 1980, 'attached enormous importance to building up the institutions of the state. . . . But he also learnt that institutions will crumble unless cemented by an ideal.' He valued Yugoslav ideals not for their own sake, 'but because he realized that it was only through them that he could acquire power'. Moreover, for Tito, 'belonging to a state was more important than belonging to an ethnic group. He did not hide his admiration for the Austro-Hungarian monarchy and its combination of law, order and local autonomy, maintaining a strong political centre' (Djilas, 1980).

During the 1950s Yugoslavia established consultative workers councils in state enterprises, devolved considerable power to local government institutions 'modelled on the Paris Commune of 1871', and abandoned the setting of obligatory physical output targets for industry and agriculture. It ceased to be a command economy. However, the Party (renamed League of Communists) maintained its virtual monopoly of power and decision-making, retained its 'vanguard' role in every secular domain and continued to imprison its domestic critics (among whom

Djilas was merely the most embarrassing). Until 1963 factory managers were still formally appointed by and responsible to Party-controlled state institutions, rather than workers' councils, and they retained the autocratic power to hire and fire employees and to make and enforce binding contracts (Singleton, 1976, 127–8). New enterprises were still founded and financed mainly by state institutions, in accordance with national economic Plans (see ibid., 130): 'The workers' council was supervised by the Party organization and its "transmission belt", the trade union' (Sirc, 1979, 39). Despite the supposed autonomy of Yugoslav enterprises, at least 50 per cent of investment resources were 'allocated from the centre', most prices were fixed by the state rather than market forces and profit-sharing contributed under 6 per cent of workers' incomes (ibid., 26, 22, 45). As late as 1961–4, 54 per cent of net enterprise income went to the state 'and only 46% was retained for payment of wages and salaries and allocation to enterprise funds' (Bicanic, 1973T, 213, 106). And so long as there was little real enterprise autonomy, the principle of workers' self-management was more apparent than real; 'Strictly speaking . . . without self-management there is no socialism' (Horvat, 1975, 127). Moreover, until 1957 82 per cent of industrial investment went into producer goods industries and under 10 per cent of total 'economic' investment went into agriculture, so prewar popular consumption levels weren't regained until about 1960 (Sirc, 1979, 34–5, 48–51); and in industry output per man was only 94 and 114 per cent of the prewar level in 1956 and 1960, respectively (ibid., 56). According to Bicanic (1973T, 78), 'a change of policy was decided in 1955, but its effect did not materialize until 1962, when the consumer goods industries began to move ahead faster than capital goods'. Unfortunately there was a renewed emphasis on lopsided heavy industrial development in the unsuccessful 1961–5 Plan, elaborated at the height of the Soviet–Yugoslav *rapprochement* (Sirc, 1979, 67–8).

However, since the decisive power struggles and ideological battles of 1963–6, in which the market socialists triumphed over the neo-Stalinists, Yugoslavia has made impressive headway towards market socialism. There has been greater enterprise autonomy, a larger decision-making and appointment-making role for workers' councils, increased reliance on market forces, less bureaucratic regulation of the economy, diminished emphasis on high-cost producer goods industries, greater realization of gains from international trade and specialization along lines of comparative cost advantage (including tourism), greater use of foreign capital and technology in joint ventures (foreigners can hold a 49 per cent stake), toleration of 100–250 strikes per annum, increased freedom of movement and emigration, increased remittances from approximately 1 million Yugoslav 'guestworkers' in Western Europe (by 1975 such remittances financed 8.6 per cent of consumer expenditure), and an impressive development of small-scale peasant agriculture alongside the inefficient and unwieldy state farms; during 1961–76 industrial labour productivity rose 4.6 per cent per annum, and personal consumption rose 6 per cent per annum in real terms (Sirc, 1979, 97–118, 193–7, 199–202, 238–9; Granick, 1975, 387–8; and see pp. 61–2 above).

Yugoslavia's educational provisions and health indicators have continued to advance and are comparable to those of its more centralized authoritarian-socialist neighbours (see Tables 2 and 3). Housing space per inhabitant rose from 8.7 m² in 1951 to 9.9 m² in 1961 and 12.2 m² in 1971, and housing rents averaged only 4 per cent of average personal expenditure in the 1970s. Moreover, by 1975 the pensions paid to Yugoslavia's 508,000 old-age pensioners averaged 74 per cent of average personal income (Sirc, 1979, 143–4).

Yugoslavia has wholly dispensed with the phalanx of central economic and social ministries characteristic of command economies. And, since major constitutional changes and policy decisions can only be made unanimously, 'every republic has, in effect, the power of veto. The process of reaching agreement on policies and solutions is sometimes cumbersome and slow', so there is much 'recourse to ad hoc and temporary measures while consensus is being hammered out' (World Bank, 1975, 42). Nevertheless, for all the drawbacks, the very weakness of the central government machinery and the difficulties of reaching consensus offer grounds for hoping that regional and local autonomy can survive attempts to revert to Stalinism.

Critics of market socialism have sometimes tried to hold it responsible for Yugoslavia's notoriously large interregional economic disparities. In fact these disparities were *already* well established by 1962, when Yugoslavia was still a *centrally* administered economy with minimal reliance on market forces, and the official gross product statistics overstate the actual disparities (e.g. by double-counting intermediate products, whose importance is greater in the more developed regions). Indeed, by 1976 Yugoslavia's interregional disparities in net *personal* income per inhabitant were remarkably modest, considering the extraordinary diversity of cultures, demographic conditions and natural endowments (Singleton and Carter, 1982, 215; Singleton, 1976, 245; Yugoslav Statistical Pocket Books, various issues):

% of Yugoslav average (per inhabitant)	Personal income 1976 (net)	Gross Material Product (at 1960 prices)				Gross Social Product (at 1972 prices)			
		1947	1952	1957	1962	1964	1976	1977	1980
Slovenia	115	175	187	182	199	185	202	200	198
Croatia	106	107	116	120	121	118	124	125	126
Vojvodina	100	109	89	109	103	111	117	118	121
Serbia proper	96	96	92	95	96	96	98	99	96
Macedonia	93	62	59	61	57	74	68	68	65
Montenegro	89	71	64	64	66	76	70	71	80
Kosovo	86	53	49	42	34	36	32	30	31
Bosnia-Hercegovina	84	83	88	74	73	70	64	65	66

Significantly, the poorer regions on the whole enjoyed higher investment rates than the richer regions, and the region most dependent on agriculture was among the richer regions. This suggests that investment rates and degrees of dependence on agriculture weren't among the major determinants of interregional disparities (Gregory, 1973, 222; Singleton, 1976, 225, 246; Yugoslav Statistical Pocket Books, various issues):

	Gross investment (% of Gross Social Product)			Capital– output ratios	Share of Gross Material Product, 1966 (% of total)	
	1953–7	1958–64	1965–9	1966–8	Agriculture	Industry
Slovenia	24	19	19	1.96	12	52
Croatia	21	27	19	1.46	18	47
Vojvodina	16	33	17	3.14	39	34
Serbia proper	28	29	22	3.96	24	42
Macedonia	32	52	41	7.62	26	40
Montenegro	92	71	35	13.09	17	43
Kosovo	18	52	46	9.34	33	38
Bosnia-Hercegovina	36	29	22	4.84	21	47

Yugoslavia's interregional disparities really widened because large-scale industrialization is by nature unevenly distributed, because investment in the poorer regions was heavily concentrated in capital-intensive producer goods industries (see Singleton, 1976, 251–2; Gregory, 1973), and because these not uncommon problems were compounded by uncommonly large cultural and demographic differences (Singleton and Carter, 1982, 215–29; Bergmann, 1975T, 132; World Bank, 1975, 370–9):

	Adult illiteracy (%)		Births per thousand persons			People of working age (%)	(%)	Participation rates (%) Male		Female	
	1961	1971	1950–4	1960–4	1975–9	1961	1971	1961	1971	1961	1971
Slovenia	2	1	23	18	18	59	56	60	59	38	38
Croatia	12	9	23	17	15	50	62	61	58	34	34
Vojvodina	11	9	23	16	14	61	63	63	60	26	27
Serbia proper	23	18	26	17	15	61	64	64	63	39	40
Montenegro	22	17	32	27	18	53	56	49	46	20	20
Macedonia	25	18	38	29	22	55	58	55	53	24	23
Bosnia-H.	33	23	38	32	18	55	57	55	51	24	23
Kosovo	41	32	44	42	34	50	50	51	43	18	8

In the 1970s economic disparities between national regions were, admittedly, somewhat larger in the multinational Federation of Yugoslavia than in the USSR, the state with which comparisons can most fairly be made (see Table 18, noting that Soviet disparities are partly offset by variations in the cost of living). However, the much older Soviet federation has had more time to bring about impressive reductions in inherited interregional economic disparities; the Soviet emphasis on centrally imposed uniformity has correspondingly reduced national/regional self-determination (although there is more than some Russophobes care to admit); and evidence presented in Chapters 2 and 9 tentatively suggested that Yugoslavia's overall personal income distribution in 1968 may have been more equal than that of the USSR in 1967 (see pp. 65–6, 161).

Some critics of market socialism and the Yugoslav system of self-management have also tried to hold the latter responsible for Yugoslavia's chronic unemployment, which stands in conspicuous contrast to the apparent absence of unemployment under the Soviet system. However, unemployment was *already* severe while Yugoslavia still had a *centrally* administered economy with minimal reliance on market forces. This was a good reason for abandoning that system in Yugoslavia, and there was no dramatic increase in registered unemployment (as a percentage of the workforce, including farm workers and excluding self-employed farmers) during the transition to market socialism and real self-management in 1965–71 (Singleton and Carter, 1982, 184; Bicanic, 1973T, 115; Granick, 1975, 394):

1961	1963	1965	1966	1967	1968	1969
6.7	7.5	7.3	7.4	8.2	9.1	7.9

1970	1971	1973	1975	1977	1980
7.5	7.2	8.5	11	12	13

The growth of Yugoslav unemployment since 1973, considerably later than the adoption of a self-managing market economy, is largely attributable to the severe impact of soaring energy costs and two world recessions on a small economy which has to import three-quarters of its oil requirements (as well as one-half of its natural gas requirements and most of its hard coal requirements), whose foreign trade has exceeded 40 per cent of Gross Domestic Material Product and whose important income from tourism and 1 million Yugoslav guestworkers in Western Europe has inevitably suffered from Western economic recession. Unlike the similarly small and mineral-deficient/trade-dependent economies of Hungary, Bulgaria, Cuba, East Germany and Czechoslovakia, the Yugoslav economy has not been 'cushioned' by high degrees of dependence on preferential access to 'soft' Soviet markets and heavily subsidized Soviet minerals: during 1973–80 the USSR took under one-quarter of Yugoslavia's exports and provided under one-sixth of its imports, on only moderately preferential terms. (The USSR has been similarly ungenerous towards the independent-minded neo-Stalinist regimes in Romania and Albania.) However, Yugoslavia's economic record before the reforms of 1965–6 suggests that she would have fared no better (and probably worse) under a more centralized neo-Stalinist system, which would have involved greater dependence on high-cost, capital-intensive heavy industries and inefficiently used imports of basic minerals. Centralized, autarkic industrialization still isn't a really viable option in Yugoslavia.

Unfortunately the USSR doesn't publish comprehensive data on the number of workers 'between jobs' (as they are euphemistically described), so we cannot make direct comparisons with Yugoslavia's published data on those 'seeking employment'. However, we do have some comparable data on annual rates of labour turnover in industry, as proportions of the industrial workforce (Granick 1975, 394; Powell, 1977, 269):

	1965	1966	1967	1968	1969	1970	1971
Yugoslavia (%)	22	18	16	15	15	17	16
USSR (%)	21	22	22	22	21	21	?

These data suggest that in both countries unemployment was to a large extent 'frictional' and that *the proportion of industrial workers 'between jobs' may have been higher in the USSR than in Yugoslavia*, remembering that Soviet unemployment normally lasted one or two months and that in Soviet Lithuania, in the late 1960s, 9 per cent of those 'between jobs' had been so for over a year (Powell, 1977, 272).

According to abstract theorizers, autonomous industrial co-operatives should be expected to maximize net revenue per member by restricting their membership/employment and by choosing capital- rather than labour-intensive technologies; and increased exposure to market forces should result in greater reluctance to expand membership or employment. But Yugoslav industrial employment expanded by a very respectable 55 per cent during 1965–79, despite increasingly difficult external economic conditions: 'few Yugoslav enterprises are ever forced into liquidation and they are rarely obliged to make redundancies. If insoluble problems arise, an enterprise in difficulty often merges with another and thereby saves the jobs at risk' (Singleton and Carter, 1982, 182, 185). Indeed, Yugoslav experience highlights 'the reluctance of self-managed enterprises to shed labour: workers do not vote for redundancies' (Nove, 1983, 138).

In 1970s Yugoslavia just over 50 per cent of the registered unemployed have been women, 'a much higher percentage than is usual' (Singleton and Carter, 1982, 184–5). This may be partly attributable to traditional male-chauvinist opposition to employment of women, but Yugoslav women may also have been unusually willing to register as 'seeking employment', thanks to the puritanical communist work ethic and the fervour of Yugoslav feminism since the Second World War (when women often participated in the Partisan movement). Moreover, by 1977 over half the registered unemployed were under 25 years old (as against one-third in 1965); and the unemployment rate ranged from only 1.7 per cent in prosperous Slovenia, where 24 per cent of the population had been under 15 years old in the 1971 census, to 21 per cent in Macedonia and 27 per cent in Kosovo where 32 and 43 per cent of the population had been under 15 in 1971, respectively (ibid., 185–6; World Bank, 1975, 373). Thus the growth in unemployment since 1973 has been aggravated by the unfavourable age structure of southern Yugoslavia, with its comparatively high birth rate. Furthermore, in 1978 the Yugoslav Council of Trade Unions complained that the economy needed an extra 400,000 skilled workers and engineers, yet only half these vacancies were being filled, because so many young Yugoslavs preferred to wait for more congenial white-collar or service sector jobs; likewise thousands of professional vacancies in small-town and rural areas were unfilled because so many appropriately qualified unemployed graduates preferred to wait for more congenial jobs (Singleton and Carter, 1982, 188). As part of the 'revolution of rising expectations', this increasing 'choosiness' is a major problem right across Europe, Russia and China, but that should not lead one to discount its contribution to the rapid growth of youth unemployment in Yugoslavia.

The growth of industrial employment in communist Yugoslavia has also been retarded by the initial neo-Stalinist overcommitment to high-cost, capital- and mineral-intensive producer goods industries, which still accounted for half Yugoslavia's industrial output in 1975 (Mayergoyz, 1978, 13). The consequent surge in fuel and raw material imports, together with underinvestment in peasant agriculture and labour-intensive consumer goods industries, has helped to generate steadily mounting trade deficits, endemic shortages and inflationary pressures, recurrent balance-of-payments problems, growing external indebtedness and disruptive 'stop-go' financial policies. During 1964–71 Yugoslavia's annual inflation rate was 13 per cent (Granick, 1975, 345), and since then it has fluctuated between 10 and 30 per cent. However, while acknowledging that inflation is a problem, it should be kept in perspective: postwar Italy, with similar long-term trends in inflation, has nevertheless managed to sustain very respectable rates of export-led economic growth; and for decades most Latin American economies have continued to expand in real per capita terms amid even higher long-term inflation rates.

Communist Yugoslavia also suffers from another legacy of her neo-Stalinist beginnings: a corrupt, repressive and doctrinaire one-party police state, against which the ordinary citizen often has little hope of redress, despite the impressive decentralization of power and decision-making. The centralized one-party police state has become a decentralized one-party police state. Yugoslavia's elective institutions have been dominated by the one and only 'vanguard and organizer of society', the League of Communists, whose members (5 per cent of the population) have been co-opted rather than democratically elected. Moreover, 'According to Amnesty International, Yugoslavia has more political prisoners than any other country in Eastern Europe' (*Sunday Times* (London), 19 September 1976); and another 1000 people were detained for 'political offences' in 1981, when the poor and largely Albanian-Muslim province of Kosovo stepped up its agitation for national autonomy, on a par with the Croats, Serbs, etc. (However, note that Kosovo cannot legitimately complain of economic neglect; its persistently high investment rates have been largely financed by federal funds, contributed by other national regions: see *Financial Times*, 7 April, 13 May, 21 May, 17 July and 8 September 1981; Singleton and Carter, 1982, 223–6.) The League of Communists also used its iron fist to crush nationalist agitation in Croatia in 1971–2 and in Kosovo in 1968, and both episodes resulted in massive purges and arrests within the respective regional hierarchies of the League (see Singleton, 1972, 1973; Cviic, 1974). Furthermore, in the 1960s, a survey of seventy Yugoslav enterprises found that two-thirds of managerial personnel were also officials of the ruling Party and/or its trade union organizations, that over one-third were Party secretaries, that nearly two-thirds were also members of the workers' self-management organs and that managerial personnel outnumbered manual workers in trade union posts (Benson, 1974, 267). However, existing Party-cum-managerial ascendancy in the trade unions and self-management organs does not preclude the possibility of eventual workers' control of the self-management system. The Constitution grants workers the formal right to elect whoever they choose to the workers' councils, which have the formal power to dismiss factory directors and their boards of management. But the proletariat will have to win many more battles before that day dawns. Meantime disciplinary matters, selection of individuals for dismissal (when unavoidable), arbitration of internal income differentials, and allocation of company housing and housing-credits seem likely to remain 'both the bread and butter of workers' management and the issues which excite real interest within the workers councils' (Granick, 1975, 382).

The growth of workers' control has also been impeded by the size of Yugoslav co-operatives. In 1958 Yugoslav industry averaged 372 persons per enterprise, as against 45 in Britain (1961), 17 in Japan (1963) and 48 in the USA (1958) (Shirokov, 1973T, 268). By 1964 Yugoslav industry averaged 540 persons per enterprise, and although this average had dipped to 530 by 1974, it was still five to twelve times the average for many Western states (see p. 147). Moreover, only 26 and 12 per cent of Yugoslav industrial enterprises employed under sixty people each in 1958 and 1970, respectively, whereas 35 per cent and 40 per cent, respectively, employed over 250 people each (Estrin, 1978, 5, 6, 38; World Bank, 1975, 120). In such large enterprises management naturally tends towards specialization, hierarchy and remoteness from the shopfloor. Managers naturally acquire 'a monopoly of the information necessary to the effective functioning of the enterprise' and the power 'to withhold or make public all the possible options open to the collective'; thus, in practice, control gravitates from the workers' councils to the executive boards, 'where manual workers are in a minority' (Benson, 1974, 261–2). Admittedly, there have been attempts to further democratize Yugoslav co-operatives. The workers' councils are 'elected by the vote of all the workers and each member serves for two years, with half the members being elected annually', and 'no person can serve more than two terms consecutively'. Since 1959 large enterprises have established lower-level organs of self-management for each section or 'basic unit of associated labour': 'Usually there are workers' councils for each unit and a separate workers' council for the enterprise as a whole. . . . The workers' council of each unit is permitted to take decisions applicable within the unit as long as their decisions do not harm other units' (World Bank, 1975, 45). Moreover, since 1968 enterprise directors have had to stand for re-election every four years (Granick, 1975, 339). However, such reforms cannot substantially alter the objective distance between the shopfloor and the specialized top-level management board, which tends to be dominated by those with political clout and/or managerial skills. Moreover, the competence of lower-level organs of self-management is necessarily circumscribed, and managerial continuity is in practice preserved by rotating senior technocratic, Party and trade union personnel between each other's posts within the same enterprise (Granick, 1975, 339). This is one reason why the smaller units and greater decentralization favoured by exponents of village communism offer more credible means of avoiding the hierarchy, inequality and workers' alienation characteristic of capitalism and state socialism. There is also some evidence that Yugoslavia's large enterprises suffer significant *diseconomies* of scale: we have already noted the relative inefficiency of her state farms (see p. 61); and in 1978 Yugoslavia's 200 largest enterprises, accounting for half her Gross Social Product, used 33 per cent more capital per employee than the average enterprise, 'but produced only 12% more output per employee than the average' (Sirc, 1981, 155). In theory, one might also expect Yugoslavia's large enterprises to indulge in considerable abuse of monopolistic power within the small Yugoslav market. However, Granick (1975, 413–20) found that 'the Yugoslav economy is quite competitive, that the many sectors of high concentration are relatively free from oligopolistic abuse because of the financial weakness of the oligopolists, and that sectors of high profit are subject to considerable invasion by enterprises seeking additional and more profitable activities'. By 1970 the scope for abuse of monopolistic power was also being limited by competition from abroad: industrial imports amounted to 60 per cent of gross industrial output (ibid., 344): 'Yugoslavia has been a member of GATT since 1965, when its tariff and trade regulations were brought into line with international practices. On the whole, Yugoslavia does not hide behind a high tariff wall' (Singleton and Carter, 1982, 243).

When Yugoslavia's enterprises and workers' councils won greater freedom to use their own resources as they saw fit, the cynics naturally predicted that they would neglect productive investment in favour of higher financial dividends for their members. In fact, although average real personal incomes rose 6.8 per cent per annum in the 1960s and 1.6 per cent per annum during 1971–5, Yugoslavia has persistently suffered from inflationary overinvestment rather than underinvestment (Sirc, 1981, 148–50, 156). Indeed, 'as much as 40% of Yugoslavia's social product was taken up by investment during the 1970s' (Singleton and Carter, 1982, 168). Such exorbitant levels of investment naturally encouraged prodigal misuse of resources, and much of this was directly or indirectly financed by irresponsible

Western and Yugoslav banks, at negative real rates of interest. There have been vain attempts to slow down the consequent inflationary merry-go-round through vague and unenforceable 'social contracts' and 'self-management agreements' on voluntary income restraint and through 'temporary' or 'emergency' price controls, but such measures merely tackle the symptoms rather than the disease (Sirc, 1981, 148–51). However, since the inefficacy of these palliatives is now beyond doubt and since its international credit rating has greatly declined, Yugoslavia may belatedly increase its emphasis on small-scale peasant agriculture and labour-intensive production of consumer goods, as against high-cost, capital- and mineral-intensive state farms and producer goods industries. Such a reorientation could substantially reduce the inflationary pressures, the shortages, the balance-of-payments problems and the chronic unemployment. Moreover, Western and Yugoslav banks could discourage profligate misuse of resources by adopting more responsible lending policies, by charging positive real rates of interest on loans and by concentrating on short-term finance for current activities (including peasant agriculture, exports and necessary imports) rather than new long-term finance for further expansion of the oversized state farm and producer goods sectors. Unfortunately Yugoslav Marxist–Leninists still tend to regard overinvestment in state farms and in producer goods industries as the 'engine of growth'. So they may well try to continue along the same old capital-and mineral-intensive growth path, by squeezing personal income and consumption levels, by increasing state control of prices, incomes, investment, imports, etc., and by thus eroding away the system of self-management and the prospects for eventual workers' control of decision-making. Moreover, Yugoslavia's Western creditors have encouraged the recent extension of state control. As the vice-premier responsible for economic affairs recently remarked, 'If Western institutions want a federal guarantee on every loan and contract, this will negate the ABC of the market economy and push us into a State economy' (*Financial Times*, 7 September 1983, 15). So Western financial institutions may well hasten the demise of Yugoslavia's market system and push her closer to the Soviet bloc, unless they radically reform their lending policies and oblige Yugoslavia to reorientate her economic stategy along the lines suggested above. Unfortunately the recent record of Western lending policies towards Eastern Europe and Latin America inspires little confidence in the capacity of Western financial institutions to act judiciously, even in their own interests: one year they act with irresponsible open-handedness, and another year they rigidly prescribe equally damaging state-administered austerity programmes, with little regard for what is economically and politically sustainable in the longer term or for the waste, discontent and disorientation engendered by 'stop-go' cycles. Indeed, these uncomprehending and unimaginative policies probably pose *the most immediate threat* to the survival of market economies, as market economies.

In sum, Yugoslavia's main systemic shortcomings have stemmed not from her latter-day pursuit of market socialism as a possible basis for real enterprise autonomy and workers' self-management, but from the tenacious political-cum-economic legacies of the preceding neo-Stalinist system, especially the doctrinaire one-party police state and overinvestment in large-scale capital- and mineral-intensive state farms and producer goods industries.

Hungary's halfway house

Several factors have favoured a gradual transition towards market socialism in Hungary since the 1960s. It is even smaller, more mineral-deficient and more trade-dependent than Yugoslavia. By the 1970s foreign trade amounted to over 70 per cent of Hungary's Net Domestic Product, despite her landlocked situation. Half her population still lives in rural areas (mainly in comparatively large villages), although most rural inhabitants now have non-agricultural livelihoods. The fertile alluvial, loessic and black soils of the Central Danubian Plain have rendered three-quarters of Hungary's land surface suitable for farming and have given it a comparative cost advantage in food production, which in the 1960s provided one-third of its employment, one-third of its GMP and nearly one-half of its hard currency earnings. Furthermore, out of the 800,000 members of Hungary's ruling Party in mid-1956, only 95,000 remained Party-members (Molnar, 1971T, 251); and this 'withering away' of the ruling Party (unlike the Czechoslovak experience of 1968–9) made it easier for the new Party leadership installed by the Soviet occupation forces to control the subsequent process of 'reform from above'. Indeed, party leader Janos Kadar, the shrewd opportunist who has ruled Hungary ever since the Soviet invasion, has found it expedient to offer his compatriots more and more economic and cultural freedoms as surrogates for more far-reaching changes in Hungary's polity and international alignment.

Since 1956 there has been diminished emphasis on (inappropriate) capital- and mineral-intensive producer goods industries, although they still accounted for an absurd 63 per cent of industrial output in 1975 (Mayergoyz, 1978, 13). And since the 1960s agriculture's share of total investment has been broadly commensurate with its contribution to Gross Material Product (see Table 10). Moreover, peasant hostility to rural collectivization, expressed in a mass withdrawal from Hungary's collective farms during 1956, was somewhat mollified by the subsequent substitution of commercial contracts for obligatory deliveries of farm produce to the state, by active encouragement of private and co-operative sidelines within the socialized sector of agriculture, by a steady expansion of collective and state farm autonomy (including greater peasant participation in farm management and responsibilities), by informal subdivision of Hungary's oversized farms into semi-autonomous sub-units, by a proliferation of village industrial co-operatives, and by a comparatively rapid expansion of farm output, farm exports and rural amenities (see Tables 10–12 and 14; and Csizmadia, 1977T; Enyedi, 1976T; Benet and Gyenis, 1977T, 10–18,

119–92; Elek, 1977; Fischer and Uren, 1973). By 1970 there was virtual parity of average urban and rural incomes, and post-1956 Hungary has developed the world's most flexible and successful system of collectivized agriculture, from which other mineral-deficient developing countries can learn a great deal. Hungary is to collective agriculture what Denmark was to private agriculture; starting from opposite poles, they have converged on Chayanov's ideal.

In 1961, under the slogan 'Those not against us are with us', Kadar also began to liberalize travel, censorship and cultural life. Finally, in 1968 the Party quietly inaugurated a carefully prepared 'New Economic Mechanism', as a major step towards market socialism. In principle, productivity growth, innovation and responsiveness were to be promoted 'by freeing enterprises to form horizontal relations with each other and with markets of final demand'; and 'The social interest embodied in the national plan was to be expressed indirectly', through 'fiscal instruments, wage and price controls, credit policy, foreign exchange multipliers etc.', which were intended to 'mould the initiatives of profit-orientated enterprises into patterns corresponding . . . to central preferences' (Radice, 1981, 130; for a full exposition, see Friss, 1971T). Provided the price structure could be made to reflect relative costs and scarcities, profits could broadly reflect enterprise performance, generate autonomous investment and bonus funds, increase responsiveness to customers' requirements and promote an increasingly efficient use of resources. Another 'virtue of coordinating a socialist economy through financial mechanisms rather than by direct physical planning lies in the freeing of central authorities from the need to make decisions concerning each production unit' (Granick, 1975, 269). By 1971 manufacturing enterprises were financing two-thirds of their own fixed investment, obligatory output targets had been abandoned, only 3–4 per cent of the intermediate goods consumed by industry were subject to central bureaucratic allocation, and Hungary was no longer a command economy (ibid., 275, 242–3, 282). Moreover, growing dependence on foreign trade increasingly exposed Hungary's economy to external market forces and competition; among other things, this obliged it to become Comecon's least inefficient energy user (see Tables 19 and 20). By 1971 Hungary's currency was semi-convertible (albeit at multiple exchange rates) and Hungarian enterprises were fairly free to deal directly with Western firms, although the state still regulated foreign trade licences, maintained specialized foreign trade corporations and enforced trade commitments to Comecon partners (Nove and Nuti, 1972, 343). It was considered 'impermissible, except in rare circumstances, to dismiss workers on any grounds other than those of gross incompetence or gross violation of factory discipline', and inefficient enterprises were usually dealt with by merger and/or redeployment rather than closure (Granick, 1975, 245–7). Contrary to fears that the new system would be plagued by immobility of labour, industrial labour turnover averaged 32–36 per cent per annum during 1968–71 (ibid., 239, 250). And yet, according to Cviic (1980, 71), 'Nearly half the population are wage-earners, which is as near to full employment as you can get.'

However, Hungary hasn't yet attained a fully-fledged market socialist system. The Hungarian polity and Hungarian industry remain essentially hierarchical and authoritarian. Enterprise directors are often influential members of the ruling Party, and they are normally Party/state appointees who work hand-in-glove with the Party hierarchy. The trade unions are still Party-controlled agencies which enforce labour discipline and administer certain social welfare provisions on behalf of the state. Hungary has nothing comparable to the workers' councils or the local and regional autonomy found in Yugoslavia, and the workers' strike weapon is conspicuous by its virtual absence. But the situation isn't hopeless. The 1967 labour code gave trade unions a 'regularly used' right to veto management decisions: 'At the national level the unions meet the government twice a year to discuss issues of economic and social policy'; and at the 1980 Party Congress the trade union overlord urged the Party to 'create conditions in which the committee of shop stewards, on behalf of the workers, can judge the work and activities of economic leaders. . . . This would make the workers' right of participation less ambiguous' (Cviic, 1980, 70). Unfortunately the size of Hungary's industrial enterprises is in itself more conducive to hierarchy, inequality and workers' alienation than to the growth of workers' participation and control. Indeed, the situation is so embarrassing that in 1973 the socialist writer Miklos Haraszti was subjected to a 'show trial' for his plain-speaking shopfloor report on the work regime at Hungary's Red Star Tractor Factory (see Haraszti, 1977T). In 1973 Hungarian industry averaged 1070 persons per enterprise, double the exorbitant Yugoslav average and ten to twenty times the average for many Western states (see p. 147). Hungary has also retained industrial branch ministries, which inevitably exercise considerable powers of patronage over the enterprises under their jurisdiction: 'the vertical relations of dependence which characterized the earlier system of directive planning have not been broken' (Radice, 1981, 133). Enterprises are under powerful pressure to conform to the perceived wishes of their economic and political overlords. More fundamentally, 'If the centre were really to withdraw from the visible tutelage of enterprises, it would lose a necessary foundation stone of the structure of political power, namely its monopoly right to form and interpret the social interest' (ibid., 135). Thus the monolithic, hierarchical polity is the ultimate obstacle to fully-fledged enterprise autonomy and socialism.

Furthermore, during 1972–7 the new system was stultified by a rampant proliferation of central controls and subsidies, because every group clamoured for special treatment, because opponents of reform claimed that it mainly benefited enterprise managers and technocrats and because world market conditions in the 1970s brought about an alarming, unavoidable deterioration in Hungary's external terms of trade (see Cviic, 1980; Buchan, 1983). However, the predictable failure of subsidies and partial recentralization to enhance either the economy's performance or the workers' position vis-à-vis managers and technocrats, together with an awareness that the relative position of workers had been much more 'inferior' under

Stalinism and that Hungary's greatly increased living standards had become the envy of the Soviet bloc, enabled the reformers to regain the initiative in 1979–80. During 1979–82 drastic domestic price increases, bringing Hungary's prices more into line with world market prices, largely eliminated market disequilibria (artificial 'shortages') and the need for cumbersome central controls and subsidies (Buchan, 1983; Nove, 1983, 125–30). The 1980 Party Congress approved a very sober Plan for 1981–5, reflecting recent increases in energy costs, slack demand for Hungary's traditional exports and the need to avoid overinvestment (and the attendant 'shortages' and inflationary pressures) if the market system is to function effectively (*Financial Times*, 1 April 1980). In 1980 most state-owned shops and restaurants were leased to small private operators, to foster more responsive cost-conscious and competitive management, and to get away from some of the 'shortages' and drab lack of variety characteristic of the retail trades in other Comecon states (*Financial Times*, 4 September 1981; Nove, 1983, 129–30). Moreover, under a law passed in 1981, 'groups of workers can lease the equipment or facilities of their State employers to perform, outside working hours, work on their own account' (*Financial Times*, 11 February 1983, 2). In 1983 Hungary also began to establish duty-free zones ('freeports') for joint ventures with Western firms; Hungary had hitherto attracted only eleven industrial joint ventures of that sort (see ibid., 4 February 1983). And according to the main Party newspaper *Népszabadság*, three out of four families actively participate in the informal 'second economy', which absorbs one-sixth of Hungary's man-hours worked and contributes one-sixth of popular consumption (Cviic, 1980, 68–70; *Financial Times* 20 November 1981, 29 July 1982). In particular, small-scale private and co-operative construction work, repair services, craft industries and taxi services are flourishing (Nove, 1983, 128; Cviic, 1980, 70). Most radically of all, the reformers are pressing the Party to permit *contested* general elections from 1985 onwards, to consolidate the process of liberalization (see *Financial Times*, 15 February 1983). This would bring Hungary closer to the status of Finland, whence Soviet occupation forces were withdrawn in 1955. But, like Finland, Hungary knows that it is 'on probation'; all concessions are conditional on 'self-censorship' and avoidance of anything that could be construed as 'anti-Soviet behaviour'.

Finally, it is encouraging to note the recent growth of Chinese interest in market socialism (see Nove, 1983, 150–1; Feuchtwang and Hussain, 1983) and China's growing reliance on market forces as stimuli to *autonomous* economic activity and greater efficiency. However, Yugoslav and Hungarian experience suggests that it is very difficult to shake off the legacies of Stalinist or neo-Stalinist systems, once they have been established. Ideally communist regimes should proceed *directly* to a decentralized and pluralistic economic–political system based on small-scale production, without first undergoing the treadmills of Stalinism.

In principle, even in its Leninist form, 'proletarian' socialism presupposes the willingness and competence of the proletariat and/or its elected management boards to take over the running of large-scale industry, transport and agriculture: 'We, the workers, shall organize large-scale production on the basis of what capitalism has already created, relying on our experience as workers' (Lenin, 1969T, 46). Moreover, if an economic system based on worker-controlled enterprises is to avoid the kinds of irresponsibility which breed ever-mounting inefficiency, production costs, waste of resources and popular disaffection, then each worker-controlled enterprise must be given to understand that it will essentially reap the rewards of its own efficiency and successes and shoulder the cost of its own inefficiency and mistakes, within a price structure which fairly reflects relative costs and scarcities; if necessary, enterprises in difficulty or in need of restructuring should be able to borrow from enterprises with surplus funds, provided they negotiate mutually acceptable terms and conditions; but it would be foolhardy to erect a system of blank cheques and power without responsibility. Unfortunately industrial labour movements have normally favoured the establishment of giant bureaucratic state enterprises which subsist on state support, which substitute state control for workers' control, and which display at least as much hierarchy, inequality and workers' alienation as do giant capitalist corporations. This preference for bureaucratic, hierarchical state enterprises seems to suggest that, in reality, Western and Leninist labour movements lack confidence in the capacity of workers to manage their own industries. Indeed, apart from Yugoslavia, the existing 'proletarian' socialist regimes haven't even attempted to use state enterprises as a preparatory transition towards autonomous workers' control of major enterprises. Admittedly, it is just conceivable that some Western labour movements really do believe in the economic viability and superiority of worker-controlled industries. If so, one could reasonably expect some Western socialist governments and trade unions to invest *mainly* in worker-controlled enterprises, to urge workers to invest their savings (including pension contributions, insurance premiums and redundancy payments) *mainly* in worker-controlled enterprises and to transform existing state enterprises into worker-controlled enterprises. After all, most Western proletariats have acquired more education, more skills, more capital assets, more political and trade union rights, and more industrial 'muscle' than Marx, Engels, or Lenin ever thought possible *under capitalism*. If workers' control of industry is a seriously intended objective, then workers must obtain as much managerial experience and control as possible, as soon as possible, before workers' control can be further pre-empted by various forms of bureaucratic or hierarchical control. The sooner and the more extensively worker-controlled enterprises can demonstrate their viability, especially in competition with capitalist and/or state enterprises, the more credible 'proletarian' socialism will become, and the more workers will join and invest in worker-controlled enterprises, and the sooner capitalism and state-run economies will be superseded by a form of socialism that would be really worthwhile. However, if industrial workers prove incapable of running their industries efficiently and without recourse to the forms of coercion and intimidation characteristic of existing 'proletarian' dictatorships, or if industrial labour movements are in fact *afraid* to take up the great challenge of setting up and running their own industries, then 'proletarian' socialism has little to offer, apart from more and more bureaucratic–hierarchical state control, which breeds its own forms of inequality, corruption and alienation. For workers' control to be really effective, workers must be willing to take *full responsibility* for their own mistakes, their own entrepreneurial risks, their own unfulfilled commitments, their own financial obligations, their own discipline and their own judgements. And fear of responsibility may be the main stumbling-block – the fundamental psychological difference between workers and entrepreneurs, which has always kept workers in subordinate roles.

12 The results of rural collectivization

Since this book began with a reappraisal of the possibilities of village-based development, it seems most appropriate to conclude with a reassessment of the actual achievements and pitfalls of rural collectivization, highlighting some of the most striking successes (e.g. in North Korea and parts of Central Asia) as well as some of the disasters (e.g. in Kazakhstan and Mongolia). The results and objectives have been too varied to support any clear-cut or dogmatic verdict on the pros and cons of rural collectivization. It is more fruitful to identify some of the forms and circumstances in which rural collectivization has been successful or unsuccessful in promoting agricultural development.

At various times and places rural collectivization has performed at least *seventeen functions*: (1) 'downward' levelling of income and wealth within the rural sector; (2) 'upward' levelling of rural access to health, education, technical and other services, helping to diffuse new techniques and crop or animal varieties, mainly through pooling and (locally) centralized management of resources; (3) the establishment of increased Party–state supervision and control of the rural population, including its work patterns and geographical/occupational mobility; (4) making sure that deliveries of rural produce to state procurement agencies and urban industry take precedence over other claims, thereby shifting almost the whole burden of adjustment to harvest fluctuations on to the rural population and creating a more stable context for urban–industrial planning; (5) 'Integrated rural development requires by its very nature a greater participation of the rural masses. Democratization, however, must be functional and not restricted to formally "progressive" institutions and legislation. In concrete terms, it means the mobilization of activity cells, a delegation of initiative, task execution and decision-making' (FAO, 1978, 310): in theory, collectivized agriculture should be able to fill the bill nicely. Unfortunately the establishment of formally participatory institutions such

as collective farms does not necessarily evoke broad and effective popular participation, especially when peasants and herdsmen have been antagonized by communist
condescension, coercion, intimidation, corruption, contempt, mismanagement,
arrogation of privileges, inequitable remuneration and inequitable urban–rural
terms of trade: in these circumstances rural collectivization has merely promoted
rural apathy and demoralization; (6) the elimination of private vested interests
which may have hitherto obstructed projects, activities and changes in land use
which could benefit the rural community as a whole; however, it should be remembered that rural collectivization can create its own vested interests in the status quo;
(7) the extraction of an 'unrequited' financial and/or goods surplus from the rural
sector, for use in urban–industrial development ('primitive socialist accumulation'); but it should be remembered that inasmuch as collectivization has *depressed*
agricultural output (e.g. in 1930s Russia), it may have reduced agriculture's
capacity to produce surpluses for use in *any* sector (see Millar, 1970–1, 1971–2;
Nove, 1970–1; Ellman, 1975); (8) the release of 'surplus' labour from agriculture
for use in other activities, through increased mechanization of agriculture and more
intensive utilization of the remaining agricultural workforce (especially women and
elderly men); but if, as many Western historians and economists believe, collectivization has *retarded* the growth of agricultural labour productivity, then it may have
retarded the rate of release of labour from agriculture; (9) the extension of cultivation
into marginal lands, where the economic/ecological risks and necessary capital
outlays may be too great for own-account farmers: thus in the Soviet 'Virgin Lands'
campaign of 1954–63, the very high risks were borne by the state; (10) the intensification of agriculture through labour absorption (e.g. in China under Mao); (11) the
intensification of agriculture through high rates of agricultural investment (e.g. in
Eastern Europe and North Korea since the 1960s, and in the USSR since 1971); (12)
the absorption of rural industries into the urban–industrial sector (e.g. in the USSR
under Stalin); (13) the promotion of rural industries (e.g. in China under Mao); (14)
the promotion of vertical agro-industrial integration (most notably in Bulgaria,
Hungary and Soviet Central Asia); (15) the 'de-nomadization' of nomadic pastoral-
ists (e.g. in Kazakhstan, Mongolia and Xinjiang); (16) large-scale agricultural
colonization or resettlement of rural populations (e.g. in western Poland, the Soviet
'Virgin Lands', Inner Mongolia and Xinjiang); and (17) mobilization of the rural
population for decentralized defence and a rural 'siege economy' (see p. 67–9 on
North Vietnam). In varying degrees the first six functions have been well-nigh
universal features of rural collectivization. The other eleven functions of rural
collectivization have been combined roughly as shown in the table on p. 196.

Rural collectivization has also assumed a wide variety of *institutional forms*:
collective farms (formally autonomous producers' co-operatives); state farms (state
enterprises based on wage labour); China's vast 'people's communes'; Bulgaria's
vast 'agrarian-industrial complexes', established in 1968–70 and subsequently
copied in parts of the USSR and East Germany; and various 'transitional forms'

(7) Primitive socialist accumulation (8) Release of 'surplus' labour (9) Extension of cultivation (12) Rural de-industrialization	European USSR, 1930s–1950s Siberia, 1930s–1953* Eastern Europe, early 1950s * Plus (16)

(11) Intensification/capital absorption
(8) Release of 'surplus' labour
(14) Agro-industrial integration
(13) Some rural industrialization
	Hungary, Bulgaria and Romania since
	   mid-1950s
	North Korea, Albania and European USSR
	   since 1960s
	North Vietnam, 1959–64 and since 1973*
	   * Plus (16)

(11) Intensification/capital absorption (8) Release of 'surplus' labour (14) Agro-industrial integration (12) Rural de-industrialization	Czechoslovakia and GDR since mid-1950s Western Poland since early 1950s* Cuba since 1970s * Plus (16)
(10) Intensification/labour absorption (13) Rural industrialization (16) Some rural resettlement	Han areas of China since mid-1950s South Vietnam and Laos since 1976

(10) Intensification/labour absorption
(9) Extension of cultivation
(14) Agro-industrial integration
	Uzbekistan, Tajikistan and Azerbaijan since
	   1930s
	Siberia since mid-1950s*
	1960s Cuba
	   * Plus (16)

(15) De-nomadization (9) Extension of cultivation (16) Massive colonization/resettlement	Kazakhstan, Kirghizia and Turkmenistan since 1930s Mongolia and Xinjiang since 1950s (Afghanistan since 1978)
(17) Decentralized defence (10) Intensification/labour absorption (13) Rural industrialization	North Vietnam, 1965–72

(mutual aid teams, purchasing co-operatives, marketing co-operatives, etc.). Collective and state farms have had widely differing degrees of autonomy: farm autonomy is greatest under market socialism and most circumscribed in the command economies, although even in the latter farms are subject to widely differing degrees of party–state supervision/control and to very varied state demands; farms in remote areas usually enjoy greater *de facto* autonomy than those near big towns; and multiproduct farms can be more 'self-reliant' than those which specialize in the production of cotton or sugar, most of which is delivered to state agencies. The average size of collective and state farms has ranged from a few hundred hectares and persons in North Vietnam, and some of the smaller communist states, to several thousand hectares and persons in Bulgaria, Romania, China and the USSR. In some areas farmwork is performed by large and highly regimented brigades, but in others farmwork is delegated to relatively small and autonomous teams. There are also wide variations in the size and importance of 'private plots' and private livestock holdings permitted to collective farmers and state farmworkers. So the average size of collective and state farms isn't necessarily a good indicator of the average size of agricultural production units. In some areas rural industries are incorporated into collective farms, in others they form separately constituted co-operatives, in others they are part of the state sector and in others they belong to people's communes or agrarian-industrial complexes; there is no consistent pattern. In the more backward communist states collective farmers' remuneration is still based on a cumbersome system of workpoints and payment-in-kind, but the more highly developed communist states (including the USSR) have gone over to monthly cash payments (advances), which are more convenient for the farmer, simpler to administer, and more conducive to proper accounting, accountability and cost control. Moreover, since the 1960s the USSR and Eastern Europe have extended to collective farmers the social insurance schemes hitherto reserved for state employees; i.e. collective farmers can look forward to a pension on reaching the age of retirement, provided they have paid their contributions. Elsewhere collective farmers have to depend on their savings and/or their relatives when they become too old to work. Furthermore, in the USSR and Outer Mongolia collectivization was preceded by the complete and permanent abolition of private property in land, without compensation. In every other communist state only the largest landholdings were expropriated and most of this land was redistributed to the peasantry and landless farm labourers as private property. In Bulgaria, Hungary, Czechoslovakia, North Vietnam, Poland, Cuba and the GDR some compensation was paid to many of the people whose land was expropriated and, except in North Vietnam, various forms of payment were made by people who received land (as formal acknowledgement that it had become their private property). In Romania, Yugoslavia, Albania, China and North Korea land was expropriated without any compensation and those who received land did not have to pay for it, but that land nevertheless remained private property. Yet, paradoxically, collectivization met with more devastating resistance in the USSR and Outer Mongolia, which abolished private property in land in 1918–22 and in 1921–4, respectively, than it did in the states which retained private property in land.

Rural collectivization has occurred in very diverse natural environments, ranging from cold temperate forests and grasslands to the deserts of Turkestan and the tropical conditions of Cuba and Indo-China. It has occurred in industrialized societies (the GDR and Czechoslovakia), as well as in various types of peasant, pastoral and plantation society. Collectivized agriculture exists in economies with widely differing productive capacities, as can be seen from the World Bank's very rough estimates of GNP per capita in 1978, expressed in US dollars (World Bank, 1980, 110–11):

Laos	Vietnam	China	North Korea	Albania	Cuba	Outer Mongolia
90	170	230	730	740	810	940

Romania	Yugo-slavia	Bulgaria	Hungary	Poland	USSR	Czecho-slovakia	GDR
1750	2380	3230	3450	3670	3700	4720	5710

Confronted by this impressive diversity, it would be foolhardy to make any doctrinaire pronouncement 'for' or 'against' rural collectivization. Nevertheless, economists and historians are doctrinally divided on the merits of rural collectivization. At one extreme there is a substantial literature extolling the alleged virtues of rural collectivization in China and/or putting forward Chinese-style collectivization as a panacea for the rural inequities and inequalities which can be perpetuated or exacerbated by capitalist 'Green Revolution' strategies aimed at diffusing higher-yielding crop strains and technologies within existing agrarian structures based on private property (see, for instance, Aziz, 1978; Byres and Nolan, 1976; Robinson, 1964, 1976, 6–14; Gurley, 1976, ch. 5; Byres, 1979; Griffin, 1979, 202–8; Griffin and Saith, 1980; Khan, 1977). It has also been argued that rural collectivization and the subsequent development of collectivized agriculture proceeded more smoothly and successfully in China than in the USSR (Nolan, 1976). Unfortunately, as indicated in Chapter 8, per capita food production and consumption has virtually *stagnated* in China since the 1930s, whereas there have been major *increases* in the USSR as well as in densely populated India, Pakistan, Indonesia, the Philippines, Taiwan and both North and South Korea (see pp. 129, 135–6 and 139–40, and Table 11). According to Chinese communist sources, the astonishingly rapid collectivization of Chinese agriculture in the mid-1950s was accomplished peacefully and 'from the bottom upwards'. But it is hard to believe that the wishes of 500 million peasants with few living traditions of communal landownership suddenly coincided with Mao's 1955 resolution 'On the co-operative transformation of agriculture' or with the Central Committee's 1958 'Resolution on the establishment of people's communes in rural areas'. Such claims are about as credible as the Stalinist insistence that nearly 100 million Soviet peasants suddenly experienced a great spiritual conversion to collectivized agriculture during 1928–33. Unfortunately there is a dearth of independent eye-witness accounts of Chinese collectivization, which would help us to assess the candour of the very rosy official accounts. 'Studies done so far have concerned themselves less with the peasant movement as such than with the Communist movement in the countryside' (Bianco, 1974–5, 313), even though the communist movement was but a drop in China's ocean of peasants. However, if there was less peasant resistance to collectivization in China than in the USSR, it may have been simply because millions of potential opponents had already been murdered and/or dispossessed, because this circumstance made the ubiquitous presence of the People's Liberation Army all the more intimidating and because most Chinese peasants had little to lose when the average Chinese farm had few livestock (Table 13) and only about 1.1 ha of cropland (Table 7). Chinese communist sources suggest that the 1949–53 'land reforms' dispossessed 20–25 million households, even though in 1949 the average 'landlord' household had owned only 7.7 ha of cropland and the average 'rich peasant' household had owned only 2.4 ha of cropland; and in 1957 Chou En-lai informed the National People's Congress that 16.8 per cent of 'counter-revolutionaries' (presumably 'landlords' and 'rich peasants') had been executed, mostly during 1950–2 (see Lethbridge, 1963, 59, 198; Gurley, 1976, 238). This supports one Sinologist's claim that over 5 million Chinese perished amid the 'land reform' (Domes, 1973T, 38). Admittedly, China seemingly avoided the widespread slaughter of livestock and contraction of farm output which accompanied Soviet collectivization. But the most obvious reason for this was that, except in Xinjiang (Sinkiang) and Inner Mongolia, few of China's largely vegetarian inhabitants can have possessed much livestock other than poultry (see Tables 8 and 13); so Han Chinese agriculture must have been only slightly dependent on livestock rearing and horse-drawn equipment. It is also doubtful whether China has less rural inequality than the USSR (see Table 18; and Vermeer, 1982; Bronson and Kreuger, 1971; Klatt, 1983, 30–2; McAuley, 1979, 29–35, 59, 65). As indicated in Chapter 8, China still has a power structure conducive to hierarchy, rural inequality and corruption, against which ordinary citizens can have little hope of redress so long as the press, law courts and police are tightly controlled by the system's chief beneficiaries, the Party apparatus. But, supposing rural China were more equal than the USSR, this would merely mean that China's peasants are more uniformly poor: in the 1970s grain output per agricultural inhabitant in China was under one-quarter of the Soviet and East European level; this disparity has steadily widened since the mid-1950s (thanks to the virtual stagnation of China's per capita grain output); and the disparity would be even wider if non-grain produce were included in the reckoning. So much for the 'success' of Chinese collectivization.

At the other extreme, most Western Sovietologists have long regarded collectivized agriculture as the major weakness or Achilles heel of the Comecon economies. They frequently point out that grain output per man-year and per hectare in communist states is generally far below Western levels, partly because Western agriculture uses far larger 'commercial' energy inputs (see table on p. 200).

Even in North America, Western agriculture has largely avoided the potential diseconomies of large-scale farming by limiting the average size of farm to a level where it can still be worked by a single family: e.g. the average 160-ha US farm is

Within agriculture, 1972–3:	Grain output per man-year (ton)	Grain output per hectare (ton)	'Commercial' energy used per hectare*
USA and Canada	67.9	3.5	20.2
Western Europe	5.8	3.2	27.9
USSR and Eastern Europe	4.1	1.7	9.3
Communist East Asia	0.9	1.8	2.4
Third World	0.8	1.3	2.2

* Mechanical traction, irrigation, fertilizer and pesticide, measured in joules × 10^9.

Source: FAO, 1976, 94, 97.

worked by an average of just 1.6 people, and only one in five US farms regularly uses hired labour. This solution to the problem of diseconomies of scale, together with high levels of formal and informal farm support, has enabled the West to achieve extraordinarily high levels of capital and energy intensity in agriculture and to become a net exporter of food (Barna, 1979, 115–25), contrary to the common assumption that Western overeating is a major cause of Third World starvation. Indeed, some of the Third World's current economic problems stem from the fact that the West is no longer a net importer of food.

Western Sovietologists have also quite rightly deplored the chaotic, impromptu and brutal implementation of Soviet collectivization during 1929–35. However, one should beware suggestions that rural collectivization was bound to be accompanied by massive resistance, coercion and losses. Wholesale collectivization was accomplished *without* widespread violence and destruction in Bulgaria, Romania, East Germany and Czechoslovakia during 1950–62, in Albania during 1956–63, in North Vietnam during 1958–66 and on Cuba's sugar plantations during 1959–63. Although collectivization did involve officially acknowledged 'excesses', 'errors', 'distortions' and 'violations of the principle of voluntariness' in parts of Czechoslovakia, East Germany and Bulgaria, such occurrences were the exception rather than the rule in those states (see Stanis, 1976T, 104, 120; Brown, 1970, 196–203; Krejci, 1972, 20; Dunman, 1975, ch. 4). Moreover, even though Eastern Europe's peasants were comparatively well endowed with livestock (see Table 13), on the whole *livestock numbers actually increased slightly during the 1950s collectivization campaign*. The decline in horse numbers wasn't a specifically East European phenomenon, and in 1960 Eastern Europe still had as many horses per inhabitant as did the rest of Europe. Moreover, it seems that the not unfavourable East European averages in Table 13 do not conceal any *national* disasters (see table on p. 201, compiled from Mitchell, 1975, 307–17; Grigorescu, 1976, 80; World Bank, 1979, 644; and FAO Yearbooks, various issues).

Several factors helped to keep down the costs of collectivization in Eastern Europe: there was relatively broad and careful preparatory discussion and briefing

Millions	Romania 1948	1951	1955	1959	1962	Bulgaria 1947	1952	1956	1961	Albania 1947–52	1951–6	1961–2	1963–4
Cattle	4.2	4.5	4.6	4.4	4.7	1.7	1.6	1.6	1.4	0.41	0.40	0.42	0.40
Sheep	(10)	10.2	10.9	10.7	12.3	8.8	7.6	7.8	9.3	1.63	1.60	1.59	1.58
Pigs	1.6	2.2	4.4	4.0	4.7	1.0	1.1	1.4	2.6	0.05	0.06	0.13	0.11

	GDR 1948	1951	1956	1961	Czechoslovakia 1947	1950	1956	1961	Hungary 1949	1952	1957	1961
Cattle	2.9	3.8	3.7	4.5	3.3	4.3	4.1	4.4	1.9	2.1	2.0	2.0
Sheep	0.7	1.2	1.9	1.9	0.4	0.6	1.0	0.6	0.9	1.5	1.8	2.6
Pigs	2.6	7.1	8.3	8.9	2.6	3.8	5.4	5.9	3.3	4.7	5.0	5.9

on the precise institutional forms and developmental functions to be assumed by collectivized agriculture in each region; there was widespread use of transitional institutions and compensation payments, recognizing that some peasants gave up much more private or personal property than others; during 1946–62 the USSR exported over 100,000 tractors to Eastern Europe; and whereas Stalin's regime had treated successful farmers as 'class enemies' who had to be annihilated by the proletariat, the East European dictatorships made more attempt to utilize such farmers in the formation of successful collective farms (see Stanis, 1976T, 47–51, 94–106, 118–25; Bermann, 1975T, 79–123; Dunman, 1975, ch. 4). There is no substantial evidence that wholesale collectivization has ever been brought about 'from below'; it has always been a high-level Party decision, implemented 'from above'. Admittedly, collectivization ought to get a smoother passage if there is broad peasant support for the ruling Party or if the peasantry in question has strong traditions of communal landownership and/or co-operative activity. But even where they exist, such advantages cannot guarantee meek compliance with the aims and methods of the ruling Party; peasant resistance soon obliged Tito's broad-based dictatorship in Yugoslavia to abandon its overzealous, heavy-handed collectivization campaign of 1948–51; and Russia's peasants fiercely resisted Stalin's collectivization campaign, because they quickly realized that it was a brutal external assault on their communal institutions and autonomy and a betrayal of the objectives for which they had fought in 1917–22.

Fortunately, as indicated above, several communist states have demonstrated that there are more humane and cost-effective alternatives to the brutal, barnstorming approach to collectivization. Furthermore, while acknowledging that Western family-based agriculture is still more productive than Soviet and East European collectivized agriculture, one mustn't exaggerate the latter's inherent diseconomies of scale and other intrinsic deficiencies. In the long term, whether we take 1909–13 or 1934–8 as our base level, the per capita availability of foodstuffs has increased even more dramatically in Russia and Eastern Europe than in Southern Europe, Ireland, or West Germany, and on a par with France (see Tables 11 and 14). Similarly, grain yields per hectare and milk yields per milch cow have increased even more impressively in Eastern Europe and in most of the Soviet republics than they have done in either Southern or North-western Europe (see Tables 12 and 14; and USSR, 1977, 347). The not unimpressive increase in average Soviet grain yields per hectare was depressed by vast, overhasty and ill-prepared Eastward extensions of Soviet agriculture into some of the potential 'dust bowls' of Soviet Asia during 1928–40 and 1953–63 (see Symons, 1972, 52, 173, 310, 129–32, 292–305). By contrast, most European states have more sensibly retreated from marginal land, thereby boosting average grain yields per hectare (see ECE, 1951; Barna, 1979, 49). This contrast was caused not by 'systemic deficiencies' inherent in Soviet agriculture, but by the deficiencies of a political system which entrusted enormous power to a few megalomaniacs and charlatans. Significantly the westernmost Soviet republics experienced much smaller extensions of cultivated area and Europe's greatest increases in grain yields per hectare (see Table 12). Moreover, the major advances in Soviet and East European agriculture occurred in the 1960s and 1970s, when Comecon began to relax its excessive emphasis on heavy industry and to assign agriculture a share of investment more commensurate with its contribution to Gross Material Product (Table 10). The consequent surge in agricultural output and yields per hectare suggests that collectivized agriculture had hitherto suffered mainly from neglect and unequal exchange, rather than inherent shortcomings. Soviet farmers, in particular, have experienced a dramatic reversal of fortunes. Their annual per capita consumption of foodstuffs has altered thus (see Morozov, 1977T, 165):

(kg)	Meat	Dairy produce	Potatoes	Grain products	Eggs (units)
1938	20.9	127	175	271	59
1971	48.5	368	200	178	291

And the proportions of collective farmers' incomes spent on major categories of consumption altered thus (ibid., 166):

(% of total)	Food	Cloth, clothing and shoes	Household goods and recreation	Social amenities
1940	67.3	10.9	1.1	4.4
1975	37.1	15.7	5.9	15.4

Moreover, if one includes 'income (in cash and kind) from private plots, there is now only quite a small difference between rural and urban incomes', and 'the long period of exploiting agriculture for the benefit of industry is over' (Nove, 1978, 7). Admittedly, Soviet agriculture still trails far behind US agriculture. In 1971–5 the 4.5 million people directly engaged in US agriculture produced approximately

15 per cent more than the 30 million people directly engaged in Soviet agriculture (USSR, 1977, 95). However, relative to US agriculture, Soviet agriculture was using under half as much 'commercial energy' per sown hectare, including one-third as much tractor-power per sown hectare and half as much fertilizer per sown hectare. Moreover, most Soviet farmland lay in Canadian – not US – latitudes; and only 1 per cent of Soviet cropland received over 700 mm of precipitation per annum, as against 60 per cent of US cropland, yet only 6 per cent of Soviet cropland was under irrigation. Further, the Soviet farm workforce was not strictly comparable to the US farm workforce, as 65 per cent of the Soviet farm workforce was female and most of the males were elderly and poorly qualified. The 5 million managers, equipment operators and other technical personnel formed the 'hard core' of the Soviet farm workforce and the true counterpart to the 4.5 million people engaged in US agriculture, whereas the 20 million women and elderly men were becoming increasingly dispensable and many of them will have been pensioned off (without replacement) by the year 2000. Also, taking food and natural fibre production as a whole, the US employed twice as much labour off-farm as on-farm, whereas the reverse was true of the USSR (see Millar, 1977, 9). Thus most of the disparity between Soviet and US output per person in agriculture can be attributed to large differences in the mixture and quality of factor inputs, rather than intrinsic ('systemic') differences in efficiency.

Collectivized agriculture has also achieved impressive output growth in North Korea, if her official agricultural statistics are to be believed. Between 1948–52 and 1976–8 grain and potato output per inhabitant nearly doubled and grain yields per hectare nearly trebled, comfortably outstripping the corresponding increases in South Korea (see Tables 11 and 12). However, as indicated on pp. 59–60, the Democratic People's Republic of Korea (DPRK) was from the outset far more industrialized than the southern Republic of Korea. In 1949 industrial and office workers made up 26 per cent of North Korea's workforce (North Korea, 1961, 9), industry contributed 33 per cent of her national income (Chung, 1974, 146), and producer goods industries accounted for 59 per cent of her industrial output (ibid., 78). For all its well-known oppressiveness, Japanese 'imperialism' had built up a substantial heavy-industrial base in mineral-rich North Korea (see McCune, 1956, 219–27; Brun and Hersch, 1976, 54–7). Indeed, by 1939–40 North Korea's per capita material product was nearly double the South Korean level, industry was contributing approximately 38 per cent of North Korea's material product, and producer goods made up 72 per cent of North Korea's manufacturing output (see Table 15; and Suh, 1978, 137–42). The post-1945 partition of Korea left 86 per cent of the peninsula's heavy industry in the North (Brun and Hersch, 1976, 119), and by 1948 North Korea was producing several times more steel, coal, electricity, chemicals, non-ferrous metal and cement per inhabitant than the South (see Table 16; and UN Statistical Yearbooks). The Korean War reduced North Korea's industrial output by 36 per cent and its agricultural output by 24 per cent during

1950–53 (Kim, 1979T, 390). But by 1956 industrial output was already 80 per cent above the 1949 level (ibid., 400), agricultural output was approximately 8 per cent above the 1949 level (ibid., 401), 27 per cent of the workforce was in industry (Kim, 1975, 188), and industry was contributing 31 per cent of national income (Chung, 1974, 147); so war damage to North Korea's economy must have been ephemeral, though the human cost was high. Moreover, since producer goods industries already accounted for 54 per cent of North Korea's much-expanded industrial output in 1956 (ibid., 79), there was absolutely no need to 'squeeze' agriculture in order to achieve rapid expansion of heavy industry. Indeed, industry was well able to assist agriculture and, possibly out of a quasi-Stalinist desire to minimize North Korea's dependence on imports, 20 per cent of state investment went into agriculture in the 1960s (ibid., 42) and 21 per cent of total investment went into agriculture during 1964–73 (Osmova and Faminsky, 1980, 357). Agriculture's share of investment was thus commensurate with its 18–22 per cent contribution to national income (Chung, 1974, 147). By 1965 North Korea had allegedly mechanized 95 per cent of ploughing, 92 per cent of harrowing and 51 per cent of fodder-making (Stanis, 1976T, 161); and by 1975 it had allegedly mechanized 100 per cent of ploughing, threshing, fodder-making and agricultural transport, 66 per cent of grain harvesting and 53 per cent of weeding (Osmova and Faminsky, 1980, 358). Between 1949 and 1960 North Korea's irrigated area had trebled, and by 1960 93 per cent of paddyland was irrigated (Chung, 1974, 49). Because North Korea is rich in chemicals and HEP potential, and because Japanese 'imperialism' left behind major chemicals and electricity industries, by 1963 North Korea's use of chemical fertilizer per hectare of farmland was approximately 300 kg (about two and a half times the West European average and fifty-three times the Third World average), 93 per cent of North Korea's villages were receiving electricity and 71 per cent of rural households were receiving electricity (ibid., 49). Moreover, possibly for reasons of military security, North Korea went in for considerable decentralization of industry after the Korean War: in the 1960s small-scale 'local industries', using locally produced raw materials, contributed just over half the output of North Korea's consumer goods industries (ibid., 70). North Korea's economic attainments also rested on her impressive educational provisions (see Table 3). However, the 1953–8 collectivization campaign was marred by the usual officially acknowledged excesses and coercion and popular resistance (see Lee, 1963a, 76–8 ff.), and even the more sympathetic Western observers of North Korea regret the extraordinary incompleteness of the economic statistics published by this supposedly well-educated society (e.g. McCormack and Gittings, 1977, 71). To quote Jon Halliday (1981, 18), North Korea remains 'a bleak, backward workhouse ruled by a megalomaniac tyrant, Kim Il Sung', and 'it is generally agreed that the political system is one of the most dreadful ever constructed in the name of socialism'. North Korean publications attribute every major decision and initiative in the history of the Korean Workers' Party and the DPRK to 'the great leader, Comrade Kim Il Sung, the sun of the nation and legendary hero' (see, for instance, North Korea, 1977T; Kim, 1979T), implicitly confirming the view that not even the Party has much of a role in decision-making in this dictatorship. This arbitrary rule makes it hard to know how much credence should be given to North Korea's published statistics, which cannot be corroborated or cross-checked.

On the whole my misgivings are directed not against rural collectivization as such, but against its frequent misuse as a framework through which 'proletarian' dictatorships have assaulted, subjugated, dragooned, or exploited peasant and pastoral communities. Some of the greatest disasters of imposed collectivization have occurred in livestock rearing societies, above all in the Soviet Republic of Kazakhstan.

Kazakhstan is an expanse of steppe, semi-desert and desert five times the size of France, stretching nearly 3000 km eastwards from the Caspian and the Volga. This region was gradually subjugated by Russia in the eighteenth and nineteenth centuries, though Kazakh hostility to Russian intrusion found violent expression during the Pugachëv rebellion of 1774 and the Muslim–Turkic uprisings of 1916–17: 'Most Kazakhs were nomadic herders who, grouped together in auls, moved with the vegetation seasons in search of pasture. . . . The aul comprised a number of kivitkas or tents, whose occupants moved their herds as a unit' (Demko, 1969, 26–7). In 1897 there were 3 million Turkic-speaking Kazakhs who were nominally of the Sunni Muslim faith, though they had few mosques and few of their women wore veils (ibid., 2, 22). During 1896–1916 Kazakhstan was colonized by 1.5 million Russians and Ukrainians, who together by 1916 constituted 35 per cent of the population and held 16 per cent of all land, including nearly 75 per cent of all cultivated land: 'Expropriation of the best grazing lands for peasant settlement created hardships for the Kazakhs. Many were forced on to marginal land' (ibid., 2, 196–7, 203). 'The first decade of Bolshevik rule proved prosperous. . . . Kazakhs and Kirghiz increased their livestock by more than one-third', and 'a decree in early 1920 ordered the return of all lands seized from Moslem households' (Dienes, 1975, 356). Until 1928 the newly established Kazakh Autonomous Soviet Republic was 'in the hands of nationalists whose chief aim was to carry out land reform at the expense of the Russian and Ukrainian colonists. . . . Russians and Ukrainians were speedily removed from their fertile fields to unproductive stony ground' (Kolarcz, 1953, 264). As late as 1927–8 livestock rearing contributed 54 per cent of material product, as against 27 per cent from crop production and 13.5 per cent from industry, while small workshops contributed 57 per cent of industrial output and 91.5 per cent of the population was still rural (Alampiev, 1959T, 175). But the brutal 1930s collectivization campaign brought catastrophe to the Kazakh herdsmen. The Kazakh population of the USSR fell by 869,000 or 22 per cent between the censuses of 1926 and 1939, whereas the USSR's total population rose by 16 per cent (Lorimer, 1946, 138). The livestock herds of Kazakhstan were largely wiped out by 1934 and took decades to recover, as the following data (from official Soviet sources, present boundaries) show:

(Millions)	1916	1922	1924	1929	1934
Sheep and goats	17.9	11.0	11.4	27.2	2.3
Cattle	5.1	3.0	4.8	7.4	1.6
Horses	4.3		2.5	4.2	0.4

(Millions)	1936	1941	1946	1951	1967
Sheep and goats	4.3	8.1	10.2	18.0	32.2
Cattle	2.7	3.4	3.6	4.5	7.2
Horses		0.9	0.9	1.5	1.1

(Muslims rarely raised pigs.)

In effect, collectivization helped to forcibly settle or resettle the Kazakhs and clear the ground for further Russo-Ukrainian colonization of Kazakhstan: the Kazakh share of the population fell from 57 per cent in 1926 to 38 per cent in 1939 and 30 per cent in 1959, while the Russo-Ukrainian share of the population rose from 33 per cent in 1926 to 48 per cent in 1939 and 52 per cent in 1959, and Kazakhstan's cultivated area expanded as follows:

	1913	1928	1932	1937	1940	1950
Million hectare:	4.1	4.2	5.3	5.8	6.7	7.8

	1953	1955	1960	1965	1970	1979
Million hectare:	9.7	20.5	28.4	30.4	31.0	36.0

Unfortunately Kazakhstan's grain yields per hectare have remained rather low:

	1928	1932	1936	1937	1938–41
Tons per hectare:	0.9	0.5	0.4	0.5	0.9

	1953–60	1961–5	1966–70	1971–5	1976–9
Tons per hectare:	0.8	0.6	0.9	0.9	1.1

According to a Soviet textbook on Kazakhstan, 'The settlement of the nomad and semi-nomad population on land opened a new channel for replenishing industrial personnel'; however, 'The nomad of yesterday had no conception of modern industrial production' and 'The new Kazakh workers could not immediately get used to working definite hours, to giving up old customs'; indeed, 'It was particularly difficult for Kazakhs to master trades in the leading industries of the Kazakh Republic', and in 1934 only 46.5 per cent of the workers in large-scale industry were Kazakhs (Alampiev, 1959T, 270–2, 288). This is another reason why Kazakhstan has been swamped by Russian immigrants, who naturally tried to monopolize urban positions. Thus while the urban population expanded from 9 to 44 per cent of the total during 1926–59, in 1959 76 per cent of Kazakhs remained in rural areas (Nove and Newth, 1967, 54). Even within the rural sector, only 26 per cent of tractor drivers were Kazakhs in 1937 (Kolarcz, 1953, 267) and 'Collectivization also had disastrous effects on the home industries . . ., the varied handicrafts which supplied the local population with many of the ordinary articles of clothing and domestic utensils'; henceforth 'The handicraft workers were obliged to seek their raw materials from the State trade organs, whose policy was to starve the private industries of raw materials. . . . Their only choice was either to enter collective farms or to become part of the industrial proletariat' (Conolly, 1967, 92).

The herdsmen of the Turkmen, Kirghiz, Tajik, Uzbek and Buryat Soviet republics, eastern Turkestan (Xinjiang), Tibet, and Inner and Outer Mongolia have had to face similar fates; and an analogous external assault on tribal–pastoral society has begun in Afghanistan since the Soviet-backed 'revolution' of April 1978 brought to power the town-based People's Democratic Party of Afghanistan, which announced in August 1979 that millions of acres had been redistributed by its land reform programme and that by 1984 1.1 million agricultural households (over one-third of the rural population) would be 'grouped into 4,500 cooperatives' (Halliday, 1980, 24; on Afghan society, see Naby, 1980; Dupree, 1980, as well as Fred Halliday's trenchant Marxist critiques of the floundering Democratic Republic of Afghanistan).

In Turkmenistan the 1930s collectivization campaign devastated the livestock herds:

(Thousands)	1916	1928	1935	1937	1940	1950	1955	1962	1977
Sheep and goats	4580	3233	1125	1694	2221	2801	3907	3481	4251
Cattle	312	368	154	198	247	257	300	364	556

This cleared the ground for substantial Russian colonization: cultivated area and the Russian proportion of the population both roughly doubled during 1926–70. And although the urban population rose from 14 to 46 per cent of the total during 1926–59, 75 per cent of Turkmen remained in rural areas (Nove and Newth, 1967, 54).

The Turkic herdsmen of mountainous Kirghizia fared likewise:

(Millions)	1924	1926	1932	1936	1940	1951	1966	1977
Sheep and goats	3.1	3.7	0.9	1.2	2.6	4.5	8.3	9.9
Cattle	0.9	0.6	0.3	0.4	0.6		0.9	0.9

Kirghizia's cultivated area more than doubled during 1926–40, but the Kirghiz proportion of the population fell from 66 to 40 per cent during 1926–59, while the Russo-Ukrainian share rose from 17 to 37 per cent. Moreover, although the urban sector expanded from 12 to 34 per cent of the total population during 1926–59, 89 per cent of the Kirghiz remained in rural areas.

The Turkic and Tajik herdsmen of Uzbekistan and Tajikistan lost around half their herds during 1929–34 (Allworth, 1967, 299–300). However, it will be shown that in these republics there were major compensating gains from collectivization.

The 1930s collectivization campaign was a more unmitigated disaster for the Buryat herdsmen of the Buryat–Mongolian Autonomous Soviet Republic, near Lake Baikal:

(Thousands)	Cattle	Sheep	Pigs	Horses
July 1928	729	898	152	214
July 1933	263	215	52	121
(Thousands)	Cattle	Sheep	Pigs	Horses
January 1946	299	465	16	56
January 1963	392	1509	152	57

In Buryatia collectivization went hand-in-hand with an assault on the Lamaist Church. Before the revolution, Buryatia had 16,000 lamas and 36 lamaseries, and 80 per cent of Transbaikal Buryats declared themselves to be Buddhist; but during the 1930s 'every single monastery in Buryatia was closed, most lamas were dispersed to live in villages, and some were killed or imprisoned' (Humphrey, 1983, 172, 419, 422). Together with relentless Russian colonization, these assaults on Buryat society reduced the Buryat population from 44 to 20 per cent of the total during 1926–59 and facilitated a several-fold expansion of cultivated area, at the expense of Buryat grazing lands. Unfortunately by 1960 this had exposed 25 per cent of Buryatia's cropland and much of her remaining pasture land to serious soil erosion, so nowadays 'the harvest per hectare is on average rather worse than it was before collectivization' (ibid., 175–7, 446). Admittedly, Buryatia's population is now predominantly urban, but only 14 per cent of Buryatia's 'workers' were Buryats in 1970 (ibid., 33).

Buryatia's experience wasn't without parallels. 'Inner Mongolia has been subjected to intensive Chinese settlement, which has meant for its indigenous Mongol inhabitants the ruthless expropriation of their grazing lands' and 'the establishment of inefficient agriculture on land best suited to a pastoral economy, leading in turn to desiccation and soil erosion' (Hambly et al., 1969, 277–8). 'The Chinese Communists have assaulted the nomads and their way of life' and 'Chinese now greatly outnumber Mongols', while 'progressive occupation of Mongolian pasture-lands by Chinese farmers apparently dooms the Inner Mongols to extinction, at least insofar as any surviving "typically Mongolian" characteristic is concerned'; indeed, 'Chinese (CCP) political control tightly integrates the Mongols into the economy and life of China', especially since 'collectivization of livestock and settlement of nomads have now been carried out' (Rupen, 1964, 302, 347).

Collectivization has played an even greater role in Chinese colonization and subjugation of Xinjiang (Sinkiang): Han Chinese made up 5 per cent of Xinjiang's 4.9 million inhabitants during the 1953 census, 38 per cent of Xinjiang's 10 million inhabitants in 1973, and 43 per cent of Xinjiang's 12 million inhabitants in 1980; the Turkic Uighurs, who made up 80 per cent of the population in 1953, have become a very subordinate ethnic minority in their own country and, as Muslims, they have been subjected to Chinese communist persecution and cultural chauvinism, especially during Mao's vaunted Cultural Revolution. The Turkic population rebelled against Chinese rule in 1954, 1956, 1958, 1959 and 1962, only to be crushed by the Chinese People's Liberation Army. With few interruptions, the government of Xinjiang has been controlled by the army, which imposed the 1950s land reforms and collectivization. The new Chinese collective and state farms have nearly trebled Xinjiang's total cultivated area since 1949, thereby encroaching on some of the best Uighur and Kazakh grazing lands. In some areas the indigenous population has been completely replaced by Chinese military–agricultural colonies and 're-education camps', mainly under the army's powerful Production and Construction Corps, which has resettled millions of ex-servicemen and 'rusticated' townspeople from eastern China in the backwoods of Xinjiang. During 1960–3 Chinese persecution and repression of ethnic/religious minorities drove some 62,000 Kazakhs and Uighurs to take refuge in the USSR, prompting China to seal off the border between Soviet and Chinese Turkestan; and since then, without allowing the indigenous inhabitants any real say in the matter, China has turned Xinjiang into her major nuclear testing ground. Xinjiang, along with Inner Mongolia and Tibet, displays Chinese communism in its true colours (on Xinjiang, see McMillen, 1979 ff.; Tekiner, 1967; Tregar, 1965, 295–7, *FT* Surveys, 14 December 1981, ix; *Central Asian Review*, 1958, 76–88, and 1967, 253–6; on China's vandalism in Tibet, see Karan, 1976, 17, 18, 26–37, 58, 59, 70).

According to Fred Halliday (1980, 22), 'Outer Mongolia has shown that revolutionary regimes can successfully develop in nomadic societies.' And Professor Wilber (1969, 170) has contrasted the disasters of collectivization in Kazakhstan with the 'success of Outer Mongolia in collectivizing nomadic tribes'. However, they fail to mention that the Mongolian People's Revolutionary Party only succeeded in collectivizing the herdsmen of Outer Mongolia in the 1950s, after it had subjected them to some major ordeals in preceding decades.

Outer Mongolia first became a Russian protectorate after the collapse of China's Manchu dynasty in 1911: 'Russia aimed to establish a viable Mongolian central government which would require a minimum of Russian financial and military aid and intervention, for the purpose of limiting Chinese influence' (Rupen, 1964, 69). 'The example of Inner Mongolia compelled the Khalkas of Outer Mongolia to recognize that Russia was less of a threat to their survival than China. . . . Regardless of the price the Mongols have had to pay for Russian protection in the twentieth century, it has at least preserved them' (Hambly *et al.*, 1969, 278).

Indeed, after Outer Mongolia was occupied by the Red Army in 1921, the ruling Mongolian People's Revolutionary Party 'followed a firm line towards strengthening its internationalist links with the Comintern and the CPSU. . . . The Red Army units which were brought into Mongolia . . . had an important role to play in ensuring the victory of the people's revolution' (Gafurov and Kim, 1978T, 153–4). 'Up to 1924, however, Mongolia nominally remained a limited monarchy headed by . . . the supreme hierarch of the Lamaist Church, which was largely a concession to the masses' backwardness, their blind faith in the sanctity of Lamaist hierarchs' (ibid., 156). In fact 'There can at that time have been little or no knowledge of Communist theory. . . . A catalogue of books printed in Mongolia since 1913 shows that the first classics of Communism did not even begin to appear in book form till 1925' (Bawden, 1968, 206). Nor was there an indigenous social/ economic basis for 'proletarian' socialism: 'There was no industry, no transport or communications' (Stanis, 1976T, 111). 'Fewer than 1000 Mongols worked in any industrial occupation in 1927' (Rupen, 1964, 208). 'The Party itself was never an effective mass organization', as 'most of the members were either lamas and minor nobility, who could not be relied on, or, when these had been purged, illiterate herdsmen' (Bawden, 1968, 276; Rupen, 1964, 195). Undaunted, Soviet backing enabled Mongolia's 'revolution' to proceed without mass support towards 'proletarian' socialism without a proletariat. In 1922 the Lamaist Church and the nobility were shorn of many privileges (Bawden, 1968, 258). In 1924, when the head of the Lamaist Church died, the Party both prevented the selection of a successor and established a secular one-party Mongolian People's Republic, whose Constitution declared all land to be state property; however, the official claim that livestock numbers fell by 29 per cent in 1924 suggests that the public response was less than enthusiastic (Rupen, 1964, 184, 207). During 1925–8 Bukharinist influences and a temporary withdrawal of Soviet troops fostered more conciliatory policies, which allowed livestock numbers, private trade and lamasary wealth to recover from the upheavals of 1921–4 (ibid., 200; Bawden, 1968, 261, 283, 290–1). But in 1929 'an offensive was launched against the feudal lords; their property and cattle were confiscated' (Stanis, 1976T, 46–7). The 1930 Party Congress also called for all-out collectivization of livestock rearing and approved 'a hopelessly ambitious five-year plan', while Party officials and 'Revsomols' (Mongolia's 'Red Guards') went on the rampage (Bawden, 1968, 303–15). The Plan called for a total of 25 million livestock by 1935, but the rapacious collectivization campaign actually reduced livestock numbers from 23.6 million in 1930 to 16.1 million in 1932 (Rupen, 1964, 231–3). 'The Church was a natural rallying point for discontent' and in 1931–2 'armed uprisings broke out, mostly in the west and centre', whereupon 'the Soviet army had to be called upon to help put down the rebels' (Bawden, 1968, ch. 8; Rupen, 1979, 60).

Ironically, though these policies obviously took their cue from concurrent Soviet policies, they were subsequently denounced by Soviet commentators. According to

Stanis (1976T, 112), 'the newly organized collective farms had no prospect of becoming socialist enterprises'; Mongolia's collectivization campaign was implemented 'mostly by administrative measures'; the Party 'regarded all lamas as exploiters and applied coercive measures to them, though many of them came from the arats [herdsmen] and also suffered exploitation by the feudal élite'; and 'the Leftists undermined the arats' trust in collective farms, thus causing the destruction of cattle in large numbers'. Naturally Professor Stanis is silent on the parallels with Soviet collectivization.

Unlike the USSR, Outer Mongolia wholly abandoned rural collectivization in the mid-1930s, and by 1938 its livestock herds had recovered (Rupen, 1964, 233). Instead the Party set about a punitive destruction of the Lamaist Church, Mongolia's only real mass organization. As late as 1930 the church still owned 14 per cent of the country's livestock, its lamas still made up 'about one-third of the male population' and, although most of Outer Mongolia's lamas married and worked for a living (mainly as herdsmen), 75,500 still resided in lamaseries. By 1939, however, hundreds of lamaseries had been forcibly closed, there were only 15,000 lamas resident in lamaseries, the Party and its army had evicted thousands of lamas from their lamaseries in mid-winter (1937–8), the church had lost all its livestock and soon only 7000 lamas remained in the surviving lamaseries (Bawden, 1968, 347–72; Rupen, 1964, 82–3, 200, 230, 244). This operation must have contributed to the significant contraction of Outer Mongolia's population during 1935–40 (see Rupen, 1979, 56–7), but it achieved the Party's purpose: by 1940 the decks had been cleared for a new 'period of socialist construction', this time employing a more 'circumspect, cautious approach' to the pivotal task of 'settling' herdsmen and 'remoulding agriculture on socialist lines' (Gafurov and Kim, 1978T, 164–9). Henceforth 'Farming associations involved every section of the arats, including the more well-to-do farmers, for there were virtually no restrictions on the admission of larger farms' (ibid., 167). But even in this conciliatory form, rural collectivization was not accomplished until 1955–9, by which time potential opposition had been thoroughly emasculated (see Stanis, 1976T, 113–16; Rupen, 1964, 292–6; Bawden, 1968, 396–404). By forcing the herdsmen to settle down, rural collectivization made room for a substantial extension of low-yield grain production (Comecon, 1979, 242, 251; FAO Yearbooks, various issues):

Annual average	1948–52	1952–6	1961–5	1966–70	1971–5	1976–8
Thousand tons	35	47	289	246	366	382
Thousand hectares	50	60	413	410	407	478
Tons per hectare	0.7	0.8	0.7	0.6	0.9	0.8

However, even in the 1970s, livestock rearing continued to contribute 75–80 per cent of gross agricultural output (Comecon, 1979, 223), and rural collectivization contributed to a long-term stagnation in Outer Mongolia's vital livestock herds (Comecon, 1979, 257–9; Rupen, 1964, 292):

(Millions)	1939	1952	1957	1960	1965	1970	1977
Sheep	16.1	12.7	13.1	12.1	13.8	13.3	13.4
Cattle	2.9	1.8	1.9	1.9	2.1	2.1	2.4
Horses	2.4	2.3	2.3	2.5	2.4	2.3	2.1
Goats	5.3	5.3	5.4	5.6	4.8	4.2	4.4

From the point of view of the herdsmen it seems there has been little to gain and much to lose from the collectivization of pastoral societies. Admittedly, such societies couldn't have been insulated from the great changes occurring in the world around them, and many of the indigenous pastoral societies of Africa and the Americas have also been overrun and/or brutally subjugated by predators. But such considerations cannot excuse the rapidity, the brutality and the predatory nature of the changes imposed on the pastoral heartlands of Asia. Rather such considerations highlight the extent to which Leninist communism is just another predatory force.

Rural collectivization has had a more positive impact on settled agricultural economies, most notably in post-1956 Hungary (see p. 188) and in Soviet Central Asia (the Soviet republics of Uzbekistan, Tajikistan, Turkmenistan and Kirghizia).

The four Soviet Central Asian republics can be regarded as thoroughly subjugated colonies, providing primary commodities for their Russian overlords and captive markets for Russian industry (see, for instance, Kolarz, 1953, 255–92; Allworth, 1967, 288, 308, 337, 344, 348). The promotion of separate Uzbek, Tajik, Kirghiz and Kazakh republics can also be seen as 'a sort of apartheid', intended to fragment the longstanding cultural unity of Turkestan by fostering new written languages and national identities which would gradually distance these new nations from one another and from the millions of Turks and Muslims outside the USSR (see Caroe, 1967, xiv–xxiv). According to Zenkovsky (1960, 1), only 40–45 per cent of the world's Turkic peoples live in the USSR. Central Asia's position also resembles apartheid inasmuch as the strict Soviet system of residence permits, which denies Soviet citizens the degree of freedom of movement which is taken for granted in most non-communist states, has helped to exclude all but a few of the USSR's 20 million Uzbeks, Tajiks, Turkmen and Kirghiz from the USSR's major urban–industrial centres. Furthermore, while Soviet Constitutions have piously proclaimed freedom of worship, some 14,000 Central Asian mosques were closed down during 1929–39, and the total number of functioning mosques in the USSR was reduced from over 24,000 in 1917 to no more than 400 in 1970 (Holt et al., 1977, 639; Schopflin, 1971, 480). Nevertheless, even though Central Asians have been denied their legitimate rights of self-determination, and even though Central Asia has mainly exported primary products in exchange for Russian manufactures, present-day Central Asia does at least constitute a strikingly successful example of socialist agricultural development, in a most inauspicious natural environment.

Soviet Central Asia had 26 million inhabitants in 1980 and occupied 1.3m. km², roughly twice the area of France. However, one-half of its territory is desert and one-third is mountain (Tuzmahamedov, 1973T, 11), so no more than one-sixth is suitable for agriculture. Central Asia was subjugated by tsarist Russia during 1865–84, and by 1913 it was supplying 60 per cent of the raw cotton consumed by Russia's burgeoning textile industry as well as silk, wool, hides, carpets, rice and fruit (see Conolly, 1967, 22–5; Allworth, 1967, 131–71, 309–14). The indigenous inhabitants were mostly Turkic Muslims, although there was a substantial Tajik (Iranian) minority and many still speak both Turkic and Farsi as well as Russian. The main written languages were Arabic (for the clergy) and Farsi (for trade and administration). The Turkmen, Kirghiz, highland Tajik and Karakalpak inhabitants were mostly herdsmen, whereas the Uzbeks and lowland Tajiks were mostly more settled farmers: 'The basic exploiter in the Central Asian village was the bai, a combination of wealthy peasant and feudal lord, who ran his household using basically the labour of métayers . . . and to a lesser extent of hired workers.' Bai households made up 13 per cent of the settled agricultural households in 1916, while 'Over 30% of the rural population led a nomadic way of life' and 'Workers . . . made up only 0.35% of the total population' (Solodovnikov and Bogoslovsky, 1975T, 39, 40, 77). However, although there was no 'proletarian' or industrial basis for socialism in Central Asia, 'Central Asia already had a history of peasant cooperation in the area of irrigation work. Peasants from one or several villages often used a single irrigation system . . . and as a rule worked the system jointly within the system of a commune of water-users' (ibid., 63). By 1913 cotton occupied 15 per cent of Central Asia's cropland (see p. 217) and the region was partly reliant on Russian grain, so the economy was all the more disrupted by Russia's involvement in the First World War and by the Russian Revolution. During 1918–22 there were various attempts to create an independent Turkistan, free from Russian control (see Zenkovsky, 1960; Pipes, 1957, chs 2, 4 and 6), so Russian colonists increasingly looked to the Bolsheviks to reimpose Russian control; the Russians won, but over 1 million Central Asians perished amid the attendant conflict and famine (see Allworth, 1967, 207–53, 284–6, 330–1). During 1923–8 there was an uneasy truce, while Central Asia's economy was slowly restored and the Bolsheviks gradually consolidated their control (ibid., 254–65, 284–8, 330–1): 'In December 1922, the land and water were nationalized, and large absentee holdings were confiscated. . . . Work animals and equipment were also confiscated from the more prosperous' (Pintner, 1953, 289). In the mid-1920s local land committees redistributed landholdings in excess of 7–10 ha of cropland per household, and tenancy was largely eliminated (see Holdsworth, 1951–2, 264; Solodovnikov and Bogoslovsky, 1975T, 53–6; Ghai and Khan, 1979, 38). Furthermore, 'by a decree of May 1924 the Soviets vested all control of distribution of water in the State', thus 'shifting the weight of economic and political power from the people to the Party' (Caroe, 1967, 153). Although this economic leverage must have facilitated collectivization, the 1930s collectivization campaign was nevertheless nasty, brutish and implemented 'from above', amid widespread opposition and slaughter of livestock (Allworth, 1967, 261–4, 289–300). Indeed, Central Asian opposition to collectivization was caught up with Central Asian opposition to the attendant extension of Russian control, Russian colonization and cotton cultivation; and when leading Uzbek and Tajik communists voiced misgivings on precisely these issues, they were promptly put on trial and executed (ibid., 261–4; Kolarz, 1953, 277–8). However, although collectivization completed Soviet subjugation of Central Asia, it was also a prelude to impressive agricultural development. And, although this agricultural development was partly a result of Russo-Ukrainian colonization in sparsely populated Kirghizia and Turkmenistan (see p. 207), Russo-Ukrainian colonization made much less headway in the more populated republics of Uzbekistan and Tajikistan, where the Russo-Ukrainian share of the population had risen to only 13.4 and 13.0 per cent, respectively, by 1970 (USSR, 1972, 544, 644).

Between 1913 and the 1970s, on official Soviet calculations, Gross Agricultural Production increased sixfold (3.0 per cent per annum) in Uzbekistan, Turkmenistan and Kirghizia, ninefold (3.7 per cent per annum) in Tajikistan, but merely threefold (1.8 per cent per annum) in Russia proper, the Ukraine and Belorussia (USSR, 1977, 277). Western sources reckon that during 1925–30 Central Asia's 'agricultural output per caput of farm population was about 80% of the all-Soviet average' and that during 1928–61 gross agricultural output increased 3.8 per cent per annum at constant 1926–7 prices in Central Asia, as against 2.2 per cent per annum in the USSR as a whole (Wilber, 1969, 199, 178–82). Under Stalin, unlike the USSR as a whole, Central Asia allocated more capital to agriculture than to industry (ibid., 194):

% of total investment, Central Asia	1928–32	1933–7	1938–40	1946–50
Agriculture	51.8	34.7	37.6	34.7
Industry	15.2	22.5	23.9	32.1
Transport and communications	17.4	14.7	8.7	6.2
Housing and services	15.6	28.1	29.8	27.0

The allocation of substantial resources to agricultural development did not detract from Central Asia's industrial development: industrial output grew 8–17 per cent per annum during 1928–40 and 6–9 per cent per annum during 1940–61, depending on the accounting conventions employed (ibid., 190–1); and Central Asia's per capita output of basic industrial products has on the whole outstripped the levels attained by the most directly comparable South-west Asian countries (Tuzma-hamedov, 1973T, 141; UN and Soviet Statistical Yearbooks, various issues):

	Uzbekistan			Central Asia		Turkey	
	1928	1940	1965	1928	1965	1964	1970
Cloth (m)	1	17	29	0.5(c)	20(c)	18(c)	6
Crude oil (kg)	0	18	171	7	665	28	98
Steel (kg)	0	2	35	0	21	13	37
Coal (kg)	0	0.5	443	49	513	237	256
Electricity (kWh)	4	73	1122	4	950	143	245
Cement (kg)	16	41	235	16	239	94	181

	Iran		Iraq	Pakistan
	1964	1970	1970	1964
Cloth (m)	—	16	5	7(c)
Crude oil (kg)	3700	6745	8172	5
Steel (kg)	0	N	N	0
Coal (kg)	7	19	N	12
Electricity (kWh)	58	248	250	34
Cement (kg)	33	100	165	15

(c) Cotton cloth only.   N = negligible.

Moreover, in contrast to the USSR as a whole, Central Asia's industrialization has been based upon textile, clothing, footwear and food-processing industries, which directly raise popular consumption levels and mainly use locally produced agricultural raw materials, and which still contributed approximately 70 per cent of Central Asia's industrial output in 1963–4 (Conolly, 1967, 128). In Uzbekistan, the largest and most industrialized of the Central Asian republics, these industries contributed 73 per cent of industrial output in 1940, 72 per cent of industrial output in 1960 and 60 per cent of industrial output in 1971 (Iskanderov, 1974, 36). Uzbekistan's chemical, engineering, metallurgical and electricity industries, which together contributed 11 per cent of industrial output in 1940, 18 per cent of industrial output in 1960 and 27 per cent of industrial output in 1971 (ibid.), have quite properly concentrated on meeting the needs of agriculture and the food and textile industries (Plotnikov, 1969, 319–26). This pattern of industrialization has naturally fostered strong 'backward' and 'forward' linkages between industrial and agricultural development, thereby helping to diffuse the benefits of economic growth (cf. pp. 58 and 146).

Agriculture's share of Central Asian investment wasn't excessive: agriculture supported 84 per cent of the population in 1928 and 57 per cent of the population in 1959 (see Table 1), so agriculture must have received far less investment per person than the non-agricultural sector. Nevertheless, agriculture was far less neglected here than in the USSR as a whole (Table 10). Indeed, while the mainstream Soviet strategy of primitive socialist accumulation involved a severe contraction of farmers' real incomes in the 1930s, the Central Asian development strategy maintained 'average gross income per household on collective farms' at relatively higher levels (Wilber, 1969, 200):

(Rubles p.a.)	Uzbekistan	Turkmenistan	Tajikistan	USSR
1937	3069	2369	1909	786

From 1935 to 1952, while the prices paid to Soviet grain and meat producers were kept artificially low, Soviet procurement agencies encouraged cotton production by paying cotton-growers reasonably remunerative prices. During 1952–60, however, the procurement prices paid to Soviet grain and meat producers were raised sevenfold and twelvefold, respectively, whereas those paid to cotton-growers rose only 7 per cent, effectively wiping out the cotton-growers' former price advantage over grain and meat producers (Nove and Newth, 1967, 59, 62; Ghai and Khan, 1979, 22–5). But one mustn't exaggerate the significance of differential price incentives in a command economy, where farms on the whole grow what they are commanded to grow (provided they have the necessary inputs). After cotton-growers lost their relative price advantage, cotton output and yields per hectare nevertheless continued their impressive climb (see below), and it should be noted that until the 1950s cotton never occupied more than one-third of Central Asia's sown area. However, from having been a net importer of cotton until the mid-1930s, the USSR has become a major net exporter of cotton since the 1960s. And Central Asia, which has produced approximately 90 per cent of Soviet cotton, has become the world's major producer of raw cotton (USSR, 1972, 216–19, and 1980, 219–20; FAO Production Yearbook, 1977):

USSR	1909–13	1924–8	1936–40	1946–50
Million tons	0.68	0.58	2.50	2.32
Tons per hectare	1.30	0.84	1.20	1.36
Million hectares	0.52	0.69	2.08	1.71

USSR	1951–5	1961–5	1971–5	1976–9
Million tons	3.89	4.99	7.67	8.67
Tons per hectare	1.69	2.06	2.73	2.88
Million hectares	2.30	2.42	2.81	3.0

1976:	USSR	China	USA	India
Million tons	8.28	6.86	6.56	3.27
Tons per hectare	2.82	1.47	1.35	0.46

1976:	Pakistan	Turkey	Brazil	Egypt
Million tons	1.47	1.34	1.11	1.10
Tons per hectare	0.84	2.10	0.66	1.95

However, despite alarmist assertions that the dramatic extension of Central Asian cotton cultivation after 1928 'squeezed out' other crops (Conolly, 1967, 82) and turned Central Asia into 'a one-crop colony' (Allworth, 1967, 288–90), the areas sown to other crops actually held remarkably steady (see, for Uzbekistan, Rizaev, 1978, 42, 46, 56, 64, 69, 161, 206; USSR, 1972, 546, and 1977, 303–4; for Turkmenistan, Turkmenistan, 1963, 76–7; USSR, 1977, 303–4; and for Tajikistan and Kirghizia, USSR, 1972, 646, 633, and 1977, 303–4):

Uzbekistan

(000 ha)	1913	1924	1928	1932	1937	1940	1945	1950	1953	1965	1970	1976
All crops	2189	1434	1873	2636	2669	3037	2392	2773	2820	3336	3476	3745
Cotton	425	268	588	990	946	924	755	1096	1153	1550	1709	1778
Other crops	1764	1166	1285	1646	1723	2113	1637	1677	1667	1786	1767	1967

Turkmenistan

(000 ha)	1913	1925	1928		1937	1940		1950	1960	1965	1970	1976
All crops	318	255	332		394	411		368	446	517	636	845
Cotton	69	63	112		157	150		153	222	257	397	491
Other crops	249	192	220		237	261		215	224	260	239	354

Tajikistan						Kirghizia						
(000 ha)	1913	1929	1940	1965	1976	(000 ha)	1913	1926	1936	1940	1965	1976
All crops	494	605	807	765	774		640	421	996	1056	1170	1283
Cotton	27	73	106	228	282		22	42	64	64	73	72
Other crops	467	532	701	537	492		618	379	932	9992	997	1011

Moreover, the foregoing data suggest that cotton must have consistently occupied under half Central Asia's irrigated land (see Timoshenko, 1953, 268; Conolly, 1967, 209):

Irrigated area	1913	1928	1932	1939	1941	1960	1964
Million ha	(2.5)	2.5	2.7	3.3	3.7	5.4	5.6

In 1976–9 Central Asia produced the following quantities of agricultural produce (USSR, 1980, 247–59, 276–7):

	Raw cotton	Grain	Vege-tables	Fruit	Potatoes	Meat	Milk
Kg per inhabitant	322	173	120	106	25	24.5	137

Clearly Central Asia is the antithesis of 'a one-crop colony'. And although livestock rearing was devastated by the 1930s collectivization campaign (see pp. 207–8), it was once again making major contributions to Gross Agricultural Production by 1961–5 (USSR, 1977, 278–9, and 1980, 224–6):

Livestock produce (Share of GAP)		Kirghizia	Turkmenistan	Tajikistan	Uzbekistan
	1961–5	56%	42%	30%	27%
	1976–9	53%	33%	30%	26%

As befits an area whose population grew 1.4 per cent per annum during 1913–39 and 3.2 per cent per annum during 1950–78 (Table 1), whose rate of natural increase was still 2.7 per cent per annum in 1979, and whose average family size (5.5 persons) was far above the Soviet average (3.5 persons) in 1979, Central Asia's agriculture has remained relatively labour-intensive. The following data show man-hours used per centner of farm produce in 1976 (USSR, 1977, 375):

	Tajikistan	Uzbekistan	Turk-menistan	Kirghizia	Ukraine	RSFSR
On collective farms:						
grain	8.8	7.4	5.8	2.1	1.4	1.3
potatoes	9.7	9.3	11.9	5.7	3.1	3.6
raw cotton	40	33	35	34	—	—
On state farms:						
grain	9.1	4.3	2.7	2.5	1.1	1.1
potatoes	6.9	8.4	—	4.8	3.2	3.2
raw cotton	32	26	25	30	—	—

However, because Central Asia has specialized in the cultivation and processing of cotton, fruit, vegetables, rice, beans and oilseeds, all of which have contributed to the region's relatively low cost of living, in the 1970s Central Asians enjoyed real incomes which were quite close to the Soviet average (see Table 18). Furthermore, by 1975 there were only modest intersectoral disparities in average monthly pay (NATO, 1979, 28, 32, 50, 53):

Rubles/month, 1975	Industry	State farms	Collective farms	Overall
Uzbekistan	152	121*	101*	137*
Tajikistan	148	111*	95*	136*
Kirghizia	154	116*	99*	134*
Turkmenistan	170	176*	121 (1974)*	158*
USSR average	162	127*	92*	146*

* Excluding income from private activities, which contributed the following proportions of collective farmers' incomes in 1974: Uzbekistan 32%; Tajikistan 25%; Kirghizia 27%; Turkmenistan 23%; and USSR 30%.

Central Asia is no longer marred by the conspicuous squalor and mendicancy characteristic of many South Asian states, and Central Asian mortality rates, health provisions and adult literacy rates compare quite favourably with those of the USSR as a whole (see Tables 2 and 3). Most remarkably for a predominantly Muslim area, 42 per cent of Central Asia's workers and white-collar personnel were women by 1979 (USSR, 1980, 392), Central Asian women seem to be almost as well educated as the men, and (at least in the major towns) women aren't afraid to go out unescorted after dark.

> The Soviet Central Asian Republics . . . have built a socialist society. . . . They were the first to demonstrate in actual practice that peoples, regardless of what stage of socio-economic development they have reached, can effect a transition to socialism, by-passing capitalism. (Solodovnikov and Bogoslovsky, 1975T, 36)

Naturally, the same Soviet textbook insists that Central Asia's successes could not have been achieved without the economic and technical assistance rendered by Russia's proletariat and heavy industries (ibid., 36–46, 70–1, 78). However, the Russian connection can be seen as more of a liability than an advantage, and Russia's Communist Party can legitimately be blamed for the major blemishes on Central Asia's otherwise impressive record: the persecution of Muslims; the predatory barnstorming approach to collectivization; the consequent human and economic losses and devastations; the lack of local autonomy and democratic rights; the excessive Russo-Ukrainian colonization of Kirghizia and Turkmenistan; the irksome controls on occupational and geographical mobility; and the irritations of alien overlordship. Moreover, the word 'assistance' is obviously intended to suggest that Russia plays a philanthropic role in Central Asia. Yet, so far as one can tell, Central Asian enterprises have paid standard Soviet prices and salaries for the Russian producer goods and technical personnel they have used, just as the Russians have paid standard Soviet prices for the Central Asian products they have used. Indeed, inasmuch as Central Asia is prevented from directly trading its relatively marketable exports for Western producer goods, it is quite reasonable to regard Central Asia as a captive supplier of primary products and as a captive market for Russia's rather old-fashioned producer goods industries. However, the importance of Russian producer goods has been reduced inasmuch as Central Asia has concentrated on relatively labour-intensive activities and local producer goods industries have concentrated on meeting local requirements.

To my mind, and in keeping with the major themes of this book, Central Asia's economic successes have been based, not on Russian aid, but on its own labour-intensive agriculture, textiles, food processing, mass education and a relatively small heavy industrial sector, whose basic *raison d'être* has been to meet the modest requirements of a rural sector which still contained 61 per cent of the population in 1975 (see Table 1). Indeed, if we ignore Central Asia's white overlords, approximately 78 per cent of the indigenous population still lived in rural areas in 1959 (Nove and Newth, 1967, 54). The Central Asian road to socialism has provided substantial confirmation that village-based development is viable, even in rather inauspicious circumstances. My advocacy of village-based development is not a form of Luddism or romantic atavism, nor is it a form of anarchism. Railways, motor vehicles, a modest urban sector, some state institutions, many social/cultural amenities, electricity and a small heavy-industrial sector can greatly assist agricultural and light-industrial development, as Denmark was the first to discover. But like Marx (see pp. 5–11 above), Herzen (pp. 29–35), Chayanov (pp. 44–7) and Gandhi (pp. 47–50), I believe that agrarian societies should be primarily concerned with rural development, if only because any other priority would mainly benefit a small minority of the population. Moreover, this book has endeavoured to demonstrate that the major socialist arguments in favour of large-scale centrally planned industrialization as a so-called 'prerequisite' for socialism and successful rural development are largely fallacious. Indeed, the costs of large-scale centrally planned industrialization and the type of state this engenders are fundamentally antithetical to any worthwhile form of socialism. Whether we look at countries as poor as communist China or as highly developed as East Germany and Czechoslovakia, it is clear that large-scale production and strong states breed functional division of labour and their own entrenched forms of hierarchy, inequality, compulsion and alienation. These major obstacles to any worthwhile form of socialism are, so to speak, rooted in large-scale modes of production and organization. Nothing can *guarantee* that decentralized small-scale communisms will succeed where large-scale state socialisms have repeatedly failed, but at least they have *some* chance of success.

Statistical appendix

(Throughout the following tables, figures in parentheses should be regarded as being very tentative.)

Table 1 Population, 1913–78

	Millions				Growth (% p.a.)		% rural†			% agricultural			
	1913*	1939*	1950	1978	1913–39	1950–78	1891	1960	1975	1910	1930	1950	1978
USSR	139	171	179	260	0.8	1.3	89	51	39	72	71(a)	54	18
Central Asia	7.3	10.5	13.7(b)	24.9	1.4	3.2	80+	66	61		84(a)	57(b)	38(c)
Kazakhstan	5.6	6.1	9.3(b)	14.5	0.3	2.4	90+	56	47		90(a)	39(b)	25(c)
Azerbaijan	2.3	3.2	2.9	5.9	1.3	2.6	(80)	52	49		65(a)	50(b)	33
Poland	29.8	35.0	25.0	35.0	0.6	1.2	(85)	53	43	76	60	53	32
Czechoslovakia	13.9	15.5	12.3	15.2	0.4	0.8	(80)	53	42	41	33	36	11
Hungary	7.8	9.2	9.3	10.7	0.6	0.5	(90)	60	52	67	51	50	17
Romania	15.9	19.9	16.2	21.9	0.9	1.1		66	55	80	72	73	49
Yugoslavia	13.0	15.6	16.2	21.9	0.7	1.1	92	72	61	82	76	67	40
Bulgaria	4.6	6.3	7.2	8.8	1.2	0.7		62	42	82	75	74	36
Albania	—	1.0	1.2	2.7	—	2.9	90+	69	62	90+	80+	74	62
Greece	5.7	7.2	7.5	9.4	0.9	0.8	87	57	35	50	48	48	39
Italy	36.6	44.2	46.7	56.7	0.7	0.7	83	41	33	58	44	42	13
Spain	20.3	25.5	28.0	36.3	0.9	0.9	84	43	30	56	50	50	19
Portugal	6.0	7.6	8.4	8.9	0.9	0.2	92	77	41	60	46	46	28
Eire	3.1	3.0	3.0	3.2	0.0	0.2	80+	54	45	60	53	46	22
Denmark	3.0	3.8	4.3	5.1	0.8	0.6	77	26	18	39	30	29	8
France	41.7	41.6	41.9	53.3	0.0	0.9	76	38	24	43	29	29	10
Germany	60.4	69.4	50.8(W)	61.3(W)	0.5	0.7(W)	70	22(W)	17(W)	35	20	16(W)	5(W)
GDR	—	—	18.4	16.7	—	-0.3		28	25	—	—	26	10
Japan	53	71	83.2	114.9	1.1	1.2	84	37	25	60	48	46	12

* 1936 boundaries. † Settlements below 10,000 people in 1891; otherwise undefined. (a) 1928; (b) 1959; (c) 1971; (W) West.

(continued)

223

Table 1—continued

	Millions				Growth (% p.a.)		% rural†			% agricultural			
	1937	1950	1960	1978	1950–60	1960–78	1950	1960	1975	c. 1936	1960	1970	1978
North Korea	7.5	9.0	10.5	17.1	1.6	2.7	80	71	57 }	75	62	55	48
South Korea	15.3	20.2	24.7	37	2.1	2.3	83	72	53	75	66	51	41
China‡	(500)	547	654	960	1.8	2.1	89	81	76	(85)	81	81	74
India	304	364	428	650	1.7	2.3	88	82	78		74	69	65
Pakistan }	66	75	45	77 }	2.5	3.0 }	92	80	73		61	59	55
Bangladesh }			51	83		2.7		95	91		87	86	84
North Vietnam }	19.0 }	13.1	16.1 }	52 }	2.1	3.0 }	92 }	87 }	83 }	90+	82	76 }	72 }
South Vietnam }		11.5	14.1		2.1						82	76	
Kampuchea	3.0	4.3	5.4	8.9	2.3	2.8	92	90	77	90+	82	78	75
Laos	1.0	1.9	2.4	3.5	2.3	2.1	94	92	89		83	79	75
Thailand	14.5	19.7	26.4	46.4	2.9	3.1	92	87	83		84	80	76
Indonesia	67	77	93	147	1.9	2.5	91	85	81		75	66	60
Philippines	15.4	20.3	27.7	46.4	3.1	2.8	87	70	64		73	53	48
Taiwan	5.5	7.4	10.8	17.1	3.8	2.5	90	65	36		50	41	33
Turkey	16.7	20.8	27.5	43.1	2.8	2.5		70	57		79	68	57
Iran	13.7	17.6	21.6	35.2	2.1	2.6	79	67	56		54	46	40
Iraq	3.7	5.2	6.8	12.3	2.7	3.3		57	38		53	47	42
Afghanistan	(11)	(12)	(14)	(16)	(1.6)	(0.7)		92	88		85	82	79
Mongolia	0.7	0.8	0.95	1.6	1.7	2.9		63	51		70	62	51
Cuba	4.4	5.5	7.0	9.7	2.4	2.0	43	49	38		39	31	25

‡ Present boundaries.

Sources: Svennilson, 1954; Mitchell, 1975; World Bank, 1978; ECAFE, 1959b; Moore, 1945; Allen, 1972; FAO, UN and Soviet Yearbooks, various issues.

Table 2   Health and health care indicators

	Deaths per 1000 inhabitants				Infant mortality (% first year)			Average life expectancy		Physicians per 10,000 inhabitants			Hospital beds per 10,000 inhabitants		
	1891–5	1909–13	1926–8	1955–9	1907–11	1926–8	1965–9	1954–7	c.1978	c.1939	c.1960	c.1978	c.1939	c.1960	c.1978
USSR	36(x)	28(x)	21(x)	8	25(x)	17(x)	2.6	65	70	8	20	35	40	80	122
Central Asia	—	17	14(a)	7						5	14	26	31		109
Kazakhstan	—	28	21(a)	8						4	15	30	39		129
Azerbaijan	—	—	15(a)	7						10	20	31	38		96
Poland	—	(23)	17	9	—	15	3.7	65	71	4	13	23	20	70	78
Czechoslovakia	(28)	(20)	16	10	(20)	15	2.4	69	70		18	30		76	78
Hungary	32	24	17	10	21	18	3.7	66	70		15	27		68	88
Romania	31	25	21	10	22	20	5.1	63	70		13	17		73	93
Yugoslavia	(29)	(24)	20	10	16	15	6.2	59	69		6	16		33(b)	60
Bulgaria	28	24	18	9	16	15	3.1	65	72		17	28		62	89
Greece	23	—	16	7	—	10	3.4	67	73		13	22		28(b)	64
Italy	26	20	16	10	15	12	3.3	68	73		16	20		69(b)	106
Spain	30	23	19	9	16	13	2.9	66	73		12	18		43(b)	53
Portugal	21	20	19	11	—	14	6.1	61	69		8	14	(25)	40(b)	53
Eire	19	17	14	12	9	7	2.3	68	73		11	12		143(b)	106
Denmark	19	13	11	9	11	8	1.7	72	74	(8)	12	20	(90)	100	97(c)
France	22	18	17	12	13	10	2.1	68	73	7	11	15		146(b)	103
GFR	23 }	16 }	12 }	11 }	18 }	10 }	2.3	68	72		15	25		100(b)	119
GDR				12			2.2	68	72		12	25		119	106
Japan	21	19	19	8	15	14		66	76	8	11	16	13	35(b)	105

(a) 1940; (b) c.1950; (c) c.1970; (x) excluding Asiatic areas.

(continued)

Table 2—continued

	Deaths per 1000 inhabitants				Infant mortality (% first year)			Average life expectancy		Physicians per 10,000 inhabitants			Hospital beds per 10,000 inhabitants		
	1935–9	1955–9	1970–5	1977	1935–9	1955–9	c. 1975	1950–60	c. 1978	c. 1950	c. 1960	c. 1978	c. 1950	c. 1960	c. 1977
Albania	17	11	7	(7)		8		56	69		3.5	10			61(c)
North Korea	19	(14)	9	8	9	6		50	63			23			
South Korea		21	9	7				50	70		3.3	5			7
China	(11)		9	8	(16)(b)		3.8	48		0.3	1.2	7	0.3		
India	23	16	16	15		15	12	41	51	1.7	1.8	2.8	4.0	4.4	7
Pakistan		17	17	14	16	11	11	41	52	0.5	0.9	2.6	0.9	2.7	5
Bangladesh		21	21	18			14	39	47			1.1			2
Vietnam			21	18			4(S)	39	(62)	0.2	0.3(S)	1.8	3.7	15(S)	35
Kampuchea	30	19	19	17		(13)		42	(45)	0.0	0.2	0.6			11
Laos		23	23	20				39	42		0.2	0.3			25
Thailand	16	10	11	9	10	5	2.7	47	61	0.8	1.3	1.2	5	8	12
Indonesia	18	19	17	14	14	(9)		39	47	0.2	0.2	0.7	6	8	6
Philippines	17	9	10	10	14	8	7.2	48	60	0.8		3.6	7	5	17
Taiwan	20	8	5	5		3	2.0	60	72		4.3	6.3			
Turkey	(13)	12	12	10				49	61	2.5	3.3	7.0	11	15	21
Iran	25	15	15	14			12	43	52	0.1	2.6	3.6	4.6		15
Iraq	4	15	15	13		4	10	44	55	0.1	1.8	4.4	10		20
Afghanistan	24	24	24	27			27	31	42		0.4	0.5			2
Mongolia	12	10	10	10				48	63	6	10	21	31	81	103
Cuba	11	6	6	6	10	4	4	60	72	8	8	9		45	44

(a) 1940; (b) c. 1950; (c) c. 1970; (x) excluding Asiatic areas; (S) South.

Sources: Mulhall, 1898; Mitchell, 1975; Lorimer, 1946; Myrdal, 1968; World Bank, 1980; Thomas, 1971; UN, CMEA and Soviet Yearbooks, various issues.

Table 3   Education indicators

	School enrolments as % of:								Higher education students as % of:					Adult literacy (%)		
	Total population					Age group			Total population			Age group				
	c.1887	c.1914	c.1928	c.1938	1970	c.1955	c.1965	c.1978	c.1914	1938	1978	c.1960	c.1978	c.1920	c.1939	c.1960
USSR	3	6	12	18	20	83	82	90	0.08	0.42	1.95	11	22	44	87	98
Central Asia	—	0.4	4.6	20	28				0.00	0.25	1.64			7	80	97
Kazakhstan	—	2	(6)	19	25				0.00	0.17	1.71			18	84	97
Azerbaijan	—	3	8	21	28				0.00	0.45	1.75			20	83	97
Poland	—	12(a)	14	14	18	68	88	88	—	0.14	1.80	9	18	—	80	98
Czechoslovakia	—	16(a)	16	16	17	79	80	78	—	0.17	1.21	11	15	95+	96	96
Hungary	12	14	16	11	15	74	82	88	0.06	0.11	1.02	7	13		93	97
Romania	2	10	12	14	16	50	89	100	0.08	0.13	0.87	5	10		(65)	89
Yugoslavia	(3)	8(a)	10	10	15	58	75	87	—	0.10	1.96	9	23		(60)	77
Bulgaria	9	14	12	16	15	72	88	94	0.05	0.16	1.62	11	22		70	91
Albania	—	—	—	7	24	64	90	88	—	0.04	1.85	5	16		(15)	71
Greece	6	13(a)	12	15	15	70	81	87	0.04	0.11	1.34	4	15	62	65	80
Italy	11	11	11	14	13	57	70	84	0.08	0.19	1.87	7	27	50	80	91
Spain	11	9	11	11(b)	18	59	75	91	0.10	0.21	1.71	4	22		75	87
Portugal	5	5(a)	6	7	13	54	67	88	0.02	0.09	0.89	4	11	36	52	62
Denmark	12	15	16	16	14	90	90	91	0.03	0.19	2.32	10	32	90+	95+	99
Eire	12	16	18	17	22	99	98	99	—	0.18	1.46	9	19	85+	90+	98
France	15	15	11	17	15	87	91	95	0.11	0.13	2.05	10	26	90+	96	99
GFR	18 }	18	17 }	14	14	87	90	77 }	0.11 }	0.08 }	1.75	6	25	95+	97+	99
GDR	}		}	15	15	79	78	96 }	}	}	2.28	16	29	95+	97+	99
UK	16	16	12	12	16	82	100	93	0.07	0.13	1.55	9	19	90+	97+	99
Japan	7	13	13	17	18	92	93	96	0.02	0.23	1.4	10	33	(75)	(90)	97

(a) 1922; (b) 1935.

(continued)

Table 3—continued

	School enrolments as % of:								Higher education students as % of:					Adult literacy (%)		
	Total population					Age group			Total population			Age group				
	1928	1937	1958	1970	1978	1955	1965	1978	1937	1960	1978	1960	1978	1937	1958	1975
North Korea	3 }	5	20	25	25	60	(80)	100 }	0.03	0.9	1.4	5 }	11 }	35	71 }	93 }
South Korea					25		72	90 }		0.40	1.0						
China	2	4	15	—	21	35	(60)	90	0.02	0.14			0.6	20+		66
India	4 }	4 }	9	12	14	25	44	53		0.26	0.75	3	8.4		24	36
Pakistan			7 }	10 }	10 }	23 }	27	32 }	0.1	0.16	0.2 }	2	2.0 }	10 }	18 }	21
Bangladesh				9	14			49			0.22 }		2.5			26
North Vietnam	2 }	3 }	9	17 }	21	20	59 }	86		0.04	0.30 }	2 }	3			87 }
South Vietnam										0.09 }						
Kampuchea			12	16		26	49	24		0.05	0.14		1.5		36	
Laos			6	9		14	32	52		0.06	0.3		0.3		28	
Thailand		9	16	17	18	46	44	62	0.04	0.18	0.5	3	5		68	84
Indonesia		3	9	13	16	37	47	61	0.04	0.05	0.22	1	2.5		47	62
Philippines	9	12	19	23	23	70	83	89	0.18	0.99	2.1	13	24	(55)	72	87
Taiwan		9	19	27	27	57	74	93	0.18	0.32	1.84	4	12	27	54	82
Turkey	4	5	13	18	21	36	54	71	0.12	0.24	0.7	3	8	21	40	60
Iran		1	8	15	21	19	40	70		0.09	0.5	1	5	(8)	15	50
Iraq		2	15	15	22	26	52	87	0.05	0.18	0.8	2	9	(8)	18	26
Mongolia		—	10	18	21	51	60	92		0.7	0.7	8	9		95	
Cuba		14	16	21	26	52	77	87	0.26	0.29	1.37	4	17	76	76	96

Sources: Mitchell, 1975; ASF, 1937; Cipolla, 1969; Grajdanzev, 1944; World Bank, 1980; E. Rawski, 1979; Marmullaku, 1975; Taiwan, 1978; Taira, 1971; Myrdal, 1968; Payne, 1973; Bharier, 1971; Gabbay, 1978; Yang and Chee, 1963; Rosenberg, 1975; Chen, 1979; Thomas, 1971; Trebilcock, 1981; UN, UNESCO, CMEA and Soviet Yearbooks, various issues.

Table 4 Landholders and labourers as percentages of the agrarian workforce (see note, p. 231)

	Landholders	Labourers	Based upon:
European			
Russia, *c.* 1900	95	5	Kovalchenko and Borodkin,
Podzols:	96	4	1980, 36–7
Central	97	3	
North-western	97	3	
Western	94	6	
Baltic	75	25	
North-eastern	98	2	
Chernozems:	97	3	
Central	98	2	
South-western	97	3	
Malorussia	97	3	
Steppes:	95	5	
Mid-Volgan	98	2	
Southern	94	6	
Poland			
1931	85	(15)	Moore, 1945, 223–6
Austria			
1902	87	13	Blum, 1978, 438
Czechoslovakia			
1930	85	15	1930s WAC, Vol. 2, 205
Hungary			
1930	61	39	Moore, 1945, 234
Romania			
1913	86	14	Mitrany, 1930, 235
Yugoslavia			
1931	91	9	Moore, 1945, 249–50
Bulgaria			
1910	93	7	Morgan, 1933, 49
1934	99	1	Moore, 1945, 251–2
Greece			
1929	(95)	(5)	Moore, 1945, 254–7
Italy			
1931	70	30	Schmidt, 1938, 10
Spain			
1966	69	31	Martinez-Alier, 1971, 19
Portugal			
1930	55	45	Moore, 1945, 264

(continued)

Table 4—continued

	Landholders	Labourers	Based upon:
Eire			
1929	79	21	1930s WAC, Vol. 3, 179
France			
1892	54	46	Clapham, 1936, 163
1929	72	28	1930s WAC, Vol. 2, 466
Germany			
1907	84	16	Blum, 1978, 438
1933	78	22	1930s WAC, Vol. 3, 43
Japan			
1929	84	16	1930s WAC, Vol. 5, 95
North Korea			
1937*	94	4	Grajdanzev, 1944, 111
South Korea			
1937*	94	4	
China, 1929–33			
22 Provinces	(85)	(15)	Buck, 1937, 196, referring to
Rice Belt:	(85)	(15)	percentages of farm work
Double-crop area	(91)	(9)	performed by family labour and
South-eastern	(88)	(12)	hired labour, respectively
Yangtze Basin	(86)	(14)	
Szechuan	(77)	(23)	
South-west	(81)	(19)	
Wheat Belt:	(84)	(16)	
Eastern	(80)	(20)	
Central	(88)	(12)	
North-western	(85)	(15)	
India, 1954–5	77	23	Griffin, 1979, 19
India, 1960–1	74	26	Sidhu, 1976, 153 and 252–5
Tamil Nadu	60	40	
Andhra Pradesh	62	38	
Mysore	76	24	
Kerala	83	17	
Maharashtra	74	26	
Gujarat	75	25	
Uttar Pradesh	79	21	
Madhya Pradesh	82	18	
Punjab/Haryana	61	39	
Rajasthan	89	11	
Jammu/Kashmir	89	11	
West Bengal	66	34	

(continued)

Table 4—continued

	Landholders	Labourers	Based upon:
India, 1960–1—*continued*			
Orissa	67	33	
Bihar	78	22	
Assam	64	36	
Pakistan			
1961	89	11	ILO, 1977, 48–9 and 155
Bangladesh			
1961	82	18	
1951	86	14	
Indo-China			
Tonkin, 1937	87	13	Poppinga, 1975T, 203
Taiwan			
1947	90	10	Cheng, 1961, 308
1952	94	6	
Philippines			
1938	40	60	Jacoby, 1949, 179
Iran			
1972	74	23	Aresvik, 1976, 101
Cuba			
1952	36	64	MacEwan, 1981, 12

* Residuals refer to *kademins* (nomadic firefield cultivators).
WAC = World Agricultural Census.

Note: 'Landholders' here refers to proprietors, tenants, sharecroppers and other 'own-account' farmers; 'labourers' refers to landless or virtually landless hired agricultural workers. People who combine 'own-account' and wagework are classified according to their main livelihood.

Table 5 Preponderant types of landholder, as percentages of all landholders (unless otherwise indicated)

	Peasant 'allotments'		Distribution of landed property, 1905 (% of total area)			Extra land rented by peasants, 1905†	Enclosed peasant holdings, late 1917 (% of total)
	Under communal ownership, 1905 (% of total)	Under joint family ownership, 1905 (% of total)	Peasant land	State land*	Other land		
European Russia							
Overall	78	22	42.6	34.6	22.8	17	11
Podzols:	—	—	—	—	—	—	—
Central	97	3	57.4	10.1	32.5	10	8
North-western	97	3	48.1	16.4	35.5	c. 11	17
Western	63	37	39.8	6.8	53.4	13	16
North-eastern	94	6	39.0	38.1	22.9	4	2
Chernozems:	—	—	—	—	—	—	—
Central	89	11	64.6	5.7	29.7	5	8
South-western	14	86	49.7	6.9	43.4	17	8
Malorussian	51	49	68.2	2.4	29.4	19	13
Steppes:	—	—	—	—	—	—	—
Mid-Volgan	98	2	57.5	20.0	22.5	13	10
Southern	98	2	54.5	4.1	41.4	29	29
Eastern	98	2	64.9	15.7	19.4	22	16

Based upon: Rubinow, 1906, 37–40; Pavlovsky, 1930, 331, 135; Kovalchenko and Borodkin, 1980, 36–7.

* 82% of state land was in the far north and north-east (mostly forest).

† As a percentage of peasant allotment land.

(continued)

Table 5—continued

	Proprietors	Mixed	Tenants	Based upon:
Poland				
1931	90	7	3	Moore, 1945, 223–6
Austria				
1890	75	?	25	Mulhall, 1896, 419
Czechoslovakia				
1930	56	36	8	1930s WAC, Vol. 2, 166
Hungary				
1890	90	?	10	Mulhall, 1896, 419
1930	86	?	9	Moore, 1945, 232
Romania				
1905	86	?	14	Mitrany, 1930, 236
Bulgaria				
1934	69	29	2	Moore, 1945, 251
Greece				
1929	80	11	9	Moore, 1945, 255
Italy				
1870:				
Piedmont	45	?	55(S)	Mulhall, 1898, 346
Lombardy	85	?	15(S)	ibid.
Parma and Modena	36	?	64(S)	ibid.
Tuscany	37	?	63(S)	ibid.
Papal States	19	?	81(S)	ibid.
	12	?	88(S)	ibid.
Naples	51	?	49	ibid.
Sicily	80	?	20	ibid.

S = mostly sharecroppers.   Mixed = ambiguous status.   'Tenants' here includes sharecroppers.

(continued)

233

Table 5—continued

	Proprietors	Mixed	Tenants	Based upon:
Italy				
1931	54	?	46(S)	Schmidt, 1938, 10
1936	46	11	43(S)	Moore, 1945, 261
1946	46(F)	—	54(F,S)	Medici, 1952, 154
Spain				
1962	52	36	12	1960 WAC, Vol. I(c), 178
Portugal				
1950	61	19	20	1950 WAC, Vol. I
1890s	75	?	25	Mulhall, 1898, 346
Denmark				
1870	34	?	66	Mulhall, 1898, 314
Ireland				
1841	under 1	?	99+	
1871	under 1	?	99+	Pomfret, 1930, 312, 83, 42, 6
1922	85	?	15	
France				
1892	61	?	39	Clapham, 1936, 161
1929	46	29	25	1930s WAC, Vol. 2, 430
Germany				
1907	73	10	17	Blum, 1978, 436
1933	93	2	5	1930s WAC, Vol. 3, 23
Japan				
1902	34	38	28	Ogura, 1968, 18
1937	31	42	27	ibid., 25

S = mostly sharecroppers. F = percentage of all farmland. Mixed = ambiguous status. 'Tenants' here includes sharecroppers.

Table 5—continued

	Proprietors	Mixed	Tenants	Based upon:
Korea				
1917	22	39	39	Suh, 1978, 81
1937	19	26	55	
South	14	27	59	Grajdanzev, 1944, 109–11
North	33	24	43	
Centre	18	26	56	
China, 1929–33				Buck, 1937, 293, 196
Rice Belt:				
Double-crop area	54	29	17	ibid.
South-eastern	38	37	25	ibid.
South-western	29	43	28	ibid.
Yangtze Basin	28	53	19	ibid.
Szechuan	57	22	21	ibid.
	42	33	25	ibid.
	41	16	43	ibid.
Wheat Belt:				
Eastern	76	18	6	ibid.
Central	80	15	5	ibid.
North-west	68	23	9	ibid.
	78	16	6	ibid.
China				
1935	47	24	29	Chinese MI, 1943, 604
1946	50	27	23	Kuo, 1976, 4
1950	42	25	33	Hsiao, 1951, 209
India				
1931	47	?	53	Parsons *et al*, 1951, 135
1951	57(F)	—	43(F)	Kotovsky, 1964, 21
1960	73	5	22	1960 WAC, Vol. V, 96

F = percentage of all farmland.   Mixed = ambiguous status.   'Tenants' here includes sharecroppers.

(continued)

235

Table 5—continued

	Proprietors	Mixed	Tenants	Based upon:
West Pakistan				
1960	35	29	36(S)	1960 ibid., Vol. I(a), 152
Bangladesh				
1960	58	6	36	1960 ibid., 149
Indo-China				
Tonkin, 1937	99	?	1	Jacoby, 1949, 142
Annam, 1937	90	?	10	ibid.
Cochinchina, 1937	65	?	35	ibid.
Kampuchea, 1937	95	?	5	ibid.
South Vietnam				
1960	24	45	31	1960 WAC, Vol. I(a), 222
Thailand				
1960	82	14	4	1960 WAC, Vol. I(b), 255
Indonesia				
1960	64	29(S)	7(S)	1960 WAC, Vol. V, 96
Philippines				
1938	49	16	35	Jacoby, 1949, 179
1950	53	21	26	1950 WAC, Vol. I
Taiwan				
1940	32	31	37	Ho, 1978, 335
Turkey				
1950	73	22	5	OECD, 1969, 304
Iran				
1960	33	11	56	1960 WAC, Vol. V, 96
Iraq				
1952	66(F)	—	34(F)	1960 ibid., Vol. I(a), 107

WAC = World Agricultural Census.   F = percentage of all farmland.   'Mixed' = ambiguous status.   'Tenants' here includes share-croppers.   S = mostly sharecroppers.

236

Table 6 Farmland per head of agricultural population (hectares)

	Cropland			Pasture and meadow		
	1891	1928	1970	1891	1928	1970
USSR	1.6	1.8	3.7	2.1	2.3	6.0
Central Asia	—	0.6	0.6	—	—	—
Kazakhstan	—	0.9	6	—	11	—
Poland	—	1.0	1.2	—	0.3	0.3
Czechoslovakia	—	1.3	2.2	—	0.5	0.7
Hungary	0.9	1.3	2.0	0.6	0.4	0.5
Romania		1.1	0.9		0.3	0.4
Yugoslavia }	1.2	0.7	0.8 }	1.0	0.4	0.6
Bulgaria		0.9	2.8		0.1	0.4
Greece	0.7	0.8	1.0	1.9	0.4	1.3
Italy	1.0	0.9	1.5	0.4	0.4	0.5
Spain	1.4	1.7	2.4	0.9	1.5	1.4
Portugal	0.7	—	1.3	—	—	0.2
Eire	—	1.0	1.5	—	2.2	4.7
Denmark	2.2	2.5	4.9	1.2	0.4	0.5
France	1.8	2.1	2.7	0.6	1.0	1.9
GFR }	1.4 }	1.6	1.8 }	0.5 }	0.6	1.2
GDR			2.2			0.7
Japan	0.2	0.2	0.3	0.0	0.0	0.0
Albania	—	—	0.42	—	—	0.45
North Korea	—	—	0.26	—	—	0.01
South Korea	—	—	0.15	—	—	0.00
China	—	—	0.24	—	—	0.40
India	—	—	0.44	—	—	0.03
Pakistan	—	—	0.54	—	—	0.08
Bangladesh	—	—	0.16	—	—	0.01
Vietnam	—	—	0.17	—	—	0.16
Kampuchea	—	—	0.55	—	—	0.11
Laos	—	—	0.41	—	—	0.34
Thailand	—	—	0.47	—	—	0.01
Indonesia	—	—	0.23	—	—	0.03
Philippines	—	—	0.48	—	—	0.04
Taiwan	—	—	0.15	—	—	0.0
Turkey	—	—	1.15	—	—	1.16
Iran	—	—	1.35	—	—	0.92
Iraq	—	—	1.14	—	—	0.92
Afghanistan	—	—	0.59	—	—	0.43
Mongolia	—	—	0.96	—	—	1.81
Cuba	—	—	1.36	—	—	0.92

Sources: Mulhall, 1896; ECE, 1951; ASF, 1937; Moore, 1945; Timoshenko, 1932; Lorimer, 1946; Taiwan, 1978; FAO and Soviet Yearbooks, various issues.

Table 7 Distribution of farms by size

	Percentage of farms not exceeding:				Average size (ha)	Based upon:
	2.2 ha	5.5 ha	10.9 ha	21.8 ha		
European Russia Peasant Allotments:						
Overall, 1877	4.4	10.6		88.4	—	Antsiferov, 1930, 23, 31;
Overall, 1905	4.7	23.3	77.9	89.4	11.1	Lenin, 1977T, 10; Jasny, 1949, 147
By region, 1905:						
Podzols:						
Central		18.8	79.7		7.9	Pavlovsky, 1930, 89–90
North-western		5.5	54.0		11.2	ibid.
Western		8.9	69.6		9.2	ibid.
North-eastern		10.0	21.6		16.0	ibid.
Far northern		17.0	38.0		22.4	ibid.
Chernozems:						
Central		22.5	76.4		7.8	ibid.
Malorussian		45.6	88.7		6.1	ibid.
South-western		57.6	90.5		5.5	ibid.
Steppes:						
Mid-Volgan		18.7	73.7		8.3	ibid.
Eastern		7.6	26.9		19.7	ibid.
Southern		20.4	64.4		9.7	ibid.

(continued)

238

Table 7—continued

	Percentage of farms not exceeding:							Average size (ha)	Based upon:
	0.5 ha	1.0 ha	2.0 ha	3.0 ha	5.0 ha	10.0 ha	20.0 ha		
Poland									
1921		26.4	33.9		64.6	87.1	96.7		Polonsky, 1975, 166; Lane and Kolankiewicz, 1973, 330;
1931			26.0		64.6				
1950(P)	6.3		25.9		57.2	88.0			Bergmann, 1975T, 154; and Moore, 1945, 82
1960(P)	9.7		32.8		63.2	89.3		4.8	Kieniewicz, 1969, 214
Russian, 1905			25		65		98	—	ibid.
Prussian, 1907			67		76		95	—	ibid.
Austrian, 1902			44		81		99	—	ibid.
Greater Austria									
1902			43.6		71.8			—	Blum, 1978, 437
Czechoslovakia									
1930	14.5		43.0		70.4		95.7	5.9	1930s WAC, Vol. 2, 166
1949	19.7		46.1		69.4	86.3	96.9	4.9	Bergmann, 1975T, 78
Hungary									
1895	22			54	73	(88)		8.9	Csizmadia, 1977T, 16; Blum, 1978, 437; Polonsky, 1975, 166
1935	(35)			68	(84)	(92)	(97)	6.1	
Romania									
1907(P)	6.6	15.1	30.3	43.9	77.2	95.4		—	Roberts, 1951, 362
1913			42.0		81.0	95.3		—	Mitrany, 1930, 240–1
1930		18.6		52.1	74.9	92.0	97.5	6.0	Roberts, 1951, 370
1948	7.3	16.8		52.7	76.0	93.8	98.5		ibid., 297

(continued)

Table 7—continued

	0.5 ha	1.0 ha	2.0 ha	3.0 ha	5.0 ha	10.0 ha	20.0 ha	Average size (ha)	Based upon:
	Percentage of farms not exceeding:								
Serbia									
1897			21.0		54.6	82.1			Milward and Saul, 1977, 448
Yugoslavia									
1931	8.0	16.8	33.8		67.8	88.3	97.1		Polonsky, 1975, 167; OECD, 1973, 29–30; Bergmann, 1975T, 133–9
1960(P)		18.0	34.9	49.9	71.2	92.8		4.3	
1969(P)		21.4	39.3	54.6	74.3	94.3		3.9	
Bulgaria									
1897	21	32	45	54	68	87	97	5.0	Bell, 1977, 13
1926		11.9	24.3	36.3	57.0	85.0	97.6	—	Rothschild, 1974, 330
1934		13.5	27.0	40.2	63.1	89.3	98.5	—	ibid.
1946		14.9	29.8		68.6	93.1	99.3	—	ibid.
Greece									
1929		37.6	59.3	72.7	87.0	95.9	98.7	4.1	1930s WAC, Vol. 3, 149–51
1961		23.0			80.8	95.9	99.3	3.2	OECD, 1969, 82
Italy*									
1930	15.7	30.6	63.3	63.3	77.0	89.6	96.1	6.7	1930s WAC, Vol. 3, 213
1961	11.6	31.2	50.3	62.1	75.7	89.1	96.0	6.3	1960 WAC, Vol. 1(c), 80
Spain									
1930	60	76.8			95	97		—	Moore, 1945, 82–83
South and centre					96	98		2.2	Vives, 1969T, 639
1959	77.4	90.2			98.1	99.1		—	Malefakis, 1970, 416

P = private properties only. * Surprisingly, detailed regional data in Medici, 1952, especially on p. 95, indicate that regional variations in the size-distribution of farms were too small for this to have been a significant source of Italy's notorious interregional economic disparities.

(continued)

240

Table 7—*continued*

	Percentage of farms not exceeding:							Average size (ha)	Based upon:
	0.5 ha	1.0 ha	2.0 ha	3.0 ha	5.0 ha	10.0 ha	20.0 ha		
Portugal, 1954(C)									
North		49.8			88.4	96.6		2.4	OECD, 1969, 161
Centre		54.1			93.2	97.8		2.2	ibid.
South		26.2			63.9	78.1		27.4	ibid.
France									
1882		38.2				84.7		8.7	Bernstein, 1899, 68
1892		39			71	85		—	Zeldin, 1979, 184
1908		37.9				83.8		—	Clapham, 1936, 184
1929		25.6			54.5	72.6	87.5	11.6	1930s WAC, Vol. 2, 428
1948		9.9			37.0	58.0	80.1	14.6	Parsons *et al.*, 1951, 537
Germany									
1895	32.7				76.4	94.4		7.8	Bernstein, 1899, 66–7
1907			58.2		74.2			—	Blum, 1978, 437
1933	36.6	44.2	54.2		70.6	83.4	92.7	8.7	1930s WAC, Vol. 2, 19
Japan									
1910	37.0	69.5	88.6	94.4				0.9	Ogura, 1968, 26, 684
1920	35.6	68.9	89.4	95.6				0.9	ibid.
1930	34.6	68.9	90.8	96.4				0.9	ibid.
1940	33.7	66.4	90.7	96.4				0.9	ibid.
1960	38.0	69.8	93.4	97.2				0.9	ibid.
Korea									
Overall, 1938(C)	34.8	63.3	83.0	93.9				1.5	Grajdanzev, 1944, 112–13
South, 1937(C)	48.8	76.4	93.0					—	Ban *et al.*, 1980, 294
South, 1960	35	71	95		100			0.5	1960 WAC, Vol. 5, 28, 30, 56

C = cropland only.

(*continued*)

241

Table 7—continued

	Percentage of farms not exceeding:							Average size (ha)	Based upon:
	0.4 ha	1.0 ha	2.0 ha	4.0 ha	6.1 ha	12.1 ha	20.2 ha		
Ireland									
1841	16.4		54.0		84.5	94.1		—	Pomfret, 1930, 42, 312
1871	8.2		20.8		49.7	73.1		—	ibid.
1911	19.7		28.0		50.0	71.5		(13)	ibid.
Southern, 1929	13.6	17.4	22.2	31.5	41.4	64.2	80.0	15.4	1930s WAC, Vol. 2, 353
Northern, 1930	20.7		29.8	42.1	52.8	74.7	87.8	—	ibid., 587
India					(10 ha)				
Overall, 1951	16.8	38.1	59.1	78.2		94.4	98.6	3.0	Ministry of Labour, Agricultural Labour Enquiry, 'Essential statistics', Delhi, 1954, as quoted in John, 1962, 103–6
South, 1951	28.0	55.1	76.0	90.0		97.9	99.5	1.8	
West, 1951	11.2	26.8	40.7	61.1		86.5	96.7	5.0	
Centre, 1951	7.4	19.7	36.1	58.2		86.6	96.2	4.8	
North-west, 1951	5.4	19.8	36.7	59.2		90.2	98.2	5.1	Sidhu, 1976, 153
East, 1951	21.4	45.8	72.2	90.6		98.6	99.6	1.8	Bergmann, 1977T, 25
North-east, 1951	14.8	41.0	66.1	86.7		98.1	99.5	3.0	
Overall, 1961	21.3	42.5	64.4			96	99	2.5	
Overall, 1971		50.6	69.7			96	99	2.3	
Pakistan				(3 ha)	(5 ha)	(10 ha)			
1960	15.2	32.8	49.4	61.4	77.0	92.0		4.1	1960 WAC, Vol. 1(a), p. 153
Bangladesh									
1960	24.3	51.6	77.9	89.3	96.5	99.5		1.4	ibid., 149

242

(continued)

Table 7—continued

	Percentage of farms not exceeding:						Average size (ha)	Based upon:
	0.3 ha	0.7 ha	1.3 ha	2.0 ha	3.3 ha	6.7 ha		
China(C)								
Overall, 1917		(36)		(62)	(87)	(97)	1.6	Tawney, 1932, 40
1934:								Chinese Ministry of Information, 1943, 547, 609, 610, based on surveys by correspondents of the National Agricultural Research Bureau of the Nationalist regime in 891 hsien in 22 provinces of China (i.e. excluding Manchuria, Sinkiang, Tibet and Taiwan)
22 Provinces		35.8	61.0	75.2	91.7		1.1	
Rice Belt:	25.7	49.5	80.5	90.5	96.6		1.1(B)	
Double-crop area								
Kwangsi	38.1	63.0	86.9	94.4	98.1		0.9	
Kwangtung	34.6	62.1	88.6	95.0	98.1		0.7	
Eastern:								(B) Buck, 1937, whose data for 1929–33 are broadly consistent with NARB findings
Fukien	34.3	62.2	87.9	94.0	98.0		0.9	
Chekiang	30.1	53.5	84.9	93.3	98.0		0.8	
Kiangsi	22.1	47.2	80.7	91.4	96.6		0.8	
Hunan	22.6	48.3	82.1	92.2	97.5		0.7	
Kweichow	27.3	49.7	80.5	81.5	97.0		1.2	
West-Central:								
Yunnan	33.2	58.0	87.7	94.5	97.9		1.2	
Szechuan	20.3	39.2	72.8	87.5	95.5		1.2	
Hupei	24.9	49.9	83.8	92.7	97.8		0.9	
South Honan	16.1	33.8	63.8	79.3	91.9		1.4	
South Anhwei	18.3	38.8	68.6	81.7	92.4		1.2	
South Kiangsu	20.2	46.4	80.9	90.5	96.7		1.1	
South Shensi	24.9	47.0	79.4	90.4	97.4		1.5	

C = cropland only.

(continued)

243

Table 7—continued

	Percentage of farms not exceeding:						Average size (ha)	Based upon:
	0.3 ha	0.7 ha	1.3 ha	2.0 ha	3.3 ha	6.7 ha		
Wheat Belt:		27.1	48.6	65.4	88.5	95.7	2.0(B)	
East-Central:								
North Honan		28.0	49.0	67.0	90.0	97.0	*	(B) Buck, 1937, whose data for
North Anwhei		27.1	49.5	66.2	89.4	97.1	*	1929–33 are broadly consistent with
North Kiangsu		24.7	47.0	64.9	89.8	96.5	*	NARB findings
North Shensi		22.3	40.8	57.2	85.0	94.0	*	
Shantung		39.3	62.7	77.6	94.0	98.5	1.1	Shen, 1951, 142, adds:
Hopei		26.4	49.5	67.5	90.4	97.0	1.5	average farm size, 1946
Shansi		18.4	37.0	53.5	81.5	92.3	2.0	Sinkiang 2.9 ha
North-west:								Manchuria 4.4 ha
Kansu		21.6	39.8	55.3	81.1	91.5	1.8	
Chinghai		20.8	43.2	59.8	87.0	95.3	3.1	
Ningsia		15.6	29.2	40.2	71.3	79.5	2.3	
Chahar		14.3	32.8	48.9	77.3	87.3	3.3	
Suiyuan		4.6	9.8	20.0	41.7	57.8	4.6	

C = cropland only. * Included with southern part of respective province.

(continued)

Table 7—continued

	Percentage of farms not exceeding:						Average size (ha)	Based upon:
	0.36 ha	1.0 ha	1.8 ha	3.6 ha	5.0 ha	10.0 ha		
Indo-China, 1937:								
Vietnam(C)								
Tonkin	61.7		91.5	97.8	98.2		1.0	Gourou, 1945T, 276–9,
Annam		69			98.6		1.2	338–40, 383–5; Jacoby, 1949,
Cochinchina(P)		33.7			71.7	86.4	9.4	142–3; Poppinga, 1975T,
Kampuchea(C)		60			94		1.1	203; Tep Youth, 1951, 174

	Percentage of farms not exceeding:						Average size (ha)	Based upon:
	0.5 ha	1.0 ha	2.0 ha	3.0 ha	5.3 ha	10.0 ha		
South Vietnam								
1960	27.0	49.0	74.5	85.8	94.7	99.0	1.6	1960 WAC, Vol. 1(a), 222
Indonesia								
1960	43.6	70.1	88.3	94.0	97.5	99.3	1.1	1960 WAC, Vol. 1(c), 72
Philippines								
1939		22.5	52.5	69	87	96	4.0	Parsons et al., 1951, 185
1960	4.1	11.5	41.1	62.3	81.0	94.4	3.6	1960 WAC, Vol. 1(c), 160
Taiwan								
1939	25.2	45.8	72	86	95	99	2.0	Ho, 1978, 351–2;
1949	28.9	56.9	85	95	99	100	1.2	Cheng, 1961, 5;
1960	37.4	66.4	91	97	99	100	0.7	Myers, 1969, 41, 47

C = cropland only.   P = private properties only.

(continued)

Table 7—continued

	Percentage of farms not exceeding:						Average size (ha)	Based upon:
	0.5 ha	1.0 ha	2.0 ha	3.0 ha	5.0 ha	10.0 ha		
Thailand								
1951		15.0	(30)	(50)	71	92	4.1	Fryer, 1970, 139
Turkey								
1960	12.9	25.0	41.0	52.3	68.9	87.0	5.5	1960: WAC, Vol. 1, 268
Iran								
1960	16.7	26.3	40.0	51.1	65.3	83.4	6.0	ibid., 96
1975		29.6	42.6		64.4	81.7	6.6	Arabadjian, 1980, 210
Iraq								
1971		20.2			49.5		9.7	Gabbay, 1978, 38

Note: Farm sizes here refer to total farm size, unless otherwise indicated. In densely populated Asian countries it makes little difference whether farm sizes refer to total farm size or to cropland as over 80 per cent of the farmland is generally cultivated. Data permitting, tenant and 'dwarf' farms are included and landless labourers are excluded. Of course, it is debatable where exactly to draw the line between 'dwarf' holdings and landless households. It seems that the greatest international comparability and consistency with Tables 4 and 5 is obtained by drawing the line at holdings of 0.1 ha, data permitting, and the availability of data reinforces my essentially pragmatic decision. One must not assume that most 'dwarf' holdings could mainly rely upon 'external' earnings in the countries under investigation – this only seems plausible in the more industrialized economies (Germany, France, Czech lands, Northern Italy, Denmark and Japan) in the early to mid-twentieth century.

P = private properties only.   C = cropland only.   WAC = World Agricultural Census.

Table 8 Grain and potatoes, as percentages of total
human calorie intake

	Mid-1930s	Mid-1960s
USSR	76	57
Poland	71	52
Czechoslovakia	55	48
Hungary	70	49
Romania	72	65
Yugoslavia	75	64
Bulgaria	76	64
Albania	—	68
Greece	61	50
Italy	65	47
Spain	57(a)	46
Portugal	60	53
Ireland	50	37
Denmark	33	28
France	51	34
East Germany }	47	41
West Germany		31
Japan	76	64
North Korea }	77	80
South Korea		90
China	76(b)	78
India		69
Pakistan }	66	75
Bangladesh		
North Vietnam		83
South Vietnam }	72	83
Kampuchea		74
Laos		89
Thailand	71	76
Indonesia	81	78
Philippines	68	69
Taiwan	71	72
Turkey	76	65
Iran	67	63
Iraq	62	57
Mongolia	—	55
Cuba	50	51

Notes: (a) Early 1930s.   (b) 1931–7.

Sources: FAO World Food Surveys; FAO Production
Yearbooks, various issues.

Table 9 Net agricultural production per person dependent on agriculture, 1924–6

European Russia and Siberia (USSR average = 100)	
North-west	100
West	103
Far north	97
Urals	131
Central industrial region	95
Central Chernozem region	90
Central Volga region	95
Lower Volga region	100
Ukraine	92
Belorussia	105
Kazakhstan	108
Siberia	154

Source: Moore, 1945, 191–2; on p. 34, Professor Moore notes that his calculations for Europe (1931–5) are not strictly comparable to those for Russia (1924–6).

Table 10 Agriculture's percentage share

	In gross investment						In Gross National Product		
	1924–8	1929–32	1933–7	1938–40	1941–5	1946–50	1913	1928	1937
USSR	58*	16	12	11	9	12	59	48	31

	In gross investment						In Gross Material Product		
	1951–5	1956–80	1961–5	1966–70	1971–4	1975–8	1950	1965	1975
USSR	14	14	16	17	20	20	38	23	17
GDR	—	10	13	14	13	11	15	16	11
Czechoslovakia	11	16	14	11	10	12	23	13	9
Hungary	17	15	17	20	20	15	29	24	18
Poland	10	13	14	16	15	16	36	23	15
Bulgaria	13	21	22	16	18	14	39	34	22
Romania	9	16	19	16	14	14	42	28	17
Yugoslavia	9	13	11	9	9	—	30(1949)	25	19
Albania	12	18	15	16	12	—	76	43	33

* Including private investment.

Sources: Gosplan, 1934; Goldsmith, 1961; Maddison, 1969; Hardt, 1974; Marmullaku, 1975; Soviet and Comecon Yearbooks, various issues.

Table 11 Grain and potato output per inhabitant (grain equivalent kg p.a.)

	1892–5	1909–13	1934–8	1948–52	1969–71	1976–8	1975–8 as % of: 1909–13	1975–8 as % of: 1930s
USSR	578	605*	520	549	794	889	147	171
Eastern Europe	(548)	605*	586(c)	553	690	856	141	146
Southern Europe	260	276*	292	235	340	341	124	117
Poland	—	—	607	782	913	916	—	151
Czechoslovakia	—	—	511	553	644	733	—	143
Hungary	650	650	720	653	922	1,195	(184)	166
Romania	780	880	571	387	658	926	(105)	162
Yugoslavia	—	469(a)	542	405	681	741	—	137
Bulgaria	—	545	503	470	794	905	166	180
Albania	—	—	(175)	199	248	370	—	(211)
Greece	210	—	200	219	387	433	—	217
Italy	224	274	285	250	317	300	109	105
Spain	350	400	410(b)	293	389	432	108	105
Portugal	173	—	214	201	227	172	—	80
Ireland	526	633	522(S)	620(S)	804(S)	590(S)	—	113
Denmark	1,005	852	604	1,065	1,396	1,380	162	228
France	655	514	465	417	714	753	146	162
West Germany } East Germany }	479 }	595 }	556	322 / 497	379 / 565	395 / 661 }	76 }	81
Japan	275	270	246	224	183	155	57	63
North Korea } South Korea }			230	258 / 233	393 / 260	472 / 271	— }	146
China(c)			273(x)	230	288	292	—	107
India			160	156	208	205	—	128
Pakistan } Bangladesh }			183 }	231	194 / 253	190 / 243	— }	119
North Vietnam } South Vietnam }			313	124 / 201	230 / 308 }	253	— }	81
Kampuchea			220	369	445	211	—	96
Laos			280	303	304	246	—	88
Indonesia			92	152	187	188	—	204
Philippines			130	176	208	216	—	166
Taiwan			200	313	290	c. 240	—	120
Thailand			214	350	437	388	—	181
Turkey			409	442	526	580	—	142
Iran			219	176	232	250	—	114
Iraq			340	272	220	147	—	43

(a) Serbia; (b) 1931–5; (c) present territory; (x) 1931–7 (Shen, 1951, 378–82); * from ECE, 1951.

Sources: ASF, 1937; Mulhall, 1896; Mitchell, 1975; ECE, 1951; ECE, 1960; ECAFE, 1959a; Shen, 1951; IEC, 1939; Taiwan, 1978; FAO, 1965; Ogura, 1968; Svennilson, 1954; UN Statistical Yearbook, 1954; Clarke, 1972; Bharier, 1971; FAO Yearbooks, various issues.

Notes: I have assumed that China's population was 500m. in the mid-1930s: Perkins, 1969, 16; and I have increased Japan's pre-1918 output data by 7 per cent to allow for alleged under-reporting: see Hayami and Yamada, 1970, 108.

FAO's 'Food Composition Tables' (Nutritional Studies No. 3, 1949) indicate that wheat, rice, rye, barley, oats, maize, buckwheat, sorghum and millet are of roughly equal nutritional value per gram and that, nutritionally, 1 g of grain is equivalent to about 4 g of potato. It is misguided to identify rice and breadgrains with human consumption and coarse grains with animal consumption. They have long been used interchangeably.

Table 12 Annual grain yields (tons per hectare)

	1892–5	1901–4	1909–13	1934–8	1948–52	1952–6	1961–5	1969–71	1976–8	1976–8 as % of: 1909–13	1976–8 as % of: 1934–8
USSR	0.7(x)	0.8(x)	0.8(x)	0.7	0.8	0.9	1.0	1.5	1.7	213	243
Ukraine	—	—	0.9(x)	1.1	1.1	1.3	1.8	2.4	2.9	322	264
Eastern Europe	—	—	1.3(c)	1.4(c)	1.3	1.4	1.9	2.4	3.2	246	267
Southern Europe	0.7	—	1.0	1.2	1.2	1.4	1.6	2.0	2.4	240	200
Other Europe	1.2	—	1.6	1.8	2.1	2.4	3.0	3.5	3.9	244	217
Poland	—	—	1.1	1.1	1.3	1.3	1.7	2.1	2.5	227	227
Austria	1.2	1.1	1.3	1.6	1.6	2.0	2.5	3.5	4.2	323	263
Czechoslovakia	—	1.2	1.4	1.7	1.7	1.9	2.2	3.0	3.8	271	224
Hungary	1.3	1.2	1.3	1.5	1.5	1.6	2.1	2.9	4.1	315	273
Romania	1.0	1.0	1.2	0.9	0.8	1.1	1.6	2.0	3.0	250	333
Yugoslavia	1.0	1.0	1.2	1.4	1.2	1.1	1.9	2.6	3.4	283	243
Bulgaria	1.0	1.1	1.1	1.2	1.2	1.4	2.0	3.0	3.5	318	292
Albania	—	—	—	1.3	1.0	1.1	1.0	1.7	2.0	—	154
Greece	0.8	—	0.9	0.9	1.0	1.2	1.5	2.0	2.5	278	278
Italy	0.7	1.1	1.2	1.6	1.6	1.9	2.2	2.8	3.2	267	200
Spain	0.6	1.0	1.0	1.1(a)	1.0	1.1	1.2	1.6	2.0	200	145(a)
Portugal	0.7	—	0.8	0.8	0.7	0.8	0.8	1.0	1.0	(125)	125
Denmark	1.6	1.8	1.9	2.6	3.1	3.3	3.7	3.9	3.8	190	146
Ireland	1.9	2.1	2.3	2.4(S)	2.3(S)	2.7(S)	3.1(S)	3.9(S)	4.3(S)	—	179
France	1.1	1.2	1.3	1.5	1.7	2.1	2.7	3.6	4.0	308	267
Germany	1.0	1.7	1.9	2.3(W)	2.3(W)	2.6(W)	3.0(W)	3.7(W)	4.1(W)	205	178(W)
				2.1(E)	2.1(E)	2.3(E)	2.6(E)	3.0(E)	3.5(E)	—	167(E)
Japan	2.3(b)	—	2.7(b)	3.0(a)	3.3	3.5	4.2	5.0	5.8	207	193(a)

(a) 1931–5; (b) official data + 7% for alleged under-reporting; (c) present boundaries; (x) official tsarist data (Wheatcroft, 1974, rejects Soviet revisions).

(continued)

Table 12—*continued*

	1931–7	1934–8	1948–52	1952–6	1961–5	1969–71	1976–8	1976–8 as % of:	
								1930s	1952–6
North Korea }	1.6	—	1.3	1.4	2.2	3.1	3.7 }	275	264
South Korea }		—	2.3	2.3	2.7	3.5	4.9 }		213
China(c)	1.5	—	1.1	1.4	1.5	1.9	2.1	140	150
India	—	0.7	0.7	0.8	0.9	1.1	1.3	186	163
Pakistan }	—	0.9	1.1	1.1	0.9	1.2	1.4 }	189	155
Bangladesh }					1.7	1.7	1.9 }		
North Vietnam }	1.2	1.9(G)	1.2	1.6	1.9	1.9 }	2.0 }	(167)	133
South Vietnam }		1.3(G)	1.4	1.3	2.0	2.2 }			
Kampuchea	0.9	1.1(G)	0.9	1.0	1.1	1.4	1.2	(133)	120
Laos	0.7	—	0.7	0.9	0.8	1.3	1.2	171	133
Thailand	—	0.9	1.3	1.4	1.6	2.0	1.9	211	136
Indonesia	—	1.1	1.4	1.5	1.5	2.0	2.5	227	167
Philippines	—	0.7	1.0	1.0	1.0	1.3	1.4	200	140
Taiwan	1.9	2.1	2.3	2.7	3.6	3.7	4.5	229	167
Turkey	0.9	—	1.1	1.1	1.1	1.4	1.8	200	164
Iran	—	1.2	1.0	1.0	0.9	0.8	1.2	100	120
Iraq	—	0.6	0.7	0.8	0.8	1.0	1.0	167	125

(G) Gourou, 1945T, 369, 371, 389.

Sources: As Table 11.

252

(continued)

Table 12—continued

Regional variations

European Russia	1911–15	USSR	1940	1976–9	China	1931–7	India	1958–61
Podzol Zone:	0.8	RSFSR	0.8	1.5	*Rice Belt:*	1.8	Overall	0.6
Central	0.8	Ukraine	1.2	2.7	Double-crop area (south)	2.3	Kerala	1.1
North-western	0.8	Belorussia	0.8	2.3	Eastern	2.2	Tamil Nadu	1.0
Western	0.8	Latvia	1.2	2.0	West-central	1.6	Mysore	0.5
North-eastern	0.7	Estonia	1.2	2.6	*Wheat Belt:*		Andhra Pradesh	0.6
Black Earth Zone:	0.9	Lithuania	0.9	2.5	Manchuria	1.2	Western states	0.6
Central	0.9	Moldavia	1.1	3.3	East-central	1.3	Madhya Pradesh	0.6
Malorussian	0.9	Georgia	0.7	2.0	North-west	1.0	Uttar Pradesh	0.7
South-western	1.2	Armenia	0.7	1.9			Rajasthan	0.4
Steppes:	0.7	Kazakhstan	0.4	1.1			Punjab	0.7
Mid-Volgan	0.7	Uzbekistan	0.4	1.9			West Bengal	0.8
Eastern	0.6	Turkmenia	0.6	2.0			Bihar	0.6
Southern	0.7	Kirghizia	0.8	2.4			Orissa	0.6
Asiatic Russia	0.6	Tadjikistan	0.6	1.3			Assam	0.8
		Azerbaijan	0.7	2.0				

Sources: Pavlovsky, 1930, 283–5; Timoshenko, 1932, 524–6; USSR, 1980, 247; Shen, 1951, 374–82; Buck, 1937, 55; Jain, 1967, 54.

Table 13 Livestock per 100 inhabitants

	Cattle	Sheep and goats	Pigs	Horses	Asses and mules	Poultry
Russia and USSR (including Latvia, Estonia and Lithuania)						
1850	35	62(x)	15	22	—	—
1887	28	55(x)	22	20	—	—
1916	43	84	15	23	—	—
1927	46	91	16	21	—	—
1938	38	61	19	11	—	—
1938*	31	42	17	11	—	—
1951*	31	54	13	8	0.5	206
1961*	35	65	27	5	0.4	241
1978*	43	56	27	2.2	0.2	364
Europe (excluding USSR, Latvia, Estonia and Lithuania)						
1850	34	78(x)	16	11	—	—
1887	30	58(x)	15	11	—	—
1913	29	45	21	6	—	—
1927	28	40	20	6	—	—
1939	27	37	21	6	—	—
1950	26	35	20	4	—	—
1960	27	35		6	—	—
1978	28	29	35	1	0.1	251
Eastern Europe (excluding USSR, Albania, Latvia, Estonia and Lithuania)						
1913	32	48	21	10	N	—
1927	29	43	20	10	N	—
1939	28	41	21	10	N	—
1950	27	36	28	7	N	185
1960*	27	37	39	5.6	N	232
1978*	30	34	48	2.8	N	342
Southern Europe						
1913	16	74	10	3	5.4	—
1927	17	69	13	3	5.9	—
1939	16	64	14	2	4.9	—

(continued)

Table 13—continued

	Cattle	Sheep and goats	Pigs	Horses	Asses and mules	Poultry
Southern Europe—*cont.*						
1950	15	65	13	2	4.5	117
1960	15	53	12	1.3	4.1	156
1978	24	40	20	0.6	1.2	200
Japan						
1937*	3	0.2	1	2	—	—
1952–6	3.3	1.5	1.1	1.1	—	45
1978	3.5	0.0	8	0.0	0.0	261
Korea (North/South)						
1952–6	5/3	0.7/0.1	6/3	0.3/0.0	N	—
1961	6/4	2.0/0.9	13/5	0.2/0.1	N	—
1978	5/4	3/0.6	11/4	0.2/0.0	N	104/83
China						
1952–6	13	13	16	1.2	2.4	62
1960	13	18	29	1.2	2.0	66
1978	10	16	30	0.7	1.4	143
India						
1952–6	53	25	1.2	0.4	0.3	25
1978	37	17	1.4	0.1	0.2	22
Vietnam						
1952–6	4.9	N	14	0.1	—	—
1978	3.3	0.4	18	0.1	—	196
Kampuchea						
1952–6	24	0.0	9	0.1	—	88
Taiwan						
1952–6	4.6	2	31	0.0	0.6	124
1977	11	9	22	—	—	253
Albania						
1952–6	32	191	5.0	3.7	5.0	73
1978	17	68	4.4	1.6	2.7	87
Mongolia						
1960*	200	1863	0.4	263	—	11
1978*	158	1198	1.8	132	—	19
Cuba						
1952–6	70	5.9	22	6.9	0.6	119
1978	59	4.6	19	8	0.3	300

Mid-summer enumerations (seasonal high point), unless marked *, to indicate winter (seasonal low point).   N = negligible.   (x) = excluding goats.

Sources: Mulhall, 1898, 111; ECE, 1951, 33; FAO, CMEA and UN Yearbooks, various issues.

Table 14 Livestock products

(a) *Average annual milk yields per milch cow*

	Litres (000s)		Tons		1976–8 as % of 1952–6
	1900–13	1934–8	1952–6	1976–8	
USSR	1.0	(1.1)	1.48	2.19	148
Poland	1.5	1.4	1.80	2.85	159
Czechoslovakia		1.9	1.61	2.99	185
Hungary	1.0	1.8	1.65	2.86	173
Romania		1.6	1.03	1.92	187
Yugoslavia		1.2	1.04	1.44	139
Bulgaria			0.62	2.23	358
Greece		0.7	0.78	1.41	180
Italy	1.5	1.6	2.59	2.71	104
Spain		1.2	1.71	2.89	169
Portugal		0.7	2.10	2.25	107
Eire	1.9	1.8	2.10	3.37	160
Denmark	2.6	3.2	3.47	4.70	135
France	1.6	1.9	2.03	2.89	142
GFR }	1.8 }	2.5	2.89	4.21	145
GDR			2.27	3.77	166
Albania			0.39	1.49	380
Japan			2.92	5.82	199
North Korea				2.00	
South Korea			2.53	2.32	92
China				0.62	
India			0.18	0.49	267
Pakistan				0.80	
Vietnam				0.80	
Kampuchea				0.17	
Philippines				1.01	
Turkey			0.51	0.59	116
Iran			0.52	0.78	149
Mongolia				0.29	
Cuba			0.59	1.07	182

Sources: ECE, 1951, 35; ECE, 1954, 9; Clarke, 1972, 137; Jasny, 1949, 190; Taiwan, 1978; FAO Production Yearbooks, various issues.

(continued)

Table 14—continued

(b) Domestic availability per inhabitant (kg)

	Meat*	Fish	Milk†
USSR			
1913	29	7	154
1928	32(C)	4	178(C)
1932	17(C)	6	113(C)
1937	18(C)	7	141(C)
1950	26	7	145(C)
1964–6	41	12.6	250
1976–9	57	17.4	319
Poland			
1934–8	26	4	120
1960	50	4.5	363
1970	61	6.3	417
1976–8	78	7.5	439
Czechoslovakia			
1934–8	33	5	150
1960	57	4.7	173
1976–8	82	5.6	218
Hungary			
1934–8	36(x)	1	152
1960	48(x)	1.5	114
1976–8	69(x)	2.6	145
Romania			
1934–8	18	2	125
1965	27		121
1975	46		160
Bulgaria			
1934–8	22	1	120
1960	33	2.0	126
1976–8	64	6.3	210

Sources: Soviet and East European Yearbooks, various issues.

Notes: (C) = Chapman, 1963, 238.   * Including offal.
(x) Excluding offal.   † Including milk products (milk equivalent).

(continued)

Table 14—continued

(b) Domestic availability per inhabitant (kg)

| | 1934–8 | | | 1962–4 | 1954–5 | |
	Meat*	Fish	Milk†	Meat*	Fish	Milk†
Yugoslavia	23	0.3	120	27	1	106
Greece	20	10	75	30	6	86
Italy	20	8	88	33	5	106
Spain	28	25	70	26		
Portugal	23	30	70	19	18	26
Eire	55	6	229	66	4	193
Denmark	75	18	249	65	15	206
France	52	11	154	77	6	167
Germany	51	12	160	65(W)	7(W)	170(W)
Japan	4	35	9	9	19	10
India	3	1	65	1	1	46
Indo-China	14	6	13	—	—	—
Indonesia	5	9	4	—	—	—
Philippines	17	17	36	14	12	—
Turkey	22	5	155	14	2	32
Iran	12	4	93+	17	—	—
Iraq	9	1	83+	20	—	—

Sources: FAO, 1952; FAO, 1946; UN Yearbooks, various issues.

Notes: W = West.   * Including offal.   † Including milk products (milk equivalent).

258

Table 15 Structure of large-scale manufacturing output

% of net manufacturing output (value added)	Consumer goods industries				Producer goods		Based on:
	Food, drinks, tobacco	Textiles, clothing, leather-ware	Paper, printing, wood-work	Pottery, glass, miscellaneous	Metals, engineering, vehicles	Chemicals, electricity, etc.	
Russia							
1887	28	39	4.5	7	19	2.5	Goldsmith, 1961
1913	30	31	9	(x)	19	11	Falkus, 1968
USSR							
1928	23	37	8	(x)	19	13	Gregory, 1970, 28
1937	12	17	7	(x)	45	18	ibid.
1955	9	16	10	(x)	52	13	ibid.
1962	10	15	7	(x)	52	16	ibid.
Poland							
1913	41	11	(m)	14	26	8(c)	Berend and Ranki,
1938	29	21	(m)	12	29	9(c)	1974T, 301
1950	38	13(t)	5	14	22	8	Mayergoyz, 1978,
1975	18	8(t)	5	14	40	13	13
Czech lands							
1885	69	24(t)	(x)	2	5	(x)	Rudolph, 1976, 42
Czechoslovakia							
1950	28	9(t)	9	17	32	5	Mayergoyz,
1975	16	6(t)	5	18	43	12	1978, 13
Hungary							
1913	42	8	3	9	29	9	Berend and Ranki,
1938	30	22	5	5	24	14	1974T, 143
1950	23	20(t)	3	11	32	11	Mayergoyz, 1978,
1975	16	5(t)	4	14	41	18	13
Romania							
1922	27	20	(m)	19	12	22	Berend and Ranki,
1938	23	26	(m)	13	17	21	1974T, 141, 301
1950	29	14(t)	11	18	21	7	Mayergoyz, 1978,
1975	14	7(t)	5	17	42	15	13
Serbia							
1913	59	9	(m)	9	20	3(c)	Berend and Ranki,
Yugoslavia							1974T, 301
1938	27	26	(m)	22	17	8(c)	
1950	20	21(t)	7	36	11	5(c)	Mayergoyz, 1978,
1975	9	12(t)	8	25	31	15	13

(continued)

Table 15—continued

% of net manufacturing output (value added)	Consumer goods industries				Producer goods		Based on:
	Food, drinks, tobacco	Textiles, clothing, leather-ware	Paper, printing, wood-work	Pottery, glass, miscel-laneous	Metals, engineer-ing, vehicles	Chemicals, electricity, etc.	
Bulgaria							
1913	58	24	(m)	8	6	4(c)	Berend and Ranki,
1938	43	22	(m)	27	6	2(c)	1974T, 301
1950	43	15(t)	10	17	10	5	Mayergoyz, 1978,
1975	24	8(t)	4	25	29	10	13
GDR							
1950	16	12(t)	6	18	32	16	Mayergoyz, 1978,
1975	17	7(t)	(x)	13	43	20	13
Germany							
1895	19	27	(m)	33	18	3(c)	Hoffman, 1958T,
1936	12	12	(m)	40	29	5(c)	tables 40–2
France							
1861–5	28	36	(m)	21	11	4(c)	ibid.
1896	13	31	(m)	36	15	5(c)	ibid.
Denmark							
1897	24	21	(m)	36	15	4(c)	ibid.
1925	30	16	(m)	25	20	6(c)	ibid.
1952	18	17	(m)	35	19	6(c)	ibid.
Britain							
1851	6	45	(m)	38	10	1(c)	ibid.
1901	14	27	(m)	30	23	2(c)	ibid.
Italy							
1903	32	38(t)	(x)	(x)	22	10(c)	Gerschenkron,
1938	22	21	(m)	15	33	5(c)	1962, 418;
1951	20	22	(m)	17	30	7(c)	Hoffman, 1958T, tables 40–2
Japan							
1900	8	51	(m)	26	10	3(c)	ibid.
1925	20	38(t)	(m)	17	18	7(c)	ibid.
1955	18	18(t)	9	4	32	19	Allen, 1972, 219
North Korea							
1930–1	21	5	3	36	4	31	Suh, 1978, 142
1939–40	11	2	2	13	10	62	
1960(G)	18	19	14	6	30	13	Chung, 1974, 79

(continued)

Table 15—continued

% of net manufacturing output (value added)	Consumer goods industries				Producer goods		Based on:
	Food, drinks, tobacco	Textiles, clothing, leatherware	Paper, printing, woodwork	Pottery, glass, miscellaneous	Metals, engineering, vehicles	Chemicals, electricity, etc.	
South Korea							
1930–1	28	10(t)	11	29	9	13	Suh, 1978, 142
1939–40	27	14(t)	6	24	12	17	
1960	40	28	(m)	17	9	6	Hasan, 1976, 68
1972	27	26	(m)	18	10	19	
Taiwan							
1954	33	25	11	(x)	8	22	Fei et al., 1979, 70
1961	30	15	14	(x)	15	25	ibid.
China							
1933	28	50	(m)	8	10	4	Liu and Yeh, 1965
1957	11	22	(m)	12	49	6	
1975(G)	12	12	3	13	37	20	Xue, 1982T, 972
India							
1951	15	55	2	(x)	18	10	Swamy, 1973, 36
1960	17	33	3	(x)	28	19	ibid.
Pakistan							
1954	15	51	4	15	7	8(c)	Myrdal, 1968, 517
Cuba							
1954	55	9	5	(x)	4	27	Newman, 1965, 35
1978(G)	44	8	6	10	13	19	Comecon, 1979, 81–5

(G) Gross output. (t) Textiles only. (m) Included with miscellaneous. (c) Chemicals only. (x) Excluded from the reckoning, for lack of data.

Note: Note that, at high levels of industrial development, the distinction between (light) consumer goods industries and (heavy) producer goods industries becomes increasingly blurred by the growing importance of 'consumer durables' such as cars and electric appliances.

Table 16 Per capita output of some basic industrial products

	Cloth (m²)	Crude oil (kg)	Steel (kg)	Coal (kg)	Electricity (kWh)	Cement (kg)
USSR						
1913	12	65	27	181	13	11
1928	19	77	29	237	33	12
1940	15	159	94	836	249	30
1971	29	1,539	492	2,615	3,266	409
1979	29	2,223	566	2,496	4,700	612
Czechoslovakia						
1913		N	88	2,678	69	
1937		1	153	2,300	273	84
1979	42	7	972	8,185	4,465	673
GDR						
1951	7(c)	N	95	8,395*	1,166	88
1971	33	N	314	15,188*	4,071	497
1979	35	N	419	15,290*	5,784	733
Hungary						
1913		N	38	480*		
1939	18	16	80	1,143*	134	37
1979	37	189	365	2,397*	2,290	454
Poland						
1938		14	41	1,089	114	49
1951	21	7	111	3,479	420	108
1979	32	9	546	6,789	3,335	545
Bulgaria						
1913		N	N	92	N	
1939		N	N	351	42	31
1979	44	28	281	3,195	3,680	612
Romania						
1938	6	420	18	141	72	33
1951	12	397	39	283	150	70
1979	37	559	586	1,486	2,944	665
Yugoslavia						
1939	8	N	15	389	71	43
1950	9	7	26	794	157	72
1979	23	187	160	1,900	2,480	410
Albania						
1938		108	N	4	9	9
1977		900		345	800	280

(continued)

Table 16—continued

	Cloth (m²)	Crude oil (kg)	Steel (kg)	Coal (kg)	Electricity (kWh)	Cement (kg)
Italy						
1913		N	25	19	55	
1939		0.3	52	71	417	114
1971	21	24	321	29	2,301	581
1979	25	30	424	33	3,173	679
Japan						
1913	(20)	N	5	402	11	
1937	60	5	62	643	441	87
1971	26	7	610	321	3,622	568
1979	23	4	963	148	5,057	761
North Korea						
1948		N	13	229	700	32
1970	30(a)	N	158	1,975	1,184	287
1976	28(a)	N	190	2,463	3,086	424
South Korea						
1948	2(c)	N	0.4	40	25	1
1970	10(a)	N	40	387	286	196
1976	27(a)	N	75	456	679	394
Taiwan						
1957	16(c)	N	9	307	269	64
1977	50(c)	N	90	178	1,785	620
China						
1957	8(c)	3	8	207	30	11
1978	11(c)	108	23	644	267	42
India						
1957	12(c)	1	4	108	33	14
1977	11(c)	16	15	156	152	30
Vietnam						
1938		N	N	123	5	14
1978	6	0.004	2	135	74	16
Mongolia						
1960	0.3	30	N	N	111	
1978	0.9	N	N	202	746	105
Cuba						
1958	15	7	N	N	215	106
1978	16	N	34	N	873	280

Sources: Mitchell, 1975; Allen, 1972; Marmullaku, 1975; Brederstein, 1975; Kim, 1979T; UN, CMEA and Soviet Yearbooks, various issues.

Notes: 'Cloth' here refers to cotton and woollen cloth, unless marked (a) for all cloth or (c) for cotton cloth only.   N = negligible.   * Mostly low grade.

Table 17 Average annual rates of economic growth (%)

	1860–1910	1913–38	1938–53	1950s	1960s	1970–8	Per capita 1860–1910	1913–38	1938–53	1960–78
USSR	2.5(a)	2.3–2.8	3.4	9.6	5.2	5.3	1.0(a)	1.4–1.9	3.3	4.3
Poland	—	—	—	8.0	4.3	7.0	—	—	—	5.9
Czechoslovakia	—	2.5	1.6(x)	7.1	3.1	4.9	—	0.2	3.0(x)	4.3
Hungary	2.4(c)	1.5	1.9(x)	5.0	3.8	5.4	1.7(c)	0.8	1.8(x)	5.0
Romania	(1.9)	—	—	7.6	9.0	10.6	(0.9)	—	—	8.6
Yugoslavia	1.6(d)	1.7	0.8(x)	7.2	5.8	5.6	0.5(d)	0.7	0.2(x)	5.4
Bulgaria	(1.4)	(3.4)	1.3(x)	9.0	5.9	6.3	(0.5)	(1.9)	0.0(x)	5.7
Greece	(2.6)	(3.3)	—	5.9	6.9	5.0	(0.7)	(2.5)	—	6.0
Italy	1.1	1.6	1.7	5.9	5.3	2.8	0.4	1.0	1.0	3.6
Spain	(0.6)	0.5	1.5(x)	5.2	7.3	4.4	0.1	−0.4	0.7(x)	5.0
Portugal	(0.9)	(1.5)	1.7(x)	4.1	6.2	4.8	0.1	0.7	0.7(x)	5.9
Eire	—	0.0	1.2(x)	1.3	4.2	3.4	—	0.2	1.2(x)	3.3
Denmark	2.9	1.8	2.2	3.2	4.7	2.7	1.9	0.9	1.2	3.2
France	1.4	0.9–1.2	2.0	4.5	5.7	3.7	1.3	0.8–1.2	1.9	4.0
GFR }	2.6 }	1.6–2.1	2.1	7.4	4.4	2.4 }	1.4	1.1–1.6	0.7	3.3
GDR }		—	—	7.4	3.1	4.7		2.6(e)	—	4.8
Japan	2.7(b)	4.0(e)	−0.2	8.6(e)	10.5	5.0	1.7(b)	2.6(e)	−1.5	7.6

(continued)

264

Table 17—continued

	1960s	1970–8	Per capita 1960–78
Albania	(7.3)	(6.7)	(4.1)
North Korea	(7.8)	(7.2)	(4.5)
South Korea	8.5	9.7	6.9
India	3.6	3.7	1.4
Pakistan	6.7	4.4	2.8
Bangladesh	3.6	2.9	−0.4
Thailand	8.2	7.6	4.6
Indonesia	3.5	7.8	4.1
Philippines	5.1	6.3	2.6
Taiwan	9.2	8.0	6.6
Turkey	6.0	7.1	4.0
Iran	11.3	7.4	7.9
Iraq	6.2	(9.5)	4.1
Mongolia	2.8	4.5	1.5
Cuba	1.1	0.4	−1.2

(a) 1860–1913: from Goldsmith, 1961. (b) 1879–1913: from Maddison, 1969. (c) 1867–1913: from Katus, 1970. (d) Serbia only. (e) Maddison, 1969. (x) 1938–50: from Bairoch, 1976.

Sources: For 1860–1953, Bairoch, 1976, and Maddison, 1969; for the 1950s, Shanks, 1973; and for 1960–78, World Bank, 1980.

Table 18 The peoples and union republics of the USSR (Census data)

| | Population | | | | | As a percentage of population, by republic: | | | |
| | Millions | | % of total | | | Titular nationality | | Russians | |
	1926	1979	1926	1979		1926	1970	1926	1970
Eastern Slavs:	114	189	77.3	77.2					
Russians(O)	78	137	52.9	52.4	Russian SFSR	78	83	78	83
Ukrainians(O)	31	42	21.2	16.1	Ukrainian SSR	81	75	9	19
Belorussians(U)	5	10	3.2	3.6	Belorussian SSR	81	81	8	10
Turkic peoples:	17	41	11.7	15.5					
Uzbeks(M)	3.9	12.5	2.7	4.8	Uzbek SSR	74	65	6	13
Turkmen(M)	0.8	2.0	0.5	0.8	Turkmen SSR	72	66	8	14
Kirghiz(M)	0.8	1.9	0.5	0.7	Kirghiz SSR	67	44	12	29
Kazakhs(M)	4.0	6.6	2.7	2.5	Kazakh SSR	57	32	20	43
Azerbaijani(Sh)	1.7	5.5	1.2	2.1	Azerbaijan SSR	62	74	10	10
Volga Tatars(M)	3.3	6.3	2.2	2.4	Tatar ASSR ⎫	45	49	43	42
Chuvash(O)	1.1	1.8	0.7	0.7	Chuvash ASSR ⎬ in RSFSR	75	70	20	25
Bashkirs(M)	0.7	1.4	0.5	0.5	Bashkir ASSR ⎭	23	23	40	40
Others	0.9	2.5	0.6	1.0					
Iranians:	1.4	3.8	1.0	1.5					
Tajiks(Sh)	1.0	2.9	0.7	1.1	Tajik SSR	75	56	7	12
Caucasians(M)	0.4	0.9	0.3	0.3					

(continued)

Table 18—continued

| | Population | | | | | As a percentage of population, by republic: | | | |
| | Millions | | % of total | | | Titular nationality | | Russians | |
	1926	1979	1926	1979		1926	1970	1926	1970
Dagestani(M)	0.6	1.7	0.4	0.6	Dagestan ASSR	65	70	12	15
Armenians(A)	1.6	4.2	1.1	1.6	Armenian SSR	84	89	2	3
Georgians(O)	1.8	3.6	1.2	1.4	Georgian SSR	67	67	4	8
Finnic peoples:									
Finns(L)	3.2	4.3	2.2	1.6					
Estonians(L)	0.1	0.3	0.1	0.1	Estonian SSR	x	68	x	25
Others(O)	0.2	1.0	0.1	0.4					
	2.9	3.0	2.0	1.1					
Baltic peoples:	0.2	4.3	0.2	1.6					
Lithuanians(RC)	0.0	2.9	0.0	1.1	Lithuanian SSR	x	80	x	9
Latvians(L)	0.2	1.4	0.2	0.5	Latvian SSR	x	57	x	30
Romanians(O)	0.3	3.0	0.2	1.1	Moldavian SSR	x	65	x	12
Germans(L)	1.2	1.9	0.8	0.7					
Jews(J)	2.7	1.8	1.8	0.7					
Poles(RC)	0.8	1.2	0.5	0.5					
Others	2.3	2.6	1.6	1.0					

Notes: National religious denominations: (O) Greek Orthodox Christians; (M) Sunni Muslims; (Sh) Shia Muslims; (L) Lutherans; (U) Uniat Christians; (RC) Roman Catholics; (A) Armenian Catholics; (J) Jews. (x) Not yet annexed by USSR.

(continued)

267

Table 18—continued

Inter-republican economic disparities (as % of USSR average):

	Average monthly wages and salaries, 1975				Collective farm incomes		GMP, 1970		Official retail prices, 1968
	All	Industrial	Agricultural	Administrative	Per man-day 1974	Per family 1970	Per man-year	Per head	
RSFSR	105	103	106	105	102	102	107	112	107
Ukraine	92	94	91	87	92	80	94	97	100
Belorussia	86	86	76	90	104	84	88	92	
Estonia	110	115	141	111	160	122	125	133	(103)
Latvia	100	95	102	100	128	115	116	132	(103)
Lithuania	97	96	92	100	124	122	106	112	(103)
Armenia	96	96	80	93	103	117	85	78	(92)
Georgia	81	85	62	86	116	105	75	73	(92)
Moldavia	80	80	78	90	92	85	78	81	(92)
Kazakhstan	102				149	148	94	82	(103)
Uzbekistan	90	90	95	93	105	188	83	61	96
Turkmenia	111	(111)	(140)	(102)	154	153	97	74	96
Kirghizia	93	95	88	93	122	93	87	67	96
Tajikistan	93	91	87	93	104	95	72	56	96
Azerbaijan	86	86	78	99	90	92	84	61	(90)

Sources: Faradzhev, 1975; NATO, 1979; Wiles, 1974; Soviet Statistical Yearbooks, various issues.

268

Table 19 Energy used per dollar of
GDP (kg, coal equivalent), 1978

Western average	1.1
Third World average	1.0
Comecon average	1.8
China	4.2
North Korea	4.4
Yugoslavia	1.2
Hungary	1.2
Albania	1.7
Bulgaria	1.9
Romania	2.7
USSR	1.8
Czechoslovakia	1.9
GDR	1.5
Poland	1.8
Cuba	1.8

Source: World Bank, 1980.

Table 20 Energy consumption per inhabitant (kg, coal equivalent)

	1960	1978
GDR	4950	7121
Czechoslovakia	4741	7531
Hungary	2072	3451
USSR	2839	5500
Poland	3107	5595
Bulgaria	1303	5020
Romania	1342	4042
Yugoslavia	872	2035
Albania	302	998
GFR	3695	6015
France	2474	4368
Japan	1171	3825
Italy	1086	3230
Spain	756	2405
Greece	460	1925
Portugal	382	1030
North Korea	989	2702
South Korea	258	1359
Taiwan	583	2202
Turkey	245	793
China	637	805
India	108	176
Pakistan	61	172
Mongolia	540	1240

Source: World Bank, 1980.

Table 21 External debt, end of 1979

	Billion US $	$ per inhabitant
USSR	10.2	39
Poland	19.5*	557*
Hungary	7.5*	700*
Yugoslavia	17	780
Romania	7*	320*
Bulgaria	4*	455*
Czechoslovakia	3.5*	233*

* Excluding debts to USSR, Comecon's 'underwriter'.

270

Table 22 Composition of merchandise exports (%)

	Manufactures		Machinery	
	1960	1977	1960	1977
From CMEA to OECD	29*	37*	6*	11*
From OECD to CMEA	73*	81*	28*	35*
USSR	35*	40*	21	19
Poland	43*	64*	28	43
Czechoslovakia	71*	76*	46	51
Hungary	60*	61*	39	34
Romania	27*	55*	17	27
Yugoslavia	44	69	15	32
Bulgaria	34*	61*	13	45
Albania	6	41	—	4
Greece	9	50	1	5
Italy	73	83	29	34
Spain	12	71	2	26
Portugal	55	70	3	15
Eire	28	55	4	15
Denmark	35	56	19	27
France	73	77	25	38
GFR	87	89	44	48
GDR	78*	82*	49*	53*
Japan	89	97	23	56
North Korea	—	18	—	1
South Korea	14	85	0	17
China	40(E)	49	1.5(E)	3
India	44	51	1	6
Pakistan	27	58	1	2
Bangladesh	—	56	—	1
Vietnam	0	56	—	0
Kampuchea	0	20	0	0
Laos	—	15	—	0
Thailand	2	19	0	2
Indonesia	0	2	0	1
Philippines	7	25	0	2
Taiwan	14	49	—	3

(continued)

271

Table 22—continued

	Manufactures		Machinery	
	1960	*1977*	*1960*	*1977*
Turkey	25	25	0	1
Iran	3	1	0	0
Iraq	0	0	0	0
Afghanistan	18	13	3	0
Mongolia	5	12*	0*	0*
Cuba	2*	13	0*	0*

* Osmova and Faminsky, 1980, 121, 174.

Notes: (E) Eckstein, 1977, 252, referring to 1959; he also gives much lower figures for manufactures in 1955 (21%) and 1966 (30%); remaining data from World Bank, 1978, 1980. 'Machinery' includes vehicles and equipment throughout.

Table 23 Impact of major diseases on Imperial Russia and the USSR, 1900–50 (cases p.a.)

	1900–5	1906–9	1910–13	1914–18	1919–22	1923–8	1929–33	1934–9	1941–5	1946–50
Malaria	3.4m.	3.4m.	3.5m.	2.3m.	3.0m.	4.7m.	4.0m.	6.7m.	3.2m.	2.2m.
Typhus	61,000	120,000	110,000	90,000	1.9m.	97,000	240,000	150,000	370,000	60,000
Typhoid	295,000	445,000	430,000	210,000	350,000	140,000	280,000	140,000	110,000	80,000
Relapsing fever	15,000	85,000	41,500	17,000	1.0m.	54,000	7,600	(4,000)	4,400	3,000
Whooping cough	360,000	446,000	470,000	(0.4m.)	(0.4m.)	343,000	450,000	400,000	270,000	230,000
Diphtheria	200,000	355,000	544,000	(0.4m.)	(0.2m.)	68,000	160,000	115,000	130,000	70,000
Scarlet fever	290,000	370,000	430,000	(0.3m.)	(0.1m.)	250,000	300,000	400,000	120,000	410,000
Smallpox	97,000	120,000	110,000	100,000	120,000	23,000	30,000	(3,500)	0	25
Cholera	(4,000)	24,100	58,500	16,000	60,000	33	0	0	40	0
All the above	4.7m.	5.4m.	5.7m.	(3.8m.)	(7.1m.)	5.6m.	5.5m.	7.9m.	4.2m.	3.1m.

Note: Based on the Soviet estimates presented in Sigerist, 1937, 229–31, 357–58; in US Office of Strategic Services Research and Analysis Report No. 1688, 'Civilian Health in the USSR: part I', October 1944, 106; and in Baroyan, 1968, 17, 49, 53, 54, 56, 63, 77, 97, 104, 109, 143. Their provenance makes it unlikely that these estimates understate morbidity in the pre-Soviet period or that they overstate morbidity in the Soviet period; Baroyan, 1968, was drawn to my attention by Steven Wheatcroft, who is carrying out some of the most interesting research in this field.

References and further reading

List of abbreviations

ASF, *Annuaire Statistique française*, Paris, 1937, volume retrospectif.
CMEA, Comecon, Council of Mutual Economic Assistance (established, 1949).
Comintern, the Communist International, 1919–43.
ECAFE, Economic Commission for Asia and the Far East, United Nations.
ECE, Economic Commission for Europe, United Nations, Geneva.
FAO, Food and Agriculture Organization, United Nations, Rome.
FT Survey, *Financial Times* Survey.
GDP, Gross Domestic Product.
GMP, Gross Material Product.
IDS, Institute of Development Studies, University of Sussex.
IEC, Imperial Economic Committee.
Inprecor, *International Press Correspondence* (Comintern weekly).
SSR, Soviet Socialist Republic.
T, translation.
WAC, World Agricultural Census.

Owing to limitations of space, this bibliography has been confined largely to works cited in the text and statistical tables, and references have been kept as brief as possible; asterisks indicate works which I found especially useful and/or stimulating in writing this book.

Adams, A., and Adams, J. (1971), *Men versus Systems*, The Free Press, New York.
Adelman, I., and Robinson, S. (1978), *Income Distribution in Developing Countries: A Case Study of Korea*, Oxford University Press.
Ahluwalia, M. (1976), 'Inequality, poverty and development', *Journal of Development Economics*, Vol. 3, pp. 307–42.

Akiner, S. (1983), *Islamic Peoples of the USSR*, Kegan Paul International, Boston.

*Alampiev, P. (1959T), *Where Inequality Is No More*, Foreign Languages Publishing House, Moscow.

Allen, G. C. (1972), *A Short Economic History of Modern Japan*, Allen & Unwin, London.

*Allworth, E. (ed.) (1967), *Central Asia*, Columbia University Press, New York.

Aman, R., and Cooper, J. (eds) (1982), *Industrial Innovation in the Soviet Union*, Yale University Press, New Haven, Conn.

Aman, R., Cooper, J., and Davies, R. (eds) (1977), *The Technological Level of Soviet Industry*, Yale University Press, New Haven, Conn.

Anderson, C., and Bowman, M. (eds) (1966), *Education and Economic Development*, Cass, London.

Andors, S. (1977), *China's Industrial Revolution*, Martin Robertson, London.

*Antsiferov, A. (ed.) (1930), *Russian Agriculture*, Yale University Press, New Haven, Conn.

*Antsiferov, A., and Kayden, E. (1929), *The Cooperative Movement in Russia*, Yale University Press, New Haven, Conn.

Arabadjian, A. (ed.) (1980), *Iran*, Nauka, Moscow.

Ardagh, J. (1973), *The New France*, Penguin Books, Harmondsworth.

Aresvik, O. (1976), *The Agricultural Development of Iran*, Praeger, New York.

Arshinov, P. (1974T), *A History of the Makhnovist Movement, 1918–1921*, Black & Red, Detroit, Mich.

Atkinson, D. (1973), 'Statistics on the Russian land commune, 1905–1917', *Slavic Review*, Vol. 32, pp. 773–87.

Auty, P. (1974), *Tito: A Biography*, Penguin Books, Harmondsworth.

Aziz, S. (1978), *Rural Development: Learning from China*, Macmillan, London.

Bailes, K. (1978), *Technology and Society under Lenin and Stalin*, Princeton University Press, Princeton, NJ.

*Bairoch, P. (1973), 'Agriculture and the Industrial Revolution', in *Fontana Economic History of Europe*, Collins/Fontana, London, Vol. 3.

Bairoch, P. (1975), *The Economic Development of the Third World since 1900*, Methuen, London.

Bairoch, P. (1976), 'Europe's gross national product, 1800–1975', *Journal of European Economic History*, Vol. 5, pp. 273–340.

Bakunin, M. (1895–1913), *Oeuvres*, 6 vols, Paris.

Bakunin, M. (1961–81), *Archives Bakounine*, 7 vols, E. J. Brill, Leiden.

Bakunin, M. (1973T), *Bakunin on Anarchy*, ed. S. Dolgoff, Allen & Unwin, London.

Balawyder, A. (ed.) (1981), *Cooperative Movements in Eastern Europe*, Macmillan, London.

Balinsky, A. (1961), 'Non-housing objectives of Soviet housing policy', *Problems of Communism*, Vol. 10, no. 4, pp. 17–23.

Ban, S., Moon, P., and Perkins, D. H. (1980), *Studies in the Modernization of the Republic of Korea,* Harvard University Press, Cambridge, Mass.

Bandyopadhyaya, J. (1969), *The Social and Political Thought of Gandhi,* Allied Publishers, Bombay.

Barna, T. (ed.) (1979), *Agriculture towards the Year 2000,* Sussex European Research Centre, Brighton.

Barnds, W. (ed.) (1976), *The Two Koreas in East Asian Affairs,* New York University Press, New York.

Baron, S. (1963), *Plekhanov: Father of Russian Marxism,* Stanford University Press, Stanford, Calif.

*Baroyan, O. (1968), *Itogi poluvekovoi borbi s infektsiyami v SSSR,* Moscow.

Bauchet, P. (1970), *La planification française,* Editions du Seuil, Paris.

*Bawden, C. (1968), *The Modern History of Mongolia,* Weidenfeld & Nicolson, London.

Baykov, A. (1946), *Soviet Foreign Trade,* Princeton University Press, Princeton, NJ.

*Bazarov, V. (1923), 'Problems of planning the economy as a whole', in *Bulleteni Gosplana,* November–December 1923.

*Bazarov, V. (1926), 'On the methodology of perspective plan formulation', in *Planovoye khoziaistvo;* trans. in Spulber, N. (ed.), *Foundations of Soviet Strategy for Economic Growth: Selected Soviet Essays, 1924–30,* Indiana University Press, Bloomington, Ind., 1964, pp. 365–77.

*Bazarov, V. (1928), 'Principles of plan formulation', in *Planovoye khoziaistvo;* trans. in Spulber, N. (ed.), *Foundations of Soviet Strategy for Economic Growth: Selected Soviet Essays, 1924–30,* Indiana University Press, Bloomington, Ind., 1964, pp. 221–9.

Beckinsdale, M., and Beckinsdale, R. (1975), *Southern Europe,* University of London Press.

Bell, J. (1977), *Alexander Stambolisky and the Bulgarian Agrarian Union,* Princeton University Press, Princeton, NJ.

Belousov, R. (1972T), *USSR Heavy Industry,* Novosti Press Agency, Moscow.

Benet, I., and Gyenis, J. (eds) (1977T), *Economic Studies on Hungary's Agriculture,* Akademiai Kiado, Budapest.

Bennigsen, A., and Wimbush, S. (1979), *Muslim National Communism in the Soviet Union,* University of Chicago Press.

Bensidoun, S. (1975), *L'Agitation paysanne en Russie de 1881 à 1902,* Fondation Nationale des Sciences Politiques, Paris.

*Benson, L. (1974), 'Market socialism and class structure: manual workers and managerial power in the Yugoslav enterprise', in Parkin, F. (ed.), *Social Analysis of Class Structure,* Tavistock Publications, London.

*Berend, I., and Ranki, Gy. (1974), *Economic Development in East-Central Europe in the Nineteenth and Twentieth Centuries,* Columbia University Press, New York.

Berend, I., and Ranki, Gy. (1974T), *Hungary: A Century of Economic Development,* David & Charles, Newton Abbot.

Bergmann, T. (1975T), *Farm Policies in Socialist Countries*, D. C. Heath, Lexington, Mass.

Bergmann, T. (1977T), *The Development Models of India, the Soviet Union and China*, Van Gorcum, Assen.

Bergson, A. (ed.) (1953), *Soviet Economic Growth*, Row Peterson, New York.

Bergson, A. (1961), *The Real National Income of Soviet Russia since 1928*, Harvard University Press, Cambridge, Mass.

Bergson, A. (1968), *Planning and Productivity under Soviet Socialism*, Columbia University Press, New York.

Bergson, A. (1978), *Productivity and the Social System*, Harvard University Press, Cambridge, Mass.

Bergson, A., and Kuznets, S. (eds) (1963), *Economic Trends in the Soviet Union*, Harvard University Press, Cambridge, Mass.

Berlin, I. (1979), *Russian Thinkers*, Penguin Books, Harmondsworth.

Berliner, J. (1957), *Factory and Manager in the USSR*, Harvard University Press, Cambridge, Mass.

Bernstein, E. (1899), *Die Voraussetzungen des Sozialismus und die Aufgaben der Sozialdemokratie*; English trans., Schocken Books, New York, 1961.

Bettelheim, C. (1976, 1979), *Class Struggles in the USSR*, 2 vols, Harvester Press, Hassocks.

Bettelheim, C., and Burton, N. (1979), *China since Mao*, Monthly Review Press, New York.

Bettelheim, C., and Sweezy, P. (1971), *On the Transition to Socialism*, Monthly Review Press, New York.

Bharier, J. (1971), *Economic Development in Iran, 1900–1970*, Oxford University Press, London.

Bianco, L. (1971), *Origins of the Chinese Revolution*, Stanford University Press, Stanford, Calif.

Bianco, L. (1974–5), 'Peasants and revolution: the case of China', *Journal of Peasant Studies*, Vol. 2, pp. 313–35.

*Bicanic, R. (1973T), *Economic Policy in Socialist Yugoslavia*, Cambridge University Press.

Billington, J. (1958), *Mikhailovsky and Russian Populism*, Oxford University Press, London.

Bizzell, W. B. (1926), *The Green Rising*, New York.

Blazyca, G. (1980), 'Polish economic development in the 1970s', *European Economic Review*, Vol. 14, pp. 101–16.

Blum, J. (1971), *Lord and Peasant in Russia*, Princeton University Press, Princeton, NJ.

Blum, J. (1978), *The End of the Old Order in Rural Europe*, Princeton University Press, Princeton, NJ.

Blyn, G. (1966), *Agricultural Trends in India, 1891–1947*, Pennsylvania University Press, Philadelphia, Pa.

Borisov, O. (1977T), *The Soviet Union and the Manchurian Revolutionary Base, 1945–49*, Progress Publishers, Moscow.

Bozyk, P. (1975T), *The Economy of Modern Poland*, Interpress Publishers, Warsaw.

Brandt, C. (1958), *Stalin's Failure in China, 1924–27*, Harvard University Press, Cambridge, Mass.

Braun, R. (1967), 'The rise of a class of rural entrepreneurs', *Journal of World History*, Vol. 10, pp. 551–66.

*Brederstein, G. (1975), 'Economic comparison of North and South Korea', *Journal of Contemporary Asia*.

Breshkovskaya, K. (1931T), *Hidden Springs of the Russian Revolution*, Stanford University Press, Stanford, Calif.

Bronson, W., and Kreuger, C. (1971), 'The revolution in Soviet farm income', in Millar, J. R. (ed.), *The Soviet Rural Community*, University of Illinois Press, Urbana, Ill.

Brown, E. (1966), *Soviet Trade Unions and Labour Relations*, Harvard University Press, Cambridge, Mass.

*Brown, J. (1970), *Bulgaria under Communist Rule*, Praeger, New York.

Brun, E., and Hersch, J. (1976), *Socialist Korea*, Monthly Review Press, New York.

Brus, W. (1972), *The Market in a Socialist Economy*, Routledge & Kegan Paul, London.

Brzezinski, Z. (1967), *The Soviet Bloc*, Harvard University Press, Cambridge, Mass.

Buchan, D. (ed.) (1983), 'Hungary: trade and industry', *Financial Times*, 10 May 1983.

*Buck, J. L. (ed.) (1937), *Land Utilization in China*, Oxford University Press, London, for University of Nanking.

Buck, J. L. et al. (1966), *Food and Agriculture in Communist China*, Praeger, New York.

Bukharin, N. (1915), *Mirovoye khoziaistvo i imperializm*, Petrograd, 1918; English trans., Merlin Press, London, 1972.

Bukharin, N. (1920, 1979T), *Economics of the Transition Period*, Routledge & Kegan Paul, London.

Bukharin, N. (1922T), *The ABC of Communism*, London, chs 1–6, 12, 18, 19.

Bukharin, N. (1925), 'Theses on the peasant question', in *Rasshirennyi plenum ispolkoma Kommunisticheskogo Internatsionala – protokoly zasedanii, 21 marta–6 aprelia, 1925*, Moscow, pp. 528–45.

*Bukharin, N. (1927), *Put k sotsializmu i raboche-krestianskii soyuz*, Moscow; reprinted in Bukharin, N., *The Path to Socialism in Russia: Selected Works*, ed. S. Heitman, Omicron, New York, 1967.

Bukharin, N. (1927T), 'Ten years of victorious proletarian revolution', *Inprecor*, 10 November 1927.

*Bukharin, N. (1928), 'Zametki ekonomista', *Pravda*, 30 September 1928; reprinted in Bukharin, N., *The Path to Socialism in Russia: Selected Works*, ed. S. Heitman, Omicron, New York, 1967.

*Bukharin, N. (1967), *The Path to Socialism in Russia: Selected Works*, ed. S. Heitman, Omicron, New York.

*Bukharin, N. (1982T), *Selected Writings on the State and the Transition to Socialism*, ed. R. Day, M. E. Sharpe, New York.

Bunin, I. (1909, 1923T), *The Village*, Martin Secker, London.

Buttinger, J. (1967–9), *Vietnam*, 2 vols, Deutsch, London.

Buttinger, J. (1977), *Vietnam: The Unforgettable Tragedy*, Deutsch, London.

*Buxton, J. (1982), 'Italian small firms', *Financial Times*, 7 December 1982.

Byres, T. (1977), 'Agrarian transition and the agrarian question', *Journal of Peasant Studies*, Vol. 4, pp. 258–75.

Byres, T. (1979), 'Of neo-populist pipe-dreams', *Journal of Peasant Studies*, Vol. 4, pp. 210–44.

Byres, T., and Nolan, P. (1976), *Inequality: India and China Compared*, Open University Press, Milton Keynes.

Campbell, R. W. (1968), *The Economics of Soviet Oil and Gas*, Johns Hopkins University Press, Baltimore, Md.

Campbell, R. W. (1972), 'Management spillovers from Soviet space and military programmes', *Soviet Studies*, Vol. 23, pp. 586–607.

Campbell, R. W. (1980), *Soviet Energy Technologies*, Indiana University Press, Bloomington, Ind.

Caroe, O. (1967), *Soviet Empire: The Turks of Central Asia and Stalinism*, Macmillan, London.

Carr, E. H. (1958), *Socialism in One Country*, Macmillan, London, Vol. 1.

Carr, E. H. (1966), *The Bolshevik Revolution*, Penguin Books, Harmondsworth, Vol. 1.

Carr, E. H., and Davies, R. (1974), *Foundations of a Planned Economy*, Penguin Books, Harmondsworth, Vol. 1.

Castro, F. (1972T), *Fidel Castro Speaks*, Penguin Books, Harmondsworth.

Castro, F. (1976), 'Main Report to the First Congress of the Communist Party of Cuba', *Granma Weekly Review*, 4 January 1976.

*Chaliand, G. (1969T), *The Peasants of North Vietnam*, Penguin Books, Harmondsworth.

Chanda, N. (1979), 'Vietnam's battle of the home front', *Far Eastern Economic Review*.

Chang, C. (1975), 'On exercising all-round dictatorship over the bourgeoisie', *Peking Review*, Vol. 14, pp. 1–10.

Chang, J. (1967), 'The industrial development of mainland China, 1912–1949', *Journal of Economic History*, Vol. 27, pp. 56–81.

Chapman, J. (1954), 'Real wages in the Soviet Union, 1928–52', *Review of Economics and Statistics*,

*Chapman, J. (1963), 'Consumption', in Bergson, A. and Kuznets, S. (eds), *Economic Trends in the Soviet Union*, Harvard University Press, Cambridge, Mass.

Chapman, J. (1970), *Wage Variations in Soviet Industry*, Rand Corporation, Santa Monica, Calif.

Chaudhuri, P. (ed.) (1971), *Aspects of Indian Economic Development*, Allen & Unwin, London.

*Chayanov, A. (1920, 1977T), 'Journey of my brother Alexei to the Land of Peasant Utopia', in Smith, R. E. F. (ed.), *The Russian Peasant*, Cass, London, 1977.

*Chayanov, A. (1966T), *The Theory of Peasant Economy*, Irwin, Homewood, Ill.

Chayanov, A. (1967), *Oeuvres choisies de A. V. Cajanov*, ed. B. Kerblay, 8 vols, Mouton, Paris and The Hague.

Chayanov, A. *et al.* (1922), *Problemy zemleustroistva, optimalnie razmeri zemledelcheskogo khoziaistva, kolichestvennyi uchet effekta zemleustroistva*, Moscow.

Chelintsev, A. (1928), *Russkoye selskoye khoziaistvo pered revoliutsiei*, Moscow.

Ch'en, J. (1979), *China and the West*, Hutchinson, London.

Chen, E. (1979), *Hyper-Growth in Asian Economies*, Macmillan, London.

*Chenery, H., and Watanabe, T. (1958), 'International comparisons of the structure of production', *Econometrica*, Vol. 26, pp. 487–521.

*Cheng, C. (1961), *Land Reform in Taiwan*, China Publishing, Taiwan.

Cheng Chu-yuan (1976), *China's Petroleum Industry*, Praeger, New York.

*Chernyshevsky, N. (1903T), *La Possession communale du sol*, Paris.

Chernyshevsky, N. (1906), *Polnoye sobranie sochinenii*, 10 vols, St Petersburg.

Chesneaux, J. (1966), *The Vietnamese Nation*, Current Books, Australia.

Chesneaux, J. *et al.* (1971), *Tradition et révolution au Vietnam*, Anthropos, Paris.

Chesneaux, J. (1973T), *Peasant Revolts in China, 1840–1949*, Thames & Hudson, London.

Chiang Kai-shek (1947T), *China's Destiny, Chinese Economic Theory*, Roy Publishers, New York.

*Chinese Ministry of Information (1943), *China Handbook, 1937–1943*, Macmillan, New York.

Christoff, P. (1961), *An Introduction to Nineteenth-Century Slavophilism*, Mouton, Paris, Vol. 1.

*Chung, J. S. H. (1974), *The North Korean Economy*, Hoover Institution, Stanford, Calif.

Cipolla, C. (1969), *Literacy and Development in the West*, Penguin Books, Harmondsworth.

Clapham, J. (1936), *Economic Development of France and Germany*, Cambridge University Press.

Clarke, R. (1972), *Soviet Economic Facts*, Wiley, New York.

Cohen, S. (1975), *Bukharin and the Bolshevik Revolution*, Vintage Books/Random House, New York.

Cohn, S. (1970), *Economic Development in the Soviet Union*, D. C. Heath, Lexington, Mass.

Cole, D., and Lyman, P. (1971), *Korean Development*, Harvard University Press, Cambridge, Mass.

Collete, J. (1964), *Politique des investissements et calcul économique*, Cujas, Paris.

*Comecon (1976T), *Statistical Yearbook of the CMEA*, IPC, London.

*Comecon (1979), *Statisticheskiy ezhegodnik stran-chlenov sovieta ekonomicheskoy vzaimopomoshchi 1979*, Comecon Secretariat, Moscow.

Confino, M. (1969), *Systèmes agraires et progrès agricole*, Mouton, Paris.

Connor, W. (1971), 'Alcohol and Soviet society', *Slavic Review*, Vol. 30, pp. 570–88.

*Connor, W. (1972), *Deviance in Soviet Society: Crime, Delinquency, Alcoholism*, Columbia University Press, New York.

*Connor, W. (1977), 'Social change and stability in Eastern Europe', *Problems of Communism*, Vol. 26, no. 6, pp. 16–32.

*Connor, W. (1979), *Socialism, Politics and Equality*, Columbia University Press, New York.

Conolly, V. (1967), *Beyond the Urals*, Oxford University Press, London.

Conquest, R. (1971), *The Great Terror*, Penguin Books, Harmondsworth.

Cox, T. (1979), *Rural Sociology in the Soviet Union*, Hurst, London.

Crick, B. (1980), *George Orwell: A Life*, Secker & Warburg, London.

*Crotty, R. (1966), *Irish Agricultural Production*, Cork University Press.

Crouzet, F. (1967), 'England and France in the eighteenth century', in Hartwell, R. W. (ed.), *The Causes of the Industrial Revolution*, Methuen, London.

*Csizmadia, E. (1977T), *Socialist Agriculture in Hungary*, Akademiai Kiado, Budapest.

*Cviic, C. (1980), 'Hungary: the quiet revolution', *The Economist*, 20 September 1980, pp. 51–71.

Cviic, K. (1974), 'Turning the clock back in Yugoslavia', *World Today*, May 1974, pp. 206–13.

Dallin, A. *et al.* (1978), *Women in Russia*, Harvester Press, Hassocks.

Dallin, D. and Nikolaevsky, B. (1947), *Forced Labour in Soviet Russia*, Yale University Press, New Haven.

Dalrymple, D. (1963), 'The Soviet famine of 1932–34', *Soviet Studies*, Vol. 15, pp. 250–84.

Danielson, N. (1902T), *Histoire du développement économique de la Russie depuis l'affranchissement des serfs*, Paris.

Darusenkov, O. (ed.) (1974), *Respublika Kuba*, Nauka, Moscow.

Das, M. N. (1961), *The Political Philosophy of Jawaharlal Nehru*, Day, New York.

Davies, R. (1980), *The Socialist Offensive: The Collectivization of Soviet Agriculture, 1929–30*, Macmillan, London.

*Dawson, W. (1896), 'The Swiss house industries', *Economic Journal*, Vol. 6, pp. 295–307.

*Day, R. (1972), *Trotsky and the Politics of Economic Isolation*, Cambridge University Press.

*Day, R. (1977), 'Trotsky and Preobrazhensky', *Studies in Comparative Communism*, Vol. 10, pp. 69–86.

Dean, G. (1972), 'Sources of technological innovation in the People's Republic of China', *Journal of Development Studies*, Vol. 9, pp. 187–99.

Debray, R. (1968T), *Revolution in the Revolution*, Penguin Books, Harmondsworth.

Defosses, H., and Levesque, J. (eds) (1975), *Socialism in the Third World*, Praeger, New York.

Degras, J. (ed.) (1960), *The Communist International, 1919–1943: Documents*, Oxford University Press, London, Vol. 2.

*Demko, G. (1969), *Russian Colonization of Kazakhstan*, Indiana University Press, Bloomington, Ind.

*Dernberger, R. (ed.) (1980), *China's Development Experience*, Harvard University Press, Cambridge, Mass.

*Deutscher, I. (1954), *The Prophet Armed, Trotsky: 1879–1921*, Oxford University Press, London.

Deutscher, I. (1959), *The Prophet Unarmed, Trotsky: 1921–29*, Oxford University Press, London.

Deutscher, I. (1966), *Stalin*, Penguin Books, Harmondsworth.

Dienes, L. (1975), 'Pasturalism in Turkestan', *Soviet Studies*, Vol. 27, pp. 343–65.

Dimaio, A. (1974), *Soviet Urban Housing*, Praeger, New York.

Djilas, M. (1957), *The New Class: An Analysis of the Communist System*, Thames & Hudson, London.

Djilas, M. (1980), 'Tito, the born rebel', *Sunday Times* (London), 11 May 1980.

*Dobb, M. (1928), *Russian Economic Development since the Revolution*, Labour Research Department, London.

Dobb, M. (1955), *On Economic Theory and Socialism*, Routledge & Kegan Paul, London.

Dobb, M. (1963), *Economic Growth and Underdeveloped Countries*, Lawrence & Wishart, London.

Dobb, M. (1966), *Soviet Economic Development since 1917*, Routledge & Kegan Paul, London.

*Dobrescu, E., and Blaga, I. (1973T), *Structural Patterns of Romanian Economy*, Meridiane, Bucharest.

Domar, E. (1957), *Essays in the Theory of Economic Growth*, Oxford University Press, London.

Domes, J. (1973T), *The Internal Politics of China, 1949–72*, Hurst, London.

Domes, J. (1977), *China after the Cultural Revolution*, Hurst, London.

Domes, J. (1980), *Socialism in the Chinese Countryside*, Hurst, London.

*Domínguez, J. (1978), *Cuba: Order and Revolution*, Harvard University Press, Cambridge, Mass.

Donaldson, R. (ed.) (1981), *The Soviet Union and the Third World*, Croom Helm, London.

*Donnell, J. (1980), 'Vietnam 1979: year of calamity', *Asian Survey*, January 1980, pp. 20–32.

Donnison, D. (1967), *The Government of Housing*, Penguin Books, Harmondsworth.

Drage, G. (1904), *Russian Affairs*, John Murray, London.

Drew, W. (1968), 'Sinkiang: land and people', *Central Asian Review*, Vol. 16, pp. 205–16.

Dryer, J. (1976), *China's Forty Millions: Minority Nationalities and National Integration in the People's Republic of China*, Harvard University Press, Cambridge, Mass.

Dubrovski, S. M. (1975), *Selskoye khoziaistvo i krestianstvo Rossii v periode imperializma*, Moscow.

Dumont, R. (1974), *Is Cuba Socialist?*, Viking Press, New York.

Dunman, J. (1975), *Agriculture: Capitalist and Socialist*, Lawrence & Wishart, London.

Dunn, S., and Dunn, E. (1967), *The Peasants of Central Russia*, Holt, Rinehart & Winston, New York.

*Dupree, L. (1980), *Afghanistan*, Princeton University Press, Princeton, NJ.

Dziewanowski, M. (1977), *Poland in the Twentieth Century*, Columbia University Press, New York.

ECAFE (1959a), *Economic Survey, 1959*, ECAFE, New York.

ECAFE (1959b), *Economic Bulletin* (June 1959).

*ECE (1951), 'Long term trends in European agriculture', *Economic Bulletin, 1951*, no. 2.

ECE (1954), *European Agriculture: A Statement of Problems*, ECE, Geneva.

ECE (1960), 'Some problems of economic development: Eastern Europe and the USSR', *Economic Survey, 1960*, ECE, Geneva.

*Eckstein, A. (1977), *China's Economic Revolution*, Cambridge University Press.

*Eckstein, A., Galenson, W., and Liu, T. (eds) (1968), *Economic Trends in Communist China*, Edinburgh University Press.

Eddy, S. (1934), *Russia Today*, Farrar & Rinehart, New York.

Elek, P. (1977), 'Hungary's new agricultural revolution', in Hajda, J., Laird, B., and Laird, R. (eds), *The Future of Agriculture in the Soviet Union and Eastern Europe*, Westview Press, Boulder, Colo.

Ellman, M. (1975), 'Did the agricultural surplus provide the resources for the increase in investment in the USSR during the First Five Year Plan?', *Economic Journal*, Vol. 8, pp. 844–64.

Ellman, M. (1979), *Socialist Planning*, Cambridge University Press.

Engels, F. (1845, 1969T), *The Condition of the Working Class in England*, Panther Books, London.

*Engels, F. (1875), 'Soziales aus Russland', *Volksstaat* (Leipzig), no. 21.

*Engels, F., and Marx, K. (1934), *Correspondence, 1834–1895*, London.

*Engels, F., and Marx, K. (1950–1T), *Selected Works*, 2 vols, Foreign Languages Publishing House, Moscow.

*Engels, F., and Marx, K. (1970T), *Selected Works*, Progress Publishers, Moscow, Vol. 3.

*Enyedi, G. (ed.) (1976T), *Rural Transformation in Hungary*, Akademiai Kiado, Budapest.

Erickson, J. (1962), *The Soviet High Command*, Macmillan, London.

Erlich, A. (1960), *The Soviet Industrialization Debate, 1924–1928*, Harvard University Press, Cambridge, Mass.

Erlich, A. (1967), 'Development strategy and planning', in Millikan, M. (ed.), *National Economic Planning*, Columbia University Press, New York.

Estrin, S. (1978), *Industrial Structure in a Market Socialist Economy*, Economics Department, University of Southampton.

Estrin, S. (1983), *Self-Management: Economic Theory and Yugoslav Practice*, Cambridge University Press.

Evans, L. (1978), *China after Mao*, Pathfinder Press, New York.

Falkus, M. (1968), 'Russia's national income in 1913', *Economica*, Vol. 35, pp. 52–73.

Fall, B. (1967), *The Two Vietnams*, Pall Mall Press, London.

Fallenbuchl, Z. (1970), 'The communist pattern of industrialization', *Soviet Studies*.

*Fallenbuchl, Z. (ed.) (1975, 1976), *Economic Development in the Soviet Union and Eastern Europe*, 2 vols, Praeger, New York.

*Fang Weizhong (1982T), 'China's economic readjustment and reorientation', in Xue Muqiao (ed.), *Almanac of China's Economy, 1981*, Ballinger, Cambridge, Mass.

*FAO (1946), *Proposals for a World Food Board and a World Food Survey*, FAO, Washington, DC.

*FAO (1949), *Food Composition Tables*, FAO Nutritional Studies No. 3, FAO, Washington, DC.

*FAO (1952), *The Second World Food Survey*, FAO, Rome.

*FAO (1960), *1950 World Agricultural Census*, FAO, Rome.

FAO (1965), *World Rice Economy in Figures, 1909–1963*, Commodity Reference Series 3, FAO, Rome.

*FAO (1971), *1960 World Agricultural Census*, FAO, Rome.

FAO (1976), *The State of Food and Agriculture, 1976*, FAO, Rome.

FAO (1977), *The Fourth World Food Survey*, FAO, Rome.

FAO (1978), *FAO Studies in Agricultural Economics and Statistics*, FAO, Rome.

Faradzhev, F. (1975), *Tempi razvitya in otrasleviye proportsii promyshlennosti Azerbaijana*, Azerbaijanskoye gosudarstvennoye izdatelstvo, Baku.

*Fei Hsiao-tung (1946), 'Peasantry and gentry: an interpretation of Chinese social structure and its changes', *American Journal of Sociology*, Vol. 52, pp. 1–17.

*Fei, J., Ranis, G. and Kuo, S. (1979), *Growth with Equity: The Taiwan Case*, Oxford University Press.

Feldman, G. (1928), 'K teorii tempov narodnogo dokhoda', *Planovoye khoziaistvo*, Nov.–Dec. 1928.

*Feuchtwang, S., and Hussain, A. (eds) (1983), *The Chinese Economic Reforms*, Croom Helm, London.

Field, M. (1967), *Soviet Socialized Medicine*, The Free Press, New York.

*Fischer, L., and Uren, P. (1973), *The New Hungarian Agriculture*, Queen's University Press, Montreal.

Fitzgerald, C. P. (1964), *The Birth of Communist China*, Penguin Books, Harmondsworth.

Fitzgerald, C. P. (1977), *Mao Tse-tung and China*, Penguin Books, Harmondsworth.

*Fitzpatrick, S. (ed.) (1978), *Cultural Revolution in Soviet Russia, 1928–1931*, Indiana University Press, Bloomington, Ind.

Fitzpatrick, S. (1979), *Education and Social Mobility in the Soviet Union*, Cambridge University Press.

Francisco, R., Laird, B., and Laird, R. (eds) (1980), *Agricultural Policies in the USSR and Eastern Europe*, Westview Press, Boulder, Colo.

*Franklin, S. H. (1969), *The European Peasantry: The Final Phase*, London.

Friss, I. (ed.) (1971T), *Reform of the Economic Mechanism in Hungary*, Akademiai Kiado, Budapest.

Fryer, D. (1970, 1979), *Emergent Southeast Asia*, George Phillip, London.

Fukutake, T. (1967), *Asian Rural Society: China, India, Japan*, University of Washington Press, Washington, DC.

Furtado, C. (1970), *Economic Development of Latin America*, Cambridge University Press.

Gabbay, R. (1978), *Communism and Agrarian Reform in Iraq*, Croom Helm, London.

Gafurov, B., and Kim, G. (eds) (1978T), *Lenin and National Liberation in the East*, Progress Publishers, Moscow.

Galeski, B. (1972T), *Basic Concepts of Rural Sociology*, Manchester University Press.

Gandhi, M. K. (1941), *Constructive Programme*, Navajivan Press, Ahmedabad.

Gandhi, M. K. (1948), *Constructive Programme*, Navajivan Press, Ahmedabad.

*Gandhi, M. K. (1959), *Economic and Industrial Life and Relations*, 3 vols, ed. V. Kher, Navajivan Press, Ahmedabad.

Ganguli, B. N. (1973), *Gandhi's Social Philosophy*, Indian Social Science Research Council, Delhi.

GDR (1977), *Statistical Pocketbook of the German Democratic Republic, 1977*, East Berlin.

Gellner, E., and Ionescu, G. (eds) (1970), *Populism: Its Meanings and National Characteristics*, Weidenfeld & Nicolson, London.

George, V., and Manning, N. (1980), *Socialism, Social Welfare and the Soviet Union*, Routledge & Kegan Paul, London.

German Institute for Economic Research (1979), *Handbook of the Economy of the German Democratic Republic*, Saxon House, Farnborough.

Gerschenkron, A. (1962), *Economic Backwardness in Historical Perspective*, Harvard University Press, Cambridge, Mass.

Gerschenkron, A. (1965), 'Agrarian policies and industrialization: Russia, 1862–1917', in *Cambridge Economic History of Europe*, Cambridge University Press, Vol. 6.

Ghai, D., and Khan, A. (1979), *Collective Agriculture and Rural Development in Soviet Central Asia*, Macmillan/ILO, London.

Ghai, D., and Khan, A. (eds) (1980), *Agrarian Systems and Rural Development*, Macmillan/ILO, London.

Gillmor, D. (ed.) (1979), *Irish Resources and Land Use*, Institute of Public Administration, Dublin.

Golan, G. (1971), *The Czechoslovak Reform Movement*, Cambridge University Press.

Golan, G. (1973), *Reform Rule in Czechoslovakia*, Cambridge University Press.

Goldenberg, B. (1965), *The Cuban Revolution and Latin America*, Praeger, New York.

Goldman, E. (1925), *My Disillusionment in Russia*, London; reissued, Apollo Editions, New York, 1970.

*Goldsmith, R. (1961), 'The economic growth of tsarist Russia, 1860–1913', *Economic Development and Cultural Change*, Vol. 9, pp. 441–75.

*Gordon, A. (1971), 'The debate on agriculture in North Vietnam', *New Left Review*, no. 68.

*Gordon, A. (1981), 'North Vietnam's collectivization campaigns', *Journal of Contemporary Asia*, Vol. 11, pp. 19–44.

Gosplan (1934), *Summary of the Fulfilment of the First Five Year Plan*, International Publishers, New York.

Gough, K. (1979), *Ten Times More Beautiful: The Rebuilding of Vietnam*, Monthly Review Press, New York.

*Gourou, P. (1945T), *Land Utilization in French Indochina*, 2 vols, Institute of Pacific Relations, New York.

*Grajdanzev, A. (1944), *Modern Korea*, John Day, New York.

Granick, D. (1951), 'Initiative and independence of Soviet plant management', *Slavic Review*, Vol. 10, pp. 191–201.

Granick, D. (1962), 'On patterns of technological choice in Soviet industry', in *American Economic Review*, Papers and Proceedings, Vol. 52, pp. 149–57.

*Granick, D. (1967), *Soviet Metal Fabricating and Economic Development*, University of Wisconsin Press, Madison, Wis.

*Granick, D. (1975), *Enterprise Guidance in Eastern Europe*, Princeton University Press, Princeton, NJ.

*Gray, J., and Gray, M. (1983), 'China's new agricultural revolution', in Feuchtwang, S., and Hussain, A. (eds), *The Chinese Economic Reforms*, Croom Helm, London.

Gregory, M. (1973), 'Regional economic development in Yugoslavia', *Soviet Studies*, Vol. 25, pp. 213–28.

Gregory, P. (1970), *Socialist and Non-Socialist Industrialization Patterns*, Praeger, New York.

Gregory, P. (1971–2), 'Economic growth and structural change in tsarist Russia', *Soviet Studies*, Vol. 23, pp. 418–34.

*Gregory, P. (1980a), 'Grain marketings and peasant consumption in Russia, 1885–1913', *Explorations in Economic History*, Vol. 17, pp. 135–64.

*Gregory, P. (1980b), 'Russian living standards during the industrialization era, 1885–1913', *Review of Income and Wealth*, Vol. 26, pp. 87–103.

Griffin, K. (1976), *Land Concentration and Rural Poverty*, Macmillan, London.

Griffin, K. (1979), *The Political Economy of Agrarian Change*, Macmillan, London.

Griffin, K. (1982), 'Income differentials in rural China', *China Quarterly*, no. 92, pp. 706–11.

Griffin, K., and Saith, A. (1980), 'The pattern of income inequality in rural China', *Oxford Economic Papers*, March 1983.

Griffiths, J., and Griffiths, P. (eds) (1979), *Cuba: The Second Decade*, Britain–Cuba Liaison Committee, Writers & Readers Publishing Cooperative, London.

Grigorescu, C. (1976), *Populatie si Economie*, Editura Academiei, Bucharest.

Grossman, G. (1977), 'The "second economy" of the USSR', *Problems of Communism*, Vol. 26, no. 3, pp. 25–40.

*Guevara, E. (1968T), *Venceremos: Speeches and Writings*, Weidenfeld & Nicolson, London.

Guevara, E. (1969T), *Reminiscences of the Cuban Revolutionary War*, Penguin Books, Harmondsworth.

Gurley, J. (1976), *China's Economy and the Maoist Strategy*, Monthly Review Press, New York.

Hajda, J., Laird, B., and Laird, R. (eds) (1977), *The Future of Agriculture in the Soviet Union and Eastern Europe*, Westview Press, Boulder, Colo.

*Halliday, F. (1978), 'Revolution in Afghanistan', *New Left Review*, no. 112, pp. 3–44.

*Halliday, F. (1980), 'War and revolution in Afghanistan', *New Left Review*, no. 119, pp. 20–41.

Halliday, J. (1970), 'The Korean revolution', *Socialist Revolution*, Vol. 1, no. 6, pp. 95–135.

*Halliday, J. (1981), 'The North Korean phenomenon', *New Left Review*, no. 127.

Hambly, G., *et al.* (1969), *Central Asia*, Weidenfeld & Nicolson, London.

Hanson, P. (1968), *The Consumer in the Soviet Economy*, Macmillan, London.

Haraszti, M. (1977T), *A Worker in a Worker's State*, Penguin Books, Harmondsworth.

*Harding, N. (1977, 1980), *Lenin's Political Thought*, 2 vols, Macmillan, London.

Harding, N., and Taylor, R. (eds) (1983), *Marxism in Russia*, Cambridge University Press.

*Hardt, J. (ed.) (1974), *Reorientation and Commercial Relations of the Economies of Eastern Europe*, US Congress Joint Economic Committee, Washington, DC.

*Hardt, J. (ed.) (1977), *East European Economies Post Helsinki*, US Congress Joint Economic Committee, Washington, DC.

*Hardt, J. (ed.) (1979), *The Soviet Economy in a Time of Change*, US Congress Joint Economic Committee, Washington, DC.

*Hardy, R. (1978), *China's Oil Future*, Westview Press, Boulder, Colo.

*Hare, P., Radice, H., and Swain, N. (1981), *Hungary: A Decade of Reform*, Allen & Unwin, London.

Harrison, M. (1974–5), 'Chayanov and the economics of the Russian peasantry', *Journal of Peasant Studies*, Vol. 2, pp. 392–417.

Harrison, M. (1976–7), 'Resource allocation and agrarian class formation', *Journal of Peasant Studies*, Vol. 4, pp. 127–61.

Harrison, M. (1977–8), 'The peasant mode of production in the work of A. V. Chayanov', *Journal of Peasant Studies*, Vol. 5, pp. 323–36.

Harrison, M. (1979–80), 'Chayanov and the Marxists', *Journal of Peasant Studies*, Vol. 7, pp. 86–99.

*Hasan, P. (1976), *Korea*, World Bank/Johns Hopkins University Press, Baltimore, Md.

*Hasan, P., and Rao, D. (eds) (1979), *Korea*, World Bank/Johns Hopkins University Press, Baltimore, Md.

*Hayami, Y. (1976), *A Century of Agricultural Growth in Japan: Its Relevance to Asian Development*, Tokyo University Press.

Hayami, Y., and Yamada, S. (1970), *Agricultural Productivity at the Beginning of Industrialization*, in Ohkawa, K., Johnston, B., and Kaneda, H. (eds), *Agriculture and Economic Growth*, Princeton University Press, Princeton, NJ.

*Haxthausen, A. von (1847–52, 1856T), *The Russian Empire*, 2 vols, London.

Heaton, W. (1980), 'Mongolia 1979', *Asian Survey*, January 1980, pp. 77–83.

Heitman, S. (1962), 'Between Lenin and Stalin: Bukharin', in Labedz, L. (ed.), *Revisionism*, Allen & Unwin, London.

Henderson, G. (1968), *Korea*, Harvard University Press, Cambridge, Mass.

*Herzen, A. (1954–65), *Sobranie sochinenii*, 30 vols, Moscow.

Hirschman, A. (1958), *The Strategy of Economic Growth*, Yale University Press, New Haven, Conn.

Ho Ping-ti (1959), *Studies on the Population of China, 1368–1953*, Harvard University Press, Cambridge, Mass.

*Ho, S. P. S. (1978), *Economic Development of Taiwan, 1860–1970*, Yale University Press, New Haven, Conn.

Hodgkin, T. (1981), *Vietnam: The Revolutionary Path*, Macmillan, London.

*Hoffman, W. (1958T), *The Growth of Industrial Economies*, Manchester University Press.

*Hohenburg, P. (1972), 'Change in rural France in the period of industrialization', *Journal of Economic History*, Vol. 32, pp. 219–40.

*Höhmann, H.-H., Kaser, M., and Thalheim, K. (eds) (1975), *The New Economic*

Systems of Eastern Europe, Hurst, London.

Holdsworth, M. (1951–2), 'Soviet Central Asia, 1917–1940', *Soviet Studies*, Vol. 3, pp. 258–77.

Holmström, S. (n.d.), *Swedish Farming*, Economic Research Institute, Stockholm.

Holt, P., Lambton, A., and Lewis, B. (eds) (1977), *The Cambridge History of Islam*, Cambridge University Press, Vol. 1.

*Holzman, F. (1955), *Soviet Taxation*, Harvard University Press, Cambridge, Mass.

*Holzman, F. (1960), 'Soviet inflationary pressures', *Quarterly Journal of Economics*, Vol. 74, pp. 167–88.

Holzman, F. (1963), 'Foreign trade', in Bergson, A., and Kuznets, S. (eds), *Economic Trends in the Soviet Union*, Harvard University Press, Cambridge, Mass.

Holzman, F. (1976), *International Trade under Communism*, Macmillan, London.

*Honey, P. (ed.) (1962), *North Vietnam Today*, Praeger, New York.

Honey, P. (1963), *Communism in North Vietnam*, MIT, Cambridge, Mass.

*Horowitz, I. (ed.) (1981), *Cuban Communism*, 4th edn, Transaction Books, New Jersey.

Horvat, B. (1975), 'An institutional model of a self-managed socialist economy', in Vanek, J. (ed.), *Self-Management*, Penguin Books, Harmondsworth.

*Hou, C. M. (1965), *Foreign Investment and Economic Development in China, 1840–1937*, Harvard University Press, Cambridge, Mass.

Hou, C. M., and Yu, T. S. (eds) (1979), *Modern Chinese Economic History*, University of Washington Press, Washington, DC.

Howe, C. (1978), *China's Economy. A Basic Guide*, Elek, London.

Hsiao, T. (1951), *Land Reform in China and Japan*, in Parsons, K., Penn, R., and Raup, P. (eds), *Land Tenure*, University of Wisconsin Press, Madison, Wis.

Humphrey, C. (1983), *Karl Marx Collective*, Cambridge University Press.

*Hunter, H. (1965), 'Transport in Soviet and Chinese development', *Economic Development and Cultural Change*, Vol. 14, pp. 71–84.

Hussain, A., and Tribe, K. (1981), *Marxism and the Agrarian Question*, 2 vols, Macmillan, London.

Hutchings, R. (1971), 'Science and technology in the Soviet Union', in Schopflin, G. (ed.), *The Soviet Union and Eastern Europe*, Blond & Briggs, London.

*Hutchings, R. (1978), 'Soviet design', *Slavic Review*, Vol. 37, pp. 567–83.

Hyde, G. (1974), *The Soviet Health Service*, Lawrence & Wishart, London.

IEC (1939), *Grain Crops*, London.

*ILO (1977), *Poverty and Landlessness in Rural Asia*, ILO, Geneva.

*International Institute of Agriculture (1939), *The First World Agricultural Census, 1930*, 5 vols, IIA, Rome.

Ionescu, G. (1970), *Eastern Europe*, in Gellner, E., and Ionescu, G. (eds), *Populism: Its Meanings and National Characteristics*, Weidenfeld & Nicolson, London.

*Ishikawa, S. (1983), 'China's economic growth since 1949', *China Quarterly*, 1983, pp. 242–77.

Iskanderov, I. (1974), *Tekstilnaya promyshlennost Uzbekistana*, Izdatelstvo 'Uzbekistan', Tashkent.

Jackson, G. (1966), *Comintern and Peasant in Eastern Europe, 1919–1930*, Columbia University Press, New York.

Jacoby, E. H. (1949), *Agrarian Unrest in Southeast Asia*, Columbia University Press, New York.

Jain, S. C. (1967), *Agricultural Development in India*, Kitab Mahal, Allahabad.

Jasny, N. (1949), *Socialized Agriculture of the USSR*, Stanford University Press, Stanford, Calif.

Jasny, N. (1961), *Soviet Industrialization*, University of Chicago Press.

*Jasny, N. (1972), *Some Soviet Economists of the Twenties*, Cambridge University Press.

*Jeffries, I. (ed.) (1981), *The Industrial Enterprise in Eastern Europe*, Praeger, New York.

Jelavich, B. (1983), *History of the Balkans*, 2 vols, Cambridge University Press.

*Jensen, E. (1937), *Danish Agriculture: Its Economic Development*, Schultz Forlag, Copenhagen.

John, P. (1962), *Some Aspects of the Structure of Indian Agricultural Economy*, Asian Publishing House, London.

Johnson, C. (1962), *Peasant Nationalism and Communist Power*, Stanford University Press, Stanford, Calif.

Jones, E. L. (1968), 'The agricultural origins of industry', *Past and Present*, no. 40.

Kahan, A. (1978), 'Capital Formation . . . in Russia, 1890–1913', *Cambridge Economic History of Europe*, Vol. 7, Cambridge University Press.

Kanet, R., and Bahry, D. (eds) (1974), *Soviet Economic and Political Relations with the Developing World*, Praeger, New York.

Kang Chao (1975), 'The growth of a modern textile industry and competition with handicrafts', in Perkins, D. (ed.), *China's Modern Economy in Historical Perspective*, Stanford University Press, Stanford, Calif.

Kantorovich, L. (1976T), *Essays in Optimal Planning*, Blackwell, Oxford.

*Karan, P. (1976), *The Changing Face of Tibet: The Impact of Chinese Communist Ideology*, University of Kentucky Press, Lexington, Ky.

Karcz, J. (1970), 'Back on the grain front', *Soviet Studies*, Vol. 22, pp. 262–94.

*Kaser, M. (1976), *Health Care in the Soviet Union and Eastern Europe*, Croom Helm, London.

Katus, L. (1970), 'Economic growth in Hungary during the age of dualism', *Studia Historica*.

Kaufman, A. (1918), *Voprosi ekonomiki i statistiki krestianskogo khoziaistva*, Moscow.

*Kaufman, A. (1962), *Small-Scale Industry in the Soviet Union*, National Bureau of Economic Research, New York.

Kautsky, J. (1968), *Communism and the Politics of Development*, Wiley, London.

Kautsky, K. (1899, 1976T), *Die Agrarfrage*, Vol. 1, abridged and trans. J. Benaji, *Economy and Society*, Vol. 5, pp. 2–49.

*Kaye, W. (1962), 'The economy of North Vietnam', in Honey, P. (ed.), *North Vietnam Today*, Praeger, New York.

Kazakhstan (1968), *Narodnoye khoziaistvo kazakhstana*, Alma-Ata.

Kennard, H. P. (1907), *The Russian Peasant*, Werner Laurie, London.

Kennard, H. P. (ed.) (1913), *The Russian Yearbook for 1913*, London.

Kennedy, M. (1957), *A Short History of Communism in Asia*, Weidenfeld & Nicolson, London.

Kerblay, B. (1962), 'L'évolution de l'alimentation rurale en Russie, 1896–1960', *Annales*, Vol. 17, pp. 885–913.

Kerblay, B. (1983T), *Modern Soviet Society*, Methuen, London.

Khan, A. R. (1977), 'The distribution of income in rural China', in ILO, *Poverty and Landlessness in Rural Asia*, ILO, Geneva.

*Khromov, P. A. (1967), *Ekonomicheskoye razvitiye Rossii*, Nauka, Moscow.

Kieniewicz, S. (1969), *The Emancipation of the Polish Peasantry*, University of Chicago Press.

*Kiernan, B., and Boua, C. (1982), *Peasants and Politics in Kampuchea*, Zed Press, London.

Kim, B. S. (1970T), *Modern Korea*, International Publishers, New York.

Kim, H. G. (1979T), *Modern History of Korea*, Foreign Languages Publishing House, Pyongyang.

Kim Il Sung (1971–5T), *Selected Works*, Foreign Languages Publishing House, Pyongyang.

*Kim, J. A. (1975), *Divided Korea: The Politics of Development*, Harvard University Press, Cambridge, Mass.

Kim, Y. C., and Halpern, A. (eds) (1977), *Future of the Korean Peninsula*, Praeger, New York.

*King, E. (ed.) (1980), *Communist Education*, Methuen, London.

King, R. (1977), *Land Reform: A World Survey*, G. Bell, London.

*Kitching, G. (1982), *Development and Underdevelopment in Historical Perspective*, Methuen, London.

Klatt, W. (1979), 'China's new economic policy', *China Quarterly*, pp. 716–33.

*Klatt, W. (1983), 'The staff of life: living standards in China', *China Quarterly*, pp. 17–50.

*Knaus, W. (1981), *Inside Soviet Medicine*, Everest, New York.

Kolakowski, L. (1978), *Main Currents of Marxism*, 3 vols, Oxford University Press.

Kolarz, W. (1953), *Russia and Her Colonies*, George Phillip, London.

Kolosi, T., and Wnuk-Lipirski, E. (eds) (1983), *Equality and Inequality under Socialism*, Sage, Beverly Hills, Calif.

Kondratiev, N. (1922a), *Rynok khlebov i ego regulirovanie vo vremya voini i revoliutsii*, Moscow.

Kondratiev, N. (1922b), *Mirovoye khoziaistvo i ego konjunkturi vo vremya i posle voiny*, Moscow.

Kondratiev, N. (1927), 'Critical observations on the economic development plan', in *Planovoye khoziaistvo*; trans. in Spulber, N. (ed.), *Foundations of Soviet Strategy for Economic Growth. Selected Soviet Essays, 1924–30*, Indiana University Press, Bloomington, Ind., 1964, pp. 438–51.

Kondratiev, N. (1935), 'Long waves in economic life', *Review of Economics and Statistics*, Vol. 17, pp. 105–15.

Kondratiev, N., and Makarov, N. (1924), *Osnovy perspektivnogo plana razvitiya selskogo i lesnogo khoziaistva*, Moscow.

Koon, W. N. (1974), *The North Korean Communist Leadership, 1945–65*, University of Alabama Press, Montgomery, Ala.

Korbonski, A. (1965), *The Politics of Socialist Agriculture in Poland, 1945–60*, Columbia University Press, New York.

Kostrowicki, J., and Szczesny, R. (1972T), *Polish Agriculture*, Adademiai Kiado, Budapest.

Koszegi, L. (1978), 'Labour turnover and employment structure in European socialist countries', *International Labour Review*, Vol. 117, pp. 305–18.

Kotovsky, G. (1964), *Agrarian Reform in India*, People's Publishing House, Delhi.

*Kovalchenko, I. (1967), *Russkoye krepostnoye krestianstvo v pervoi polovine XIX v.*, Moscow.

*Kovalchenko, I., and Borodkin, L. (1980), 'Agrarian typology of the Gubernia of European Russia at the end of the 19th century', *Soviet Studies in History*, Vol. 19.

*Kozlowski, Z. (1977), 'Socialism and family farming', *Osteuropa Wirtschaft*.

Krader, L. (1966), *Peoples of Central Asia*, Indiana University Press, Bloomington, Ind.

Krasin, L. (1924), *Planovoye khoziaistvo i monopoliya vneshnei torgovli*, Moscow.

Krasina, L. (1929), *Leonid Krasin: His Life and Work*, London.

Kravchinsky, S. (Stepniak) (1888), *The Russian Peasantry*, London, New York, 1905.

Krejci, J. (1972), *Social Change and Stratification in Postwar Czechoslovakia*, Macmillan, London.

Kroef, J. M. van der (1980), *Communism in Southeast Asia*, Macmillan, London.

*Kropotkin, P. (1899, 1907), *Fields, Factories and Workshops*, London.

*Kropotkin, P. (1902), *Mutual Aid*, London.

*Kropotkin, P. (1906T), *The Conquest of Bread*, London; first published in France, 1892.

*Kropotkin, P. (1927), *Kropotkin's Revolutionary Pamphlets*, ed. R. Baldwin, New York.

*Kuark, Y. T. (1963a), 'North Korea's industrial development during the postwar period', *China Quarterly*, no. 14, pp. 51–64.

*Kuark, Y. T. (1963b), 'North Korea's agricultural development during the postwar period', *China Quarterly*, no. 14, pp. 82–93.

Kuo, L. (1976), *Agriculture in the People's Republic of China*, Praeger, New York.

*Kuznets, S. (1966), *Modern Economic Growth*, Yale University Press, New Haven, Conn.

Kwon, D. Y. (1975), 'North Korea's economy and foreign liabilities', *East Asian Review*, Vol. 2, no. 4.

*Kýn, O. (1975), 'Czechoslovakia', in Höhmann, H.-H., Kaser, M., and Thalheim, K. (eds), *The New Economic Systems of Eastern Europe*, Hurst, London.

*Lampe, J., and Jackson, M. (1982), *Balkan Economic History, 1550–1950*, Indiana University Press, Bloomington, Ind.

Lampert, E. (1965), *Sons against Fathers*, Oxford University Press, London.

*Landes, D. (1969), *The Unbound Prometheus*, Cambridge University Press.

Lane, C. (1978), *Christian Religion in the Soviet Union*, Allen & Unwin, London.

Lane, D. (1976), *The Socialist Industrial State*, Allen & Unwin, London.

Lane, D. (1978), *Politics and Society in the USSR*, Allen & Unwin, London.

Lane, D., and Kolankiewicz, G. (eds) (1973), *Social Groups in Polish Society*, Macmillan, London.

Lang, N. (1975), 'The dialectics of decentralization: economic reform and regional inequality in Yugoslavia', *World Politics*, Vol. 27, pp. 309–35.

Lange, O. (1936–7), 'On the economic theory of socialism', *Review of Economic Studies*, Vol. 4, pp. 53–71, 123–42.

Lardy, N. (1978), *Economic Growth and Distribution in China*, Cambridge University Press.

Lardy, N. (1980), *Regional Growth and Income Distribution*, in Dernberger, R. (ed.), *China's Development Experience*, Harvard University Press, Cambridge, Mass.

Lattimore, O. (1962), *Nomads and Commissars: Mongolia Revisited*, Oxford University Press, London.

*Lazarcik, G. (1974), 'Agricultural output and productivity in Eastern Europe', in Hardt, J. (ed.) *Reorientation and Commercial Relations of the Economies of Eastern Europe*, US Congress Joint Economic Committee, Washington, DC.

Leasure, J., and Lewis, R. (1966), *Population Change in Russia and the USSR*, State College Press, San Diego, Calif.

Leasure, J., and Lewis, R. (1968), 'Internal migration in Russia in the late nineteenth century', *Slavic Review*, Vol. 27, pp. 375–94.

Lebl, A. (1981), 'Energy review: Yugoslavia', *Financial Times*, 30 December 1981.

Le Duan (1965), *On the Socialist Revolution in Vietnam*, 2 vols, Foreign Languages Publishing House, Hanoi.

Le Duan (1971), *The Vietnamese Revolution: Fundamental Problems and Tasks*, International Publishers, New York.

*Lee, C.-S. (1963a), 'Land reform, collectivization and peasants in North Korea', *China Quarterly*, no. 14, pp. 65–81.

Lee, C.-S. (1963b), 'Politics in North Korea: pre Korean War', *China Quarterly*, no. 14, pp. 3–16.

Legget, G. (1981), *The Cheka: Lenin's Political Police*, Oxford University Press.

Lenin, V. (1948T), *Imperialism: The Highest Stage of Capitalism*, Lawrence & Wishart, London.

Lenin, V. (1960–70T), *Collected Works*, 55 vols, Foreign Languages Publishing House, Moscow.

*Lenin, V. (1964T), *The Development of Capitalism in Russia*, 1908 edn, Progress Publishers, Moscow.

Lenin, V. (1968T), *Left-Wing Communism: An Infantile Disorder*, Progress Publishers, Moscow.

Lenin, V. (1969T), *State and Revolution*, Progress Publishers, Moscow.

Lenin, V. (1972T), *On the Development of Heavy Industry and Electrification*, Progress Publishers, Moscow.

*Lenin, V. (1975T), *Selected Works in Three Volumes*, Progress Publishers, Moscow.

Lenin, V. (1976T), *The Agrarian Question and the 'Critics of Marx'*, Progress Publishers, Moscow.

*Lenin, V. (1977T), *The Agrarian Programme of Social Democracy in the First Russian Revolution, 1905–1907*, Progress Publishers, Moscow.

Leontief, W. (1945), 'Scientific and technological research in the USSR', *Slavic Review*, Vol. 4, pp. 70–9.

Leontief, W. (1946), 'Soviet planning: the problem of economic balance', *Russian Review*, Vol. 6, pp. 26–36.

Leontief, W. (1977, 1978), *Essays in Economics*, 2 vols, Blackwell, Oxford.

Leptin, G., and Melzer, M. (1978T), *Economic Reform in East German Industry*, Oxford University Press.

*Leslie, R. F. (ed.) (1980), *The History of Poland since 1863*, Cambridge University Press.

Le Thanth Khoi (1978), *Socialisme et développement au Vietnam*, Presses universitaires de France, Paris.

Lethbridge, H. (1963), *The Peasant and the Communes*, Dragonfly Books, Hong Kong.

Leung, C. (1980), *China's Railway Patterns and National Goals*, Geography Department, University of Chicago.

Levesque, B. (ed.) (1978), *The USSR and the Cuban Revolution*, Praeger, New York.

*Levine, N. (1975), *The Tragic Deception: Marx contra Engels*, Clio Books, Santa Barbara, Calif.

*Lewin, M. (1967), 'Who was the Soviet kulak?', *Soviet Studies*, Vol. 18, pp. 189–212.

*Lewin, M. (1968T), *Russian Peasants and Soviet Power*, Allen & Unwin, London.

Lewis, J. (ed.) (1974), *Peasant Rebellion and Communist Revolution in Asia*, Stanford University Press, Stanford, Calif.

*Lewis, P. (1973), *The Peasantry*, in Lane, D., and Kolankiewicz, G. (eds), *Social Groups in Polish Society*, Macmillan, London.

Lewis, R. (1979), *Science and Industrialization in the USSR*, Macmillan, London.

Leys, S. (1978T), *Chinese Shadows*, Penguin Books, Harmondsworth.

Liang, E. (1981), 'Market accessibility and agricultural development in prewar China', *Economic Development and Cultural Change*, Vol. 30, pp. 77–105.

*Liao Jili (1982T), 'On the question of restructuring China's economic system', in Xue Muqiao (ed.), *Almanac of China's Economy, 1981*, State Council of the People's Republic of China/Ballinger, Cambridge, Mass.

*Liashchenko, P. (1949T), *History of the National Economy of Russia*, Macmillan, London.

Lincoln, W. (1977), *Nikolai Miliutin*, Oriental Research Partners, Mass.

Lipski, W. (1969T), *Agriculture in Poland*, Interpress Publishers, Warsaw.

Lipton, M. (1978), *Why Poor People Stay Poor*, Maurice Temple Smith, London.

Littlejohn, G. (1977), 'Chayanov and the theory of peasant economy', in Hindess, B. (ed.) *Sociological Theories of the Economy*, Macmillan, London.

*Liu, T.-C., and Yeh, K.-C. (1965), *The Economy of the Chinese Mainland*, Princeton University Press, Princeton, NJ.

*Liu, T.-C., and Yeh, K.-C. (1973), 'Chinese and other Asian economies: a quantitative evaluation', *American Economic Review*, Papers and proceedings, Vol. 63, pp. 215–23.

Lockett, M. (1983), 'Enterprise management', in Feuchtwang, S., and Hussain, A. (eds), *The Chinese Economic Reforms*, Croom Helm, London.

Lomax, Bill (1976), *Hungary 1956*, Allison & Busby, London.

*Lorenz, C. (1982), 'Manufacturing: a modest role', *Financial Times*, 23 November 1982.

Lorimer, F. (1946), *The Population of the Soviet Union*, League of Nations, Geneva.

Lucey, D., and Kaldor, D. (1969), *Rural Industrialization*, Geoffrey Chapman, London.

McAlister, J., and Mus, P. (1970), *The Vietnamese and their Revolution*, Harper Torchbooks, New York.

*McAuley, A. (1979), *Economic Welfare in the Soviet Union*, Allen & Unwin, London.

*McCormack, G., and Gittings, J. (eds) (1977), *Crisis in Korea*, Spokesman Books, Nottingham.

McCune, S. (1956), *Korea's Heritage*, C. E. Tuttle, Vermont.

MacEwan, A. (1981), *Revolution and Economic Development in Cuba*, Macmillan, London.

McGrew, R. (1965), *Russia and the Cholera*, Madison & Milwaukee, New York.

McLellan, D. (1971), *The Thought of Karl Marx*, Macmillan, London.

McLellan, D. (1977), *Engels*, Collins/Fontana Modern Masters, London.

*McMillen, D. (1979), *Communist Power and Policy in Xinjiang, 1949–77*, Dawson, Kent.

Maddison, A. (1969), *Economic Growth in Japan and the USSR*, Allen & Unwin, London.

Maddison, A. (1971), *Class Structure and Economic Growth: India and Pakistan*, Allen & Unwin, London.

Madgearu, V. (1930), *Romania's New Economic Policy*, London.

Madison, B. (1968), *Social Welfare in the Soviet Union*, Stanford University Press, Stanford, Calif.

Maenchen-Helfen, D., and Nicolaievsky, B. (1976T), *Karl Marx*, Penguin Books, Harmondsworth.

*Ma Hong (1982T), 'On China's new strategy for economic development', in Xue Muqiao (ed.), *Almanac of China's Economy, 1981*, State Council of the People's Republic of China/Ballinger, Cambridge, Mass.

Makarov, N. P. (1926), *Organizatsiya selskogo khoziaistva*, Moscow.

Male, D. (1971), *Russian Peasant Organization before Collectivization*, Cambridge University Press.

Malefakis, E. (1970), *Agrarian Reform and Peasant Revolution in Spain*, Yale University Press, New Haven, Conn.

Malet, M. (1983), *Nestor Makhno in the Russian Civil War*, Macmillan, London.

Mao Tse-tung (1955T), *Selected Works*, 5 vols, International Publishers, New York.

Mao Tse-tung (1961–5T), *Selected Works*, 4 vols, Foreign Languages Press, Peking.

Mao Tse-tung (1969T), *The Political Thought of Mao Tse-tung*, ed. S. Schram, Penguin Books, Harmondsworth.

Mao Tse-tung (1970T), *Mao Papers*, ed. J. Chen, Oxford University Press, London.

Mao Tse-tung (1974T), *Mao Tse-tung Unrehearsed*, ed. S. Schram, Penguin Books, Harmondsworth.

Mao Tse-tung (1977T), *A Critique of Soviet Economics*, Monthly Review Press, New York.

Marcuse, H. (1958), *Soviet Marxism: A Critical Analysis*, Routledge & Kegan Paul, London.

*Marmullaku, R. (1975), *Albania and the Albanians*, Hurst, London.

Martin, F. (1964), 'The information effect of economic planning', *Canadian Journal of Economics and Political Science*, Vol. 30, pp. 328–42.

Martinez-Alier, J. (1971), *Labourers and Landowners in Southern Spain*, Allen & Unwin, London.

Marx, K. (1852), *The Eighteenth Brumaire of Louis Bonaparte*, English trans., Allen & Unwin, 1926, and Progress Publishers, Moscow, 1977.

*Marx, K. (1867, 1976T), *Capital*, Penguin Books, Harmondsworth, Vol. 1.

Marx, K. (1969T), *Theories of Surplus Value*, Progress Publishers, Moscow, Vol. 1.

Marx, K., and Engels, F. (1848), *The Communist Manifesto*; English trans., London, 1888.

*Marx, K., and Engels, F. (1934T), *Correspondence, 1846–1895*, London.

*Marx, K., and Engels, F. (1935), *Sochineniya*, Progress Publishers, Moscow, Vol. 27.

*Marx, K., and Engels, F. (1950–1T), *Selected Works*, 2 vols, Progress Publishers, Moscow.

Marx, K., and Engels, F. (1952T), *The Russian Menace to Europe*, The Free Press, Glencoe, Ill.

Marx, K., and Engels, F. (1960), *Werke*, Dietz Verlag, Berlin, Vol. 8.

*Marx, K., and Engels, F. (1970T), *Selected Works*, Progress Publishers, Moscow, Vol. 3.

Massell, G. (1974), *The Surrogate Proletariat: Moslem Women and Revolutionary Strategies in Soviet Central Asia*, Princeton University Press, Princeton, NJ.

Mathieson, R. (1975), *The Soviet Union*, Heinemann, London.

Matthews, H. (1970), *Castro*, Penguin Books, Harmondsworth.

Matthews, M. (1978), *Privilege in the Soviet Union*, Allen & Unwin, London.

Mavor, J. (1925), *An Economic History of Russia*, 2 vols, Dutton, New York, and Dent, London.

Maxwell, N. (ed.) (1979), *China's Road to Development*, Pergamon, Oxford.

Mayergoyz, I. M. (ed.) (1978), *Ekonomicheskaya geografiya zarubezhnikh sotsialisticheskikh stran*, Moscow University Press.

Medici, G. (1952), *Land Property and Land Tenure in Italy*, Edizione Agricole, Bologna.

Medlin, W., Carpenter, F., and Cave, W. (1971), *Education and Development in Central Asia*, E. J. Brill, Leiden.

Medvedev, R. (1979T), *On Stalin and Stalinism*, Oxford University Press.

Mellor, R. (1971), *Comecon: Challenge to the West*, Van Nostrand, New York.

Mellor, R. (1975), *Eastern Europe: A Geography of the Comecon Countries*, Macmillan, London.

*Mendels, F. (1972), 'Proto-industrialization', *Journal of Economic History*, Vol. 32, pp. 241–61.

Mesa-Lago, C. (1968), *The Labour Sector and Socialist Distribution in Cuba*, Praeger, New York.

Mesa-Lago, C. (1978), *Cuba in the 1970s*, New Mexico University Press, Albuquerque, NM.

*Mesa-Lago, C. (1982), 'The economy', in Domínguez, J. (ed.) *Cuba*, Sage, Beverly Hills, Calif.

Metzer, J. (1974), 'Railroad development and market integration: the case of tsarist Russia', *Journal of Economic History*, Vol. 34, pp. 529–91.

Mikhailovsky, N. (1888), *Sochineniya*, St Petersburg, Vol. 2.

Mikhailovsky, N. (1897), *Sochineniya*, St Petersburg, Vol. 4.

Mill, J. S. (1891), *Principles of Political Economy*, 1891 edn, London.

Millar, J. R. (1970), 'A reformulation of A. V. Chayanov's theory of peasant economy', *Economic Development and Cultural Change*, Vol. 18, pp. 219–29.

*Millar, J. R. (1970–1), 'Soviet rapid development and the agricultural surplus hypothesis', *Soviet Studies*, Vol. 22, pp. 77–93.

*Millar, J. R. (ed.) (1971), *The Soviet Rural Community*, University of Illinois Press, Urbana, Ill.

Millar, J. R. (1971–2), 'The agricultural surplus hypothesis: reply to Alec Nove', *Soviet Studies*, Vol. 23, pp. 302–6.

Millar, J. R. (1977), 'Prospects for Soviet agriculture', *Problems of Communism*, Vol. 26, no. 3, pp. 1–16.

Miller, M. (1926), *The Economic Development of Russia, 1905–14*, P. S. King, London.

Milward, A., and Saul, S. B. (1977), *The Development of the Economies of Continental Europe, 1850–1914*, Allen & Unwin, London.

Mintz, S. (1973), 'A note on the definition of peasantries', *Journal of Peasant Studies*, Vol. 1, pp. 91–106.

Mintz, S. (1977–8), 'A note on Unseem's "Peasant involvement in the Cuban revolution"', *Journal of Peasant Studies*, Vol. 5, pp. 482–4.

*Mitchell, B. (1975), *European Historical Statistics*, Macmillan, London.

Mitrany, D. (1930), *Land and Peasant in Romania*, Yale University Press, New Haven, Conn.

Mitrany, D. (1951), *Marx against the Peasant*, University of North Carolina Press, Chapel Hill, NC.

Mokyr, J. (1974), 'The Industrial Revolution in the low countries', *Journal of Economic History*, Vol. 34, pp. 365–91.

Molnar, M. (1971T), *Budapest 1956: A History of the Hungarian Revolution*, Allen & Unwin, London.

Mongolian People's Republic (1976T), *History of the Mongolian People's Republic*, Harvard University Press, Cambridge, Mass.

Moore, B. (1973), *Social Origins of Dictatorship and Democracy*, Penguin Books, Harmondsworth.

*Moore, W. (1945), *Economic Demography of Southern and Eastern Europe*, Geneva.

Moorsteen, R., and Powell, R. (1966), *The Soviet Capital Stock, 1928–1962*, Irwin, Homewood, Ill.

Morgan, O. (ed.) (1933), *Agricultural Systems of Middle Europe*, Macmillan, New York.

Morozov, V. (1977T), *Soviet Agriculture*, Progress Publishers, Moscow.

Morris, M. D. (1963), 'Towards a reinterpretation of nineteenth century Indian economic history', *Journal of Economic History*.

Morris, M. D. (1968), 'Trends and tendencies in Indian history', *Indian Economic and Social History Review*, Vol. 5, pp. 319–88.

*Mulhall, M. G. (1896), *Industries and Wealth of Nations*, London.

*Mulhall, M. G. (1898), *The Dictionary of Statistics*, 4th edn, London.

*Murphey, R. (1977), *The Outsiders: Western Experience in India and China*, University of Michigan Press, Ann Arbor, Mich.

Murray, R., White, C., and White, G. (eds) (1981), *Socialist Transformation and Development in the Third World*, Harvester Press, Brighton.

Myers, R. (1969), 'Taiwan', in Shand, T. (ed.), *Agricultural Development in Asia*, Australian National University Press, Canberra.

Myers, R. (1970), *The Chinese Peasant Economy*, Harvard University Press, Cambridge, Mass.

Myers, R. (1975), 'Cooperation in traditional agriculture', in Perkins, D. (ed.), *China's Modern Economy in Historical Perspective*, Stanford University Press, Stanford, Calif.

Myrdal, G. (1968), *Asian Drama*, 3 vols, Random House, New York.

Naby, E. (1980), 'The ethnic factor in Soviet–Afghan relations', *Asian Survey*, May 1980, pp. 237–59.

Nadkarni, M. (1978), *Socialist Agricultural Price Policy*, People's Publishing House, Delhi.

Nakamura, J. (1966), *Agricultural Production and the Economic Development of Japan*, Princeton University Press, Princeton, NJ.

*Nanda, B. (1974), *Gokhale, Gandhi and the Nehrus*, Allen & Unwin, London.

Narkiewicz, O. (1976), *The Green Flag*, Croom Helm, London.

*NATO (1979), *Regional Development in the USSR: Colloquium*, NATO, Brussels.

Needham, J. (1954–83), *Science and Civilization in China*, 5 vols, Cambridge University Press.

*Newman, P. (1965), *Cuba before Castro: An Economic Appraisal*, Prentice-Hall, India.

Nolan, P. (1976), 'Collectivization in China: some comparisons with the USSR', *Journal of Peasant Studies*, Vol. 3, no. 2.

Nolan, P., and White, G. (1979), 'Socialist development and rural inequality', *Journal of Peasant Studies*, Vol. 7, pp. 3–48.

North Korea (1961), *Facts about Korea*, Foreign Languages Publishing House, Pyongyang.

North Korea (1977T), *The Outline of Korean History*, Foreign Languages Publishing House, Pyongyang.

*Nou, J. (1967), *Studies in the Development of Agricultural Economics in Europe*, Almquist & Wiksells, Uppsala.

Nove, A. (1959), *Communist Economic Strategy*, National Planning Association, Washington, DC.

Nove, A. (1964), *Was Stalin Really Necessary?*, Allen & Unwin, London.

Nove, A. (1970–1), 'The agricultural surplus hypothesis', *Soviet Studies*, Vol. 22, pp. 394–401.

*Nove, A. (1972), *An Economic History of the USSR*, Penguin Books, Harmondsworth.

*Nove, A. (1977), *The Soviet Economic System*, Allen & Unwin, London.

Nove, A. (1978), 'Agriculture', in Kaser, M., and Brown, A. (eds), *The Soviet Union since the Fall of Khrushchev*, Macmillan, London.

*Nove, A. (1979), *Political Economy and Soviet Socialism*, Allen & Unwin, London.

*Nove, A. (1980), 'Problems and prospects of the Soviet economy, *New Left Review*, no. 119, pp. 3–19.

*Nove, A. (1983), *The Economics of Feasible Socialism*, Allen & Unwin, London.

Nove, A., and Newth, J. (1967), *The Soviet Middle East*, Allen & Unwin, London.

Nove, A., and Nuti, D. M. (eds) (1972), *Socialist Economics*, Penguin Books, Harmondsworth.

*Nuti, D. M. (1981), 'Industrial enterprises in Poland, 1973–1980', in Jeffries, I. (ed.), *The Industrial Enterprise in Eastern Europe*, Praeger, New York.

Nyerere, J. (1968), *Freedom and Socialism*, Oxford University Press, London.

*OECD (1969), *Agricultural Development in Southern Europe*, OECD, Paris.

OECD (1973), *Agricultural Policy in Yugoslavia*, OECD, Paris.

Ofer, G. (1973), *The Service Sector in Soviet Economic Growth*, Harvard University Press, Cambridge, Mass.

*Ogura, T. (ed.) (1968), *Agricultural Development in Modern Japan*, Fuji, Tokyo.

*O'Hagan, J. P. (ed.) (1978), *Growth and Adjustment in National Agricultures*, Macmillan, London.

Ohkawa, K., Johnston, B., and Kaneda, H. (eds) (1970), *Agriculture and Economic Growth*, Princeton University Press, Princeton, NJ.

Oldham, C. (1973), 'Science and technology policies', in Oksenberg, M. (ed.), *China's Development Experience*, Praeger, New York.

Olsson, C.-A. (1968), 'Swedish agriculture', *Economy and History*, Vol. 11, pp. 67–107.

*Oshima, H. (1961), 'A new estimate of the national income and product of Cuba in 1953', *Food Research Institute Studies*, Vol. 2, no. 3.

Oshima, H. (1965), 'Meiji fiscal policy', in Lockwood, W. (ed.), *The State and Economic Enterprise in Japan*, Princeton University Press, Princeton, NJ.

*Osmova, M., and Faminsky, I. (eds) (1980), *Ekonomika zarubezhnikh stran: Sotsialisticheskie stran*, High School Press, Moscow.

*Owen, L. (1963), *The Russian Peasant Movement, 1906–1917*, Russell, New York.

Parker, W. (1968), *An Historical Geography of Russia*, University of London Press.

Parsons, K., Penn, R., and Raup, P. (eds) (1951), *Land Tenure*, University of Wisconsin Press, Madison, Wis.

Pasquier, A. (1961), *L'Economie du Portugal*, Paris.

Patnaik, U. (1978–9), 'Neo-populism and Marxism', *Journal of Peasant Studies*, Vol. 6, pp. 376–420.

Pavlovsky, G. (1930), *Agricultural Russia on the Eve of the Revolution*, Routledge & Kegan Paul, London.

Pavlowitch, S. K. (1971), *Yugoslavia*, Praeger, New York.

Payne, S. (1973), *History of Spain and Portugal*, University of Wisconsin Press, Madison, Wis., Vol. 2.

Perkins, D. (1969), *Agricultural Development in China, 1368–1968*, Edinburgh University Press.

*Perkins, D. (ed.) (1975), *China's Modern Economy in Historical Perspective*, Stanford University Press, Stanford, Calif.

Perkins, D. (ed.) (1977), *Rural Small-Scale Industry in the People's Republic of China*, University of California Press, Berkeley, Calif.

*Perrie, M. (1976), *The Agrarian Policy of the Russian Socialist Revolutionary Party*, Cambridge University Press.

*Pethybridge, R. (1974), *The Social Prelude to Stalinism*, Macmillan, London.

Pichon Loh (ed.) (1965), *The Kuomintang Debacle of 1949*, D. C. Heath, Lexington, Mass.

Pintner, W. M. (1953), 'Initial problems in the Soviet economic development of Central Asia', *Journal of the Royal Central Asian Society*, Vol. 40, pp. 284–97.

Pipes, R. (1957), *The Formation of the Soviet Union*, Harvard University Press, Cambridge, Mass.

Pipes, R. (1960), 'Russian Marxism and its populist background', *Russian Review*, Vol. 19, pp. 316–37.

Pipes, R. (1964), 'Narodnichestvo: a semantic inquiry', *Slavic Review*, Vol. 23, pp. 441–58.

Pisarëv, D. (1955–6), *Sochineniya*, 4 vols, Moscow.

Planning Commission, Government of India (1958), *The New India*, Macmillan, London.

Planning Commission, Government of India (1966), *Material and Financial Balances*, New Delhi.

Plekhanov, G. (1974T), *Selected Philosophical Works*, Progress Publishers, Moscow, Vol. 1.

Plotnikov, N. (1969), 'Transformation of the Uzbek Republic', in Robinson, E. A. G. (ed.), *Backward Areas in Advanced Countries*, Macmillan, London.

Poland (1976), *Poland 1976: Statistical Data*, Central Statistical Office, Warsaw.

Polish Academy of Sciences (1974T), *Polska 2000*, Warsaw.

*Pollitt, B. (1976–7), 'Problems in enumerating the "peasantry" in Cuba', *Journal of Peasant Studies*, Vol. 4, pp. 162–80.

Pollo, S., and Puto, A. (1981T), *History of Albania*, Routledge & Kegan Paul, London.

Polonsky, A. (1975), *The Little Dictators*, Routledge & Kegan Paul, London.

*Pomfret, J. (1930), *The Struggle for Land in Ireland, 1800–1923*, Princeton University Press, Princeton, NJ.

Poppinga, O.-H. (1975T), 'North Vietnam', in Bergmann, T., *Farm Policies in Socialist Countries*, D. C. Heath, Lexington, Mass.

*Post, J. (1976), 'Famine, mortality and disease', *Economic History Review*, Vol. 29, pp. 14–37.

Powell, D. (1977), 'Labour turnover in the Soviet Union', *Slavic Review*, Vol. 36, pp. 268–85.

Preobrazhensky, E. (1922, 1973T), *From NEP to Socialism*, New Park Publications, London.

Preobrazhensky, E. (1922T), *The ABC of Communism*, London, pt II.

Preobrazhensky, E. (1925–7), 'Economic notes'; trans. in Preobrazhensky, E., *Crisis of Soviet Industrialization*, ed. D. Filtzer, M. E. Sharpe, New York.

*Preobrazhensky, E. (1926, 1965T), *The New Economics*, Oxford University Press, London.

*Preobrazhensky, E. (1979T), *Crisis of Soviet Industrialization*, ed. D. Filtzer, M. E. Sharpe, New York.

Price, R. (1977), *Marx and Education in Russia and China*, Croom Helm, London.

Price, R. (1979), *Education in Modern China*, Routledge & Kegan Paul, London.

Prout, C. (1983), *Market Socialism in Yugoslavia*, Oxford University Press.

Qi Wen (1979T), *China: A General Survey*, Foreign Languages Press, Peking.

*Radice, H. (1981), 'The state enterprise in Hungary', in Jeffries, I. (ed.), *The Industrial Enterprise in Eastern Europe*, Praeger, New York.

Radkey, O. (1955), 'Chernov and agrarian socialism before 1918', in Simmons, E. J. (ed.), *Continuity and Change in Russian and Soviet Thought*, Harvard University Press, Cambridge, Mass.

Radkey, O. (1958), *The Agrarian Foes of Bolshevism*, Columbia University Press, New York.

Radkey, O. (1963), *The Sickle under the Hammer*, Columbia University Press, New York.

Radkey, O. (1976), *The Unknown Civil War*, Hoover Institution, Stanford, Calif.

Rashin, A. (1958), *Formirovaniye rabochego klassa Rossii*, Sotsekgiz, Moscow.

*Rawski, E. (1979), *Education and Popular Literacy in Ching China*, University of Michigan Press, Ann Arbor, Mich.

*Rawski, T. (1979), *Economic Growth and Employment in China*, Oxford University Press.

Rawski, T. (1980), *China's Transition to Industrialism*, University of Michigan Press, Ann Arbor, Mich.

Riazanov, D. (ed.) (1924), *Arkhiv K. Marksa i F. Engelsa*, Moscow, Vol. 1.

Rifkin, S., and Paterson, E. (1974), *Health Care in China*, Christian Medical Commission, Geneva.

Rimlinger, G. (1971), *Welfare Policy and Industrialization*, Wiley, London.

Risquet, J. (1970), 'Sobre problemas de duerza de trabajo y productividad', *Granma*, 1 August 1970.

Ritter, A. (1974), *The Economic Development of Revolutionary Cuba*, Praeger, New York.

*Rizaev, G. (1978), *Sotsialisticheskoe selskoye khoziaistvo Uzbekistana*, Izdatelstvo 'Uzbekistan', Tashkent.

Robbins, R. G. (1976), *Famine in Russia, 1891–1892*, Columbia University Press, New York.

Roberts, H. (1951), *Romania: Political Problems of an Agrarian State*, Yale University Press, New Haven, Conn.

Robinson, G. T. (1932), *Rural Russia under the Old Regime*, Longman, London.

Robinson, J. (1964), 'Chinese agricultural communes', *Co-Existence* (May).

Robinson, J. (1965), 'The Korean miracle', *Monthly Review*, January 1965.

Robinson, J. (1969), *The Cultural Revolution in China*, Penguin Books, Harmondsworth.

Robinson, J. (1976), *Economic Management in China*, Anglo-Chinese Educational Institute, London.

*Rosenberg, W. (1975), 'Economic comparison of North and South Korea', *Journal of Contemporary Asia*, Vol. 5, pp. 178–202.

*Rosovsky, H., and Ohkawa, K. (1961), 'Indigenous components in the modern Japanese economy', *Economic Development and Cultural Change*, Vol. 9, pp. 476–501.

Rothschild, J. (1974), *East Central Europe between the Wars*, University of Washington Press, Washington, DC.

Roubquain, C. (1944), *Economic Development of French Indochina*, Oxford University Press, London.

Rubel, M. (1947), 'Karl Marx et le socialisme populiste russe', *La revue socialiste* (May).

Rubinow, I. (1906), *Russia's Wheat Surplus*, US Department of Agriculture, Bureau of Statistics, B.42, Washington, DC.

Rudolph, R. (1976), *Banking and Industrialization in Austria–Hungary*, Cambridge University Press.

*Rupen, R. (1964), *Mongols of the Twentieth Century*, Indiana University Press, Bloomington, Ind., Vol. 1.

*Rupen, R. (1979), *How Mongolia Is Really Ruled*, Hoover Institution, Stanford, Calif.

*Ryan, T. M. (1978), *The Organization of Soviet Medical Care*, Blackwell & Robertson, Oxford and London.

Sabsovich, L. (1929), *SSSR cherez 15 let*, Moscow.

Samli, A. (1978), *Marketing and Distribution Systems in Eastern Europe*, Praeger, New York.

Sanders, A. (1968), *The People's Republic of Mongolia*, Oxford University Press, London.

Sanderson, F. (1978), *Japan's Food Prospects and Policies*, Brookings Institute, Washington, DC

Scalapino, R., and Lee, C.-S. (1972), *Communism in Korea*, 2 vols, University of California Press, Berkeley, Calif.

Schapiro, L. (1970), *The Communist Party of the Soviet Union*, Methuen, London.

Schapiro, L., and Reddaway, P. (eds) (1967), *Lenin*, Pall Mall Press, London.

Schmidt, C. (1938), *The Plough and the Sword: Land, Labour and Property in Italy*, Columbia University Press, New York.

*Schnitzler, J. (1856–69), *L'Empire des tsars*, 4 vols, Paris.

Schopflin, G. (ed.) (1971), *The Soviet Union and Eastern Europe*, Blond & Briggs, London.

Schram, S. (1967), *Mao Tse-tung*, Penguin Books, Harmondsworth.

Seers, D. (ed.) (1964), *Cuba: The Economic and Social Revolution*, University of North Carolina Press, Chapel Hill, NC.

Seers, D. (1974), 'Cuba', in World Bank, *Redistribution with Growth*, IDS/Oxford University Press, London.

Seton-Watson, H. (1952), *The Decline of Imperial Russia*, Methuen, London.

Shabad, T. (1969), *Basic Industrial Resources of the USSR*, Columbia University Press, New York.

Shaffer, H. (ed.) (1977), *Soviet Agriculture*, Praeger, New York.

*Shand, T. (ed.) (1969), *Agricultural Development in Asia*, Australian National University Press, Canberra.

Shanin, T. (1971a), 'Socio-economic mobility and the rural history of Russia, 1905–1930', *Soviet Studies*, Vol. 23, pp. 222–35.

Shanin, T. (ed.) (1971b), *Peasants and Peasant Societies*, Penguin Books, Harmondsworth.

Shanin, T. (1972), *The Awkward Class*, Clarendon Press, Oxford.

*Shanin, T. (1973–4), 'The nature and logic of peasant economy', *Journal of Peasant Studies*, Vol. 1, pp. 62–80, 186–206.

Shanin, T. (1981), 'Marx and the peasant commune', *History Workshop*, no. 12, pp. 108–28.

Shanks, M. (1973), *The Quest for Growth*, Macmillan, London.

*Shen, T. (1951), *Agricultural Resources of China*, Cornell University Press, Ithaca, NY.

Shirokov, G. (1973T), *Industrialization of India*, Progress Publishers, Moscow.

Short, P. (1982), *The Dragon and the Bear*, Hodder & Stoughton, London.

Sidhu, B. S. (1976), *Land Reform, Welfare and Economic Growth*, Vora, Bombay.

Siebel, D. (1975), 'Planning in France', in Bornstein, M. (ed.), *Economic Planning*, Harvard University Press, Cambridge, Mass.

Sigerist, H. (1937, 1947), *Socialized Medicine in the Soviet Union*, Gollancz, London.

Sik, O. (1967T), *Plan and Market under Socialism*, Academia, Prague.

Sik, O. (1971T), 'Economic impact of Stalinism', *Problems of Communism*, Vol. 20, no. 3, pp. 1–10.

Sik, O. (1972T), *Czechoslovakia: The Bureaucratic Economy*, International Arts and Sciences Press, White Plains, NY.

Sik, O. (1976T), *The Third Way*, Wildwood House, London.

Simkovitsch, V. (1906), 'The Russian peasant and autocracy', *Political Science Quarterly*, Vol. 21, pp. 569–95.

Simmons, E. J. (ed.) (1955), *Continuity and Change in Russian and Soviet Thought*, Harvard University Press, Cambridge, Mass.

Simms, J. (1977), 'The crisis in Russian agriculture at the end of the 19th century', *Slavic Review*, Vol. 36, pp. 371–98.

Simms, J. (1982), 'The crop failure of 1891', *Slavic Review*, Vol. 41, pp. 236–50.

Singleton, F. (1972), 'The roots of discord in Yugoslavia', *World Today*, April 1972, pp. 170–80.

Singleton, F. (1973), 'Yugoslavia and market socialism', *World Today*, April 1973, pp. 160–8.

*Singleton, F. (1976), *Twentieth Century Yugoslavia*, Macmillan, London.

*Singleton, F., and Carter, B. (1982), *The Economy of Yugoslavia*, Croom Helm, London.

Sinha, R. (1974), 'Chinese economic performance', *World Today*, January 1974, pp. 33–42.

*Sirc, L. (1979), *The Yugoslav Economy under Self-Management*, Macmillan, London.

Sirc, L. (1981), 'The industrial enterprise in Yugoslavia', in Jeffries, I. (ed.), *The Industrial Enterprise in Eastern Europe*, Praeger, New York.

Skilling, G. (1976), *Czechoslovakia's Interrupted Revolution*, Princeton University Press, Princeton, NJ.

*Skrubbeltrang, F. (1953), *Agricultural Development and Rural Reform in Denmark*, FAO, Rome.

Smith, A. (1983), *The Planned Economies of Eastern Europe*, Croom Helm, London.

*Smith, C. (1982), 'Why Japan still thinks small', *Financial Times*, 26 April 1982.

*Smith, R. E. F. (ed.) (1977), *The Russian Peasant*, Frank Cass, London.

*Smith, T. C. (1969), 'Family farm by-employments in preindustrial Japan', *Journal of Economic History*, Vol. 29, pp. 687–715.

Snow, E. (1972), *Red Star over China*, Penguin Books, Harmondsworth.

Snow, E. (1974), *China's Long Revolution*, Penguin Books, Harmondsworth.

Sokolnikov, G. (1922), *Gosudarstvennyi kapitalism i Novaya Finansovaya Politika*, Moscow.

*Sokolnikov, G. (ed.) (1931T), *Soviet Policy in Public Finance*, Stanford University Press, Stanford, Calif.

Solodovnikov, V., and Bogoslovsky, V. (1975T), *Non-Capitalist Development*, Progress Publishers, Moscow.

*Solomon, S. G. (1977), *The Soviet Agrarian Debate, 1923–1929*, Westview Press, Boulder, Colo.

Solomon, S. G. (1978), 'Rural scholars and cultural revolution', in Fitzpatrick, S. (ed.), *Cultural Revolution in Soviet Russia, 1928–31*, Indiana University Press, Bloomington, Ind.

Solzhenitsyn, A. (1974–6T), *The Gulag Archipelago*, 3 vols, Collins/Fontana, London.

*Spulber, N. (ed.) (1964T), *Foundations of Soviet Strategy for Economic Growth: Selected Soviet Essays, 1924–1930*, Indiana University Press, Bloomington, Ind.

*Stalin, J. (1952–5T), *Works*, 13 vols, Foreign Languages Publishing House, Moscow.

Stalin, J. (1973T), *The Essential Stalin*, Croom Helm, London.

*Stanis, V. (1976T), *The Socialist Transformation of Agriculture*, Progress Publishers, Moscow.

Starr, S. (1978), 'Visionary town planning', in Fitzpatrick, S. (ed.), *Cultural Revolution in Soviet Russia, 1928–31*, Indiana University Press, Bloomington, Ind.

Stavis, B. (1978), *The Politics of Agricultural Mechanization in China*, Cornell University Press, Ithaca, NY.

Stepniak, S. (S. Kravchinsky) (1888), *The Russian Peasantry*, London, New York, 1905.

*Stipetić, V. (1975T), *Yugoslavia's Agriculture, 1945–1975*, Kommunist, Belgrade.

Strauss, E. (1969), *Soviet Agriculture in Perspective*, Praeger, New York.

Strumilin, S. G. (1928), *Ocherki sovetskoi ekonomiki*, Gosplan, Moscow.

*Strumilin, S. G. (1962T), 'Economics of education in the USSR', *International Social Science Journal*, Vol. 14, pp. 633–46.

Stuart, R. (1972), *The Collective Farm in Soviet Agriculture*, D. C. Heath, Lexington, Mass.

*Suh, S.-C. (1978), *Growth and Structural Changes in the Korean Economy, 1910–40*, Harvard University Press, Cambridge, Mass.

Sun Yat-sen (1927T), *San Min Chu I. The Three Principles of the People*, Commercial Press, Shanghai.

Sutton, A. (1968–72), *Western Technology and Soviet Economic Development*, 3 vols, Stanford University Press, Stanford, Calif.

Svennilson, I. (1954), *Growth and Stagnation in the European Economy*, ECE, Geneva.

*Swamy, S. (1973), *Economic Growth in China and India, 1952–1970*, University of Chicago Press.

Sweezy, P., and Huberman, L. (1969), *Socialism in Cuba*, Monthly Review Press, New York.

Symons, L. (1972), *Russian Agriculture*, G. Bell, London.

Symons, L., and White, C. (1975), *Russian Transport*, G. Bell, London.

Taira, K. (1971), 'Education and literacy in Meiji Japan', *Explorations in Economic History*.

Taiwan (1978), *Taiwan Statistical Data Book*, Taipei.

Tanzania (1969), *Second Five-Year Plan, 1969–1974*, 4 vols, Dar es Salaam.

Tanzania (1974–5), *Economic Survey*, Dar es Salaam.

Tawney, R. H. (1932), *Land and Labour in China*, Allen & Unwin, London; reissued, 1964.

Taylor, F. W. (1929), 'Guidance of production in a socialist state', *American Economic Review*, Vol. 19, pp. 1–8.

*Tegoborski, M. L. de (1855T), *Commentaries on the Productive Forces of Russia*, 2 vols, London.

*Tekiner, S. (1967), 'Sinkiang in the Sino-Soviet conflict', *Bulletin of the Institute for Study of the Soviet Union*, Vol. 14, pp. 9–16.

Tendulkar, D. (1960–3), *Mahatma*, 8 vols, Government of India, New Delhi.

Tep Youth (1951), 'Land tenure in Cambodia', in Parsons, K., Penn, R., and Raup, P. (eds), *Land Tenure*, University of Wisconsin Press, Madison, Wis.

Textor, L. (1923), *Land Reform in Czechoslovakia*, Allen & Unwin, London.

Theriot, L., and Matheson, J. (1979), 'Soviet economic relations with non-European CMEA: Cuba, Vietnam and Mongolia', in Hardt, J. (ed.), *The Soviet Economy in a Time of Change*, US Congress Joint Economic Committee, Washington, DC.

*Thomas, H. (1971), *Cuba*, Eyre & Spottiswoode, London.

Thorner, D. (1965), 'A post-Marxian theory of peasant economy: the school of A. V. Chayanov', *Economic and Political Weekly* (Bombay).

*Thorner, D. (1966), 'Chayanov's concept of peasant economy', intro. to Chayanov, A., *The Theory of Peasant Economy*, Irwin, Homewood, Ill.

Tiltman, H. (1934), *Peasant Europe*, Jarrolds, London.

Timoshenko, V. (1932), *Agricultural Russia and the Wheat Problem*, Stanford University Press, Stanford, Calif.

Timoshenko, V. (1953), 'Agricultural resources', in Bergson, A. (ed.), *Soviet Economic Growth*, Row Peterson, New York.

*Tocqueville, A. de (1856, 1856T), *L'Ancien Régime et la Révolution*, Paris, London.

Tolstoy, L. (1900T), *The Slavery of Our Time*, London.

Tolstoy, L. (1967T), *Tolstoy on Education*, University of Chicago Press.

Tomasevich, J. (1955), *Peasants, Politics and Economic Change in Jugoslavia*, Stanford University Press, Stanford, Calif.

Tomiak, J. (1972), *The Soviet Union*, World Education series, David & Charles, Newton Abbot.

Toye, H. (1968), *Laos*, Oxford University Press, London.

Trebilcock, C. (1981), *Industrialization of the Continental Powers*, Longman, London.

Tregar, T. (1965), *A Geography of China*, University of London Press.

Treml, V. (1975), 'Alcohol in the USSR', *Soviet Studies*, Vol. 27, pp. 161–77.

Trotsky, L. (1904), *Nashi politicheskye zadachi*, Geneva.

*Trotsky, L. (1906, 1962T), *Results and Perspectives*, New Park Publications, London.

Trotsky, L. (1909, 1922), *1905*, Moscow; English trans., Penguin Books, Harmondsworth, 1973.

Trotsky, L. (1919–20, 1961T), *Terrorism and Communism*, University of Michigan Press, Ann Arbor, Mich.

*Trotsky, L. (1923, 1965T), *The New Course*, University of Michigan Press, Ann Arbor, Mich.

*Trotsky, L. (1926T), *Toward Socialism or Capitalism?*, International Publishers, New York.

*Trotsky, L. (1928T), *The Real Situation in Russia*, New York.

Trotsky, L. (1930, 1962T), *The Permanent Revolution*, New Park Publications, London.

Trotsky, L. (1931T), *Problems of the Development of the USSR*, Militant Press, New York.

*Trotsky, L. (1937), *The Revolution Betrayed*, New York; reprinted, Pathfinder Press, New York, 1972.

*Trotsky, L. (1945T, 1953T), *First Five Years of the Communist International*, 2 vols, Pioneer Publishers, New York.

Trotsky, L. (1975T), *My Life*, Penguin Books, Harmondsworth.

*Trotsky, L. (1980T), *The Challenge of the Left Opposition, 1926–27*, Pathfinder Press, New York.

Trouton, R. (1952), *Peasant Renaissance in Yugoslavia, 1900–1950*, Routledge & Kegan Paul, London.

Tsang, C.-S. (1968), *Society, Schools and Progress in China*, Pergamon, Oxford.

Tucker, R. (ed.) (1977), *Stalinism: Essays in Interpretation*, W. Norton, New York.

Turcan, J. (1977), 'Observations on retail distribution in Poland', *Soviet Studies*, Vol. 29, pp. 128–36.

Turkmenistan (1963), *Narodnoye khoziaistvo Turkmenskoy SSR*, Ashkabad.

Turley, W. (ed.) (1980), *Vietnamese Communism in Comparative Perspective*, Westview Press, Boulder, Colo.

Turpin, W. (1977), *Soviet Foreign Trade*, D. C. Heath (Lexington Books), Lexington, Mass.

Tuzmahamedov, R. (1973T), *How the National Question Was Solved in Soviet Central Asia*, Progress Publishers, Moscow.

Unseem, B. (1977–8), 'Peasant involvement in the Cuban revolution', *Journal of Peasant Studies*, Vol. 5, pp. 99–111.

USSR (1957), *Dostizheniya sovetskoy vlasti za sorok let v tsifrakh*, Statistika, Moscow.

USSR (1960T), *Outline History of the USSR*, Foreign Languages Publishing House, Moscow.

USSR (1972), *Narodnoye khoziaistvo SSSR, 1922–1972*, Statistika, Moscow.

*USSR (1977), *Narodnoye khoziaistvo SSSR za 60 let*, Statistika, Moscow.

USSR (1977T), *History of the USSR*, 3 vols, Progress Publishers, Moscow.

*USSR (1980), *Narodnoye khoziaistvo SSSR v 1979*, Statistika, Moscow.

Utechin, S. (1958), 'The Bolsheviks and their allies after 1917', *Soviet Studies*, Vol. 10, pp. 113–33.

*Van Dyke, J. M. (1972), *North Vietnam's Strategy for Survival*, Pacific Books, Calif.

Vanek, J. (ed.) (1975), *Self-Management*, Penguin Books, Harmondsworth.

Vasilieva, E. (1976T), *The Young People of Leningrad*, International Arts & Sciences Press, New York.

*Venturi, F. (1966T), *Roots of Revolution*, Grosset & Dunlap, New York.

*Vergopoulos, K. (1977–8), 'Capitalism and peasant productivity', *Journal of Peasant Studies*, Vol. 5, pp. 446–65.

*Vermeer, E. (1982), 'Income differentials in rural China', *China Quarterly*, no. 89, pp. 1–33.

Vilson, I. (1869), *Obiasneniia k khoziaistvenno-statisticheskomu atlas evropeiskoi Rossii*, St Petersburg.

Vives, V. (1969T), *An Economic History of Spain*, Princeton University Press, Princeton, NJ.

Volin, L. (1970), *A Century of Russian Agriculture*, Harvard University Press, Cambridge, Mass.

Voline (1975T), *The Unknown Revolution, 1917–1921*, Black Rose Books, Montreal.

*Von Freyhold, M. (1979), *Ujamaa Villages in Tanzania*, Heinemann, London.

Von Laue, T. (1963), *Sergei Witte and the Industrialization of Russia*, Columbia University Press, New York.

Vorontsov, V. (1882), *Sudby kapitalizma v Rossii*, St Petersburg.

Vorontsov, V. (1886), *Ocherki kustarnoi promyshlennosti v Rossii*, St Petersburg.

Vorontsov, V. (1892a), *Itogi ekonomicheskogo issledovania Rossii: Krestianskaya obshchina*, St Petersburg.

Vorontsov, V. (1892b), *Progressivniye techeniya v krestianskom khoziaistve*, St Petersburg.

Vucinich, W. (ed.) (1968), *The Peasant in Nineteenth Century Russia*, Stanford University Press, Stanford, Calif.

*Wada, H. (1981), 'Marx and revolutionary Russia', *History Workshop*, no. 12, pp. 129–50.

Wadekin, K.-E. (1982), *Agrarian Policies in Communist Europe*, Allanheld, Osmun, Totowa, NJ.

Walicki, A. (1969), *The Controversy over Capitalism*, Oxford University Press, London.

Walicki, A. (1970), 'Russia', in Gellner, E., and Ionescu, G. (eds), *Populism: Its Meanings and National Characteristics*, Weidenfeld & Nicolson, London.

Walicki, A. (1975T), *The Slavophile Controversy*, Oxford University Press, London.

Walicki, A. (1979T), *A History of Russian Thought*, Oxford University Press.

*Walker, K. (1981), 'China's grain production: 1975–80 and 1952–57', *China Quarterly*, no. 86, pp. 217–47.

*Walker, K. (1982), 'Interpreting Chinese grain consumption statistics', *China Quarterly*, no. 92, pp. 575–88.

Warren, Bill (1980), *Imperialism: Pioneer of Capitalism*, New Left Books/Verso, London.

Warriner, D. (1962), *Land Reform and Development in the Middle East*, Oxford University Press, London.

Warriner, D. (1969), *Land Reform in Principle and Practice*, Oxford University Press, London.

Warshaw, S. (1975), *Southeast Asia Emerges*, Diablo Press, Calif.

Waswo, A. (1977), *Japanese Landlords*, University of California Press, Berkeley, Calif.

Webb, A. (1911), *The New Dictionary of Statistics*, London.

Webb, B., and Webb, S. (1936), *Soviet Communism*, 2 vols, Charles Scribner's Sons, New York.

Weidemann, P. (1980), 'The origins of agro-industrial development in Bulgaria', in Francisco, R., Laird, B., and Laird, R. (eds), *Agricultural Policies in the USSR and Eastern Europe*, Westview Press, Boulder, Colo.

Weisskopf, T. (1980), 'Patterns of economic development in India, Pakistan and Indonesia', in Dernberger, R. (ed.), *China's Development Experience*, Harvard University Press, Cambridge, Mass.

*Wheatcroft, S. (1974), 'The reliability of Russian prewar grain output statistics', *Soviet Studies*, Vol. 26, pp. 157–80.

Wheeler, G. (1964), *The Modern History of Soviet Central Asia*, Weidenfeld & Nicolson, London.

Wheelright, E., and McFarlane, B. (1970), *The Chinese Road to Socialism*, Monthly Review Press, New York.

White, C. (1975), 'Impact of Russian railway construction on the market for grain', in Symons, L., and White, C., *Russian Transport*, G. Bell, London.

*White, C. (1982), *Debates in Vietnamese Development Policy*, IDS, University of Sussex, Brighton.

White, G. (1983), 'Urban employment', in Feuchtwang, S., and Hussain, A. (eds), *The Chinese Economic Reforms*, Croom Helm, London.

Wilber, C. K. (1969), *The Soviet Model and Underdeveloped Countries*, University of North Carolina Press, Chapel Hill, NC.

Wilczynski, J. (1969), *Economics and Politics of East–West Trade*, Macmillan, London.

Wilczynski, J. (1972), *Socialist Economic Development and Reforms*, Macmillan, London.

Wilczynski, J. (1974), *Technology in Comecon*, Macmillan, London.

Wilczynski, J. (1977), *Economics of Socialism*, Allen & Unwin, London.

Wiles, P. (1974), *Distribution of Income: East and West*, North Holland, Amsterdam.

Wiles, P. (1975), 'Recent data on Soviet income distribution', *Survey*, no. 96, pp. 28–41.

Williams, H. (1914), *Russia of the Russians*, Pitman, London.

Wilson, D. (ed.) (1977), *Mao Tse-tung in the Scales of History*, Cambridge University Press.

Witt, N. de (1961), *Education and Professional Employment in the USSR*, US Government Printing Office, Washington, DC.

Wittfogel, K. (1957), *Oriental Despotism*, Yale University Press, New Haven, Conn.

Woerlin, W. (1971), *Chernyshevsky*, Harvard University Press, Cambridge, Mass.

Wolf, E. R. (1966), *Peasants*, Prentice-Hall, Englewood Cliffs, NJ.

Wolf, E. R. (1973), *Peasant Wars of the Twentieth Century*, Faber, London; paperback edn.

Woodcock, G. (1963), *Anarchism*, Penguin Books, Harmondsworth.

Woodside, A. (1976), *Community and Revolution in Modern Vietnam*, Houghton Mifflin, Boston, Mass.

*Woollacott, M. (1980), 'Vietnam: the enduring struggle', *Guardian*, 28 May 1980.

World Bank (1974), *Redistribution with Growth*, IDS/Oxford University Press, London.

World Bank (1975), *Development with Decentralization*, Johns Hopkins University Press, Baltimore, Md.

World Bank (1978), *World Development Report, 1978*, Oxford University Press.

World Bank (1979), *Romania: Industrialization under Socialist Planning*, World Bank, Washington, DC.

World Bank (1980), *World Development Report, 1980*, Oxford University Press.

*Wos, A., and Grochowski, Z. (1978), 'Case study of Poland', in O'Hagan, J. P. (ed.), *Growth and Adjustment in National Agricultures*, Macmillan, London.

*Wuorinen, J. (1965), *A History of Finland*, Columbia University Press, New York.

Wynia, G. (1978), *The Politics of Latin American Development*, Cambridge University Press.

*Xue Muqiao (ed.) (1982T), *Almanac of China's Economy, 1981, with Economic Statistics for 1949–1980*, State Council of the People's Republic of China/Ballinger, Cambridge, Mass.; especially 116–27, 299–339, 959–87.

Yaney, G. (1971), 'Agricultural administration in Russia', in Millar, J. R. (ed.), *The Soviet Rural Community*, University of Illinois Press, Urbana, Ill.

Yang, K., and Chee, C. (1963), 'The North Korean education system', *China Quarterly*, no. 14, pp. 125–40.

Yanowitch, M. (1977), *Social and Economic Inequality in the Soviet Union*, Martin Robertson, London.

Zaionchkovsky, P. (1954), *Otmena krepostnogo prava v Rossii*, Moscow.

Zaleski, E. (1971T), *Planning for Economic Growth in the Soviet Union*, University of North Carolina Press, Chapel Hill, NC.

Zaleski, E. (1980T), *Stalinist Planning for Economic Growth, 1933–1952*, Macmillan, London.

Zaleski, E., *et al.* (1969), *Science Policy in the USSR*, OECD, Paris.

Zasloff, J., and Brown, M. (1980), 'Laos 1979: caught in Vietnam's wake', *Asian Survey*, February 1980.

Zasloff, J., and Langer, P. (1970), *North Vietnam and the Pathet Lao*, Harvard University Press, Cambridge, Mass.

Zauberman, A. (1975), *The Mathematical Revolution in Soviet Planning*, Oxford University Press, London.

Zeitlin, M., and Scheer, R. (1963), *Cuba*, Grove Press, New York.

Zeldin, T. (1979), *France 1848–1945: Ambition and Love*, Oxford University Press.

Zeman, Z. (1969), *Prague Spring*, Penguin Books, Harmondsworth.

Zenkovsky, S. (1960), *Pan-Turkism and Islam in Russia*, Harvard University Press, Cambridge, Mass.

Index